£3.50

William Robinson 1838–1935

William Robinson
1838–1935

Father of the
English Flower Garden

by

MEA ALLAN

faber and faber

First published in 1982
by Faber and Faber Limited
3 Queen Square London WC1
Printed in Great Britain by
Ebenezer Baylis and Son, Limited
The Trinity Press, Worcester, and London
All rights reserved

British Library Cataloguing in Publication Data

Allan, Mea
William Robinson 1838–1935.
1. Robinson, William
2. Gardeners—Great Britain—Biography
I. Title
635′.092   5B63.R/

ISBN 0-571-11865-8

For
Philip
Iris
and
Peter

Contents

Illustrations

List of Illustrations

Line Drawings

The floral tailpieces are illustrations from Robinson's *The English Flower Garden*

Acknowledgements

It is to two people in particular that I am most indebted for facts, hitherto unknown, about William Robinson. One is Lieut.-Colonel Philip Haslett whose father was Robinson's cousin, medical adviser and confidant. Most obligingly Philip roamed Ireland to piece together fragments of Robinson's early life, finding to his delight other members of the family. Details of his later life were revealed by Iris Poynter to whom 'Robbie' was both hero and playmate and who was never tired of listening to reminiscences about him told to her by her Aunt Mary Gilpin. I must add a third, namely Mrs Mary Taylor, widow of Geoffrey Taylor whose chapters about William Robinson evoked an indignant letter from Miss Sarah Robinson. I am indebted to Mrs Taylor for the kind loan of this letter which revealed facts that would otherwise have never come to life. In this connection I was also given help by Mrs Ruth Duthie who put me on the trail, initially by an article in *The Journal of the Garden History Society*. All gave me kind encouragement when it was doubtful if William Robinson would ever emerge from the mists of his private past.

My first sight of Gravetye Manor, where Robinson created his world-famous Sussex garden, was equally unpromising. The footsteps of the master were all but obliterated. Gone were the occupants of the carefully planned borders; the pergolas once clothed with a riot of clematis and roses were rotting and rocking on their foundations. When I asked (for the purpose of a gardens guide I was writing) if I might walk round the place, permission was given, though reluctantly. That was in 1968 when the new owner was still transforming the lovely old house to a hotel and country club before recovering the garden from wartime and post-war neglect. Now it is different. Although compromises have had to be made, the garden is back to being the floriferous place Robinson planned. The lake he drained now again reflects the house from across the Alpine Meadow. The Heath Garden has been replanted, the amazing walls of the fruit garden have been repaired and again hold trained young trees. William Robinson would have applauded, and all who knew him in person or through his books must thank Peter Herbert.

Acknowledgements

No list of acknowledgements would be complete without mention of Will Ingwersen, that famous alpinist whose nursery is in the heart of the Gravetye Estate. He has known Gravetye for over half a century and as an impressionable lad knew Robinson for a decade. To him I am indebted for interesting anecdotes.

A working gardener is a good judge of his master's character and whether that master is any sort of gardener himself. Percy Picton, Bob Snashfold, and Harry Pattenden and his brothers helped me build up the picture not only of the man but of the once-energetic gardener who though confined to his chair could not resist poking out a stray weed with the end of his stick. They respected him for his knowledge of plants and how he liked to grow them. They knew him as a man who had done great work for gardens.

Miss Lily Suddaby was one of Robinson's nurses and was with him at his death. Though now ninety-one, at the time of writing, her memories of her patient are clear. She knew him over a period of twelve years. Adeline Astbury, his secretary, is likewise able to recall those far-off years. She remembers an employer kind to the point of indulgence, a man who fought his infirmities with indomitable and uncomplaining courage. I am grateful to both of them for their help.

To other members of the old Gravetye staff I am grateful for help, including Mrs Robert Snashfold (*née* Henley), and Mrs Branch (*née* Findley), whose father was head gardener at Duckylls Park (one of his duties being to grease the knees of the tame flamingoes there in winter); and to Mrs Joan Duffett, daughter of Sydney Terry, for many years chauffeur.

I thank the relations of William Robinson who still live in Ireland, particularly Belinda Mahaffy; and in England, Canada and Australia the three sisters of Philip Haslett, who all contributed childhood memories. I am indebted to their cousin Mrs Kenneth D. James for directing me to the letters and family photographs collected by her mother. For the loan of other letters and material I am grateful to Bernard Gilpin and his wife Elizabeth.

My thanks go also to the following: Patrick Bowe; The Lady Freyberg; William Harris and his daughter Mrs Audrey Malan; Mrs E. N. Johnsen; Arthur L. Rolls; Donald K. Roy, Mount Royal Cemetery Company and Crematorium Limited; Peter Taylor who generously gave me some Robinson papers; Mr and Mrs Adrian W. Thorpe; Madame Roger de Vilmorin; Robert B. Walpole; Mrs Oonah Walsh-Kemmis and her son Peter; the Marquess of Waterford; and many residents of West Hoathly, Sussex.

For other material I am indebted to the Arnold Arboretum and Gray

Acknowledgements

Herbarium of Harvard University; the University Botanic Garden, Cambridge; the National Botanic Garden, Dublin (Glasnevin), in the person of Dr E. C. Nelson; Mrs Mavis Batey of the Garden History Society; the Royal Botanic Gardens, Kew; Dr Brent Elliott, of the Lindley Library, Royal Horticultural Society; the Massachusetts Horticultural Society; and Mrs Elizabeth Atchison, librarian, the John Innes Institute, and the Gardeners' Royal Benevolent Society.

The following libraries all gave help: that of the Linnean Society; the Belfast Public Library; the British Museum (Natural History) and Newspaper Libraries; Cambridge University Library; Lowestoft Central Library and that of the Borough of Marylebone; the National Library, Dublin; that of the Royal Borough of Kensington and Chelsea; the Tunbridge Wells Reference Library with particular thanks to Miss Jean Malden; and the Victoria Library, Westminster.

Thanks are also due to the Public Record Office; the Record Office of Belfast and those of the Counties of East Sussex, Kent, Suffolk and West Sussex.

Among the others who supplied information were the British Medical Association; Anton G. Spicer of Spicer-Cowan Limited; the East Grinstead Society; William Robinson's publishers John Murray and Frederick Warne; Kenneth C. Prevette and Horace Carter of the Cremation Society; Braund & Hill and Hugill & Co., solicitors; the Standard Life Assurance; the Shipwrecked Fishermen and Mariners' Royal Benevolent Society; the Sussex and Montreal newspapers, and *The Field* and *The Times*; the Forestry Commission and their head forester Kenneth Most who is in charge of the Gravetye Estate woodlands; and David Chambers, head gardener, Gravetye Manor.

Special thanks go to Peter Herbert for kind hospitality at Gravetye and the loan of precious Robinson books; and to J. S. L. Gilmour for his meticulous care in reading the typescript. In this connection I wish to record thanks to my editor at Fabers, Eileen Brooksbank. A welcome grant from the Phoenix Trust assisted with the expenses of research and I thank the Managing Trustees for making this path more easy.

My sincere thanks go to Alpha Data Services for compiling the index, saving very many valuable hours and headaches.

Finally I thank my friend and colleague Grace Woodbridge for all her help throughout the making of this book. It could hardly otherwise have come into being.

Illustration Acknowledgements

It is to Lieut.-Colonel Philip Haslett that I am chiefly indebted for the loan of photographs illustrating the life of William Robinson and the

Acknowledgements

making of Gravetye; but also to other members of the Robinson family and to Iris Poynter and her cousin Bernard Gilpin. Later photographs of the Gravetye garden are from a series taken by the late Donald F. Merrett.

Mystery attaches to the Carolus-Duran portrait. The painting was last known to be in the possession of Miss Sarah Handfield Robinson of Surrey but was not bequeathed to anyone in her will. The Robinson family would like to know of its whereabouts.

The photograph of Curraghmore, taken by *Country Life*, is reproduced by courtesy of the Marquess of Waterford. The plan of the Royal Botanic Society's garden, Regent's Park, was kindly supplied by the Marylebone Library.

To the Royal Botanic Gardens, Kew, I am indebted for the pictures of Henry Vilmorin and Charles Sprague Sargent. The picture of Napoleon III at the 1867 Paris Exhibition is by permission of the Bibliothèque Nationale, the two of Pierre Barillet-Deschamps and Edouard André kindly given by the Service Technique des Parcs, Ville de Paris. Those of the Mushroom Cave, the Pyramidal Pear, and the Square des Batignolles are from the second edition of William Robinson's *Parks and Gardens of Paris*, and are reproduced by permission of Macmillan, the publisher. 'Agave telegraphica' came from William Robinson's publication *The Garden*.

Other delightful line drawings are from various of William Robinson's books, including his periodicals. Those illustrating the alpine trip are from *Alpine Flowers*; others from *Gravetye Manor*, *The Wild Garden* and *Wood Fires*, all by permission of John Murray.

Several of William Robinson's old gardeners kindly helped with snapshots of him, Percy Picton supplying the photograph with Sir Frederick and Lady Moore.

I gratefully thank Mrs Adrian W. Thorpe for the photograph of 28 (now No. 9) Scarsdale Villas.

Many of the old photographs, including two lent by William B. Harris of Moatlands, required special treatment and for this I am grateful to Peter Herbert of Gravetye, who also generously supplied the Barry Hicks colour photograph that appears on the jacket. In addition, Peter Herbert kindly provided prints of the Francis Dodd etching of William Robinson (discovered by Will Ingwersen in a second-hand bookshop), and my favourite picture of him, with the Irish twinkle in his eyes, which endeared him to so many people throughout his long and useful life as a pioneer of the principles that make the English flower garden what it is and beloved across the world.

Author's Introduction

For long there has existed a gap among the biographies of gardeners famous for the contributions they have made to horticulture. The contribution William Robinson made was second to none. *The English Flower Garden*, first published in 1870, is still regarded as the gardener's bible; while in *Alpine Flowers* his principles of good alpine gardening—in natural conditions in a properly constructed rock garden—preceded Reginald Farrer by thirty-seven years. 'No burrs, clinkers, vitrified matter, portions of old arches and pillars, broken-nosed statues, etc., should ever obtain a place in a garden devoted to alpine flowers' might be Farrer himself speaking. And just as Robinson's aims were to uproot the idea that a flower garden was necessarily a set piece, usually geometrical, placed on one side of the house; to sweep away 'railway embankment' terraces; flower beds on the lawn crowded together like tarts on a pastrycook's tray and, worst horror of all, carpet-bedding where flowers were planted to make carpet-like patterns (and dare one plant rear an inch taller than its regimented neighbours, it was mercilessly beheaded)—so in *The Wild Garden* he promoted the virtues of natural planting in neglected places in almost every kind of garden, in woods and copses, along verges and the margins of shrubberies, suggesting how all these could be planted for beauty, without further care or cost; even meadows which would be cropped for hay. Here, before it was time for the scythe, would be naturalized drifts of the blue anemone, crocuses, snowdrops, narcissus, grape hyacinths, Stars of Bethlehem, scillas and wild tulips. There, in the shade of trees, replacing weeds and brambles, would spread the graceful fronds of Solomon's Seal, patches of cyclamen and primroses, honeysuckles, wild roses and foxgloves. A cloud of daffodils would clothe a mound.

He gave us the herbaceous border: he called it the mixed border. This new kind of planting meant the elimination of the digging up of the flower garden in a repetitive programme of summer bedding replacing spring bedding, annuals and biennials. Once planted, the herbaceous border could go on year after year in its own natural sequence of flowering.

So with his natural rock garden, natural wild garden and natural flower garden William Robinson let us look at flowers and admire them for their own sake.

His ideas were revolutionary. He established them through his books and through the gardening periodicals he founded: they are now accepted as the principles of good gardening. By such changes wrought do we assess greatness, and William Robinson who gave the most was unquestionably the greatest of British gardeners.

Yet not one biographical study of him has appeared in print. Why? The little that has been written about him in surveys of gardening history acknowledges some of this greatness but is condemnatory of a supposed crotchety and quarrelsome nature. The late Geoffrey Taylor, from whom other writers have taken their cue, says that 'even his surviving friends speak of him as a crusty old man'. So was it because he was, reputedly, 'difficult', an unattractive subject repelling investigation, that he was so largely neglected? One well-known lady gardener even spoke to me of him thus: 'Writing about *that* man . . . that vicious man! How horrible!'

Or was it because his birth and early years were shrouded in mystery, which baulked writers of a beginning to their story, a mystery Robinson did nothing to dispel and indeed impishly encouraged with the statement that he was the son of a farm labourer?

One cannot write a biography founded on 'It is said . . .' or on conjecture which may be wrong or misleading. The fact was there were no facts with which to re-create the complete story of his life and the logic of his behaviour. For Robinson's activities were wildly out of context: a poor young Irishman fleeing to London—and soon becoming a voice in the affairs of the Royal Botanic Society. A lad 'of peasant stock' (it was said) becoming fluent in French, able to converse with and question the nurserymen of the Seine Valley whose methods he admired, becoming a friend of the famous Vilmorin family, at the same time covering the horticulture of the great Paris Exhibition of 1867 for *The Times*, *The Gardeners' Chronicle* and *The Field*.

The truth had to come out sometime, and it is hardly surprising that Geoffrey Taylor who wrote inaccurately about Robinson's character and family background should be the means of bringing the truth into the open. Two chapters in his book *Some Nineteenth-Century Gardeners* (1951) evoked an indignant letter from Miss Sarah Handfield Robinson denying that William Robinson, her first-cousin-once-removed, was any 'peasant boy', and proving her statement by giving an account of their family connections. Geoffrey Taylor never published this letter.

But much remained to be discovered, and later when other

investigators joined the field a few more facts emerged. I had begun to piece the whole jigsaw together from Robinson's first gardening days at Curraghmore, County Waterford (not at Ballykilcavan, as is always said) to Gravetye Manor in Sussex. Obvious sources of material had been left unresearched, and these yielded much information. Finally a chance meeting landed his family right in my lap, so to speak, and this was a marvellous piece of serendipity.

It is now my good fortune to present William Robinson as descending from the parents he did, growing up in a tragic household and clouding his own future by a foolish act of destruction, but, clinging to the career he decided to follow, forging on to success. He might never have risen above adversity had it not been for two people who early recognized his genius and helped him on his way. But the genius was of William Robinson's own making. It was based (for all that has been written of his alleged crotchetiness) on his kinship with nature and the motto by which he lived: in his own words—love flowers and everything that grows.

I

Curraghmore and the Beginning

It was in County Down in Northern Ireland that William Robinson was born, on the 15th of July 1838. The countryside is varied in its scenery: from the wild granite uplands at its centre to the fertile valleys below; from the low-lying fields around Strangford Lough to the Mourne Mountains made famous in song. They rise in sharp peaks culminating in Slieve Donard from whose summit on a clear day can be seen the English Lakes, Wales, and the Scottish Isle of Arran across the Irish Sea. One day William was to cross that stretch of water, to become England's greatest gardener and author of the most widely read gardening book ever written.

He had a hard start in life, going out to work as soon as he was old enough. There was need of the few shillings he could earn, for his father, a land agent, for whom he was named, had deserted his wife Catherine and their young family and eloped with Lady St George, the wife of his employer. So states the entry in the family Bible. They decamped to America.

He started his gardening career at Curraghmore, seat of the Marquess of Waterford, his first job being to carry water from the River Clodiagh, which runs through those gardens, to the glasshouses. This is recorded in *Gardening Illustrated* in the obituary of its founder, William Robinson. He had a fondness for the place, for when the fifteenth edition of *The English Flower Garden* was published he sent a copy to the head gardener there for the use of the present young men in the bothy; 'for,' as he said, 'I once lived in that bothy myself.'

It was after Curraghmore that he became a student gardener at the National Botanic Garden, Dublin. Frances Garnet, later Viscountess Wolseley, related in her diary under the date 10 March 1898 that 'Mr Robinson, the great gardener . . . was good enough to spend some hours of the afternoon in our new little garden at Farmhouse, giving me advice. . . . What a clever successful man he is! From a gardener's apprentice at Glasnevin he has risen to owning three gardening papers, to manage the garden part of "the Field" and to have a fine country place at Gravetye in Sussex.'

Curraghmore and the Beginning

We know that William went to Ballykilcavan, there rising to be foreman. But it cannot be doubted that it was at Glasnevin he gained his thorough knowledge of plants and planting. Although the Ballykilcavan estate was fairly large, according to the 1791 survey by Edward Walsh of part of the demesne comprising 151 acres and including 'the different borders adjoining the Garden', the garden was no show place, for Loudon does not mention it in his list of good gardens in the neighbourhood. So it is unlikely that the head gardener at Ballykilcavan was anything more than just a competent man able to manage an ordinary country-house garden.

William's employer was the Rev. Sir Hunt Johnson-Walsh, Bart., vicar of the parish of Stradbally since about 1820. The Walsh family had settled in County Kilkenny at the end of the twelfth century and remained there till the reign of Charles I, when they removed or were transplanted to the Queen's County (Leix). They were landowners, clergymen of the Irish Church, army men of high rank. The Walsh Papers reveal that they managed their affairs efficiently.

William was the eldest of the family of three children and would have been about ten when their father left them, throwing them 'on the mercies of relations'. The Robinsons of Bloomfield, County Sligo, came to their rescue in the persons of the children's Uncle Joseph and Aunt Sarah, daughter of Colonel Charles Handfield who was Commissary-General in Ireland; and if Milton was right when he said 'The childhood shows the man, as morning shows the day', then the boy William was open and quick to respond, sure of himself and that what he liked should be liked by others, delighted when they did, argumentative when they did not. But this was understandable: he had an eye for beauty, a sense of fitness and rightness. There was a touch of genius in the boy. What, Sarah wondered, would be its flowering? Fate had given his Irish eyes a look of divilment that was a merry challenge to authority, and Sarah Handfield Robinson was something of a rebel herself. She took to him and was ever afterward his friend. It was she who suggested gardening as a beginning for him. She was a keen gardener herself and was delighted when her suggestion met with William's approval.

Horticulture in Ireland had taken a vigorous step forward in these years. With new plants to be grown: dahlias from Mexico, chrysanthemums and tea roses from China, and other floral wonders—for wonderful they certainly were—new gardens sprang up to accommodate them, spurred by the famous premiums offered by the Dublin Society (Royal in 1820) which encouraged the formation of smaller societies. The (Royal) Horticultural Society of Ireland, founded in 1816

1 Curraghmore, home of the Marquess of Waterford, where young William Robinson began his career—carrying water to the greenhouses from the River Clodiagh. (Photograph by *Country Life*)

2
William's aunt
Sarah Handfield Robinson
who was the spur
to his ambition

with the aim of protecting professional standards, was remodelled in 1830. Three years earlier the Botanic and Horticultural Society was formed in Belfast to establish a botanic garden. Dublin already had Glasnevin.

Then came the advent of the modern greenhouse, made possible by the facts that glass could now be made in six-foot sheets and cast-iron frames could be curved. In 1845 with the tax on glass finally lifted, the price fell. This gave a fresh impetus to the growing of tender fruits for the table, exotics to decorate the drawing-room, and a constant supply of plants for bedding-out. At Kylemore Castle in Connemara there was a range of twenty-one greenhouses heated by three miles of hot-water pipes.

Ballykilcavan had nothing like that, despite the assertion of Geoffrey Taylor of a 'considerable range of glasshouses' there. Mrs Oonah Walsh-Kemmis, great-grand-daughter of William Robinson's third employer, is emphatic that the gardens of Ballykilcavan were never 'grand', nor among the several notable ones in the district; it was her old home and so far as she knows there never was any extensive range of glasshouses but merely the few usually to be found in the gardens of Irish country houses, for the growing of grapes, peaches, and house plants. If Robinson's hatred of bedding dates back to Ballykilcavan days, as seems from his covert and overt allusions to it, there must have been a greenhouse devoted to the trays of seedlings whose destiny was the floral carpeting of bare beds waiting to receive them. And of course the inevitable pelargonium cuttings. Robinson had nothing against these plants with their 'numerous beautiful varieties', at least in the early editions of *The English Flower Garden*—apart, that is, from commenting that without pelargoniums bedding-out might never have become fashionable (which could be read both ways). But it is interesting that in the fifteenth edition he leaves them out altogether, jumping from the paulownia tree to pennisetums. Today, ironically, there is only one greenhouse at Ballykilcavan and that is in a state of decay.

For part of the Robinson legend is the story of how William left Ballykilcavan. It has become somewhat magnified into a tale of terrible destruction, though basically the story is true. Mrs Walsh-Kemmis heard it from her aunt who lived most of her life at Ballykilcavan and died there in 1953 at the age of ninety-one. Her aunt was therefore born in 1862, just a year after William took his departure from the place one cold winter's night, and she was the member of the family most interested in the garden and its history.

The winter of 1860–1 was one of the severest on record, the frost lasting from the 20th of December to the 5th of January. William, now twenty-two, had been unhappy at Ballykilcavan for some time (he was probably bored with an uncreative and unscientific garden that could not compare with Glasnevin), and Aunt Sarah Robinson did not see why he should not seek work elsewhere. She persuaded him to leave, and it was on one of these bitter days that he came to an open quarrel with the head gardener, that night forsaking the greenhouses in his charge and taking the road to Dublin on foot. Legend says that beforehand he drew out the fires and opened the windows, so that houseful after houseful of precious plants perished in the cold. The story as told to Mrs Walsh-Kemmis by her aunt has no such melodramatic climax. She said there was a dispute and some damage was done, but it can have been no scene of carnage or William would not have dared to present himself to his old chief, Dr David Moore, Glasnevin's revered director.

David Moore, fifty-three at this time, was a Scot born at Dundee as a Muir but changing the spelling of his name when he went to Dublin as assistant to J. T. Mackay, Director of the University Botanic Garden. In 1838 the Royal Dublin Society elected him to the charge of their garden at Glasnevin and soon with his energy and ability he raised it from comparative insignificance to being one of the foremost botanic gardens, enriching it with many plants of his own collecting. He represented British horticulture at the Paris Exhibition of 1867 and was one of the delegates at the botanical congress there, both of which William attended as horticultural correspondent of *The Times* and *The Gardeners' Chronicle*.

The portrait of David Moore, to whom Joseph D. Hooker as Director of the Royal Botanic Gardens, Kew, dedicated Volume XCIX of *Curtis's Botanical Magazine*, shows a rugged alert face with keen discerning eyes: not the sort of man to be fooled by any young man diverging from the truth, or to be bothered by trivia. Whatever account William gave of his misbehaviour at Ballykilcavan would be believed, and accepted as—if not justifiable—at least understandable. We know that Moore at once became a friend and that he gave him the introduction that was to set his feet on the next rung of the ladder. He too saw that young William Robinson was worth encouraging.

2

The Regent's Park

Dr Moore could not have sent him to a happier place. Where could a young man bent on a career in horticulture find such fulfilment in the day's work, such inspiration for tomorrow's, as in the Royal Botanic Society's garden in Regent's Park under its energetic and imaginative curator, Robert Marnock? Here was the *genius loci*, a force that directed everything about the place with the quiet voice of authority; and whereas John Lindley at the Horticultural Society's garden at Chiswick was (as William Robinson later wrote) 'hated by the gardeners, Mr Marnock, in the Regent's Park, had their good will'. It was an understatement: Marnock was a loved figure arousing affection wherever he went, and much respected. In January 1846 he had been admitted a Fellow of the Linnean Society.

He and Moore were two of a kind. Both Scots of nearly the same age, David Moore had left Dundee for Dublin, Robert Marnock his native Aberdeenshire to be gardener at Bretton Hall, Wakefield. After four years there he won a competition for designing the new botanic garden at Sheffield and was made its first curator. In 1839 on the founding of the Royal Botanic Society of London he repeated the performance by winning not only the competition for the best design for laying out the eighteen acres of its grounds but, again, the curatorship—this on the recommendation of the revered John Claudius Loudon.

It is interesting to compare his design with the stilted conformity of others submitted, many of them by leading architects such as Edward Lapidge, Alfred Bartholomew, and Wyatt Papworth. Even Henry Laxton, F.L.S., Architect and Landscape Gardener, did not win a place with four designs. But then Marnock was a gardener (a term he preferred to horticulturist) who believed that a garden should be a place where plants look as if they were growing in their natural environment.

The state of the garden-to-be when the Society took it over was unpromising, the soil stiff clay, but under Robert Marnock's supervision it was transformed. The joy of all the visitors when they first came was something to see, and they could hardly believe that this beautiful garden was wholly artificial. For Marnock's design was deceptively simple in its natural flowing lines: the lake with its curving shores populated by water plants and hanging trees (where no lake had been before), its marvellously contrived hills and dales, its walks and flower borders. Even the Order beds showing the different plant families were an ornament. These in most botanic gardens are, even today, straight and uniform with no pretence to artistry; but here they were of all shapes and sizes, and the larger the Order the larger the bed, an arrangement which not only impressed upon the students the relative sizes of the Orders but made the beds attractive to the ordinary unscientific visitor.

Marnock had also used great imagination when planning the difficult boundary. The Garden was contained in a circle, the Inner Circle in which was to have been built a palace for the Prince Regent and now is Queen Mary's Garden with one of the finest rose collections in Britain. By clever siting of trees and shrubs the circular outline was smudged, making the Garden seem twice as large and cutting it off from public view. Up to 1838 the ground had been occupied by a nurseryman by the name of Jenkins. A number of his trees remained, some of them of good height, and this was an inducement to the Royal Botanic Society when they were looking for a site for their garden.

It was to this sylvan retreat 'entirely removed from the slightest evidence of proximity to a town', as A. D. Webster wrote of it, that William Robinson came with his letter of introduction. Marnock, now sixty-one, had an experienced eye for a good gardener. He noted as they walked round how attentively the young man listened to what he was saying, how eager were his questions. Some of the older tenants among the trees were specimens of weeping ash and weeping elm, and as Marnock explained how he had been able to incorporate these in his design he could see the younger man's eyes flash with appreciation. After a chat, when it was Marnock who fired the questions, on every aspect of gardening including the sort of knowledge William had on plants of all kinds and their culture, he knew that here was a gardener worth having; and William had been well trained indeed or he would not have pleased this perfectionist of a curator.

In creating the lake Marnock had piled the dug-out earth into a large irregular mound sloping naturally down to the water. The ascent of this mound with its natural rough grass was one of the great attractions to visitors, for the view from its summit of Primrose Hill and other neighbouring hills and more distant country. Also on the summit was an anemometer for measuring the velocity of the wind, and a sunshine recorder. Nearby were earth thermometers from three inches to sixteen feet deep. Daily records of all the instruments were kept from readings taken three times a day, later to be printed in the Society's *Quarterly Record*.

When William was duly engaged Marnock assigned him to the herbaceous ground and here were meteorological instruments and appliances. William was more much interested in the plants.

February of 1862 was so mild that the springtime season was a fortnight early, and at the Garden Committee's meeting on the 22nd Marnock asked for permission to engage a man to assist Mr Robinson who was now able to tackle the clearing of the Herbaceous Garden. He got his man and the work proceeded smoothly.

William began to appear regularly in the Committee's minutes. At the meeting of the 28th of June it was agreed that one or two small collecting boxes, besides the large one previously asked for, should be obtained for the use of Mr Robinson. These were not for collecting money but to be used as vasculums for collecting plants, showing that William extended his work into the field, and indeed he became an authority on British wild flowers. In his foreword to the tenth edition of *The English Flower Garden* (meticulously he always called these 'Forewords') he tells how at the Regent's Park there was at that time a small garden of British plants which he had to keep up, and this led him into the varied country around London, 'from the orchid-flecked meadows of Bucks to the tumbled down undercliffs on the Essex coast, untroubled by the plough'.

The same meeting gave him more power over his domain in the Garden. He had been horrified at the way the students, on the hunt for plant material for their studies, heedlessly cut off the flowers to such an extent that little seed was left to ripen, and rare species were therefore being threatened with destruction. The thoughtless vandals were medical students of London University, for plants were then part of the *materia medica*.

The Secretary, to whom William had complained personally, took up the matter himself. This was James de Carle Sowerby, eldest son of the great James Sowerby who illustrated the volumes of *English Botany* and other valuable works. In future, the meeting decided, the existing regulations would be enforced in a Notice ruling that the plants were not to be cut by any person; that any student breaking this rule would be reported and would be liable to have his admission order stopped; and that application for flowers etc. for study might be made to Mr Robinson, the Foreman of the Educational Department.

For by this date William had risen in the world.

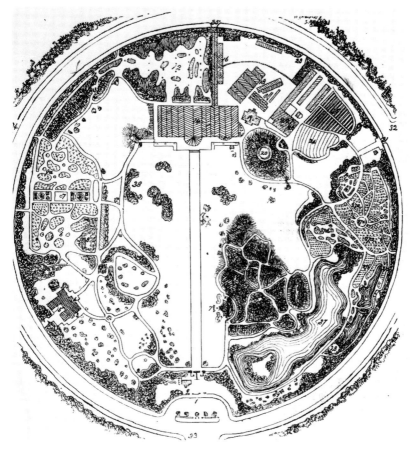

3 Robert Marnock's plan for the Royal Botanic Society's Garden.
It won him not only the competition but the curatorship.
He went on to become England's leading garden designer

It was a blow when in February of the following year, 1863, the curator announced his intention of retiring. For some years Marnock's outside interests away from the Garden had gradually been expanding, and these were now tending to come into conflict with the duties he owed to the Society. These other interests concerned other gardens. In 1853 he had laid out the grounds of the Villa San Donato, near Florence, for Prince Demidoff, and having successfully designed both the Sheffield Botanic Garden and the Regent's Park Garden and regularly coming into contact with wealthy Fellows of the Society it was natural that he should often be asked to design or redesign their gardens.

William's thoughts were also turning to other gardens, but for other reasons. He was anxious to increase the number of species in the Garden, in order to make the collections in his charge as complete as possible. Already he had planned a tour that would, he thought, bring the desired results. Botanic gardens all over the world worked an exchange system, as they still do, distributing to each other their seed lists of plants mainly of botanical interest, of which they have a surplus: they are not the sort of seed lists that would interest the weekend gardener. They also exchange living plants. William proposed to visit the botanic gardens of Scotland and Ireland: Edinburgh and Glasgow, Belfast and Dublin. 'I believe,' he wrote in a memorandum to the Garden Committee, 'I could thoroughly examine their Collections and accomplish my objects for twelve pounds.'

There was no hesitation in giving him a cheque for this amount. It was a bargain, for William managed to include Hull, York, Liverpool and Manchester, coming back laden with plants and promises of more.

'Most of the Curators of the gardens I visited had been to the Regent's Park and received duplicate plants,' he wrote in his report, 'so that I will have no difficulty of obtaining the plants I want.'

There was only one confession of failure he had to make: having visited many more places than originally intended, he had spent three pounds more than was granted! At their meeting of the 26th of September 1863, it was recommended that the extra three pounds be paid him.

Before he left, Robert Marnock paid William a handsome compliment. He told the May 22nd meeting: 'I have found Mr Robinson to be a very fit person to manage the medical and herbaceous gardens, and a zealous botanist. His wages at present are twenty-five shillings a week, and as he has asked for a rise I would recommend the Committee to add five shillings, which he thinks would be sufficient to keep him in the service of the Society for some years.'

This statement must have jolted the Committee uncomfortably, for they were well aware by this time of William Robinson's value to them, and was it not natural that a young man of his capabilities should wish to improve himself? They had no hesitation in agreeing that the services of Mr Robinson ought to be retained, and accordingly directed that his wages be raised to thirty shillings. Ordinary gardeners of two grades were receiving eleven shillings and twelve-and-sixpence at that time. In 1866 even Kew gardeners were paid only twelve shillings a week, three shillings less than the men at Regent's Park in that year. Amazing to think that in 1861 the weekly labour cost to the Society's Garden was only twenty-eight pounds.

William left in August and was away for a month. The tour proved to be the key to the wider world he was soon to enter, and one day capture.

He set off on his adventure as excited as a schoolboy and soon spellbound by the magic of travel.

'One fine August morning,' he wrote, 'I started from King's Cross on a botanical tour full of "great expectations", which were more than realised. After sweeping by the hills of Barnet through the then golden prairies of Lincolnshire, and across the Humber I safely landed in Hull.'

4 William Robinson at twenty-six. He had been in England less than three years and was already Foreman in charge of the Educational and Herbaceous Department in the Royal Botanic Society's Garden, Regent's Park

It was late in the day but he could not rest until he had found the Botanic Garden and introduced himself to James Craig Niven, the Dublin-born son of Ninian Niven who was curator of Glasnevin for four years from 1834. David Moore had succeeded him in 1838. James Niven specialized in alpines, those mountain plants on which William himself was to become an authority, later writing a book about them. Told that the curator was somewhere in the rock garden, William found him 'in the vicinity of his Saxifrages', and preliminaries were soon cut short by William's delighted exclamation at sight of a bed of diminutive ones. Dropping on his knees he began examining them, the finest collection he had ever seen. There were upwards of 120 species and all were well labelled. Among them William was pleased to find some from the mountains of Killarney. Others were from the Scottish Highlands, the Alps, the Pyrenees, and from almost every northern peak—and here they all were, near neighbours and in the most perfect health. Never had he seen anything prettier than the little frosted silvery masses of such species of saxifrage as *caesia*, *diapensoides*, and *caryophyllata*. He thought how remarkable it was that these lovely things were not more appreciated and cultivated. They were always so neat and pleasing to the eye, keeping their foliage throughout the year and giving forth their numerous flowers as gaily as many other plants which were soon ragged and decaying.

The sedums were his next favourites, about sixty species here, and then sempervirens. Of the beautiful spring-flowering drabas there were healthy tufts of *boetica*, *tridentata* and *ciliaris*, with nine commoner species. *Dolomiaea lucida* he did not much take to: it was in bloom but was 'decidedly more curious than beautiful'. The androsaces included the too little-known *lanuginosa*. 'What an admirable basket-plant it would make for the school greenhouse!' he exclaimed.

The Hull Botanic Garden was one of the oldest in the provinces, having been established in 1812. For many years it was a prosperous institution, but after a rival sprang up in the form of the Zoological Garden the town seriously considered doing away with it. Then with the British Association deciding to hold its 1853 Meeting in the ancient borough the town hastily put its scientific house in order. Niven, then superintendent of the herbaceous department at Kew, was given the curatorship and the task of remaking the Garden to something worthy of its bygone fame.

Among the herbaceous plants William found many that were interesting. One was *Thapsia garganica*, the Drias-plant, which had such a miraculous reputation for healing among the ancient Moors that they struck them on the reverse of their coins. There was also the curious *Megacarpea polyandra* of enormous pinnate leaves, a plant 'which is so remarkable a divergence from the hexandrous character of Cruciferae,' remarked William Robinson the botanist.

This exhilarating start of his tour was followed by a visit to York to see the Museum gardens but chiefly to visit James Backhouse and his son of the same name who were to become his close friends.

The Museum was that of the Yorkshire Philosophical Society. The grounds in which it stood rose boldly from the River Ouse and contained picturesque ruins of Roman fortifications and the very beautiful remains of the Abbey of St Mary. There was a good collection of fossil ferns and cycads in the Museum, and out of doors was the small botanic garden. Unfortunately Henry Baines the curator was unwell and could not see him, and his assistant was fern-hunting in the Highlands. So, without a guide, William suspected he was missing much of interest. But he enjoyed the ferns in the glasshouses, and from what he wrote about them it is evident that he knew enough to recognize rare ones like *Llavea cordifolia*. The British ferns were well represented and nearly all the curious varieties he had seen shown in London were among them.

Next he went to the Backhouse nurseries. They were about a mile west of York, on an incline sloping to the south and commanding a wide view over rich and fertile countryside. The exhibit James Backhouse and his son had put up at the Horticultural Society's show only a few weeks ago had given William some indication of what he might expect to see. He was quite unprepared for what he did see. In blocks of glasshouses from 70 to 160 feet long were orchids from Brazil and New Granada, India and the East Indies: laelias; cattleyas including the rare and exquisite rose-brown and red-purple *schilleriana*; gorgeous-foliaged anoectochili growing like weeds, some filling specimen pans with their gold and silver-veined leaves and producing 'an indescribably beautiful effect'; in the main hothouse a superb display of tropical plants such as a new dipladenia of large deep-rosy-crimson flowers, the *schottii* variety of *Allamanda cathartica* everywhere showing its golden-yellow trumpets and the dazzling scarlet Passion Flowers of *Passiflora raddiana* from Brazil hanging from the rafters.

Then came the ferns.

William had 'a vague notion of great Ferneries and so forth, but,' he wrote, 'I was utterly unprepared for such a fascinating imitation of wild Nature as that which stretched for 70 feet before me, and which may be likened to a concentrated New Zealand or Australian Fern ravine, everywhere charmingly diversified and draped with graceful verdure.' The filmy ferns, for instance, were not isolated like some green disease in a house of their own. Just as it would be in their natural environment, 'Ferns large and small, massive and delicate, filmy and arborescent', were mingled together, the tree ferns six to nine feet high with crests ten, fifteen, eighteen feet across throwing feathery canopies gracefully aloft and almost hiding the roof. There was a 'glen' twenty feet wide constructed of seventy tons of massive stones, with a small sheet of water half-hidden among the surrounding boulders, into which gushed a charming little cascade. All around grew the ferns in wild profusion.

Revealing is a glimpse of the young William Robinson performing the dull routine of gardening of his early days. For of the wonderful spectacle of this great fern house he wrote: 'To one like myself, fresh from the region where monotony holds almost undisputed sway; where

[31]

"decided" colours take a too decided lead, the relief afforded by this exquisite touch of nature, and sudden collapse of pot, bench and regulation, could only be equalled by a sudden transfer from a Bedfordshire Cucumber field to a Gentian-covered Alp.'

Even more spectacular was what was referred to as the 'Trichomanes house' where grew a wondrous collection of these and hymenophyllums, both filmy ferns but grown in a place specially designed where their beauty was exquisitely and naturally displayed. It was unquestionably the most remarkable and interesting garden structure in England at that time. No bricks or even cement had been used to build it but 120 tons of rough sandstone skilfully placed together to form a narrow crevasse reaching some ten feet underground and reminding William of the rocks 'under which I had crept years ago on the shattered sides of the Scalp Mountain in Wicklow.' Iron bars spanned the chasm, bearing the slabs of thick glass that formed the roof and let in the minimal light required. The floor of rough stone slabs was always moist from the natural drainage of the water: in rainy weather the whole place filtered water through its rocky sides and the floor became a veritable watercourse, clean and pure-looking as a mountain streamlet.

The whole was made in the shape of a horseshoe, one arm being for tropical species, the other for ferns from cool regions. A huge stone arch divided the two and by means of a heated tank at the tropical end and a cool current of air from the open arch, two different climates were created. The cool current continually passed under the other, in the opposite direction, in passing condensing the vapour of the upper warm current so that everything within its range was incessantly covered with dew. 'And such dew! Every fern, nay every pinnule and every particle of moss was radiant with tiny drops that glistened like polished diamonds and emeralds, for the reflection of light—now green, now gold—on these living gems was wonderful. And yet this moisture, incessant day and night, scarcely touches them. They would not bear it, so delicate is their texture. It stands upon their tiny hairs, hardly touching the real substance of the frond. Even the sprinkling of the finest watering can or the thinnest misty spray is too much, so admirably are their delicate forms fitted by the hand of the great Creator to be nurtured by evening dews, and defended by the deep recesses and intense shade of tropical forests from the storms and tempests which abundantly assail the elevated and robust forms of vegetation.'

So wrote William Robinson of his first experience of a great nursery. As he said: 'Accustomed to see but very few species of these rare plants in gardens generally, and the scarcity of them even in the very best places, small wonder it is that an ordinary son of Adam should feel an alarming gushing up of ignorance in the midst of the delights of such a scene.'

There were more delights outdoors: acres of fruit trees, a frame ground where rare British orchids were grown, and finally the alpine rockery reached by a path winding above a timber-line of conifers, just as it might be in the European Alps. It looked utterly natural with its cliffs and ravines, small lake with a rocky island, and a gloomy gorge, all giving a range of homely terrains for mountain plants. Four hundred tons of crag rose in the most varied and ragged forms to twenty or twenty-five feet in height, surrounding and hemming in the placid sheet of water, with every sort of nook, aspect, fissure, soil, shade or shelter that one could wish for the numerous and in many cases not easily pleased gems that were flourishing among the rocks: the Killarney Fern of bright green fronds nestling under a slab of rock overhanging the water, providing this filmy inhabitant with its moisture and protection; the exposed ledge where the Alpine Forget-me-not was thriving 'as if on its native Ben Lawers'. One could look over the water to the inhabitants of Southern Europe and Madeira—mesembryanthemums and cyclamens, while in cool and shady spots were plants from the Arctic regions of Spitzbergen and Melville Island. On one hand was a blue carpet of *Gentiana verna* beside a little chalky bed of the Bee orchid; on the other *Primula farinosa* in fruit, and below, cropping out vigorously from under large stones on the little island, beautiful hardy North American and Siberian cypripediums.

How often in the future he was to wish for a magic carpet to take him on a 'rapid ride to York', to spend an hour among the delicately beautiful transparencies of the tropical fernery, but, for a real feast of interest, to settle down amidst the 'heaven-kissing gems' of the great Alpine Rockery there.

3

Plants and Plant Men

It was natural that after the excitements of the Backhouse nurseries Edinburgh should be something of an anticlimax. Not the city itself, nor its neighbourhood which was 'a delightful one for the lover of rare and beautiful hardy plants'. The pure air and very sandy soil in which the plants flourished no doubt tended to make it so pleasant; though the immediate reason so far as William was concerned was that 'many of the nurserymen and amateurs of Edina are not in the habit of measuring their horticultural excellence by the number of Tom Thumbs and Purple Kings they can marshall out by the 1st of June each year.' (Ballykilcavan's bedding-out routine still haunted him.)

At York he had met William Mackenzie Stark, an authority on mosses who had a nursery in Edinburgh. He gave William the names of a few places where he would find some interesting plants, particularly recommending him to see Mr Tait of Dickson's extensive nursery in Leith Walk. William felt well rewarded for his visit. American plants were a speciality of this excellent and well-kept nursery, but even more rewarding was a visit to a place he would never have thought of including in his tour—the Dean Cemetery—except that the superintendent had been employed at the Comely Bank and Edgehill nurseries and was a 'rare-plant man'. His plants certainly were interesting and he had almost every hardy ornamental tree and shrub procurable. But what intrigued William was the way they were planted all about the cemetery, making it 'decidedly a garden', and with fine clumps of *Lilium eximium* in all its snowy beauty, other kinds of lilies and an abundance of the very best Perpetual and Tea roses. Simple spring flowers were much used for the decoration of the graves, he was told.

Just as the Backhouse nurseries were to inspire William Robinson to write his first book on plants, so the Dean Cemetery was to spark off another idea. But that was to come much later.

The Comely Bank nursery was a place that frequently came into the conversation when William inquired, 'Have you such and such a plant?' If the answer was No, inevitably the rider would be, 'But you would find it at Comely Bank.' Founded by James Cunningham, on his death becoming Cunningham, Fraser & Co., the nursery retained its reputation for the good things and rarities that had made it famous.

But I have the uneasy feeling that William, while appreciating the efficiency of the place and its great range of plants, did not find it altogether inspiring and perhaps even made fun of its superlatives. The houses and sheds, he wrote, surpassed in magnitude and strength those generally found in nurseries, as much as did the boundary wall (twelve feet high) a wooden fence. There was a 'Leviathan shed used for packing which would make a tolerable barrack, being 120 feet long, 50 feet wide and almost strong enough to stand a seige.' But perhaps the Edinburgh winds accounted for that. Certainly everything was of the very best; and despite the fact that the rare silvery-leaved *Geranium argenteum* could not be increased sufficiently to supply its numerous admirers, it was a nursery affording a treat for the lover of rare plants 'for which the term interesting is altogether too weak.'

On a brilliant afternoon he popped out to Dalkeith on a very rickety sort of railway, found the 'guiding mind' of David Thomson, the head gardener, away from home, and began a rapid walk round the place, starting at Thomson's house.

This was the renowned garden of the Duke of Buccleuch, and it presented a view more interesting to William than the Bay of Dublin, the Bay of Naples or any such famous scene. For here was the horticultural wealth of Dalkeith Park spread below as if it were a picture on a single page, a picture surrounded by a margin of richly coloured flower beds all beautifully arranged. There were streets of glasshouses, bright and perfect-looking and again filled with colour—from 50,000 flowering plants.

From the eminence on which the mansion stood he climbed down to the great square kitchen garden and began a tour of the glasshouses. There was nearly a mile of them, and with the afternoon becoming spent his walk through them had to be a quick one. He was interested in the fact that in the two houses in which apricots, pears, peaches, plums and cherries were grown no heating was used. Apart from the main vineries he had time to cast only a glance over the rest of the houses, for the great circular conservatory was beckoning him to a distant part of the demesne, an elaborately ornamented and costly structure containing palms, medicinal plants and a mixed collection of exotics. He went back to the main part of the garden to make notes on the ribbon borders. These were more effective than any he had seen elsewhere and presented a welcome change from ordinary 'ribboning'.

Plants and Plant Men

The secret was the judicious use of *Centaurea ragusina*, a silvery-leaved plant Thomson used for toning down glaring colours. If bedding there had to be, this was the bedding system seen at perfection. There was only one border given up to the primitive colours red, blue and yellow, and in William's opinion it was the least beautiful of the lot. He was convinced that if only one of Mr Thomson's displays could be seen side by side with the usual bedding plot, it would lead the way to revolt.

The entrance gate to Edinburgh's Royal Botanic Garden was very like that of a nunnery, thought William, and very unlike that through which one would expect to enter a great national garden.

He found himself in a sort of botanical college and was first introduced to the very useful museum recently established by the botany professor, John Hutton Balfour. Before touring the glasshouses he was taken round the Order beds, which were arranged under both the Natural and Linnaean systems. Hardy exotics were growing in two different soils, a light sandy soil and a heavy clay, plants perishing in one garden surviving in the other, and—'Awful to relate,' (wrote William with tongue in cheek) 'there were no "Calcies", no "Tom Thumbs", no "Verbenias" covering acres.' For the Edinburgh Botanic Garden was a real garden, its well-kept grounds illustrating the world's vegetation; and from what he was told by James McNab, who had succeeded his father, William McNab, as curator, some of the borders in which were the best hellebores and some fine varieties of *Orobus vernus* produced a display of good hardy species that no gardener in the neighbourhood of London could excel.

The Edinburgh Garden at that time was famed for its medicinal plants and tropical fruits, and William was enthusiastically led to inspect them, 'doubtless missing numerous plants more likely to attract a general plantsman,' he wrote ruefully. However, as he was spending a week in Edinburgh there was plenty of time to come back and compile his list of desiderata.

The Glasgow Garden from want of funds was not in first-rate condition, he found, although he had already had some interesting plants from it.

He hurried over the rest of his Scottish tour. Perhaps he was homesick for Ireland, for he wrote: 'So next for my gleanings on the shores of "yon sweet Dublin bay".'

With his feet on his native heath William became lyrical about the beauties of Glasnevin and was staggered at the number of people who visited it 'from the many fair streets and suburbs of Dublin and the many foul alleys on the banks of Liffey'. Ten to fifteen thousand and upwards on a single Sunday! What attracted so many from a city whose population was a mere tenth of that of London?

There were exotic tree ferns, quaint and beautiful forms of cactus in Richard Turner's elegant curvilinear hothouse (of which the Turner hothouse in the Regent's Park Garden was almost a twin). There was a tropical and hardy aquarium, the lack of which to William Robinson deprived a botanic garden of a quarter of its interest. 'I am very fond of water plants,' he declared, and here at Glasnevin grew the rarely seen Water Chestnut with the American Lotus blossoming rich and fragrant. Nymphaeas were well represented and beautifully grown, the Sacred Bean 'nobly done'.

Outdoors were thirty acres of interest: the conifers of all sorts which grew superbly at Glasnevin, the groves of the forest giants of Europe and America, down to carpets of the tiniest heaths; lilies, medicinal herbs, water plants like *Hottonia* and *Villarsia* growing richly along the banks of Tolka, in all so many plants and *good* plants that the names of those he wanted filled a notebook. Remembering that a great philosopher had written of the 'eternal verities', William had recently arrived at the conclusion that good plants are the 'eternal verities' of respectable gardening. He was to receive more plants from Glasnevin than from any other botanic garden on his tour.

But he was scathing about the new Palm House he had heard about. Previously the first object to strike the visitor was the Octagon, one of the oldest glasshouses and built to accommodate the finest Norfolk Island Pine in the United Kingdom (unfortunately broken and destroyed while being conveyed to its new home!). William had expected that it would make sad comparison with the new house. To his amazement it looked almost classical, the new Palm House astoundingly ugly. 'It is as if,' he wrote, 'the demon of bad taste had ... built his temple in the central scene of a beautiful garden, in the midst of the elegant leaf-builders, and over a host of graceful Palms!'

Beauty had its revenge: in 1883 the atrocity was so damaged by gales that it had to be taken down.

Because of the expense of making a collection of orchids, botanic gardens could not compete with such orchidists as Robert Warner of Chelmsford, John Day of Tottenham and Turner's of Manchester who were the great cultivators of their day. Glasnevin, however, had an extensive collection with many new and rare kinds. Above them, running along the roof and hanging from the rafters was the largest Pitcher Plant William had ever seen, while each pillar had a different species of hoya wreathed round it.

Plants and Plant Men

He went to and fro: indoors to avoid a shower, outdoors again. Glasnevin was a great garden for herbaceous plants. William wrote of it: 'They muster a goodly army in the natural arrangement, make a very select company in the reserve garden, display a numerous and still choicer band in the borders that surround the two great ranges of glass, marshal scores of the really useful individuals in the economical garden, and present the most ornamental and graceful species here and there throughout the garden.' He was in military mood!

He was particularly struck by the fact that so many tender and even stove plants were growing happily outside. *Clerodendron foetidum (bungei)*, for instance, was in luxuriant tufts, each shoot forming a flower truss: it grew wild in some parts of the garden. *Sauromatum guttatum* was quite hardy here and *Helianthus orgyalis (salicifolius)*, with the Compass Plant of the American Indians.

The sight of these exotics acclimatizing themselves seemed to William to 'ring a note of preparation for sub-tropical gardening elsewhere'. He was to write a book on the subject.

A really worthy national garden, he summed up Glasnevin, extolling its beauties over and over in what he later wrote about it, remembering as clearly as if he were there again the visits he had made in the ten days he was in Dublin, scenes of beauty that sparked off many ideas. 'I must apologise for sundry digressions,' he wrote. 'But where is one to talk if not in a garden after his own heart?'

After such a floral and botanical feast it was restful to visit Kilakee on the ruin-crested hill of Montpellier which looked down upon Dublin seven miles away. Its exquisitely terraced flower garden, its picturesque and densely wooded glen with the brawling little falls of a rivulet, the huge and precipitous banks of rhododendrons, and—to his joy—a mixed border of roses and herbaceous plants ('which I was glad to find had not been sacrificed to the mania of red, yellow and blue') filled an enchanting day.

When its owner, Colonel White, bought the estate the 500 acres of its demesne were a barren waste supporting only a few miserable cottiers; before he died it had become a most beautiful scene with woodlands and gardens of every kind. After his tour of these delights William sat down on a rustic chair to survey it all, writing, 'I know of no better example of the advantages of extensively planting and draining a barren and elevated district than is afforded by this demesne.' Had he been able to look into the future he could have been speaking of himself and his own demesne fifty years on.

When he visited the garden at Rockville, still in the neighbourhood of

Dublin, he found something so remarkable that after his article about it appeared in *The Gardeners' Chronicle* the leader-writer filled three more columns with the subject, urging everyone who could do so to try a similar experiment.

The something so remarkable was indeed a glimpse into the future—double-glazing. It was the invention of Rockville's owner, the wealthy Thomas Bewley. *The Gardeners' Chronicle* hailed it as a minor scientific discovery destined to play a very important part in the future of plant culture. It had every virtue: saving fuel, retaining moisture and maintaining equable humidity, doing away with shading, and slowing the increase of heat in warm weather.

The reverse effects in winter were equally advantageous: the thermometer rarely went below 48°F and it took three or four nights of severe frost to bring the temperature down from 54°. Were the fire to be let out or neglected for a whole night the plants would suffer no damage. William found this particularly interesting. Perhaps he was thinking of Ballykilcavan.

Bewley had tried the experiment on his fern house, which was sixty feet wide and forty-eight feet long. He was now going to use it for his beloved orchids whose houses were part of the 'vast indoor department which quite absorbed my time and taste,' as William wrote, first proceeding to a house of gorgeous cattleyas. The Bewley orchids were 'valuable enough to make a ducal garden famous', a collection begun seriously in 1861 when William had seen a range of houses being built especially for them.

Before visiting Manchester he had thought London the worst place in the world for plants, but he was mistaken. He left a London whose plane trees were remarkably healthy and verdant: he now saw gaunt skeletons flit by, whose last leaves of life were shed. On the road to Todmorden there were even more dead trees and William feared for what he might see in Manchester's botanic garden.

Manchester, however, was not the blackest of cities, and the botanic garden was pleasantly situated at a considerable distance from its busy and smoky parts. Various surprises awaited him: the redoubtable 'Victoria' (the vast water lily) though grown under difficulties in a lean-to was in a far better state than the one in his own Regent's Park; ferns were exceedingly well done, and the display of gladiolus the finest he had seen in any public garden. There were few treasures, the garden being almost wholly an ornamental one, but, even so, he expected he would have a few dozen good plants. What was the biggest surprise was meeting 'a gentleman named Leeds' who kept a little botanic garden of his own at Longford Bridge, Stretford, near the River Mersey. William found it well worth visiting, for it was full of rarities. Edward Leeds, a stockbroker, spent all his leisure time growing old florists' flowers such as auriculas, carnations, pinks and tulips, and raising daffodils, concentrating on improving the white and pale-coloured varieties. One day his collection was to become famous as the *Leedsii* Division of Narcissus.

He was back in London in September, just in time to write the report of his successful journey for the Garden Committee meeting on the 26th. Robert Marnock presented it, the last time he would do so before his retiral, though he would continue to manage the exhibitions. Appointed to superintend the Garden was Thomas Don, an efficient administrator though not to be compared with Robert Marnock. He was given the office of superintendent, not curator.

William had accomplished much in the month he had been away, acquainting himself with the botanic gardens of England, Scotland and Ireland, as well as many of the best private gardens, seeing what new plants were being grown and how they were cultivated, comparing garden with garden, and meeting curators and private owners, a gardening fraternity.

He could now look at the Regent's Park Garden with fresh eyes, and he lost no time in reporting that the Economical Border was useless and from the mixture of trees and herbs anything but pleasing to look at. He proposed to remove any suitable plants to the Medical Garden and give up the Economical arrangement altogether.

As foreman in charge of the educational and herbaceous department William was now allowed to write his own reports. Some of these reports made Thomas Don's hair stand on end, such was the vehemence adorning Mr Robinson's recommendations. The report Don read to the Garden Committee on the 9th of July 1864 ran as follows:

> I think it my duty to call attention to the positive good that would be done to the neighbourhood of the Medical Garden by the removal of the wretched old experiment, called a greenhouse, which is now an object of ridicule there. The house is perfectly useless as a plant-growing house, is the most paltry affair of the kind to be seen in any Botanic Garden of the United Kingdom, and if it could not be made use of in the much wanted addition to the stove I again say it would be a great improvement to my department if the spot of earth occupied by the said structure were laid bare.

Added Thomas Don:

> I should not myself report to the Committee in the above Language,
> but do not feel authorised to alter the reports of the foremen. I
> therefore copy them exactly as they are handed to me.

Mr Robinson (less than three years in London) was now embarked
on a campaign of improvements, some radical, all sensible. Because of
the pressing want of somewhere to grow and exhibit the British ferns, he
proposed making a hardy fernery on the east side of the archway
leading to the Mound, where they could properly be seen and admired
by the many people who hardly noticed them in their present
unsatisfactory place by the Bridge. He had plenty of rough stones and
he had the labour. By the sole purchase of some new soil the job could
be done for twelve pounds.

The Committee approved.

He indented for, and got, 4,000 iron labels to replace the old wooden
ones, a decided advantage in every way.

He wanted unsightly hedges removed and replanted with improved
varieties, one to be dwarf so as to give sufficient shelter but not obscure
the view. Thomas Don concurred with some of this, but his foreman did
not get his dwarf hedge. Don lacked Mr Robinson's far-seeing
imagination.

During this time valuable plants were coming in from Kew,
Glasnevin, Hull and Glasgow, Belfast and Liverpool, and from private
gardens. At the meeting of the Council on the 10th of August 1864
James de Carle Sowerby was pleased in presenting his annual report to
remark that the usual number of plants donated to the Society had been
greatly increased by Mr Robinson, the Society's gardener, whose visits
to these gardens, with the view to arranging exchanges, had been so
successful. Consequently the systematically arranged part of the
garden was improving and had provided good materials for study to the
amount of 26,140 specimens to eleven professors and the teachers of two
schools of art.

'It has been a pleasure,' he told the Council, 'to see those pupils who
have access to the garden in the morning, lying in twos and threes on
the grass with their books and plants in hand, studying the structure of
the flowers and preparing for competitive examinations.'

By 'the Society's gardener' was meant the head gardener. The other
foreman was in charge of the glasshouses. The Garden had a total staff
of thirty-four men and two boys in summer, twenty-six men and two
boys in the winter.

[41]

William's world was expanding fast. He wrote up his gardens tour in *The Gardeners' Chronicle* where it ran in twenty-six issues, from November 1863 to the end of January 1865. He was also writing on Oxford's Botanic Garden, which he visited in June 1864, and this prompted a new series of visits—round the London parks. These were fair game for his critical pen in denouncing the monotonous repetition of bad blue, gamboge, and scarlet. But they were of use, jolting his mind to the contrast of what might be done in gardens, if plants were allowed to grow as they were meant to grow—naturally.

What a scene of beauty a garden might then present!

4
William Robinson F.L.S.

In 1865 and to May of the following year William was consolidating his position both with the Royal Botanic Society and as a regular writer on special plants and on different kinds of gardens.

He was extending the plant-exchange system, now with gardens abroad. In February, as he reported to the Garden Committee, he had received an offer from Mark John M'Ken, curator of the Botanic Garden of Natal, a country where there were some good plants as yet unintroduced. William recommended that a flora of South African plants be consulted so that a list of wanted plants could be compiled, with the request that only those specified be sent. In exchange, a case of roses or other plants wanted in the Natal garden could be sent.

Another offer had come from a plant hunter travelling in the United States. Plants had come from France; and he had heard from James Duncan, curator of the Mauritius Botanic Garden, that the Wardian cases of plants sent him had arrived safely and were being returned with the best plants the Mauritius garden had, including the orchid which was exciting everybody's admiration—*Angraecum sesquipedale* of huge six-rayed flowers like stars, formed of snow-white bracts. Its two nectaries were eleven and a half inches long, requiring, as Charles Darwin predicted, a moth with a proboscis of that length to pollinate it. There was such a moth: *Xanthopan morgani praedicta* had a proboscis of exactly the right length.

He had spent some days in February visiting the London nurseries, giving *The Gardeners' Chronicle* readers a timely look at the winter flowers to be enjoyed in the glasshouse, for 'The snow is in the fields and parks, its black sludge in the streets; frost, sleet and rain succeed each other rapidly and regularly.' Outdoor attractions were out of the question, so it was indoors to see cinerarias in brilliant bloom at Woodroffe's nursery in the Harrow Road, the early pelargoniums just beginning to open, and *Acacia drummondii* in flower.

Henderson's nursery in Pineapple Place close by Hall Road, just off the Edgware Road, was always the most interesting to William because of its age, standing, associations, and even the name of its location. It specialized in hiring flowering pot plants to London halls and drawing-rooms, and so more attention was paid to winter and early spring-flowering plants than at other nurseries. On this day 200 pots were absent, lending their beauty elsewhere, yet there was still a very good display in the Show House, the Tussac-grass in flower, *Rhododendron variabilis*, pretty bouquets of mixed bulbs in rustic and earthenware pots, and, most beautiful ornament of all, standards of *Viburnum tinus virens*, a compact sheet of fragrant white blossoms.

In Wellington Road, E. G. Henderson's nursery rewarded him with an arctic ramble among the bloom of an unequalled collection of cyclamens, with a more tropical scene at Low's nursery at Clapton. William thus described it: 'Anybody writing of antipodal scenery without having the advantage of travel among Dicksonias, should at once go to the Clapton nurseries, where three rows of Tree Ferns in a long house will afford a most essential perspective. Looking lengthwise or sideways the effect is remarkable. It would be pardonable absent-mindedness in a man to peer through the stems for an aborigine and his "gin" or squaw in this house. I was on the point of doing so,' he joked, 'when my eye caught the roof of an adjoining house, and the illusion was dispelled.'

Veitch's nursery in the King's Road, Chelsea, was the climax of his tour, for here was everything of elegance and grace that could be hunted up anywhere. The space occupied by palms, cycads, tree ferns and tender pines along the corridor and adjacent houses was very large, 'and yet, winter or summer the scene is ever grateful to the eye and mind; because, group the plants as you may, the "lines of beauty" are ever there; arrange them as you may, the mystery and indefiniteness which constitute beauty of vegetation in its highest sense, cannot be extinguished. Such a scene can have no effect on the mind but an elevating one; nobody was or ever will be repelled by it. It is only by freely intermingling such plants with free-flowering ones, that you can get the supremest beauty of vegetation—not that which pleases a class, however large or learned, but all mankind. This I say advisedly and I take this opportunity to utterly repudiate the false notion that it is by colour alone we can attract the non-gardening community. Therefore, I urge that every conservatory or house for exhibiting plants in their best state, should have in it a large proportion of ever-verdant and gracefully habited species, which are incapable of being trained in ugliness, and moreover always ready to intensify by contrast the beauty of free-flowering plants.'

This, at the age of twenty-six, was William Robinson's testament of beauty.

William Robinson F.L.S.

The snow eventually cleared away, the sun came out, and gardens began to burgeon. Making day trips to Cliveden to see how spring gardening was done at this vast place where Robert Marnock had laid out the flower garden, and to Wilson Saunders' garden at Reigate, and the Royal Gardens at Frogmore, he wrote a series of articles on 'Spring Flowers and Spring Gardening', 'Spring and Early Summer Flowering Plants', and 'Beautiful Hardy Plants for the Select Spring Garden', articles which had an impact on the floricultural world, as the leader-writer of *The Gardeners' Chronicle* acknowledged. Letters came from all quarters, asking what had happened to 'Primroses, Polyanthuses, Auriculas, and other ancient favourites' which in these days of the bedding-out system had been allowed to go very much out of sight and therefore out of mind. 'It has been discovered,' added the leader-writer with some irony, 'that our grandfathers had fine flowers, though they lived before the appearance of Dahlias and Verbenas.' Older florists wished they could recover the massive Grand Admiral auricula which they remembered as one of the finest plants they ever saw.

The articles certainly gave birth to a resurgence of interest in long-neglected plants. The leader ended: 'It is something that cultivators who have been too much engrossed with the autumnal flower garden, should become aware of the fact that there are numerous classes of hardy plants which are quite as interesting and attractive, if not so brilliant and showy as their special favourites. We trust that the interest which has been awakened in spring flowers will not wear off without practical results.'

William hoped so, too. It became part of his life-work to see that it did not.

He did not lose sight of his garden duties for the Society, in May able to report that the Medical Garden was now in an excellent state of usefulness for the students, reporting also that the old fernery near the bridge was now a home for British orchids, and that they were doing well.

He was anxious to visit the great private botanical gardens, proposing to the Garden Committee that he would begin with the famed garden at Dangstein, then to Bicton near Exeter, and Elvaston, Chatsworth and others. The Herbaceous Division did not now want very many plants, so he would pick up plants for the glasshouses and Ornamental Department. He asked for ten pounds towards his expenses.

As always, Thomas Don had written William's request into his general report. He continued: 'Mr Robinson wants so few plants for the

Herbaceous Department, they can be had by writing for. The Houses and Ornamental Department he has nothing to do with and Plants can be procured for them when required.'

This snub did not weigh with the Committee. They agreed that Mr Robinson should go on his tour. The only concession made to Don was that five pounds and not ten pounds should be provided towards defraying his expenses.

At Dangstein, Lady Dorothy Nevill's place of plant-treasures near Midhurst in Sussex, he kept a tryst with a plant introduced in 1861. He was all agog to see it and surprised when he did, for the eight tiny seedlings were little more than an inch high, yet each was perfectly developed in its own small way. They were of *Darlingtonia californica*, a species of Pitcher Plant which was to be of personal interest to him. 'I found it on the Californian Sierras,' he wrote in his catalogue of *Alpine Flowers*, 'about little springs on the hills thickly tufted among the common Rush.' This was a trip to come. He had tried raising it from seed but the results were a weedy failure. Here they were as healthy as the other sarracenias on the bench. They looked like up-ended slugs, bright green, with little pocket-handkerchiefs in their mouths.

He spent the whole day at Dangstein and into the evening, in order to see the Moonflower come into bloom, *Ipomoea bona-nox* (now called *Calonyction aculeatum*). This was an event at Dangstein, breathless moments of watching it unfold to huge deliciously fragrant flowers of transcendently beautiful pure white. Several of Lady Dorothy's guests came out to see the spectacle, who 'would not think of hothouses after supper for anything else except the night-blooming Cactus, and that,' wrote William, 'is a poor thing compared to this creeper, which keeps expanding its flowers after dark for nearly the whole year round.'

He spent three days at Bicton; there was so much to see. The flower garden was bounded by two long walls running down to the church built by Lady Rolle in memory of her husband, and these walls were entirely clad by one plant alone, *Magnolia grandiflora*, whose flowers scented the valley for a mile around. The head gardener's description of the perfume reminded William of Thomas Moore's poem *Lalla Rookh*, whether 'The perfume breathing round, Like a pervading spirit', or sleeping and waking in scented airs, amid 'a wilderness of flowers'.

Conifers were here, there, and everywhere, and had been grown from seed. Current was the belief in the degeneracy of conifers from home-grown seeds, but there were hundreds of perfect specimens here raised in this way. There were also noble plants of *Abies cephalonica* (William called them *Picea cephalonica*, the name used in his day) and deodars, struck from cuttings. Today, Bicton's pinetum contains some of the largest and finest specimens in Britain.

It was not the glasshouses that interested William in this garden. More to the point was that looking out through the glass one could see dark, very dark and healthy beds of evergreen, composed of Lady Hume's Blush and the old white and other camellias. They were densely studded with buds, and if the blooms were to get hurt by spring frost there were plenty ready to unfold the day after.

The flower garden gave him more pleasure than he thought possible for such a place. This was a confession, for it was 'mechanical landscape gardening'. He was delighted that 'the beauty of vegetation obliterates the geometrical lines and twirlings of man'. It was 'an open-air drawing-room, but not one in which interest of detail is sacrificed to general effect.' Every good flower garden should be interesting in its details, he added, while agreeable in its general effect, and 'There is nothing to prevent it being so—absolutely nothing. English flower gardening must come to this—it is coming to it.' By his efforts, it could be added.

Robert Pince's nursery at St Thomas, Exeter, was his next call, a firm specializing in fuchsias, in 1842 having raised the hybrid *exoniensis* of three-inch-long scarlet sepals and purple petals. Then it was to Elvaston Castle in Derbyshire.

Conifers were popular at this period, as evergreens to make winters more cheerful than could the bare boughs of leaf-shedding trees. Variegated and coloured sports that appeared in their seed beds were seized upon by the nurserymen, to be propagated and advertised. William Barron, gardener to the Earl of Harrington at Elvaston, had built up a superb collection and was the author of *The British Winter Garden: A Practical Treatise on Evergreens*, published in 1852.

A visit to the botanic garden at Sheffield was especially interesting because of its associations. 'The moment you enter on the lawn you are reminded of the Botanic Gardens, Regent's Park—and not unnaturally, of course, as Mr Marnock laid out both.' It was a most pleasant garden with a handsome range of glasshouses filled with plants suited to a botanic garden but with plenty of showy ones among them.

On the 14th of October Thomas Don reported to the Garden Committee that Mr Robinson had been visiting many of the great gardens and had already received plants from them. From Sheffield had come an established plant of *Sarracenia purpurea*, and from Lady Dorothy Nevill's garden he expected some valuable and rare medicinal plants. When a fortnight later her plants arrived they proved to be treasures indeed: the true Ebony (*Diospyros ebenus*), the famous

William Robinson F.L.S.

Hippomane mancinella (the Manchineel or Mazanilla tree), the Cuba Bast Plant (*Hibiscus elatus*), and the Hand Plant (*Cheirostemon platanoides*), with other very rare medicinal plants. Many good plants had also come from the Royal Botanic Garden at Edinburgh, including the Crown or Brown Peru Bark (*Cinchona condaninea*, now *C. officinalis*), one of the important trees in India and other tropical countries because it contains anti-malarial quinine.

During 1865 William was not only regularly contributing to *The Gardeners' Chronicle* but, as the year went on, answering queries in the 'Home Correspondence' columns, and all with the voice of authority. He found it exhilarating to communicate his thoughts to the public; and always with the giving of advice it was from the depths of sincerity, feeling that he had things to say that must be said for the future health of good gardening. He began to think that one day he would like a 'Gardeners' Chronicle' of his own to manage, that would concentrate on garden plants and all things pertaining to gardens and gardening, leaving out the chats about apiaries and agricultural matters.

By this time he numbered among his friends and acquaintances many influential people. They were Fellows of the Royal Botanic Society ('Royal' long before the Horticultural Society was given the accolade), or of the Linnean and other learned societies, or leading botanists with whom he was associated in his work, or whose gardens he had visited or whom he met at the R.B.S. shows. They were an ever-widening circle.

One was Charles Darwin who was in the thick of experiments for his monumental book *The Effects of Cross- and Self-Fertilisation*. So was William! For in a letter to the Society's young foreman Darwin asked if he had the aquatic plant *Euryale ferox*. If so, and 'if it produces more than one flower at a time, I wish you would cross some & fertilise some others with their own pollen, in order to see, when the seed is counted (which I would undertake), whether the cross aids at all in increasing fertility.'

Darwin was staying at Queen Anne Street with his brother Erasmus, and wrote later, 'I was very sorry to have missed seeing you & hope I shall be more fortunate when I may next be in London.'

It was good at Exhibition-time to see Robert Marnock again. Much out of London these days, he was adding to the list of gardens he was designing in that happy manner in which his work was always done. Breadth of treatment and grace of outline were his hallmark, with natural gradations of colour and arrangement. They were gardens of the greatest charm, for he was both artist and gardener, a happy combination.

William Robinson F.L.S.

He not only designed gardens. The Exhibition tent 'which has enabled us all to see and enjoy the delightful assemblage called a "Flower Show" to the best advantage' was also designed by him. The first of its kind, it was much more a tent-garden than a mere tent. The idea soon spread 'and no doubt all our great shows will be arranged on the same principle,' as William wrote. The Royal Horticultural Society, marquee by marquee, eventually brought all the floral exhibits of the Chelsea Show under one canopy, this in 1951 when it introduced an enormous tent which, covering more than three acres, was the largest stretch of canvas in the world.

The summer of 1865 was a warm one, ideal weather for Exhibition Week. S. Reynolds Hole, then Vicar of Caunton, was there and William was conducting him round some of the exhibits when Hole began fanning himself with his hat. What happened then is best told in Dean Hole's own words, written in 1900.

They were sitting in the shade of a tree.

I had retired with my friend from the heat of the Exhibition tents when he first announced, as we sat, *subtegmine fagi*, his intention to edit a weekly newspaper exclusively devoted to horticulture. At that time there was only one hebdomadal publication on the subject which kept within the boundaries of the garden, and this the *Gardener's Magazine*, although it was conducted by a most zealous and capable editor, Mr Shirley Hibberd, had not the circulation which it deserved. *The Gardeners' Chronicle*, admirable then as now, and supported by a very large staff of efficient contributors, was combined with an *Agricultural Gazette*, and many of the pleasant practical pages of the *Cottage Gardener* were devoted to beehives and cocks and hens.

I therefore welcomed with acclamation Mr Robinson's proposal to establish a newspaper which would treat of the garden and the garden only, and so far as other topics were concerned should 'brook no rival near its throne.'

I was impelled to stronger motives and happier anticipations to express my sympathy, and to promise such help as I could give, as I knew that my companion was resolved to maintain against all comers the superiority of the Natural to the Artificial system, of the English to the Italian style of garden, and that he had not only the will but the power. He believed as I believed, in Tennyson's words: 'Great Nature is more wise than I.'

Robert Marnock encouraged him. He knew about publishing, having edited *The Floricultural Magazine* for four years, and having been associated with Dr Richard Deakin in Volume I of his *Florigraphica Britannica*.

[49]

William Robinson F.L.S.

It was the Dean-to-be who suggested the title of the newspaper-to-be. In his book of *Memories* Dean Hole gives a briefer version of that hot day at the Exhibition.

> ... I sat down with my friend, William Robinson, under a tree in the Regent's Park, and suggested THE GARDEN as a title for the newspaper which he proposed to publish and which has been so powerful in its advocacy of pure horticulture of the natural, or English, school, free from rigid formalities....

William's next step was breaking free from his own rigid formalities. On the 12th of May 1866 he handed in his resignation, couched in these words:

> Wishing to devote myself to the study of our Great Gardens and to the Literature of Horticulture for a year or two, I beg to resign my situation here—desiring to leave as soon as may be convenient to the Society.
>
> I desire to heartily thank you for the encouragement and courtesy shown to me during the time I have had charge of the botanical department and but for which I could have done but little for its improvement.

He left Regent's Park on the 26th of June, and he left it with an inch or two added to his stature. On the 19th of April something very pleasant had happened: he was elected a Fellow of the Linnean Society. The citation read as follows:

> Mr William Robinson of the Royal Botanic Society's gardens, Regent's Park, a gentleman much attached to the study of Natural History, especially Botany, being desirous of becoming a Fellow of the Linnean Society of London, we, the undersigned, beg to recommend him as deserving that honour, and likely to prove a useful and valuable member.

He had ten sponsors, an almost unheard-of number. The list of their names reads like a star cast. The first two were James Veitch, the great nurseryman and father of a race of nurserymen, and Charles Darwin (whose *Origin of Species* William found 'inexplicable'). Three were professors to whom he had supplied student plant material: John T. Boswell Syme, lecturer in botany at Charing Cross Hospital and Westminster; Robert Bentley, botany lecturer and professor of botany at King's College; and Dr Maxwell Tylden Masters, scientific editor of *The Gardeners' Chronicle* and lecturer at St George's Hospital; with the Revd. William Williamson Newbould, an original member of the Ray

Society; Dr Richard C. A. Prior, traveller in South Africa, Canada and Jamaica, who had recently published *Popular Names of British Plants*; Thomas Moore, curator of the Chelsea Physic Garden; William Bull, one of the first sixty recipients of the Royal Horticultural Society's Victoria Medal of Honour; and the man who had put William Robinson's feet on the first rung of the ladder—Dr David Moore of Glasnevin, Ireland's National Botanic Garden.

5
'From our
Special Correspondent'

Much in the horticultural air was talk of the great French International Exhibition, to take place in Paris in 1867. But, as the leader-writer of *The Gardeners' Chronicle* complained on the 15th of December 1866, information about it was not only exceedingly meagre and unaccountably tardy, but altogether unsatisfactory so far as English exhibitors were concerned.

'Months and months ago,' he recalled, 'the English cultivators were invited to pledge themselves to become exhibitors, and up to the present time they have sought in vain for anything like a detailed schedule or guide, such as would enable them to set about definite preparations.'

True, in this month of December they had received a general programme covering the whole period from April to the end of October, but so 'general' that it was utterly useless as a guide in preparing plants for the respective shows. A detailed schedule was promised before the end of July 1866. It had not been forthcoming. How was it that the French horticultural press had the schedule and not those invited to exhibit as foreigners? 'Anyway, thanks to the French journalists, we were enabled some two months ago, to give much fuller information than what was contained in the official document only now issued in England.' Though, it was added, even that information was incomplete and practically useless, the number of plants in the respective classes not being stated. Unless this information was supplied to them immediately it would be impossible to prepare the plants for exhibition.

William Robinson, however, was well on the way to preparing himself. The fact of the forthcoming Exhibition had been one spur to his leaving Regent's Park, for various aspects of French gardening had been claiming his interest for some time. It had started with some old French garden books he had found in the Botanic Society's library, and when writing up the Irish gardens in 1864 he had compared the 'chaste' and beautifully executed geometrical garden at Kilakee with the 'polychromatic' style of the French parterre. This kind of thing, he remarked, might have been desirable in La Quintinye's time (when seventeenth-century France was in a comparatively rude state) 'to encourage the draughtsman in ground and gravel, and astonish the natives with elegant twirlings on mother Earth'. In the present day, and in England where it was almost impossible to get away from all sorts of artificiality, it could only be productive of what it had already yielded—'an abundant crop of well-deserved ridicule'.

William wanted to see what the French were up to now in their gardening. Hints of it appeared from time to time in the horticultural papers: the mode of cultivating asparagus as practised by Louis L'Hérault of Argenteuil, for instance; and the way the Parisian nurserymen used plants with decorative foliage. He hired a tutor to teach him French, a lady *emigrée* who worked him hard so that he would be conversant enough with the language to ask questions of the French nurserymen and understand their answers. Time was short, only seven months before he would have to be in Paris.

He filled up the time profitably by writing up a round of gardens for *The Gardeners' Chronicle*, in June revisiting Cliveden and Bicton, the latter particularly to see the four acres of its vegetable garden and the methods by which James Barnes produced year-round crops of lettuces, cabbages and spinach. The entire ground was trenched once a year, and for every crop, so that some parts were trenched three times annually. He successfully cultivated ginger, grew pineapples in the open from May until October, and produced plentiful crops of apricots and a continual abundance of mushrooms. Grapes, strawberries and figs were grown in a range of glasshouses.

On the way to Cliveden William dropped in to see Berry Hill, near Maidenhead, not expecting to see much in the way of unusual plants but delighted with the charm of the place. It had been laid out by Robert Marnock, and this was sufficient to account for its beauty. It was everything that William Robinson asked of a garden. The following paragraph in which he compared its attractiveness with—inevitably— the artificialities of what passed for good taste demonstrated the great principles William Robinson was to teach.

> British horticulturists, and indeed intelligent Britons generally, are ardently devoted to the English or 'natural' style of garden design; and it is not too much to suppose that if every city or town in these islands was embellished by a public garden laid out on the opposite principle of making steps, stones and statues, and pagodas, pedestals, pounded brick, and polychrome, ten times more conspicuous than the natural ornaments of a garden, it would not alter our love for the natural in garden design. And yet the taste lives

under difficulties, not from opposition of other schools but from the barbarous and strait-laced designs that are passed off as representative of this style.

Who, he asked, had not seen 'ornamental water' looking as if it had been designed after an antique pie-dish slightly bent in the baking? Who had not seen the undulating ground that here and there went off at a tangent, as if the superintendent of a gang of railway navvies had now and then replaced the landscape gardener for a few hours? Who had not witnessed the painful mixture of the geometrical and 'English style' that was so common?

It is of great importance to English horticulture that the most tasteful examples of what foreigners call the 'English garden', and the most correct principles of designing should be made known.

Meanwhile, he was off to the Lake District for a week with James Backhouse junior and Robert Farmer. They were going to explore the hills for alpines, starting with the craggy slopes of Helvellyn.

Robert Farmer was an alpine specialist whose house, The Hill, Hornsey, was within a pleasant walk of St Paul's, as William described it. His garden was remarkable, merely being two little rocky beds not more than five feet across in the widest part. Yet even on the July day William saw it, when alpine plants are usually out of flower, these two little beds were full of bloom. *Calandrinia umbellata* on tiny prominences was a show of brilliant crimson-magenta flowers. The little dark purple bells of the rare *Campanula pulla* hung over such things as that gem among sedums—*brevifolium*, and fairy bushes of *Alyssum spinosum*, evergreen, or more correctly ever-silvery. And this was only one small patch in that jewel of a garden which William had visited several times during the fifteen months since it was created.

'It rained all the time we stopped in the Lake District,' was the mournful report of *The Gardeners' Chronicle* correspondent, 'except when it "snawed whiles" and poured down big hailstones.' On the afternoon of the 16th of June some of the high mountains were covered with snow, and a striking sight it was to see, as they drove to Ambleside from the direction of Keswick, the lower summits free of it and the countryside in summer green.

They found the rare and beautiful *Lychnis alpina* of pale purple heads, *Silene acaulis* covering four miles of the higher slopes above Ullswater with firm, dense, bright-green mossy tufts dotted over with reddish-purple flowers, a lovely little alpine plant that turned the crumbling and awesome mountainsides into beauty. William was no mountaineer but he had implicit faith in his friend James Backhouse. 'Some of the gorges, though deep,' he wrote, 'are not much wider than a chimney, so that in climbing one could lay hands on both sides. This was in some cases a comfort, as things now and then looked dangerous, and I was many times indebted to Mr Backhouse, who is a safe mountain-climber, as to where to place my feet.'

Having collected a harvest of plants the three parted, William to visit Crewe Hall, Biddulph Grange, Knypersly for its orchids and fine fruit houses, and on to the magnificent flower and fruit garden at Trentham—all in Staffordshire. At Biddulph he was much impressed with the saucer-like flowers of the large-flowered clematis, writing that these noble climbers should oftener be seen. One day he was to specialize in them.

Alpines continued to command his interest, for he had the idea that once on the Continent he could plan a journey farther afield into Switzerland to see the mountain flowers on their homeland Alps.

Gardeners everywhere at that time were awaking to the fascination of these little plants, due to the stimulus of seeing them at such places as Hull. At the Museum gardens at York the collection had recently been wonderfully increased. But they took some knowing. Soon, William hoped, people would learn how to grow them properly, for rarely were they successful in England—so that 'many of the gems of the most exquisite of all known plants . . . will, ere long, be seen in perfection in our gardens.'

Early in 1866 he was writing a series of articles on specialist subjects for *The Gardeners' Chronicle*. On the 31st of March he dealt with 'Hardy Edging Plants', starting with the neat little hedge of box and quoting John Parkinson who wrote that 'it is of excellent use to border up a knot, and a marvellous fine ornament thereunto', glancing too at strawberry edgings running round the kitchen-garden squares; the Sea Pink, gentian, and dwarf campanulas margining the flower borders of a more recent era of gardening, and the present-day phase of edging-hunting for something different. He recommended some original edgings: *Alyssum spinosum* for one, a shrubby alpine with small silvery leaves; the variegated Cocksfoot Grass; *Sempervivum californicum* for its bluish leaves tipped with chocolate, and some of the encrusted saxifrages which he thought would made very charming and hardy edgings.

On the 28th of April he deplored the fact that there was not a genus more beautiful that was more neglected than the iris. Other neglected plants made a feature for the 22nd of December issue, and by then he was almost ready to pack his bags for Paris.

'From our Special Correspondent'

He was well equipped. In his June and July tour he had studied English methods of cultivating fruits and vegetables: he now knew what he should look for in France. Since 1863 he had been all over England, Scotland and Ireland, looking at flower gardens in private hands and in public parks and botanic gardens, and this included every type of gardening from the growing of alpines whose homes were wind-swept mountainsides to the culture of exotic plants from the tropics. All this would provide comparisons with anything he found in France. Now he was ready, and he was crossing the Channel three months before the Exhibition would open, in order to have a good look round, acclimatize himself and visit some of the nurseries which would be exhibiting their products.

He went armed with commissions from *The Field*, *The Times*, and *The Gardeners' Chronicle*, to write up the Paris Exhibition from the horticultural point of view, particularly with regard to aspects of French gardening which would be valuable for gardeners in England.

But William's plans included more than the Exhibition. France, not merely Paris, was his objective. As he himself said: 'I went to France in January, 1867, with a view to study the horticulture of the country so far as possible, while continuing my connection with the horticultural press.'

His first despatch for *The Gardeners' Chronicle* was date-lined February 16. He wrote it from the rooms he had engaged at 26 rue Bonaparte, not far from St-Germain-des-Près. Here he had been 'hibernating for a month past', as he put it, the weather being fully as disagreeable as the weather he left in England. But at last 'the Lilac buds are beginning to swell,' he wrote, 'there are a few spring flowers to be seen in the Jardin des Plantes; the Wallflowers and various other spring-blooming things, considerably used in Paris squares, &c., are assuming a deeper green preparatory to blooming; the birds are singing merrily in the Tuileries Gardens; the Parisians beginning to crowd the Avenue des Champs Elysées on fine days; in short, one is pleasantly reminded that

> To mute and to material things
> New life returning Summer brings;

and the bright blue sky and gladdening sun of this morning reminded me that it was a capital one on which to see the establishment from which many of the gardens, parks, avenues, and squares in and around Paris, are supplied with plants.'

He was referring to the famous Jardin Fleuriste de la Ville de Paris, otherwise called La Muette, the subject of his first article. It was at

Passy and although no longer in existence is commemorated in the Métro station bearing its name.

'Many English horticulturists have an idea that French gardening is "behind the age",' he began, 'but a single visit to this establishment would leave a very different impression.'

He had imagined Le Jardin Fleuriste to be a kind of large propagating house and was surprised to find that in addition to the plants used for bedding it had a magnificent collection of exotics that would have done credit to any national botanic garden.

'Imagine yourself,' he invited his readers, 'prepared to visit a "propagating establishment", and then ushered into a magnificent span-roofed curvilinear Camellia house—quite a grand conservatory of Camellias, with, on one side, a great conservatory filled with Aralias, Yuccas, Beaucarneas, Tree Ferns, Nicotianas, Dasylirions, Dracaenas, and a host of such plants all in fine condition; and, on the other side, another very fine span-roofed structure for Palms. And such a noble collection of healthy Palms in a fresh green state!'

He was struck with the closeness of the pots to each other—efficient economy of space, he called it, such as he had never seen in England. (Nowadays we know that some plants, such as saintpaulias, are 'sociable', prospering better when their leaves touch each other.) Under the benches were packed quantities of caladiums, fuchsias, cannas and arums, while shelf above shelf accommodated a multitude of other plants. The place was a hive of activity. The potting shed had a great wide bench in the centre around which sixty men could work.

The method of propagating was quite different from how it was done in England. No pans were used but very minute pots, a shade larger than a thimble, and into each a cutting was placed and the little pots stood on tan and covered with large bell-glasses.

Walking from one house to another William was dazzled. Bedding plants were raised by the half-million but also rare plants and scores of different species of aralia, oreopanix, anthurium, zamia and ficus—and all to supply one city with plants for decorating its gardens, civic dinner tables and other indoor functions. The Hotel de Ville alone could be supplied with 10,000 plants for a single occasion.

The man responsible for all this productivity was the brilliant Pierre Barillet-Deschamps who had made the beautiful Promenade des Quinconces at Bordeaux. Following this success he was engaged by Baron Haussmann, architect of the New Paris (as it was called) transformed by Napoleon III.

In his second 'Letter from Paris' William went on to describe the floral feast that awaited the dignitaries invited to dine at the Hotel de

Ville. It could hardly be anything but a criticism of the English way of doing things, and he knew what he was talking about, for he was able to compare home efforts with the displays of plants at the last ball of the Paris season.

Like St Paul delivering a homily he began with a compliment: 'You can grow good plants in England without doubt—nobody denies that merit to English gardeners, but,' he added, 'nowadays when the taste for having plants indoors is becoming so prevalent it is not enough to have good specimens; we should know also how to arrange them tastefully.'

Conservatories in England were occasionally well arranged, he allowed, and there were some nurserymen who arranged plants nicely for balls and other indoor functions, but 'it is rare to see anything really well done in that line, while the way plants are arranged at the Linnean and Royal Societies and other important places, on special occasions, is almost sufficient to prevent people tolerating plants indoors at all.' William Robinson never minced his words when he was waging war on what was ugly, or, if not quite ugly, what could have been done better, much better.

He described the scene in the Salle St Jean as set for the ball. It was breathtaking in its beauty. Flowers were everywhere, never stuck about in solitary pots, never shouting a blast of mere colour, but always set, like jewels, among the green of leaves. They were massed together to form set pieces in mirror-lined alcoves where their beauty was endlessly duplicated in reflections. Not a flower-pot was showing, not a bare stem. Mosses and ferns filled the gaps. The regal leaves of palms made a framework above. Yet all these were the ordinary flowers and plants to be found in English greenhouses, but here arranged with exquisite grace.

Bouquets, posies and buttonholes were the subject of 'Letter from Paris, Number III'. The flower shops were selling plants not so different from what could be seen in Covent Garden, except that in most of them not only flowers but yuccas, dracaenas and young palms were for sale, attesting how thoroughly the French people were awake to beauty of form. William hoped that these would soon be offered cheap by English nurserymen. Forced lilac was much in evidence, particularly white lilac, and of the hardy spring flowers the violet—*la Violette*—was the darling. The flower-shop windows were purple with them, the street barrows covered with them, the streets themselves filled with their fragrance. Some people were buying bunches as big as a saucer, and old flower-women were dividing the larger bunches into

5 (*left*) Pierre Barillet-Deschamps (1824–1873), creator of the great
boulevards, squares and parks of Napoleon III's New Paris
(*Service Technique des Parcs, Ville de Paris*)

6 (*right*) Anglophile Henry Vilmorin, scion of France's greatest
horticultural family and close friend of francophile William Robinson.
(*Royal Botanic Gardens, Kew*)

very small ones to suit poor purchasers, and putting a couple of
snowdrops, a cyclamen or two or a primrose in the centre of each little
bunch.

During recent winters some of the London seed shops had been
selling what to William were 'ridiculous bunches of Everlastings and
Grasses', the "Everlastings" being mostly marigolds, geraniums, and
double zinnias dried into an ugly rigidity, the grasses mostly of a weedy
type.

'Very few would appear to know anything about the beauty, the
extraordinary beauty that may be made by a combination of the best of
both,' William addressed himself to these shops. 'The Parisians use but
a few kinds—the old Stipa and the fairy-like Agrostis nebulosa, with
one or two more; but they arrange these in bunches almost as graceful
as the tail of a bird of paradise.'

But he had nothing good to say of the way Everlastings were used in
French cemeteries. 'Next to seeing the contents of a hundred morgues
"laid out", the great spread of decaying Everlastings is the most ghastly
sight. They hang them on the poor little wooden crosses, they pile them
inside on the covered tomb, they hang them on the few green bushes,
they sling them under little spans of glass placed purposely over many
tombs to protect the Immortelles from the weather, and in every other

[59]

way, till in every part and particularly the part where the second and third class departed are buried, there is scarcely anything to be seen but Everlastings in every stage of decay, the *coup d'oeil* being most depressing to anybody used to green English or Irish churchyards.'

It was a relief to visit the Exhibition grounds and to report that everything was progressing rapidly, nothing as yet fit to be described, 'though some of your readers may have long ago read descriptions of fish gliding about in aquariums that were not then even moist.' He could, however, safely say that the permanent or outdoor features of the gardening part of the Great Exhibition would be interesting, beautiful, and instructive. Already there was quite a display of glasshouses— twenty-six of them, from handsome large conservatories to propagating houses. But the whole would not be seen in perfection for two months to come.

This gave William leave for a trip into the country. He went with Henri de Vilmorin to see his late grandfather's estate at Des Barres, near Nogent-sur-Vernisson. Philippe-André de Vilmorin, a great lover of trees who had died in 1862, had created a magnificent arboretum there, which he wished to be given to the State. It had been handed over the year before. Seeing it, William fell under the spell of forests, appreciating too the value to a nation of such an experimental plantation where both conifers and broad-leaved trees could be grown in the poor gritty soil common to much of France.

It was Des Barres which inspired his own plantings of trees when he came to his Sussex kingdom of Gravetye.

6

The International Exhibition, 1867

In order to understand the Paris of 1867 which William Robinson saw we have to look at that great city as it was in the Second Empire when Napoleon III was finishing his vast schemes of rebuilding. From 1853 to 1862 a transformation had been taking place on a scale of unparalleled magnificence. Under the direction of Georges Eugène Haussmann crowded masses of dwellings in warrens of tortuous streets had been replaced by broad boulevards and avenues—twenty-two of them—spacious squares, and palatial buildings. Parks too: the Bois de Boulogne, the Bois de Vincennes, the Parc Monceau—all had been made or made anew. Paris had become a city of gardens and palaces.

It was Pierre Barillet-Deschamps who, in creating the new boulevards, the new squares and parks, waved a wand whereby large trees appeared as if by magic, as if they had been growing there all their lives. He did it with a machine which uprooted and transplanted them, while his method of raising multitudes of plants in the glasshouses ('le système Barillet') spread instant colour and leaf in all the gardens. He planted trees along the Champs-Elysées and made a great belt of gardens on either side. More trees appeared along the banks of the Seine—planes, chestnuts, robinias, and ailanthus, the Tree of Heaven. Here and there was a glorious *Paulownia imperialis*, in William's estimation the best tree of all, especially when he saw them in flower in May, decked in royal purple.

And it was Barillet who in 1867 turned the Champ de Mars, scene of Napoleon Bonaparte's military reviews, into a fairy-like garden as a setting for the Exhibition.

It had rained, it had even snowed, it had rained again, right up to the day before the formal opening. Horses were knee-deep in mud near the entrance on Saturday afternoon; on Sunday it was dark with a cutting wind. Nobody believed that by Monday morning the hopeless confusion would have vanished and the sun be shining.

The outdoor part of the Exhibition was arranged round the main building in four quarters of which one was occupied by the horticultural section, and this was the first time in any international exhibition that horticulture had been given a place of such importance. In the centre was a noble conservatory rightly called the Serre Monumentale. Around it was a landscape of undulating ground with water, rockwork, grottoes, trees and shrubs, all in the 'English' style and exceedingly well done, reported William, the only thing badly done being the water, which was a repetition of the sort of lake he had seen in almost every 'English garden' around Paris—a regular serpentine quite unlike the meanderings pursued by natural water. But there were noble groups of magnolias, many in flower, large beds of hyacinths in full bloom, fine plantations of young shrubs and interesting hollies, with an enormous and handsome specimen of *Thuja gigantea* dominating the scene. All that was wanting, thought William, was that there should be plants in the flower borders and green grass where it was intended green grass should be (it was to be sown tomorrow, he had heard). When this was done he was sure that no horticulturist would be ashamed at the sight presented by the garden department of the first Great Exhibition at which it had a place.

It was a good thing that the outdoor part of the horticultural section was well done, for the Flower Show was nowhere to be found on the first day, with the exception of a few dozen dishes of apples and pears, though William was delighted to see that Joseph Knight, one-time head gardener at Dalkeith and now of Pontchartrain, had a fine show of well-grown roses coming into flower. He began to understand the necessity for having fifteen-day shows. There were to be ten of these, covering five months.

What interested William most was a beautiful fruit garden displaying the most extraordinary and perfect examples of training that he had ever seen, in fact had any idea existed.

The Second Show was not much of an improvement on its predecessor, nor was it likely that there would be much in the way of a Flower Show before the 1st of May. William had been horrified that Messrs Veitch were almost the only British exhibitors, even although they had some nice new plants on view, particularly several beautiful crotons, John Gould Veitch's introductions from the South Sea Islands. William practically dismissed the Show. He still had nothing to report that was acceptable to *The Times*, which did not print a first article till the 9th of May. Apart from some remarkable cacti—'Great cockscomb Mammillarias sheeted over with white spines stand upon comparatively slender legs or bodies of other genera'; 'a specimen of *Echinocactus pottsii*, a globular mass, a foot in diameter and ten inches deep, in robust health, not standing on its own feet however, but supported upon three legs of a comparatively slender-stemmed species'—there was hardly anything worth noticing. William went off to the Parc des Buttes Chaumont to meet Edouard F. André, chief superintendent of all the outer or suburban gardens and squares of Paris.

Napoleon III's great face-lift of Paris was not even finished while the Exposition was going on. At one end of the new park Barillet had created around it was the École Militaire, at the other 'a high rising ground known as the Trocadero' from which you could see nearly all Paris. This had been mined in a thousand places and acres of its soil removed to make a commanding slope right in front of the Exposition. On this they were now planting shrubs. The whole face of the rising ground opposite the Champ de Mars had in fact been altered within the past eight years. (The Champ de Mars itself was to be altered in 1889 when the Eiffel Tower was erected to commemorate the centenary of the Revolution.)

William's article describing the Third Show filled more than two closely packed columns in the May 4 issue of *The Gardeners' Chronicle*. Readers must have detected a whoop of joy.

'At last,' *W.R.* exulted, 'we have something like a Flower Show!'

The new plants shown were remarkable for any exhibition. Again Messrs Veitch were the main exhibitors, but one by the name of Linden had come up with 'an extraordinary thing in the way of Tradescantia with noble leaves a yard or so long and 7 inches broad, a vein of dull purple along the margin, the bases of the leaves clasping the stem like a Billbergia.'

Always on the look-out for things to interest English gardeners William was fascinated by M. Rousseau's method of cultivating truffles. He had ploughed up a lot of inferior waste land and sown it with acorns gathered from an oak wood in which truffles grew, in seven years being rewarded by an abundant crop of more than fifty pounds of truffles per acre. 'Are there not many wastes in England in which the plan might be tried?' asked *W.R.*

Window-gardening was a branch of horticulture much better done in Paris than anywhere else, and William decided to devote an entire Letter to it, giving a list of all the plants in this class. Charles Truffaut, a genial and excellent horticulturist of Versailles, told him that he invariably sold 5,000 of one species alone for this purpose, and that kind not cheap either—*Dracaena terminalis*.

The kinds of plants to be grown were as varied as the window-gardens themselves, one of the simplest 'gardens' being a sponge squeezed almost dry and sown with seeds of millet, red clover, barley-grass, rice and oats. Soon tender leaves would shoot and grow rapidly to form a drooping mass of living green.

The French use of the hose was surprising. 'If there be one thing the corps of men under M. Barillet do better than another,' wrote William, 'it is watering the gardens thoroughly with the hose, a thing the British gardener has not yet learnt with rare exceptions. The consequence is that the reserve garden looks as fresh as a bit of Killarney after a May shower.'

On the 10th of May a letter went from Printing House Square addressed to 'Mr Robinson, Rue Bonaparte No. 27, Paris.' It was signed by Mowbray Morris who was manager of *The Times* from 1847 to 1873 and brother-in-law of the editor.

My dear Sir,

Your first letter was published yesterday & you will naturally expect that I should say something about it.

I think it on the whole a good letter, its chief merit being that it is practical and judicious in the selection of topics. Its chief fault is in the style which is rather obscure. The sentences are involved and not always grammatical, & the reader can hardly in all cases seize the meaning at a first glance; a grave defect in newspaper writing which, before all things, should be clear and easily understood.

We hope soon to hear from you again.

The Letter in question was a telescoped account of all that had happened so far at the Champ de Mars, though it was a long piece taking up more than a column. This was not bad going for a first contribution to *The Times*.

The weather was 'of the vilest description' for the start of the Fourth Show, and the roses and many other things being exhibited in the open were covered with waterproof canopies to protect them. Previously Paris had enjoyed days that were exceptionally hot. London had shared both the wet and the heat, and William was at pains to point out that there was a closer similarity between the two climates than was generally supposed. On the 16th of May, with the dismally wet weather back again, he fled with his friend Knight to see what went on at Pontchartrain. Nothing much was happening at the Show, which started as usual in an unfinished state. Its main features were palms, azaleas, rhododendrons and other greenhouse plants; roses, herbaceous and annual plants outside. The large conservatory was now quite different from how it looked ten days ago, but even with palms and azaleas predominating the effect was bad—'unmitigatedly bad', William denounced it. He hoped it could be improved.

He was much cheered by the Fifth Show, for 'if there be any one thing the French grow pre-eminently well in their gardens, it is hardy fruit, especially Apples and Pears.' The finer apples commanded an extraordinary price in the Paris markets in the spring, and fine French pears were often to be seen at Covent Garden and at some of the English fruit shows. One of the most extensive features in the reserve garden at the Exposition was the fruit garden. M. Barillet told him that it was not at all as good as it should be, and William—who had been visiting some of the private gardens and nurseries—agreed, though telling his readers that so extensive and interesting was it that it would probably please the English horticulturist more than anything else at the Exhibition. The rest of this Letter was devoted to French fruit culture, ending with a note about the beds of annuals, which were pleasing everybody. They were the prettiest things in the garden, 'and about the prettiest things I have ever seen in any garden,' William declared. One bed, displayed by the Vilmorin nurseries, was made up of a great number of the newer kinds—'the dwarfs, and margined and ameliorated annuals, so much brought out of late.' He had a bouquet for English nurserymen. 'The gorgeous Pavilion-like tent that abuts against the central conservatory is now finished and its floor covered with numerous beds of fancy and other geraniums. Very pretty and useful for the show but not nearly so well grown or finished as Messrs Turner Bailey and other English nurserymen are wont to stage them.'

Roses monopolized the Sixth Show with fine-leaved plants and a few miscellaneous things. But 'the Roses are not equal to our own in quality, and the effect they produce is not nice, in consequence of their being closely placed, without green, on wide benches. As for the plants shown as standards in the open ground, they are simply ordinary French nursery stock. The strawberries were very good when fresh, but look badly at present, as many things do after being a few days exposed. Bulbous Irises, Ranunculus, good Shaddocks, &c, are also shown, but nothing worth speaking of, or from which one could take a hint.'

There were a few neat orchids; the house for aquatic plants was now in working order but barely worth mentioning; by far the best new plant was *Nierembergia frutescens*. After a few lines of description William ended his despatch.

'This is all that need be said about the present meeting. It is much more profitable to go into the country now and then, and also to the public gardens, &c., than to spend much time at the Exposition. I have visited the Asparagus-growing region since I last wrote, of which I shall give some particulars at another time.'

It was these out-of-town visits and tours round the Paris parks that were to supply meat for William Robinson's first two books.

Meanwhile he had four more shows to describe and was glad the Seventh *série* was more interesting. M. Linden was showing a selection of his unsurpassed and rare collection of medicinal plants, and nearby were magnificent tree ferns with pygmies a foot high but still with graceful fronds. Among the new roses Prince Humbert seemed to William the most remarkable, a magnificent and distinct rich dark variety. A host of species and varieties of begonias was sad to look at; but a bank of dwarf plants of oleander, beautifully flowered at about fifteen inches high, self-coloured and striped, and rich rose with a small white streak down the petal, was a challenge. 'These are plants which we certainly do not do justice to in England, while the French enjoy them in all stages—from the gigantic specimens placed out with the orange trees in the Luxembourg Gardens to the pretty and most useful sizes I have just alluded to.'

The most interesting thing shown at the Eighth *série* was a large collection of extraordinary seedling gloxinias. They were as good as they were entirely new in style, and the admiration of everybody. 'This popular plant is in fact enobled,' was how William put it. They had been bred a few years before at Bougival by Jules Vallerand, gardener to M. Carcenac. He crossed a pale lilac *Sinningia speciosa* dotted with dark violet with an erect-flowered form and obtained a race of finely spotted and marked flowers. They reminded William of *Achimenes* 'Ambroise Verschaffelt', and he marvelled that all these exquisite varieties had sprung from a single seedling. 'If I say that some of them do not look like Gloxinias at all, but like the flowers of a Dipladenia, it may seem exaggeration, but it is nevertheless a fact; and as really good things are sure to spread, there will probably be, ere long, an opportunity of seeing them in England.'

Gloxinia is the florists' name for the *speciosa* species of the genus *Sinningia* (the true *Gloxinia* being a different plant). *Achimenes* is nearly related. All belong to the same family. M. Vallerand's spotted beauties were not long in crossing the Channel.

It was now August, the flowers of high summer were past and William thought to interest his readers with a description of some of the garden tools and accessories on show. It was time to sow seed for winter and early-spring lettuces, so how better to protect and help them grow than

[66]

7 The Emperor Napoleon III and his Empress
distributing prizes at the Exposition Universelle, Paris 1867.
(Bibliothèque Nationale)

by covering them with a *cloche*? This was the large glass cover used in all French gardens, as big as a beehive and shaped like a bell—hence its French name. Oddly, while we call it a cloche, the French now call it by its English translation, 'bell'! Acres of them were to be seen in the market gardens around Paris, bringing on the fine Cos lettuces and other saladings of which large quantities would be exported to England.

There was also the *sécateur*, and William declared that this was an instrument every gardener should possess. The '*Sécateur* Vauthier' had been described in *The Gardeners' Chronicle* in 1862, the '*Sécateur* Lecointe' in 1865, yet English gardeners were still prejudiced against it. William himself had believed in 'a good knife above all' before coming to France, but seeing how easily and effectively secateurs were used by the French fruit-growers, cutting 'as clean as the best knife-man with the best knife ever whetted', he was at once converted and hastened to convert others. It was not long before secateurs became an indispensable tool in the hands of the British gardener. (British gardeners had used secateurs since the sixteenth century, as we learn from William Robinson's own paper, *The Garden*, Volume II, page 549, but the idea had not stuck.)

At the same time as the Tenth Show was going on, a botanical congress was taking place. William covered the event as Press and was delighted that David Moore was one of the delegates. During their stay in Paris they visited various interesting gardens, one excursion being to Verrières, the country house of Madame Elisa Vilmorin whose speciality was strawberries. She wrote a monograph on them.

Verrières was about twelve miles from Paris, and before breakfast their appetites were sharpened by the morning air and by a pleasant walk in the very pretty countryside. They came back to 'a magnificent *déjeuner*' set out for them in a circular clearing in a grove. A bed of flowering plants was in the centre, with clumps of the fine tall grass *Panicum altissimum* to give it grace. Around this the tables were placed, and a prettier spot or happier reunion could not be found.

'We were of all parts,' wrote William, 'from St Petersburg to the Cape of Good Hope, spoke a variety of tongues, from musical Italian to our own "hoarse northern gutteral"; had widely diverse ways of saying grace, and yet each one said that the day was one of the most agreeable he had ever spent.

'Verrières is a sort of botanist's home. I have been there a good many times now, and never yet found it without several botanists enjoying the interesting garden and cordial hospitality of Madame Vilmorin and M. H. Vilmorin.' Elisa de Vilmorin was the widow of Louis who had died in 1860. Henri, who later anglicized his name, was their twenty-four-year-old son.

After that magnificent breakfast they had a long walk through a large wood planted with rare trees from all over the world, returning to 'an equally *recherché* luncheon'. William thought they could have seen a little more of the fine trees and plants at Verrières, 'had our reception not been so cordial and the wines and fruits and other viands, not so particularly good.' But, he added, 'Even botanists are human.'

He could not resist adding a description of the dessert plates beautifully painted by Madame Vilmorin, each with a different design of flowers and leaves and true in every line and tint. He was enchanted with them. 'This kind of thing is the antithesis of "Brummagen"—it is real taste,' he declared.

As for the Tenth Show, he singled out the gladioli for special praise. The first prize had been awarded to Eugène Souchet, head gardener at the Palais de Fontainebleau whom William had recently met and of whose magnificent collection he promised a description later. It was the last of the fortnightly horticultural shows, though the Exhibition itself would not close until the end of October.

Summing it up, he wrote in *The Times* that 'French horticulture is, generally speaking, less advanced than our own, but in some respects it is far superior.' It was in the edible department that the French excelled, with their magnificent apples and pears. For flavour and beauty there were 'such as we never produce by the ordinary way of growing apple trees, training a single shoot along a wire supported about one foot from the ground, grafting those little apple trees on a stock called the "Paradise", which induces a dwarf habit and early fertility so that they bear fine fruit at two years of age.'

This lauding of the cordon system began a correspondence in *The Times*, and for months it raged in the horticultural papers. 'A London Market Gardener' told *The Times* correspondent to read what the books said! Retorted William: 'Why should I consider garden books—in most cases a generation behind their time— when it is clear to me that some of the modes of culture pursued in this country (France) are well worthy of our immediate adoption, and likely to improve our gardening, and even our food resources.'

He went on believing in the system. When he came to establish his own fruit garden in Sussex he engaged a French expert to train his apples and pears in just the same way.

7

'I am in love with several peach trees...'

The pleasantest house to visit out of Paris was certainly that of the Vilmorins at Des Barres. 'I was lucky enough to be taken there by my very kind friend M. H. Vilmorin,' William recounted of his first visit. Louis's son Henry was an enthusiastic student of conifers, and of alpines—he was to found the famous Alpine Garden at Verrières. In March William had met Charles de Vilmorin, now retired after twenty-six years in the navy. On his shore visits Charles too had fallen victim to the spell of fine trees, particularly those on the shores of the Black Sea where he had command of a ship.

With Henry on one side of him and Charles on the other 'I had guides who made me so much at home in every way,' wrote William, 'that I did not know whether most to admire their kindness or the valuable and interesting experimental plantation of trees.'

Though trees were the theme there were other things to see at Des Barres. 'Immediately on going outside the house towards the woods, I happened to look down among the Violets and Moss, to be astonished at the quantities of Cyclamen hederaefolium, perfectly naturalised and quite wild-looking, about the plantation near the house, the leaves being large and fat, and the plants as happy-looking as possible, on ground nearly purple with the Sweet Violet. What a pretty sight this cyclamen must prove in Autumn!

'And of course,' he added, 'it may be naturalised in England quite as well as here. I particularly allude to this because it reminds me of the many beautiful things that may be naturalised about English plantations and shrubberies—in the neighbourhood of every country house. There are some things like this Cyclamen, the Apennine Anemone, and not a few beautiful bulbs and herbaceous plants, which without requiring any attention would prove a perpetual source of interest and beauty, and so planted many of them would thrive much better, and look much better, than in the border or any other position in which they are cultivated.'

What a crowd of fresh ideas kept rushing into his head! Almost at every step. Naturalizing cyclamen, filling plantations with an array of beautiful bulbs and even herbaceous plants. . . . Pictures kept forming in his mind's eye like coloured patterns in a kaleidoscope. One day these thoughts were to materialize in the revolutionary idea of a 'wild garden'.

For this was the very essence of his third book, to be published three years hence.

Another of William's favourite gardens was that of the Palace of Fontainebleau where Eugène Souchet was superintendent and famous for the magnificent varieties of gladiolus he raised. He made many visits there, on one occasion with Charles Moore, brother of David Moore of Glasnevin, who was director of the Sydney Botanic Garden. He had come from Australia to see the Exhibition and was pleased to find that many of the ravines in the remoter parts of the Fontainebleau forest were remarkably like those inhabited near the coast by the Australian tree ferns.

In April William went to see gardens where vegetables and fruit were forced for market, and thanks to an introduction from Henry Vilmorin he was able to look over what was 'almost the best' of them. This was on the outskirts of Paris, and here considerable numbers of pineapples were grown, though 'the less said about them the better', was William's comment. The plants were too old, they were not forced in a congenial tropical heat, as in England, and were not fed freely throughout the season. Vines were forced in long narrow frames and the grapes had been cut in March, but again the French were as much behind us in this as they were superior to us in growing peaches.

There were good crops of cucumbers and melons. These were grown in the narrow rough frames so popular in France and were heated. The winter treatment of frames was simple and neat. They were covered with straw mats called *paillassons*, made by tying little bundles of straw about as thick as a finger in three rows, the ties interlaced to make a mat three or four feet wide. These were flexible and much cheaper than the mats used in England. As for asparagus: 'I never knew what asparagus was till I came here,' declared William. 'I have heard good authorities say that a French market-gardener can readily take twice as much off a given space of ground as a London market-gardener.' The sticks were grown to the thickness of a good-sized eel and were in deep sandy soil. A book on asparagus-culture was to result by James Barnes with himself as co-author.

To mushrooms he was to devote a special article (and later another book). They were grown in obsolete mines and so plentifully that 'in the middle of winter a Frenchman who dines for a franc and a half in a restaurant gets a nice little lot of them with his kidneys, and a toothpick into the bargain.'

Pears would be ripe in June and would be sold in their pots—'I suppose to the rich Russians and Americans who don't mind eating gold, especially while sojourning here.'

He visited the nurseries of Jamain & Durand at Bourg-la-Reine and the private garden of an amateur at Chatillon, both a little south of Paris. The extensive nurseries were among the largest in France training apples as cordons and pears as dwarf pyramids. William thought to ask the exact meaning of a cordon, deriving from the French word for cord or rope. He wrote to Professor de Breuil, the leading authority on fruit culture in France. The reply was simply a tree confined to a single stem. Where there were two branches Professor de Breuil used the expression 'double cordon'.

One day he went to the Luxembourg to hear a lecture by Auguste Rivière, author of *Arboriculture fruitière*. It started at nine in the morning and was attended by several hundred people. William had heard a few lectures in England but none so useful to the horticulturist as this one. It was thoroughly practical and was illustrated by a fine peach tree brought in bodily in full flower.

Occasionally he refreshed himself with visits to other kinds of nurseries, to Antoine Chantin's, for instance, where ferns, caladiums and other plants with ornamental leaves were grown. On that particular day he called in at the cemetery at Montparnasse and was shocked to see broken-up gravestones bearing the date 1860 and thereabouts being used as rubble to make a new drive. They had come from ground that had not been paid for in perpetuity. William had read and admired Lyell's story illustrating that all flesh is grass, but, he remarked wryly, 'I never knew what a poor, transient, weedy kind of grass is the flesh of the lords of creation till I came here.' The sad experience haunted him.

A highlight was the fruit garden at Montreuil where the Napoleon peach was growing. The place was also interesting as being a school for training young gardeners. He visited it on the 23rd of June, a large garden consisting simply of a series of oblong spaces surrounded by peach walls. A very old man dressed in a blouse was moving along the walls nailing in the shoots here and there, and with him moved a dozen young men, his pupils. This was the owner, the distinguished M. Lepère. He had a class twice a week. William was astounded, asking his readers if anybody had ever heard of an unusually successful English market-gardener or fruit-grower calling a class round him at a low fee or none at all. He feared that English cultivators were too jealous of 'the

8 A mushroom cave at Montrouge 'just outside the fortifications' of Paris.
William Robinson thought that England should copy, and in 1870 wrote a
book on mushroom culture

secret'. 'The French, though proud of their success in this way, are careful to give it the fullest possible ventilation, and those who attend here cannot fail to learn the culture of the Peach as well as need be, for the master glides along the wall and stops and nails in the shoot and cuts out the foremost branches here and there that are not wanted for next year's work, and, in short, does and explains everything before his pupils. He has been cultivating peaches here for a couple of generations and certainly has reason to be proud of the result.'

Lepère asked about the state of gardening in England and William told him we could beat him in most things but not with the peach, and that he, M. Lepère, was indisputably the Emperor of Peach Growers.

1 The Napoleon Peach Tree

Actually the famous Napolean peach, whose branches were trained to form the Emperor's name, though in good health was looking a little weak about the central letters. A far finer object in William's eyes was the specimen trained to form the owner's name—LEPERE.

'I am in love with several peach trees I have seen here,' he exclaimed to his readers, and much as he admired them when in fruit, 'to see them when in flower in Spring must be much more beautiful.'

He had rarely found anything that better repaid a journey than this garden at Montreuil, and having spent the whole day in it he came to the conclusion as to why the peach was so successfully cultivated there. 'It appears to me that the cultivators pay thorough and constant attention to its wants, with which lifelong experience has made them familiar. They take great pains to have the sap equally distributed, and succeed more perfectly than we do.'

He was varying these out-of-town trips with visits to the Paris parks, which he wrote up with his usual critical verve. Having done his rounds at the Exhibition to see what was new he would call on one of his new friends: Auguste Neumann who was deputy chief of the glasshouses at the Jardin des Plantes, and Bernard Verlot, head of the

School of Botany there; Edouard André, superintendent of the Paris parks, Auguste Rivière of the Luxembourg. His book on the Paris parks and gardens remains a classic and is a rare study of the social conditions of the times as well as a fascinating slice of nineteenth-century horticultural history.

9 Edouard André (1840–1911), superintendent of the Paris Parks and creator of parks and gardens not only all over France but in Holland, Austria, Russia, Bulgaria and Italy (*Service Technique des Parcs, Ville de Paris*)

There were also three great shows to cover, apart from the Exhibition: the Versailles Flower Show, the Great Rose Show at Brie Comte Robert, and the Great Fruit Show at the Pomological Congress.

The flower show was held in the great gardens of Versailles and lasted five days. William found it much prettier than anything at the Exhibition, the best things being grouped in a large circular tent where a charming scene was made by a free mingling of ornamental-leaved plants among azaleas and other brilliant flowers. He was pleased that the fine-leaved plants from Pontchartrain were so good. They 'would have been considered remarkable in any show, being in fact the finest kinds known and very well cultivated.' Beds of these alternated with beds of roses, rhododendrons and other shrubs. The result was pleasing, in fact the whole show was a feast of colour and interest, with one little exhibit deserving special notice. This was a large collection of very dwarf rhododendrons used three deep as an edging of a bed. Each little plant bore one good truss of flowers and could be almost exactly compared with the strong-flowered but dwarf hydrangeas sold with a single truss in Covent Garden. They were obtained by grafting short shoots with plump buds on small plants of *Rhododendron ponticum*. William thought they could be highly useful in England.

[75]

He never forgot he was Irish, and so as to give his readers a picture of the Great Rose Show at Brie he asked them to imagine they were at Donnybrook Fair, the 'mildest possible corner' of it, telling them to arrange it round a grassy yard or the corner of a field, extract all the 'divilment' out of it, and place a great oblong tent at one end. For the Rose Show was held in connection with the *fête* of the place and was simply an affair of little gaming tables, gingerbread stalls, a travelling theatre, and a very small establishment for telling fortunes, with various other contrivances for fooling the rustics out of their money.

On the 19th of September the French pomologists held an exhibition of fruit in the hall of the Société Imperiale et Centrale d'Horticulture de France, and this was later moved in entirety to the Exposition. The displays of fruits in more than 2,000 dishes were tremendous. As William wrote: 'To describe individual fruit or dishes of fruit would merely be to give a string of adjectives filling many columns. Some of the exhibitors were showing several hundred kinds of pear, and the marvel was that with few exceptions they were all of superb quality.' It was not only the extent and the character of the displays that astonished the English visitors but the size of the very large varieties like Uvedale's St Germain and the greater depth and beauty of colour of the smaller and medium-sized varieties.

Not all agreed about their excellence. The London trade journals immediately took sides. The French pears were 'coarse, granular and insipid' according to 'London Market Gardener' in *The Times*. One contended that the heat of the Continental sun made the French pears hard, another that it was this same heat that gave them their superiority. William's retort was 'If, according to some, we have the finest climate for the Pear, how is it that we do not grow it as cheaply and as well as the French? How is it that Covent Garden is obliged to buy so largely from them?'

The controversy went on for months in the horticultural press, one of the protagonists being none other than Thomas Rivers of Sawbridge-worth, a leading fruit nurseryman. It was still raging in December 1867 when on the 7th of that month William's last 'Letter from Paris' appeared in *The Gardeners' Chronicle*. He had been scourged for 'libelling' English gardeners, and his editor urged him to take a stand. He signed his name to the following paragraph:

And now for a time I bid goodbye to French horticulture. I have not devoted articles to the abuse of its failings—and they are many, inasmuch as I had not space to follow the unusual course of describing the bad. But I must protest against the charge of having 'libelled' the merits of English gardeners; anything I have done in the matter has originated in quite an opposite feeling—a wish for their improvement in some few points. Any little work I have done in France must be regarded as merely preparatory, and I hope to some day traverse every part of Europe interesting for its horticulture, with means and opportunities for observation, which I possessed in but a slight degree in Paris.

As to the little already done with French gardening, I am anxious to hear any further objections, answer any inquiries, or be corrected on any point in which I am in error.

The editorial management moved in to support him in these words:

We can abundantly confirm our correspondent's statement that he has not sought to uphold French at the expense of English gardeners or gardening. He has given his own opinions as to certain matters in which he considered we might learn from our neighbours, but he has even more sedulously and frequently called attention to the general superiority of British horticulture. Our correspondent is responsible for his own opinions, but it will, we are sure, be admitted, that he has done good service by his narrative of horticultural doings and horticultural facts, in and about Paris during the 'Exhibition' season.

Even this was not enough to quell the controversy. Father and son became opponents, Thomas Rivers castigating '*WR*', his son Thomas Francis upholding him, this in *The Times*. Finally Rivers *père* gracefully bridged the abyss. 'We are, perhaps,' he said, 'like steel and flint, and if we do not strike too hard, we may emit a few genial sparks.' He agreed with '*WR*' in some respects, disagreed with him in others, but it was clear that he respected him. They became good friends and in 1873 '*WR*' dedicated the third volume of *The Garden* to him, 'in recognition of his many and great services rendered to horticulture.'

Speaking 'as one of that numerous class who had not the opportunity of seeing for themselves', D. T. Fish, head gardener at Hardwicke House, Bury St Edmunds, was merely grateful for being able to look at things French through the excellent medium that *The Gardeners' Chronicle* had provided. 'We have,' he said, 'done Paris and its environs on the wings of his pen, and I for one am pleased to confess that I have enjoyed the imaginary journey.'

William himself, when the shouting died down, was content to quote from Francis Bacon's *Essay on Travel* when he said:

And let it appear that he doth not change his Country Manners for those of Forraigne Parts: But only prick in some Flowers of that he hath Learned abroad into the Customes of his own country.

8

Gleanings from the Alps

He had spent nearly a year in France. Now it was home to write a book. Not, however, the first of his books to be published, which was *Gleanings from French Gardens*, but one on alpine flowers suitable for gardens. This explains the seeming anachronism in the first edition of *Gleanings*, an intimation by Frederick Warne the publisher that *Alpine Plants* by W. Robinson, F.L.S. would be ready in November. For this under the title *Alpine Flowers for Gardens* was not published until March 1870, the same year as *The Wild Garden*. Yet another book, *Mushroom Culture*, came between.

The pros and cons of French and English gardening were still being argued, each critic discussing a single aspect of the subject or approaching it from his own point of view. William decided that the only way to present the subject clearly and as a whole was to make a book of it.

In March 1868 *The Gardeners' Chronicle* heralded the forthcoming *Gleanings*, mentioning that the book would be copiously illustrated. The review in the May 23 issue declared that William Robinson by his own over-positive views had again laid himself open to criticism. The critic, who was anonymous, while praising him as 'a diligent and accurate observer' who had succeeded in showing how British and French gardeners could learn from each other, said that had the author waited till time and larger experience had convinced him that some of his opinions must be modified, at the same time showing his opponents that others of his opinions were correct, he would not have exposed himself to so much hostile criticism. 'As it is, he has had to run the gauntlet of ridiculous misrepresentation, and of a style of criticism for the bitterness and acrimony of which there is no excuse whatever.'

But the reviewer had 'no doubt whatever that Time, the softener, will show that British gardeners have much for which to thank the author of the present volume.'

Such is the hard and hilly road of the pioneer, who has to declare his beliefs without compromise if his message is to rouse an audience to lend a listening ear!

The book was a compilation of all he had seen and studied in Paris and on his out-of-town forays, written in a more literary style than his Paris Letters and much more considered. Additional were two chapters on subtropical gardening, to do which he had left Paris in August for six weeks in order to examine what subtropical gardening was done in Britain and so compare it with the extent to which it was done around Paris. In October 1866 in *The Gardeners' Chronicle* he had written an article on the famous subtropical garden in Battersea Park. But a single article was not enough to encompass all William's thoughts on the subject, though Battersea remained the best example of the style under the influence of its superintendent John Gibson, a former protégé of Joseph Paxton, who had seen most of its exotic trees and plants growing in their far-distant native lands.

It was not just the display of flowers of the most brilliant kinds that interested William, or that some, like the dracaenas, had richly coloured leaves, but that flower-colour and leaf-colour were always relieved and complemented by the many greens of leaves and fronds like those of palms, tree ferns, bananas and aralias. This form of gardening originating on the Continent and brought to perfection in and around Paris was an innovation which had been making its way in England during the last few years.

It had been objected, however, that these ornamental plants were so tender and expensive as to make 'subtropical gardening' impossible for most British gardeners. But why, asked William, confine ourselves to these? No effect given by costly 'subtropicals' was superior to what could be produced by hardy plants combined with those exotics which could be raised cheaply and were as free in growth as common 'bedding stuff'. In any case, he added, what was important was what the system had taught us.

He summed up the lesson. 'Well, then, subtropical gardening has taught us that one of the greatest mistakes ever made in the flower garden was the adoption of a few varieties of plants for culture on a vast scale, to the exclusion of interesting variety and too often of beauty or taste.'

The thoroughly practical William Robinson went on to list and describe suitable subtropical plants available from seed catalogues of the current year.

Gleanings from French Gardens was published in April 1868 and William was happy to send an inscribed copy to Reynolds Hole 'as a small testimony of the great pleasure I have derived from your writings—and for long before I ever thought of becoming a writer on gardening matters or any others'.

[79]

His letter was written in May from 28 Scarsdale Villas, Kensington, W., his London home for many years. The street has been renumbered and it is now 9 Scarsdale Villas, a substantial three-storeyed house with a semi-basement, four bedrooms and a large drawing-room running from the bow window at the front through to a small conservatory overlooking the long narrow garden at the back.

Meanwhile he was not long in England. In June he was off to the Continent—to France to look again at fruit culture, to Switzerland to look at alpine flowers on their native mountains.

He had seen enough of alpines, in places like the Backhouse nurseries and Hull Botanic Gardens, to fall in love with them, Ruskin's 'heaven-kissing gems', to William himself 'the most exquisite of all plants'. In the Lake District he had climbed high enough, to places only daringly accessible, to know the thrill of discovering them in cracks and crannies of the rocks or sunning themselves on ledges.

Finally, what Ruskin had written about mountains and mountain plants had drawn him like a magnet, and Ruskin had placed them in an idyllic setting.

> The best image which the world can give of Paradise is in the slope of the meadows, orchards, and cornfields on the side of a great Alp, with its purple rocks and eternal snows above . . .

So there was a book to be done, to dispel the erroneous idea generally held that the plants of alpine regions could not be grown in gardens. But to grow them well, the gardener must know in which kind of terrain the plant had its home, in which kind of soil. He must breast in imagination the winds of these uplands, as they did, must shelter in the lee of a rock-face, as they did. He must glimpse a particular alpine treasure revelling in a boggy hollow. He must watch with drawn breath the snow melting around the warming bud of a soldanella as the purple fringed helmet thrust its way upward to light and sun. He must understand these small people of the mountain, which are small because they flatten themselves against the unruly elements.

It was William's first excursion in an alpine country, a brief one but long enough for him to absorb the spirit of the mountains and convey it to those who could know it no other way. He called this dealing with 'one of the many texts that may be read in the great book of the Alps'.

He came through France to Geneva, and his first day's work was devoted to the ascent of the Grande Salève overlooking Lac Léman. Ruskin had climbed it in 1863 when he was living at Mornex. Though not a great mountain, and with green meadows instead of snow at its summit, it was nearly 5,000 feet high, to the athletic William Robinson

10
28 Scarsdale Villas,
W. (now Number 9)
where William Robinson
established himself in
1868, employing a
gardener and a
housekeeper

a way of commencing training for more serious work. He rose early, to be at the foot of the mountain before six o'clock. It was a few miles' drive through a June morning aglow with sun on lake, hills and far-off Alps, in an air fragrant with flowers.

The first part of the ascent was through meadows where pinks, harebells, sages and pea-flowers made a gaily coloured carpet, but soon the cultivated land was left behind and he and his guide were on the hem of an immense belt of hazel and copse-wood spangled with numerous little bright-green patches of grass. Here a nightingale was singing and white-headed eagles were floating aloft, now over the lake and now over plain and hill, sometimes on motionless wing, silently gliding along on the look-out for prey, and here the air was fragrant with lily of the valley.

Up and up they went to a rocky scene of gorges and precipices where every crevice held some plant and the ledges were clothed with the greenest grass or with bushes. Few alpines were to be seen as yet. As William explained, many of the most delicate and minute of these would grow well in such spots, but the long grass and low wood would soon overrun them. However, among the copse-wood which had its home on the shattered flanks of the mountain were numbers of beautiful flowers that could be termed sub-alpine, and occasionally plants of diminutive size near the top of the mountain were here larger. He pointed out that plants occurring at such heights should interest home gardeners because they flourish under conditions like those of the greater part of Britain. Scores of these copse-herbaceous plants could be grown, that now rarely found a home in our gardens.

Genista sagittalis was one, making bushy masses of yellow flowers, and here forming the very turf in some places. Neat dwarf bushes of *Cytisus sessilifolius* were common, 'and soon,' he wrote in delight, 'I gather my first wild Cyclamen.' Lily of the valley made a carpet under the brushwood, Martagon lilies shot up here and there among wild orchids, the great yellow gentian began to be plentiful as he climbed yet higher, and *Globularia cordifolia* was in sheets of blue.

After a walk of three hours he and his guide reached the top. They would have reached it sooner had they not stopped so often to admire the view. From the bottom of the mountain the summit seemed barren of all but stunted vegetation, but at close quarters it was an immense plateau miles long covered with the freshest green studded with flowers.

He was pleased to meet with his first silvery rockfoils in a wild state, having long held that these—so often kept in pots, even in botanic gardens—require no such attention and can safely be grown in the open. Here they were in every sort of place: at the bottom of small narrow chasms; under the shade of bushes; in little thimble-holes on the surface of the rocks, and sometimes in a flaccid condition from the drought; and here and there among short grass and fern where the soil was a little deeper.

2 The Alpine Journey:
Setting off

3 The Alpine Journey:
With his guide

One of the most beautiful of all the alpine flowers was of course the gentian. 'Its vivid blue and peerless beauty stamp themselves on the mind of the Alpine traveller, as deeply as the wastes of snow, the silvery waterfalls, or the dark plumy ridges of pine,' he wrote. It was 'a little gem of life in the midst of death, buried under the deep all-shrouding snow for six or even eight months out of the twelve.' In the high Alps this brilliant blue spring gentian would still be under the snow. In the pastures below it was already out of flower and in seed.

Now descending the other side of the Salève he saw Lac Léman spread out before him, reflecting in its celestial calm the vast ranges of snowy mountains. Viewing the scene, any traveller would have had a rose-coloured impression of the Alps. In William's case, this impression was to be considerably modified, as he wrote, in the forty-eight hours ahead.

He was referring to the scene two days later when he and his guide were walking along the Saas valley. With its deeply-worn river bed and vast sides of gloomy rock it looked anything but a cheerful pass to the Monte Rosa district whither they were bound. Fortunately there were distractions from the forbidding landscape and greying skies, for here were countless tufts of the Cobweb House-leek. It was the first time, again, William had met it in the wild, and there were thousands of its rosettes in almost every chink of rock, in the spaces between the stones that propped up the pathway, and spreading in cushions over the bare boulders.

The scenery was now becoming more and more rugged, and after a walk of nearly two hours they reached a village with a very poor inn where they had some black bread and wine. By this time a misty rain had begun to fall; and bearing in mind the long valley they had to traverse before reaching a place where they could stay for the night, they resolved to move on as quickly as possible, shutting their eyes to all the interesting objects around them. A soaking rain helped them to carry out this part of the plan.

On they went, eyes fixed on the stony path and well aware of how dangerous it had become, the valley narrowing as they progressed, the sides almost perpendicular now and of loose stones. Presently they came to a little rough weather-beaten wooden cross.

'Why a cross here?' William wanted to know.

'That great rock you see,' said the guide, pointing to a boulder as big as a cottage, 'killed a man returning from the market in the valley.'

How innocent looked the boulder now, having come to rest on a little lawn of rich grass and bright flowers on the other side of the torrent across which it had leapt on its headlong career down the mountainside.

Ten minutes later they came to a group of three more rough wooden crosses. These marked the spot where two women and a man had been buried by an avalanche.

The rain turned to snow but they were emerging into a region abounding with flowers where there were caves lined with the little yellow *Viola biflora*. Every cranny was golden with it, and at the entrance of one of the caves were the crimson blooms of William's first alpine rhododendron. Here and there, weighed down by the snow, were the handsome flowers of a crimson pedicularis and in almost every place where a little soil was gathered were the beautiful soft-crimson white-eyed flowers of *Primula viscosa*.

4 The Alpine Journey: A Welcome Fire

[84]

Saas was the goal, attained after plodding for several hours, feet saturated and chilled with deep snow-water. They reached it as night was closing in, by which time nearly a foot of snow had fallen. Gone were William's hopes of seeing the plants of the High Alps in this region, so rather than return by the same long and dreary valley he determined to cross the Alps and descend into the sunny valleys of Piedmont.

Next day they set out for Mattmark, nearly nine miles away, more than 7,000 feet up and above the timber-line. It was here they found the rare *Ranunculus glacialis* in full beauty, some of the flowers measuring nearly an inch and a half across. Wrote William: 'This is the plant which Mr Ruskin met with high up among the icy rocks, near the margins of the snowy solitude of the Alps, and which pleased him so much there.' It has been described as the delight and despair of alpine gardeners, resisting all attempts to persuade it to display the beauty which is breathtaking in its natural habitat. William wrote that it is easily raised from seed and that it will thrive in a cool spot in deep gritty soil, moist during the warm months.

He was referring to Ruskin's mention of the Arctic Buttercup in his *Modern Painters*, though Ruskin described the flower as 'wan and corpselike' in its paleness.

Other rare plants were discovered by lifting cushions of snow off them: uncommon saxifrages, the pretty little *Chrysanthemum alpinum*, a pink flax and a spectacular *Polygala chamaebuxus*; *Senecio uniflorus* of deep orange flowers and the most silvery of leaves, with that alpine treasure the beautiful *Eritrichium nanum* half an inch high making cushions of sky-blue flowers.

They were the first strangers to cross the Pass of Monte Moro into Italy that year. The snow here was eighteen inches deep, so that it was impossible to gather any plants. This was unfortunate, as the neighbourhood of the little lake of Mattmark was said to be very rich in plants. However, there was quite enough to do to ascend Monte Moro with its thick coating of snow. Arrived at the cross which marked its top a magnificent alpine prospect burst upon them: great mountains with snowy heads in range after range, on the Swiss side nothing but snow on peak or in hollow; on the Italian side a deep valley among the white-topped mountains, flushed with green meadows. The contrast between the valley and the great uplands of snow was very beautiful.

As they descended from the path and left the snow behind them flowers began to appear again, a minute gem, the silvery *Androsace imbricata*, growing on the hollowed flanks of the rocks. William noted that the tufts, not more than half an inch high, sent their roots far into the narrow chinks. These having a downward direction, the rainwater could reach the roots from above. Their silvery rosettes were more delicately chiselled than the prettiest encrusted saxifrage; their flowers had the purity of a snowdrop, and occasionally the blushes of the alpine primrose. They are the smallest of beautiful flowering plants, growing on the very highest spots of the Alps where vegetation exists, and carpeting the earth with loveliness wherever the sun has sufficient power to lay bare for a few weeks in summer a square yard of wet rock-dust. *Silene acaulis* was everywhere, and no description, wrote William, can convey an idea of the denseness of its flowers. Starved between chinks, its cushions are as smooth as velvet, one inch high—though perhaps a hundred years old—and so tightly covered with bright rosy flowers that the green was often eclipsed.

The Piedmontese meadows were blue with forget-me-nots and strange harebells, enlivened by orchids and jewelled here and there with St Bruno's lilies whose flowers were nearly two inches long and as pure white as the snows on Monte Rosa, each petal having a small green tip like the Spring Snowflake, but purer, and golden stamens. To William, the pleasure of finding so many beautiful plants, rare in cultivation, growing in the long grass under conditions very similar to those of our own meadows, was even greater than the meeting with the diminutive gems on the heights, confirming, as they did, his conviction that no flowers grow in those mountain meadows that cannot be grown equally well in the rough grassy parts of British pleasure-grounds and copses. One day he was to prove it for himself.

He had not mapped out the journey to the last detail, preferring to wait on the weather and consult his guide. Now they resolved to descend into the plains of Lombardy, cross the lakes of northern Italy, go as far as Lecco on Lake Como, and climb Monte Campione to find *Silene elisabethae*, a plant as rare as it was beautiful, carrying enormous ragged flowers of brilliant magenta-crimson.

There were plenty of other good things but not a sign of what they had come to find. A treasure was the tiny *Saxifraga caesia*. In little indentations in rocks it sometimes looked a mere stain of silvery grey, like a lichen, but on the ground it spread into dwarf silvery cushions from an inch to four inches wide. It seemed quite indifferent as to where it grew. He even found it in a channel which in winter was a torrent after heavy rains and thaws.

'One would think,' William wrote, 'that coming from habitats so far removed from all that is common to our monotonous skies, it would be impossible to keep these little stars of the earth in a living state; but our climate suits them well, and they are the chief stay of the cultivator of alpine plants. In autumn, when most plants quail before the approach of darkness, winter, and frost, and casting off their soiled robes, the Rockfoils glisten with silver and emerald when the rotting leaves are hurrying by before the stiff, wet breeze.'

They spent the whole day on Monte Campione, collecting a harvest of plants but never finding the beautiful silene. Finally, waiting as long as they dared before night came on, they decided that there was nothing for it but to give up the hunt. It was a terrible disappointment, having climbed so high and searched so long.

They were descending the mountain down a long and rocky chasm formed of a vast bed with banks of shattered rock when to William's delight they discerned a little plant with a few leaves growing from a chink on a low mass of rock, and by carefully breaking away tiny chips they succeeded in getting it out intact, roots and all. A persevering search in the immediate neighbourhood produced a few more specimens, not yet in flower but the flower-stems pushing up. One was growing in the flaky rock without a crumb of soil. William marvelled that a plant could adapt itself to two entirely different environments: he had so recently seen the silene growing perfectly well in sandy soil in a warm nook in Edmond Boissier's garden in Switzerland.

It was in triumphant mood that they began their long trudge down the mountain, along the valley and on to the hilly road that brought them to their quarters at half-past nine, after nearly twenty hours of walking.

9

The Parks and Gardens of Paris

He made a leisurely return to Paris. On the 3rd of July he was at Dijon, writing about the many small regional schools established to spread a knowledge of rural economy. A few had specialist aims, one being L'École Régionale de la Saulsaie in the department of Ain, a couple of hours' journey by rail and carriage from Lyons.

At first sight it was not reassuring. Typically French was the 'want of finish which we Britons are in the habit of putting on country seats, farms, and gardens, and a hungry look about the place, if we may so speak.' However, any garden was interesting to William and worth visiting because of what it could teach or suggest.

The growing of pears and apples was taught here, two methods being used. Grown against the wall, and even on trellises, both trees and fruit of the Doyenne d'Hiver pear were in perfect condition. There was a marked difference between these and the same variety grown away from shelter and protection. In fact the free-standing trees were a total failure this year because of the cold rains at the time of flowering.

'It is to well-managed walls we must look for the main improvement of the culture of our finer fruit,' William pointed out. 'Here the French actually find that walls are not only a benefit but a necessity for some hardy fruits, yet we have been going on for years planting pears in quantity away from walls, and paying little attention to the kinds that ought to be planted against them.'

The original specimens of the Palmette Verrier were to be seen here. This was a 'simple, noble, and beautiful form' of espalier like a many-branched candelabra, named in honour of the late head of the fruit-growing and gardening department here.

A variation of supporting the trees against the trellis was to plant a row and train their branches in a criss-cross to form a living trellis, each tree thus supporting and being supported by its neighbours. It had been said that the branches would be destroyed by friction: there was ample evidence that this was not the case, even with the strong winds that were nearly always blowing. When William mentioned the objection to the head gardener he was much amused and simply pointed to a fine line of espalier apples eight feet high, mutually supporting each other without the slightest injury.

Another method, particularly applied to pears, was cultivating the trees in pyramids. William had seen these pyramidal pear trees in the gardens of even very humble amateurs, and if they never bore a single fruit they were beautiful in themselves. 'I have met with few "avenues" that afforded me more pleasure,' he wrote, 'than a short one of pyramid pear-trees leading up through a little town garden within the walls of Paris.'

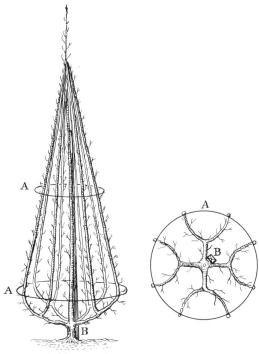

5 A Pyramidal Pear

When he came back to England at the end of the year he brought with him as a present for fruit-growing friends 3,000 apple trees, most of them grafted on the true Paradise stock but some on the Doucin or English Paradise. 'The difference in roots and vigour of stem,' he wrote, 'is quite enough to show the cause of failure of those who attempted the cordon with the Doucin.' He backed up his claim with photographs showing the system of close pruning, entirely different from the English method. These would 'almost furnish as good an idea of the early spring aspect of the trees ... as if you were in the garden where they were grown.' He added, 'I think it will be admitted they are such as the best of gardeners might be proud of.'

In his Letter from Paris series written at the time of the Exhibition William had described some of the new Parisian gloxinias. He was now again based at Paris and on the 27th of September went out to Bougival, their birthplace, to see what fresh varieties Jules Valleyrand had been raising.

He had a feast of them. About forty flowers were spread out before him: the tube waxy white and with an irregular belt of light purple spots fading into a limb of translucent palest lilac; with the tube and throat of rich purplish-rose gradually merging into light-purple spottings on a white ground, the dottings near the margin of the limb being perfectly clear and distinct; the tube reddish, the veins enclosing dense lines of reddish spots, all merging at the throat into a band of rich rosy crimson, the limb dotted all over with clear rosy spots, deep towards the throat, light and delicate at the margin—and so many more glorious gloxinias in endless variety that he gave up describing them. The newest had markings of true blue, and rich deep and well-defined rosy crimson throat-belts.

He went with M. Courtois-Gérard, a well-known seedsman, writer and grower of the Rue du Pont Neuf, on a round of market gardens to see the earlier stages of cloche culture. It was the 6th of October and in some gardens the cloches were not yet at work. Other gardens were preparing an early stock of the winter lettuce and the plants were already under their cloches. In one garden was a large crop of cabbage lettuces, three plants under each cloche. Other cloches protected germinating seeds, while seed of the lettuces destined for the London market would be sown on or about the 9th of the month. William wrote that it would be impossible to find anything more pleasing in the way of culture than the sight of the first crop of lettuces, not one leaf disfigured by even a speck, the plants rolling out their young hearts so vigorously that they would be fit for market at the end of the month.

'It is impossible to exaggerate the importance of this culture for a nation of gardeners like the British,' William emphasized, 'and if it were the only item that we could adopt from the French gardeners with advantage, it would be well worth writing about. "Enormous" was the English equivalent of the term used by one market gardener in describing to me the quantities of lettuces sent from these gardens, and the visits of the traders who come to search for them. To say that it would not succeed in England as well as around Paris, is a mistake.'

He promised to publish a list of fifty of the best Paris market gardens,

11 The Square des Batignolles in Napoleon III's New Paris,
which put London's squares to shame

so that those interested could go and study cloche culture in person.
Then 'we shall see whether prejudice or truth shall win the day,' said
William Robinson.

Contrasts always fascinated him. Methods, practices and differences:
there was always a proper way of doing a thing, which would produce
good results, and if not done in this way had better be scrapped—and
immediately, and a campaign started to banish it for ever.

　　In another sphere no greater contrast could be found than the city
squares of London and Paris. To William the London squares had a

ghoulish loneliness, the best effort in planting them being—apart from the trees—the 'scraggy hedges of miserable privet'. What a contrast to the squares of Paris with their carpets of fresh grass between mixed beds of flowers and clumps of fine-leaved plants such as acanthus and yucca, the trees usually clothed with climbers, generally ivy but occasionally aristolochia and clematis. They were open to the street, not railed off like the London squares to which admittance could be gained only by the wealthy residents of the surrounding houses.

Although he had made a detailed study of the Paris parks and public gardens William had half-ignored the existence of these squares, thinking they would contain little of interest. Now taking a look at them he found that each could occupy him for a whole morning.

He selected two as giving his English readers a good idea of what might be done to improve their counterparts across the Channel.

One was the Square and Tour St Jacques. The famous old tower with its carven stone figures and leaves was all that remained of a church and had been hidden from view by tall buildings. Now, surrounded by a green and brilliant garden, it was one of the most beautiful and interesting objects in Paris, the open space a source of pleasure and benefit to the people living in the neighbourhood. The first thing that struck the visitor was the freshness of everything, the neat way it was kept, and the numbers of people enjoying it. There was a belt of grass of varying widths, kept well watered, and here and there large beds of flowers or palms. There were clumps of shrubs and plenty of seats and chairs, so that hundreds of people could sit around. Remarked William: 'The richest of our nobles has in his flower-garden no better treasures than are here spread for all who will enjoy it.' He added: 'People who sneer at what they call Haussmannisation would do well to ponder.'

The Square des Battignoles was much larger and entirely different. It was laid out as a vale down which meandered a streamlet ending in a pool. The grassy sides sloped up to dense plantations. Plane trees had honeysuckles trained up them. The whole place was superbly planted. Moisture-loving plants, choice shrubs, exotics, fine trees and brilliant portulacas and other flowers: all contributed to a scene of sylvan and floral delight. William did not doubt that if one of these squares could be dropped into the West Central district of London, the owners of those squares would soon want to follow the French example.

All this—parks, gardens, squares, tree-lined boulevards and avenues—was to go into a book of more than 500 pages and crammed with illustrations. William called it 'Notes on a Study of Paris Gardens', but its full title was *The Parks and Gardens of Paris considered in relation to the Wants of Other Cities and of Public and Private Gardens*. It was first published in May 1869 by John Murray; the second edition, revised, seventh thousand, by Macmillan in 1878.

He dedicated the book to Vernon Lushington, Q.C., the Deputy Judge Advocate-General who was soon to become Secretary to the Admiralty. Judge Lushington was the soul of hospitality and was to gather round him some of the great thinkers of the day: Carlyle and Ruskin and most of the Pre-Raphaelite Brotherhood of painters—

12 Vernon Lushington, Q.C., in whose rooms at Oxford the Pre-Raphaelite Movement was born. Though not a member of the Brotherhood, William Robinson was the advocate of natural gardening. 'I should like to make you head gardener of London,' Lushington told him

Holman Hunt, D. G. Rossetti and J. E. Millais, to name the three founders of the movement in revolt against the 'grand style' and dedicated to a 'return to nature'. The Brotherhood had been formed in 1848, and two years later appeared the first number of their organ, *The Germ*, with its motto 'To encourage and enforce an entire adherence to the simplicity of nature.'

It is not surprising that William Robinson became an adherent of the new philosophy, for the motto could have been his own. In his sphere he was the great encourager of the natural style of gardening; and if this principle failed to instil itself into the minds of those who professed to be good gardeners professional or amateur, he was ready to enforce it with all the might of his pen.

Vernon Lushington's acknowledgement of the dedication reveals much of William Robinson.

[93]

The Parks and Gardens of Paris

87 Eccleston Square
21 May 1869

Dear Robinson,

Thank you for your noble book. I hope it will do a great deal for us poor Londoners, & others in populous city pent. I hope also it will find you a position to do much more good.

I have read your introduction with a great deal of pleasure;—and indeed I greatly admire your free & energetic handling. And so far as I have a right to any opinion on the subject, I think you are worthy of all confidence. I sh^d like to make you Head Gardener of London!

What I am going to say is a mere outsider's opinion, but it may be of use to you. I think your book is too profuse in illustrations. Of useful illustrations you can't have too many; but here views of gardens, and garden work wh. you *don't* recommend for imitation, are cumber and cost both you & the purchaser money.

With all good wishes
truly yours
Vernon Lushington

The illustrations had caused William much concern. Two separate reviews of the book appeared in *The Gardeners' Chronicle*, the 'second and best' censuring him for reproducing the woodcuts from A. Alphand's *L'Art des Jardins* without acknowledgement. But, as William wrote to John Murray on the 23rd of June, 'they are quite wrong as I shall prove in the G. Chronicle. Of the 430 cuts there are only 10 from this book & for the use of these I paid the owner cash long before the book went to press and indeed before I received the electros.'

By now William was on friendly terms with John Murray and was preparing a plan and planting scheme for the garden at Newstead, the Murray home at Wimbledon. Already he was beginning to stock it, writing on the 16th of June that a friend had despatched some seeds 'selected with a view to carrying out my "naturalisation" scheme that you seemed to like.' That Murray was no gardener is evident from William's detailed explanations. 'Other plants of equal importance are not so quickly raised from seed—or are not worth raising in that way—Lily of the Valley, Solomon's Seal & hardy bulbs for example.' Plants of these could be bought from a nurseryman. As for the seeds sent, they should be sown *at once* in some spare place in the kitchen garden, in shallow little drills.

The Parks and Gardens of Paris

I owe you an apology for not having asked your permission to inflict such a great seed-sowing hardship upon you and, secondly, for not accompanying the seeds with some idea of what I meant. I was however, away at York when they were sent to you by a friend or I shd. have done these things & perhaps sorted the seeds into two groups.

His planting plan was still secret.

It may not be amiss to remark that the scheme we are preparing is utterly unknown to gardeners and therefore you must not be surprised if your man does not at first enter into the spirit of it.

He listed some of the plants he would like to use, 'giving preference of course to such things as Mrs Murray and you admire most.' One beautiful plant, the Caucasian Borage,[1] was best used as carpeting under trees, 'and there is not a bare or unpromising spot in or near a garden or a grove which may not be embellished in the most charming way with suitable plants.' But, he added, 'I despair of fully explaining my meaning until I get the idea explained in a book or, better still, till one or more gardeners show the system in perfection.'

Murray took the hint. The book was *The Wild Garden, or the Naturalisation and Natural Grouping of Hardy Exotic Plants with a Chapter on the Garden of British Wild Flowers.* It appeared in 1870, with no dedication. The fourth edition was inscribed to S. Reynolds Hole, now Dean of Rochester, 'by his friend the author'. In 1899 Dean Hole was to return the compliment, when he dedicated his book *Our Gardens* 'To William Robinson, author of "The English Flower Garden", with admirations of his genius, congratulations on his success, and pleasant memories of his friendship'.

Advertising the book in 1881 Robinson dropped the mention of British wild flowers and substituted 'being one way onwards from the Dark Ages of Flower Gardening, with suggestions for the Regeneration of the Bare Borders of the London Parks.' The many illustrations by Alfred Parsons were engraved by Huyot, Pannemaker, Hyde, Kohl and Lacour.

William Robinson as an author was prolific in 1869. *Gleanings* went into a second edition and Murray had such faith in *Parks and Gardens of Paris* that he put out an edition of 5,000 copies. The book was divided into two parts, the first describing the new Paris 'in language so precise and yet so picturesque that Paris seems to pass before us as in a moving panorama,' wrote a critic; the second twelve chapters devoted to the

[1]I think Robinson here means the Cretan Borage.

important part horticulture played in satisfying the hunger of the Parisians, even to the cultivation of fruit on railway embankments. The book delighted Austen Henry Layard, excavator of Nineveh who was Paris-born. In a letter to Murray William wrote that 'A friend has irreverently suggested that I ought to give her Britannic Majesty's first commissioner of works, the Rt. Hon. A. H. Layard, a commission on the sale of my book for, said he, "he is a walking advertisement for you"! It is very kind of him!' Though, added the author, 'it would be more agreeable to be introduced to such important people through a better book!' A modest remark for, as we have seen, the book was well received.

William was also busy with another author's book. From the industrious pens of the Loudons, the great John Claudius and his wife Jane, had poured forth two constant streams of botanical and horticultural knowledge. Jane had published *The Amateur Gardeners' Calendar* in 1847, and with a new edition needed William took on the job of revision, contributing besides a useful introduction and articles on questions that had more recently arisen. Among these were ground vineries, orchard houses, subtropical gardening, large-flowered clematis, and the training of cordons.

The new edition, published in 1869 by Frederick Warne, was welcomed as 'a healthy sign of the times, showing that a taste for horticulture is spreading amongst the middle classes who, in these days of fierce competition and commercial antagonism, need more than ever such soothing, softening, elevating influences as the culture of a garden affords.'

There was no end to the busyness of the Robinson pen in 1869. *The Field* promoted him as horticultural editor of its section 'The Garden', and he was still contributing to *The Gardeners' Chronicle*, one article being on mushroom culture, which became a chapter in *Parks and Gardens of Paris* and finally a small book. The article evoked spirited correspondence, dealing as it did with the French method of growing *Agaricus campestris* in caves some seventy or eighty feet below ground. Andrew Turnbull, gardener to James Brunton of Broomlands, Kelso, took up this aspect, pointing out that the silver mines of frigid Siberia were the great depots for receiving law-breakers, and wondering whether our own Government could not transport 'some of our finely-nursed convicts' to the caves under the bleak hills of Derbyshire and elsewhere to grow mushrooms for the million.

Alpine Flowers for English Gardens was in the making and like *The Wild Garden* to be published in 1870. In June, lacking descriptions of some plants he had not seen in bloom, he went to York, to the Backhouse nurseries where the younger James was now in charge: his father had died in January. W. H. Hooper drew and engraved nearly all the illustrations. Others were done by John Wood Whymper, father of Edward Whymper, that giant among alpinists who in 1865 had made the first ascent of the Matterhorn, four of the woodcuts coming (by permission) from *Peaks, Passes and Glaciers*, the anthology of mountain experiences which preceded the *Alpine Journal*.

Among those whom William thanked for their help on the book was James Atkins of Painswick who out of long study and deep knowledge of them had taught him to love cyclamens. Atkins was a bulb man, his name personified in that lovely tall snowdrop *Galanthus nivalis* 'Atkinsii', which E. A. Bowles regarded as the finest of all. Thomas Moore also came in for special mention, William's botanical mentor on this and other books. Moore had also generously supplied him with a selection of ferns most likely to succeed in places exposed to wind and sunshine, as these, for variation in the rock garden, were included in the book.

It was a 'purely garden book', the first to deal with alpine plants as a garden subject, and divided into two useful parts: chapters on the culture and siting of alpine plants; and a descriptive catalogue that was no mere listing of what was suitable to grow in the garden. For in it William recorded his days among the Alps and his delight in finding various plants there, but also in 'Mr Peek's garden at Wimbledon' where a Ground Pine Moss flourished; describing too a lost erythronium which he rediscovered in the Redwood forest of Mendocino County, California.

But that was another story, involving another rediscovery that was to be a turning-point in his life.

10

A Visit to America, 1870

It is amazing how alpine plants inspire the beholder to poetry: William Robinson caught the fever, as had John Ruskin, as Reginald Farrer was to do in the future.

What are alpine plants? Here is William Robinson's answer to his own question.

'The word *alpine*,' he wrote, 'is used to denote the plants that grow naturally on all high mountain-chains, whether they spring from hot tropical plains or from green northern pastures.' This is an interesting note. Joseph Hooker in his ascents of the Himalaya saw how the vegetation changed from dense jungle in the heat and humidity of the plains, to where, 4,000 feet up in the climate of an English spring, oaks were in flower, birches bursting into leaf, and violets everywhere; finally in the heights, the winter of the tropics, finding the lichen *Lecanora minuata*, a little crimson plant he had last seen in the Antarctic.

William Robinson described their terrain as he knew it in Switzerland.

> Above the cultivated land these flowers begin to occur on the fringes of the stately woods; they are seen in multitudes in the vast pastures which clothe many great mountain-chains, enamelling their soft verdure; and also where neither grass nor loose herbage can exist; or where feeble world-heat is quenched and mountains are crumbled into ghastly slopes of shattered rock by the contending forces of heat and cold; even there, amid the glaciers, they spring from Nature's ruined battle-ground, as if the mother of earth-life had sent up her loveliest children to plead with the spirits of destruction.

He had loved the high Alps and their flowers. He now set his sights on mountains farther afield, in a country he had thought of very often, for personal reasons, America.

The year was 1870 and William Robinson was now thirty-two. He had achieved much in the nine years since he had left Ireland. Indeed, his career had been meteoric. In five years he had won independence as a freelance writer, and here he now was—author of five books on horticulture and a much-respected authority. He was ready to conquer a fresh field.

Long ago, in Regent's Park days, he had confided to the future Dean Hole his ambition to found a horticultural journal of his own. It was no mere ambition to become a newspaper proprietor: what he now needed was a platform for his ideas, to spread them as far and wide as successful circulation could reach; and he would be able to choose his contributors from a consortium of friends who were experts on every aspect of gardening. Not only British horticulturists but French. Perhaps he could add American?

We know from Sarah Robinson's letter to Geoffrey Taylor that Aunt Sarah Handfield Robinson of Bloomfield paid all the expenses for William and his brother James to go to America to find their father, which they did. They demanded money from him, she said, and returned quite well off.

That was in 1870. In 1871 William Robinson founded *The Garden*.

New things awaited him in the New World. Of that he felt sure, writing, 'When starting for the "great country", as Americans justly call theirs, I said to myself, Here we break new ground in this as in many other matters.'

He voiced his repugnance of the Old World, its dirt and decay. America would be quite different, a clean new country where land was still so abundant that there would be room in the cities for a few trees and other vegetation here and there to make them more fitting abodes for intelligent beings than the human burrows of the old countries.

Alas! 'No "rookery" of the old countries is fouler than the tenement houses in New York,' he mourned when he saw it. 'No large city I have ever seen in Europe is so devoid of squares or open spaces.' In fact, 'New York, the chief city of the States, is, in some respects, the most disagreeable and filthy city I have ever seen.' Apart from its length, the famous Broadway was inferior to some of the second-rate Paris boulevards. In the more fashionable parts of the town the streets were clean, but in hundreds of others the filth was woeful, the people in the habit of throwing their refuse into the streets, the municipality allowing it to lie there and rot.

In other respects, he was glad to discover, the island city was attractive: it was built on a noble harbour, and Central Park was magnificent. Its design surpassed that of any park in London.

A long train journey awaited the two brothers, that would take them across the continent to San Francisco. But first William must establish himself a little in this huge unknown land. He knew he must visit Dr Asa Gray, the doyen of American botanists, who would be sure to help him with useful introductions. So his first excursion was to Cambridge, Massachusetts, where Gray was Harvard's Professor of Natural History. Gray was also President of the American Academy of Arts and Sciences.

At sixty years old he was a genial bearded man who received William kindly and took him home to meet his wife. William was captivated by her, instantly warmed by her welcome, for she greeted him as if he were an old friend; and she was small and pretty, with thick dark hair and bright eyes. She could talk and listen, laugh and be serious, and somehow she made him feel that their home was his too—and he wished it were. Later he was to write to his distinguished friend, 'Kindly remember me to Mrs Gray—I sometimes regret, & I may as well confess it, that nearly all the nice women I have ever seen were married, though it is very rare indeed that one of them is secured by a botanist, who, like myself, is frequently obliged to console himself with flowers of a less exalted type.'

Poor William! Such consolation was to be his lot for the rest of his life.

But the visit was fruitful in other ways. Asa Gray lived up to his reputation by giving him every introduction he could wish. He was going to California? So he must meet Mr Bolander and Dr Kellogg. Both were Californian botanists and it might be possible for Dr Kellogg to show him some of the mountain plants of the Sierras. German-born Henry Nicholas Bolander was the State botanist of California, and about the same age as William, thirty-nine to William's thirty-two. Albert Kellogg was older and had turned from medicine to become a pioneer botanist. And he must not miss seeing the Hunnewell place. This, William decided, he would visit on the way back.

Meanwhile, California called, which for ever afterwards was to be William's 'beloved' country.

It was a journey that was almost historic, for America's first transcontinental railroad had been completed only the year before, in May 1869, when the United Pacific Railroad was connected with the Central Pacific at Promontory, Utah, fifty miles west of Ogden. It ran from Baltimore to San Francisco via Chicago. Baltimore was also the railhead for the more local and early railroads. William travelled on the New York Central line from Boston to Chicago, there picking up the great transcontinental train.

Chicago was then one of America's great cities, in Europe reputed to be *the* great city of the West, and by some unhappy mistake often called 'The Garden City'. William found it a sad repetition of the seamy side

A Visit to America, 1870

13 Asa Gray, doyen of American botanists, who
befriended William Robinson when he went to the
United States to find his long-lost father

of New York with not even the benefit of being broken up by that city's
grand rivers and estuaries. Added to which there was a terrible
population of rats hiving under the wooden footways. But at least two
parks were in course of construction, tree-planted boulevards being
made to link them, and work begun on improvements to the suburb
which one day, William rightly guessed, would be densely covered with
houses.

His first stunning experience was the great American desert, the best
preparation one could have, he thought afterwards, for the startling
greenness of the vegetation and giant tree-life that was to greet him in
the Sierras. It was all dust and dreariness, the desiccated earth looking
as if sprinkled with salt, here and there in favoured places a few tufts of
brown grass but generally nothing better than starved wormwood that
seemed afraid to put forth more than a few small grey leaves. The arid
hills were scored with terraces worn by the waves of ancient seas, a few

thin tufts of alders and poplars marking their hollows; and along the streams of undrinkable water coursing through the valleys a fringe of willows. This desert country could be summed up as a vast ash-pit several hundred miles across, dusted with a few light-grey weeds that were scarcely distinguishable from the parched earth.

The train began its long ascent of the Sierra, passing through dark-ribbed tunnels, the long covered sheds which guarded it from the snow in winter. When dawn broke it was as if to a new world, for gone were the dust and dreariness, the harshness of rock and hopelessness of barren soil. Instead, near at hand, a giant pine tree rushed up like a huge mast, and all around and in the distance were great pines grouped in stately armies, filling the valleys and cresting the wave-like hills.

The western slopes of the great chain of the Sierras were clothed with even nobler trees and richer verdure. There the thousands of mountain gorges, the flanks of every vale and every one of the innumerable hills were densely populated with stately pines and glossy evergreens. It was like an ocean of huge land-waves over which the spirit of tree-life had passed.

'The autumn days I spent among these trees were among the happiest one could desire,' wrote William, 'every day glorious sunshine and the breeze as gentle as if it feared to overthrow the dead trees standing here and there, leafless, and often barkless, but still pointing as proudly to the zenith as their living brothers.'

Everywhere he went, wandering away from the little rough dusty roads, he came upon these dead monarchs of the forest, 'now given back to the dust from which they had gathered so much beauty and strength,' as he wrote.

We must presume, since Sarah Handfield Robinson said so, that William and his brother met their father, were well received by him and were not sent away empty-handed. It can be asked how a runaway Irishman accumulated enough wealth to satisfy two sons. We may also ask why San Francisco? We know that Father William Robinson deserted his family when they were quite young, and we know from what Sarah Robinson, their cousin, said, that William never mentioned his father. If he were ten years of age or thereabouts William would be old enough to remember him and young enough never to forgive. This would bring us to 1848 when San Francisco became a gold boom-town with people pouring into it from every quarter. Few cities contain a more cosmopolitan population, and it has always been a mecca for the Irish.

This could be the whole explanation, but there is no doubt that it was after his visit to America that William Robinson was able to finance the founding of *The Garden.*

Meanwhile, with his journal already in the making, if only in imagination, he bethought himself of an interesting series for it. He had written up the parks and gardens of Paris and the parks and squares of London: the parks of the great cities of America must also be of interest to gardeners. And he could add a chapter on the mountain plants of America in the next edition of *Alpine Flowers* (which is what he did). What he had so far glimpsed of them, even along the sides of the railroad as the train climbed up into the Sierras was promise enough.

And so it proved. He had made contact with Albert Kellogg and the two of them went off on a plant-hunting expedition in the White Mountains. On the summit of the Sierras they found a pretty little shrublet which William thought deserved to be introduced into Britain. 'Growing as they do on some of the coldest mountains of the world I have little doubt that they will prove as easy to cultivate as many other American bushes which thrive in our gardens.' Kellogg knew it as *Bryanthus*, the Rocky Mountain Heath, but did not know the species, and William wrote to Asa Gray to ask where he had described any members of the genus, 'so that I may be able to determine my plant.'

Bryanthus is monotypic, the only species being *gmelinii*. It was introduced into Britain, though only recently and from Japan, the American plants having failed to establish themselves.

Otherwise, the vegetation on the summit was not luxuriant, as was to be expected; for there, as on any high mountain range, is the 'frost that burns and the wind that shears', as William wrote. A solitary pine bold enough to plant itself among the rocks was so contorted that it looked as if inhabited by demons. Others which had succumbed to the enemy were a mere few blanched branches sticking up from the earthless granite.

The beauty of the mountain woods was wonderful to William. In some parts the scene was finer than in the most carefully planted park, for the pines were not crowded together as in the Eastern States; and often, near the crest of a knoll, each tall tree would show clear against the sky. Beneath them was always a rich undergrowth of evergreens.

But grand as were the pines and incense cedars, the evergreen oaks matched them in beauty. One with large shining leaves, yellowish beneath, and long acorns in thick cups covered with a dense and brilliant fringe of fur, was the most beautiful oak he had ever seen. Then, one day in a deep valley darkened by the shade of giant specimens of the incense cedars he was astonished to see an arbutus some sixty feet high, quite a forest tree. This was Menzies' arbutus, commonly known by the old Mexican name of Madrona, and a handsome tree it was with its cinnamon-red bole and branches. Here and there, too, the Californian Bay (*Oreodaphne californica*) formed glossy laurel-like bushes. Shrubs abounded, ceanothus and the manzanita (*Arctostaphylos manzanita*) being predominant, while beneath them and all over the bare ground were the dried stems of the numerous bulbs and annual flowers that made a living carpet of brilliantly coloured stars and bells in spring.

It was not all trees, parched desert and arid upland. In complete contrast were the bogs and their plants. Most dramatic were the vivid blooms of the Cardinal Flower (*Lobelia cardinalis*), springing erect from wet peaty hollows and growing even along the sides of the railroads. Where the forest vegetation disappeared the Pitcher Plant (*Sarracenia*), Golden Clump (*Orontium*), Water Arum (*Calla palustris*), and a host of other handsome and interesting bog plants covered the ground for hundreds of acres, with perhaps an occasional splendid bush of the Laurel Magnolia (*Magnolia glauca*).

Snow fell early and deep on the Sierras, he was told by Dr Kellogg, the boles of the higher trees often covered with it to a depth of up to twenty-five feet, and on the 15th of November when they went to hunt for alpines a foot or two had already fallen. They were in time to see a patch of alpine plants here and there before they were tucked in under their wintry shroud. Among the rocks and boulders on exposed spots were brown tufts like withered moss, some of them low cushions, others looking as if moss had assumed a shrubby habit and died full of years at three inches high on a gouty stem nearly as thick as a finger. These were little phloxes withered almost beyond hope by the heat of summer, but on pulling one up he saw that the old roots were sending out a mass of fragile feeders in the snow-moistened earth, and that in the very centre of each juniper-like truss of prickly leaves was a small speck of green. He was told that some twenty feet of snow would be piled here by successive falls. When it melted in spring and the sun warmed the saturated earth these mites of phloxes would break into blossom, the dead 'moss' changing to bright shining green, to be covered by a sheet of flowers. The alpine phloxes of the Rocky Mountains were as indispensable to a choice collection of alpine plants as the gentians or primroses of the Old World.

Everywhere on bare places were dwarf penstemons two to five inches high, and these were among the most beautiful of the rock plants, in colours more delicate than those of the tall garden species. Their blues and purples had an irridescence not to be found in any other flower he knew. *Penstemon humilis* was a treasure abundant about Pike's Peak.

A gem of a rock plant was an eriogonum, the Umbrella Plant, carrying umbels of primrose yellow springing from dull brownish leaves two inches high. Far away, on a bare gravelly hillside, they could see vivid red tufts, and these proved to be another equally beautiful eriogonum, with leaves of deep blood colour.

What William longed to find in its wild state was the Californian Pitcher Plant, *Darlingtonia californica*, and when they were up about 4,000 feet he came upon it growing among bushes of ledum. With their yellow pitchers ready to trap unsuspecting insects, they looked like a lot of Jargonelle pears.

While in California he visited the Chinese gardens. They bore, he thought, a striking resemblance to French ways in their thorough culture, absolute cleanliness, and instant supplies of water, suggesting to him some old-world connection between the two. He also looked up Henry Bolander, who gave him some dried plant specimens for Asa Gray. William was becoming quite a courier, for Gray had asked him to take a box of apples for Joseph Hooker at Kew.

He was back at the Westminster Hotel, New York, on the 30th of November, with only a few days to pack in more visits before he sailed on the 7th of December.

One visit was to the Hunnewell Arboretum at Wellesley, Massachusetts. H. H. Hunnewell, a banker and railroad builder, gave him another warm American welcome. He had started his garden in 1851, transforming forty acres of his large estate into a place of such beauty and interest that visitors came from afar. Spectacular was the Italian garden overlooking Lake Waban, with its topiary of fantastical shapes, the finest collection in America. More to William's liking was the splendid collection of rhododendrons and azaleas, again the finest in the whole country. At the time Hunnewell began planting them it was not known which species would thrive in the trying climate of New England, and so far north. He proved that hundreds of kinds were adapted to outdoor culture in that climate. Another 'first' was the pinetum which for long was unsurpassed for the numbers of species and varieties it contained.

'I was charmed with the place & proprietor!' William wrote, thanking Asa Gray for this happy introduction.

If the American cities disappointed him, their parks did not. Neither did the American cemeteries, to which he applied one of his favourite adjectives—'noble'. These were the most creditable city improvements yet carried out by the Americans, and as great an advance upon ours as it was possible to imagine. Some were as large as national parks and as full of flowers and trees as a choice garden. Even small country villages had followed the examples of the cities, and instead of the old-fashioned 'God's Acre' there were imitations of Greenwood, Mount Auburn, and Philadelphia's Laurel Hill which occupied a beautiful and commanding site. On his way to visit Robert Buist, the well-known nurseryman there, he passed at Mount Vernon yet another large and ornamental cemetery, each family possessing quite a little garden of its own.

All too soon for William, he and James were climbing aboard the *China*, bound not for England but for Ireland. Their mother was still alive, and although William kept contact with her, on his rare visits home and regularly writing to her, there was much that was new to tell her.

I I

The Founding of *The Garden*

He had lost some of his heart to America; and in answer to Asa Gray's promise that a welcome would be awaiting him should he return, he wrote, '*Of course* I will go again to America & next time for a year or more if necessary.'

Something of America travelled with him: Dr Gray's box of apples for Dr Hooker, with plants for himself and a bunch of papers on the Californian flora, all accompanied by a kindly note. Six days out from New York William wrote his thanks. 'The ship is plunging a good deal,' he apologized in explanation of his jerky handwriting.

He was also taking home photographs of the Californian trees and wished for a true and good photograph or sketch of the American Elm of which Oliver Wendell Holmes was so fond. He had read the books of the famous 'Autocrat'.

'You did not name O. W. Holmes among the *gardeners* you were kind enough to ask me to meet but I think from his books he must be a true gardener! I wish very much to see him—another Boston treat deferred.'

The photographs were for his new periodical, he confided. He thought the American Elm 'not at all sufficiently well known to the Britishers', and that it was better to show a picture of a fine specimen in its native land rather than one in an English garden, adding, 'I am not sure that I could find any such specimen in our gardens or groves as I saw at Boston.'

The magnificent White Elm (*Ulmus americana*) was introduced into Britain in 1752 but unfortunately it is rarely good here and is the most susceptible of all to Dutch Elm disease.

Asa Gray replied that Dr Holmes had only a very small photograph of the tree; but a copy of this would do very well, William wrote back, with a word as to the height of the specimen. Oliver Wendell Holmes became a contributor to *The Garden*, in its first issue writing on 'Planting Trees'.

Between his return home in December 1870 and the launching in November 1871 of what William called his 'newspaper' came the publication of two more books: *Hardy Flowers* and *The Subtropical Garden*. The first was published by Macmillan, the second by John Murray. For although Murray published most of his books William liked to shop around.

It was not unusual in those days for an author to buy the paper for his own book, engage an artist and even have the book printed at his own expense. What he could not do, lacking the trade facilities, was market the book. William followed the procedure up to the point where he needed the imprint of a good publisher. Mainly he favoured Murray, and having wooed him into accepting the book he then had to commission him to publish it. He himself had the benefit of all the sales less the commission.

In *Hardy Flowers* he put forward a new principle of gardening. This was the herbaceous border: he called it the 'mixed border'. True, there had been mixed borders before, and this was to beg the question—what had he to offer that was new? He explained that 'in most cases when people discuss this question, the old mixed border seems to represent their ideal of the highest beauty to be attained by the use of the hardy herbaceous and alpine flora of our gardens. To me it has a very different and a very much wider and nobler aspect.'

He told his readers how during the past eight or nine years he had sought hardy plants of all kinds 'unremittingly', and previously had seen some good old-fashioned mixed borders, but never had he seen any border display a tenth of the beautiful plants it might have had, or one really worthy of a beautiful garden.

The culmination of his search was a checklist published in April by John Murray under the title 'Catalogue of Hardy Perennials, Bulbs, Alpine Plants, Annuals, Biennials Etc.' Included were plants out of place in the garden proper, for instance many of the asters and solidagos; but, as he explained, 'I am not without hope that my *Wild Garden* will be effective in pointing out the true home for those and numbers of the other members of the flora of cold and temperate regions.' Laudable was the addition of trees, shrubs and other plants native to Britain, as being too much neglected in gardens and as being field plants quite common in one district which could be choice garden rarities in another, just as plants hardy in America and Europe could be considered rarities in England. He was careful to add that recommending for cultivation all the plants he had enumerated was 'no part of my plan—it would be rash to say one-fifth of them were worthy of that.' Of the 10,000 listed he selected 1,400 for his book.

The checklist was unique; nothing like it had been done since William Townsend Aiton's *Hortus Kewensis* (1810–13), and that dealt

14 'A beautiful accident', an engraving from a sketch by Alfred Parsons, showing a colony of *Myrrhis odorata* and white harebells growing naturally in a shrubbery

only with plants grown at Kew and only 5,500 species.

The principle presented in his book anticipated the work being done today in the field of garden design and landscape gardening by such dedicated plantsmen as Christopher Lloyd who at Great Dixter has created the most outstandingly beautiful herbaceous border that even William Robinson could wish for. 'Many combinations of the utmost beauty' were what was required by the author of *Hardy Flowers*. Good 'association' was emphasized, the contrast of one plant—flower and leaf—with another. The mixed border must therefore be an 'infinite variation' of choice hardy herbaceous plants, bulbs and alpines, with room for the newest sedum or silvery saxifrage, the latest delphinium, phlox or gladiolus. It could also be of shrubs, but again in endless variety, varied also by the introduction even of pegged-down roses, and certainly by lilies 'stolen in' here and there. Lillies again in gardens where rhododendrons were massed, the bold and tall heads of *Lilium tigrinum* 'Fortunei' and *Lilium superbum* relieving the dull summer greenness of the rhododendrons, while the rhododendrons obligingly hid the withering leaves of the lilies.

The book was divided into three parts, the first devoted to layout, choice of plants and culture, the main part being descriptions of hardy flowering plants of all kinds, the remainder handy indices listing such things as 'Dwarf Hardy Perennial and Alpine Plants with Fern-like or graceful Leaves and suitable for Association with those distinguished by beauty of Flower in borders, the rock-garden etc.'. There was an index to the families of the plants described, a glossary and finally an index to their English names.

This last, the use of English names in place of botanical names, became a William Robinson fetish, and with some he came unstuck. For however well-known in their day were Spiked Button Snake-root and Sundrops these were not names that have stood the test of time. What was a poor foreigner to make of Burchell's Flame-flower? How identify Pine Barren Beauty if faced with it in one of his books? With all his understanding of people and plants European he should have known better. Latterly in such charming works as *Home Landscapes* and *Gravetye Manor* William Robinson dispensed with Latin names—if not altogether, with few exceptions when he found that for the sake of absolute identification a particular plant had to bear its universal label. Nor could he make a translation of such names as globularia, fuchsia, draba or dracocephalum. Linnaeus would have sighed with despair.

We have already glimpsed the makings of *The Subtropical Garden*, inspired by John Gibson's plantings in Battersea Park: his palms, tree ferns, bananas, aralias, dracaenas and other exotics with richly coloured leaves and flowers. But here again was William Robinson's plea for diversity: the introduction into the garden of plants with large and graceful foliage but grown in association with the brilliant flowering plants common in gardens though frequently lacking beauty of form. Thus form and colour could effectively be wedded.

The success of subtropical planting was achieved not only at Battersea but, as he tells us in a foreword, in his own homeland.

> Since writing the preceding remarks I have visited America, and when on my way home landed at Queenstown with a view to seeing a few places in the South of Ireland, and among others Fota Island, the residence of Mr Smith Barry, where I found a capital illustration of what may easily be effected by hardy plants alone. Here is an island planted with a hardy bamboo (*Bambusa falcata*), which thrives so freely as to form great tufts from 16 ft to 20 ft high. The result is that the scene reminds one of a bit of the vegetation of the uplands of Java, or that of the bamboo country in China. The thermometer fell last December (1870) seventeen degrees below freezing point, so that they suffered somewhat but their general effect was not much marred.

He added that the scene surpassed even Battersea Park but was simply the result of selecting from the rich store of subtropical plants those that were hardy.

With a flood of colour to choose from in flower and leaf he warned against the kind of 'geometro-picturesque' planting seen in some of the London parks—long straight lines of the same species, or the 'twisting masses' of carpet bedding. The day would come, he prophesied, when we would be as anxious to avoid these formal twirlings as we were to have them 'perpetrated' now by 'landscape-gardeners of great repute applying wallpaper or fire-shovel patterns to the surface of the reluctant earth'.

As usual, the book contained a wealth of information, and, as always, there were valuable appendices.

The 'Catalogue' by 'Mr Robinson, whose literary activity is worthy of comment', earned a mere mention in *The Gardeners' Chronicle*. *Hardy Flowers* did better with two columns devoted to it as 'one of the best of the many books its writer has produced', describing it as 'the result of study and application over a considerable period', of especial value being the information indicating the best situation for each plant. The appearance of *The Subtropical Garden* at the season when the planting of the flower garden was engaging attention was very opportune. It should form part of every garden library, said the critic.

Now in 1871 came his great venture as a newspaper proprietor. He was comfortably settled at 28 Scarsdale Villas with two servants. One was Thomas Spanswick who had come to him from the Royal Botanic Society, Regent's Park. William had first known him in 1865 as a half-crown a week gardener in his own Herbaceous Department. He came in May of that year when the flood of new plants was arriving. Thomas's wife Harriet was his housekeeper. Their daughter, Harriet Louisa, was three years old.

He opened an office at 37 Southampton Street, Covent Garden, just off the Strand, and there on the 25th of November was born *The Garden*, which he was to edit for the next twenty-nine years. Everybody who was anybody in the gardening world at some time wrote for it or read it. A weekly costing fourpence, it was value for money, bringing to the reader the expertise of not only leading British horticulturists but of those in Europe and America. William himself set the pace in the first issue with a leader on 'The Pathway to Noble National Gardens', in which he discussed how in large cities like London, New York or Paris the thousands of acres 'already rescued from our mighty deserts of slate and brick' might be so treated that they could be of fullest value to the public, not only as fields of health but as schools of delightful instruction. He spoke passionately from personal experience in declaring that no public park in any of these cities represented even a tithe of the beauty and interest of which they were capable under a system which he went on to expound. William Robinson was in his stride, a godlike figure who viewed nature within the confines of a garden, viewed too a garden within the boundless universe of nature, and drew them skilfully together. His was a synoptic eye, seeing how they might be blended to make a perfect whole.

He saw what was bad and condemned it: vast surfaces were almost totally neglected or only garnished with a few commonplace trees; and if a favourite spot was embellished at great expense during the summer months with tender plants, the remainder was usually uncared for, and this was 'like embellishing a man fluttering in rags with a costly buttonhole bouquet'.

The system he proposed was to treat all the public parks and gardens of a city as a whole, and to establish in each a distinct type of vegetation. One park might be devoted chiefly to noble deciduous trees; a suburban one like Richmond to evergreen forest trees. Or the planting might be treated geographically, a small square or park with British trees, shrubs and other plants; another with European, another with American, and so on.

This system would free parks superintendents from paltry rivalry in the matter of bedding displays. Each could select a botanical family, or even flora, and develop its beauty and variety. He thought that in the vast expanse of our public gardens there was not one interesting and important branch of aboriculture which could not be developed in this way. The best results would be obtained in botanic gardens, most of them not large enough for the proper grouping and arrangement of even a single family of trees. For 'Generally our present botanic gardens give no more idea of the variety, beauty and majesty of vegetation, than the fountain basin does of the wild tossing of a wind-tortured sea.' None worthily represented the vegetation of even Europe alone! What could we see of the beauty and character of any one large family of trees by planting them all at regular intervals in a plot! This was good enough if we had no higher objective than collecting specimens to illustrate the grammar of botanical nomenclature. But if our aim was to show the inexhaustible beauty and dignity of the vegetable kingdom, then, said William Robinson, we must disentangle ourselves from such small notions. And, clearly, the way to do this was to treat our public gardens (both botanic gardens and parks) as a whole; stamp on each some distinguishing feature—'from the smallest square with a complete collection of Ivies or Hawthorns, to the noblest park adorned with the trees of a hundred hills.'

It was one idea.

The Founding of 'The Garden'

These he never lacked. Nor, when an empty space in the dummy called for a filler, was his pen ever still. He hid his identity under a series of pseudonyms: E+++++ in the December 2 issue was himself as Editor, as was Conductor, and (of course) W.R. Some articles though unsigned were recognizably his. In fact one could be forgiven for thinking that *The Garden* was simply a platform for the ideas of William Robinson. Certainly he could air them well through this medium, and he never let an opportunity slip when by comment or criticism he could urge reform or improvement.

The Garden served another purpose. It was a trial ground for exercising principles he later expanded to become books. Thus, articles on smoke pollution in cities, American cemeteries, garden design—all were precursors of future books, while the descriptions of plants old and new, established and recently introduced or bred, rewritten and occasionally quoted from their authors, formed the plant catalogue for *The English Flower Garden* in all its expanding fifteen editions. *The Garden* also provided many of the beautiful illustrations for this book.

He employed several artists. Alfred Dawson was one who illustrated *The Parks and Gardens of Paris* and *Alpine Flowers*. Alfred Parsons had illustrated *The Wild Garden* and worked for him till his death in 1920. Henry George Moon who was to join the staff of *The Garden* in 1880 did drawings for the third edition of *Alpine Flowers*. C. Pochon did many others for the alpine book. Armand Kohl was almost constantly employed from the time of that book through to *The English Flower Garden*. Edward William Cooke, R.A. drew for *The Garden*. Later, H. G. Moon and the American W. E. Norton were to spend an idyllic year at Robinson's Sussex home, painting the garden in all its moods and the flowers in all their seasons.

Another *Garden* artist was Frank Miles. This was George Francis Miles, R.A., who took him to see Ruskin's collection of pictures. Miles had the greatest admiration for his Editor and in a 'long talk with Ruskin told him of the splendid work you are doing among the people and his delight is intense.'

There was room for prose and poetry in *The Garden*, as well as for sound common-sense instruction. The following, on page 2 of the first issue, is sheer magic—though not a step removed from William Robinson's 'natural' thinking, nor in fact from reality. It was written by Oliver Wendell Holmes.

I don't know anything sweeter than this leaking in of Nature through all the cracks in the walls and floors of cities. You heap up a million tons of hewn rocks on a square mile or two of earth which was green once. The trees look down from the hillsides and ask each other as they stand on tiptoe, 'What are these people about?' And the small herbs at their feet look up and whisper back, 'We will go and see.' So the small herbs pack themselves up in the least possible bundles, and wait until the wind steals to them at night and whispers, 'Come with me.' Then they go softly with it into the great city—one to a cleft in a pavement, one to a spout on the roof, one to a seam in the marble over a rich gentleman's bones, and one to the grave without a stone where nothing but a man is buried—and there they grow. . . .

In such charming prose he sees the invasion of Nature, ending with the trees themselves.

Wait long enough and you will find an old doting oak hugging a huge worn block in its yellow underground arms: that was the corner-stone of the state-house. Oh, so patient she is, imperturbable Nature!

Holmes also treated the readers to a poem on 'Violets'.

The Garden was not above reflecting William Robinson's love of fun. Reynolds Hole, writing from Caunton Manor, addressed a Letter to the Editor which was published in December. It related how in the spring the Dean was perturbed by a proposal to erect a line of telegraph poles along the road in front of his house, and how a kind friend who was a lieutenant in the Royal Engineers and engaged in supervising the work turned the Dean's annoyance into laughter. He wrote, sending a neat illustration:

Knowing you to be pre-eminent as a horticulturist, I beg to bring to your notice a magnificent species of the Aloe tribe (Agave telegraphica).

This highly ornamental plant flourishes best by the side of roads and on railway embankments, and I can strongly recommend it to your notice, feeling it would succeed admirably at the edge of the high-road at the foot of your lawn, where it would be seen to great advantage from your drawing-room windows . . .

The Dean's reply was that he thought this beautiful plant would succeed best if it were 'pegged down and layered'. He was delighted when it was found that this could be done, the telegraph wires laid out of sight, underground.

His kind friend was Herbert Jekyll, younger brother of Gertrude Jekyll who was not yet famous in the gardening world but was making a name for herself as a painter. She was to become a contributor to *The Garden*, first visiting William Robinson at his office in January 1875.

The Founding of 'The Garden'

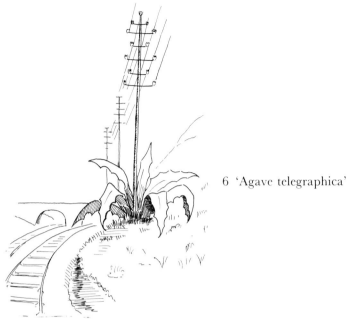

6 'Agave telegraphica'

Dean Hole also contributed a series called 'The Six of Spades', later to be a book, which was a *pot pourri* of gardening expertise and delightful reminiscence. The series recorded the activities of the Dean's club of that name whose six gardener members met on winter evenings to discuss such subjects as boilers, flues and stoves; disbudding, stopping and pruning; soils, sand and peat; and traps for earwigs. The meetings were held in his garden-house, a 'warm and cosy chamber' where 'Before our blazing fire, which roars a hearty bass to the mirthful tenor of the kettle, is a table for our pipe and glass...'

The contributors to *The Garden* were indeed a star-studded cast: among them David Moore of Glasnevin; John Ruskin; Henry Nicholson Ellacombe, Canon of Bitton; George Paul, the rosarian; James Britten who with G. S. Boulger was to compile the invaluable *Biographical Index of British and Irish Botanists*; James Russell Lowell, the American poet, essayist and diplomat; and, with other French experts, Charles Baltet and his old friend Edouard André, head gardener of Paris.

It was fitting that the motto of the paper should be the quotation from Shakespeare, who had a remarkable knowledge of gardening and plants,

> This is an art
> Which does mend Nature: change it rather: but
> The art itself is Nature.

For this exactly expressed William Robinson's ideas.

The newspaper seemed all set for success, and its founder looked eagerly and ambitiously forward, writing to Asa Gray, 'It is my present intention to have one edition of my "Garden" specially prepared for the American climate & to issue it simultaneously in America & England.'

Though this never happened, the English edition of *The Garden* travelled across the Atlantic. Oliver Wendell Holmes called it a 'beautiful journal' and wrote that it was as 'widely acceptable in your country as *ours*', which was a graceful transposition.

12

A Toast to the Queen of Spades

An editor is always on the look-out for features to keep his readers happy and to attract new ones. Much in the public eye at this time was George Maw whose business was pottery but who far preferred plants. In 1871 he had accompanied Joseph Hooker, head of Kew, and John Ball the scientist, politician and alpine climber, on an expedition to the Atlas Mountains, then one of the world's least-known regions. From there, as from Greece and other places where he had collected, Maw brought home new plants to enrich the garden surrounding his beautiful sixteenth-century house, Benthall Hall in Shropshire. William decided that the description of the interesting garden of this famous man would be enjoyed by his readers.

It could be compared, he found, with William Borrer's wonderful botanic garden at Henstead in Sussex and Wilson Sanders's collection at Reigate but was far richer than either in interesting and hardy plants, and here the charms of association were woven around them: with a houseleek from the Atlas, a sedum from the Sierra Nevada, rock roses from Gibraltar, an iris from Tangiers and a primrose from the Alps—all collected by him. Every step brought some distant part of the earth before the visitor, 'in the person of one of the earth children.' His collection of alpine plants was amazing. At the time of William's visit there were eighty species of saxifrage in flower, including *maweana* of large waxy white flowers discovered by him in North Africa and named in his honour.

It was at Benthall that William met with 'one of the first attempts to *cultivate* alpine plants in a worthy manner'. Familiar were the wretched examples sent to shows, even by notable growers. Rarely could one know from any specimens in their collections that these plants were specially distinguished by spreading out into cushions of the most vivid colours, or have the faintest notion of their true habit of beauty. Maw had the secret of making them feel at home.

A series in the early issues of *The Garden* was devoted to descriptions and views of smaller gardens, as being more useful to the majority of readers and often better laid out.

[117]

One was at Newstead, Wimbledon, that of his publisher John Murray who in a comparatively few years had transformed a bare piece of heathland with a rich collection of healthy young conifers and shrubs. Choice American plants were a dominant feature.

A most attractive small garden was at Sheen Lodge, admired by many a visitor to Richmond Park, for it nestled on the fringe of the undulating ground near the Sheen Gate. Its owner was Richard Owen, Hunterian Professor at the Royal College of Surgeons, and the house had been given to him by Queen Victoria in 1852. Professor Owen was no stranger to William Robinson, who had often supplied him with plant material in Regent's Park days.

The garden was simple and unpretending, with a lawn 'unbroken by geometrical twirlings'; and the beautiful creeper-covered cottage seemed to spring out of a bank of flowers, for instead of being surrounded by a bare gravel walk there was a wide border filled with rhododendrons, spiraeas, lilies and foxgloves, tall evening primroses and other herbaceous plants. Nearby stood a noble *Gleditschia triacanthos* of graceful ferny foliage and stately height.

William had sent Owen a copy of *The Wild Garden* in 1871, a gift the professor much appreciated, for thinking he ought to make more of his plantation through which rambled grass walks he asked William to pick up suitable bulbs and tell him their proper treatment. After that there were frequent visits to Sheen, by himself or with such congenial friends as Vernon Lushington.

The paper was not, of course, only about visiting gardens. A brisk exchange took place on the subject of 'practical' gardeners versus 'scientific' men. This subject, wrote Editor Robinson in a leader of May 1872, was of the greatest importance to horticulture. Yet in no horticultural periodical had it ever been discussed. He pointed out that we lost much by the wrongful use of words, and how greatly we impeded progress both in horticulture and botany, by using false distinctions as to knowledge and the means of adding to it.

> It should be clearly understood by all men that all knowledge is the same in kind; that there is no real difference between 'science' and practice, and that what is sound in theory must be sound also in practice, and *vice versa*. . . . The old meaning of the word science is knowledge; the modern meaning is the same.

Such an expression as 'It is right enough in theory, but wrong in practice' was simply nonsense; and 'It is mere theory' was often the silly comment on some simple statement, the truth of which could be put to the test in the garden. To say that the author of a proposition was 'not a practical man' or not a 'scientific' one, was an easy but ungenerous and unworthy way of saving ourselves the trouble of investigating whether he was right or wrong.

Who was to blame for this state of things? Chiefly the class of botanists and 'scientific' men who did not rise higher than mere technicalities and their application.

'We might suppose that the Royal Horticultural Society would not propagate errors of this kind. But this is precisely what it does, and at the great Birmingham meeting' (he was referring to the Royal Horticultural Exhibition to be opened by Prince Arthur of Connaught the following month) 'there is to be a scientific and a practical congress. Addresses are also to be given on separate days on "recent progress in scientific" and "recent progress in practical" horticulture, as if these terms did not mean one and the same thing.'

Another item of current interest to readers of *The Garden* was the Ayrton Affair which had started in 1871. Acton Smee Ayrton was the First Commissioner of Works in the Gladstone administration. Described as 'a repulsive blunt-mouthed creature with the proverbial skin of a rhinoceros', Ayrton detested gardeners, in his re-election speech of 1869 warning 'architects, sculptors and gardeners' that they would be kept in their place. He aimed preposterous charges of incompetence against the illustrious Joseph Dalton Hooker who had succeeded his father as Director of Kew. He failed, for the weight of science in the persons of such great leaders as Charles Darwin, T. H. Huxley and Sir Charles Lyell forced Gladstone to remove Ayrton from the Board of Works and elevated Hooker to the highest position a man of science can hold—presidency of the Royal Society.

The battle—of scientific men against non-scientific and non-gardening—was faithfully reported week by week, and in this case the editor of *The Garden* upheld science. He recognized that Kew was, as it still is, a scientific establishment where botanists and gardeners could study plants in their dried state in its Herbarium, could read about them and see illustrations of them in its library, and in the Gardens see them as living beings, growing, flowering and fruiting.

But William Robinson had his own quarrel with Kew. Its gardens were a disgrace. Never, he declared, in the history of the world had a nation been so liberal to a public garden as England had been to Kew. He quoted the figures, which in those days amounted to a princely sum. Yet, 'Ask any orchid-grower as to the state of the orchids at Kew and the extent of the collections, and he will most probably laugh with derision.' There were scores of collections better grown and richer. 'Then go out of doors and look at the flower gardening.' We would see that Kew was an age behind some of the London parks, and could anything be more discreditable to the gardening of England than the general state of the plants in pots? Further, what about recent introductions? 'Nobody thinks of looking to Kew for them,' he deplored. 'If we seek new conifers, or new and rare ferns, or new alpine plants of any class, we all have one or more gardens associated in our minds with such novelties, but we do not think of Kew in connection with them.' The best collections of plants, and the best grown, were not, he declared, under the control of the botanists proper 'but in charge of our gardeners amateur and professional.' Likewise our 'scientific' horticulture; that is, our best and most advanced gardening.

What he advocated was simply that the gardens should be run by gardeners, a Backhouse, a Moore or a Niven, in other words no mere cultivator but a really accomplished botanic gardener.

Design entered into the argument. Kew in some respects was superior to any other botanic garden in the world, but in the matter of design was 'no higher than a chess board'. It was devoid of picturesque beauty, though the Paris botanic garden was infinitely worse! The Royal Horticultural Society's garden at South Kensington was specially designed for flower shows, and experience elsewhere had taught that the happiest effect was achieved with an open lawn where crowds could promenade and from it view the features of the garden. What had been done to meet this want? A geometrical garden, an idiotic maze, an avenue of Lombardy poplars cutting off the view! The only public garden showing any judgement or insight into what a garden should be was the small garden of the Botanic Society in the Regent's Park, which in its general design 'has helped to keep a true spirit of landscape gardening from slumbering among us during one of the most marked periods of retrogression that it has ever lived through.'

Thus William Robinson the evangelist, seizing the opportunity to convert even Kew to his principles of good gardening and good garden design.

France had always held a special lure for him, particularly its capital. He had been back to Paris in March 1870, and again in November of the following year, and his article in the December 2 issue of *The Garden* gives a vivid picture of the city as it was after the seige and after the carnage and destruction during the Commune. Yet he was able to compare it hopefully with what he had seen in March. Then the once-beautiful Bois de Boulogne had presented a scene of desolation where the large forest trees had been felled to make the gigantic barricades and fortifications that still surrounded the city and intersected the streets. Now the empty places were covered with fresh vegetation, with the most curious effect caused by the scarlet tints of the American oaks *Quercus coccinea* and *Quercus rubra*. Thousands of these trees had been sent from the United States by André Michaux to de Sahme, *ancien conservateur* of the Bois. Though cut to the ground they had thrown out fresh shoots and these now formed a stunning field of scarlet foliage.

William's beloved Parc Monceau had not suffered much, but gone were all the beautiful-foliaged and flowering plants which had so delighted Parisians and their visitors. In their place were a few species pelargoniums, ageratums and chrysanthemums 'not better than those to be seen in a London shopkeeper's garden'. These two great head gardeners Barillet and André had resigned and the promenades and plantations were now in the hands of a roads-and-bridges engineer who knew nothing about horticulture. 'So,' lamented William, 'the fair days of public gardening in Paris are past.'

But in May 1873 when he saw Paris again the magnolias had recovered and were about to break into flower.

William Robinson is recorded by the Gardeners' Royal Benevolent Society as being the first subscriber to make a substantial annual donation to its funds. This was in 1869. Soon he was elected to the Society's Committee and in 1872 was invited to propose the loyal toast to the sovereign, Queen Victoria, at the annual dinner. He was to remain a supporter of the G.R.B.S. to the end of his life, finally leaving to it half the residue of his estate—a considerable sum, for he died a wealthy man. He also bequeathed to it the manuscripts, plates, wood blocks, copies of and copyright in *The English Flower Garden*, directing that fresh editions be published for the Society by John Murray, the first part remaining as far as possible as he had written it, the second part to be kept up to date as each new edition was required. In 1956 Murray brought out the sixteenth edition. It was revised by Roy Hay.

William's speech at the dinner was one of graceful allusion. He came 'as a gardener, with gardeners in my head and gardeners in my heart—I had almost said the Queen of Spades', but he was quite prepared to defend this designation because, firstly, Queen Victoria was patron of the Gardeners' Benevolent Institution; because the florist, loving peace and order, regarded the rose as the Queen of his garden; and because, like the Queen of Spades in the popular game of bézique, Her Majesty held supremacy over all other Queens.

(His speech was given in more clement circumstances than those at Birmingham when the recent Royal Horticultural Society's Exhibition was opened by Prince Arthur 'with a grace which charmed us all and a spirit which no deluge could depress'. The Queen's Weather had declined to exert itself for her younger son, and the rain not only penetrated the canvas but dripped from sunshade and umbrella, turned the 'richest cake into Sponge, and completely demoralised the mint sauce.')

A cry for peace was in the air. Voicing a tribute to the army, the navy and the reserve forces through whom we were enjoying safe tranquillity, William hoped 'our eyes shall never see a Prussian uniform among our German asters'. In 1866, only six years before, Prussia had annexed the Duchy of Hanover which previously had belonged to Britain's royal family. He went on '... and our ears shall never hear Yankee Doodle played amid our American plants', for excitement was running high regarding the American claims under the Treaty of Washington. He added a series of military puns, saying he would be vexed if we imported the foreign *grape*, the Cannon Ball *Muscat*, and if our peas were *shelled* by the hands of the artillery rather than by the hands of the cook. The only *pistils* should be within the flowers, and there should be nothing more martial than *Maréchal* Niel (the reference was to the climbing noisette rose introduced in 1864).

He kept up his friendship with Reynolds Hole and dedicated Volume II of *The Garden* to him in 1872. Two years later he wrote a pleading letter to Mrs Hole. For William Robinson at thirty-five years of age was in search of a new housekeeper—or a wife, and Mrs Hole was evidently able to produce at least the first, for thus he replied to a letter from her:

Dear Mrs Hole,
I shall be glad to see the person you kindly write about as soon as I return. In *this* case I shall dispense with a certificate of youth and beauty! In another (which I need not particularise) by no means! We are never satisfied alas! I now begin to long for somebody to superintend the domestic department if I may put it in that prosaic way. I think I must appeal to my friends! ...

The letter was date-lined Bray, Dublin, Nov. 4th, 1874.

Mrs Spanswick had disappeared from the scene. It was about 1873 that William moved from Scarsdale Villas and took up residence at 37 Southampton Street, the address of *The Garden* office. We know from the street directory that he was living there in 1879 and that his housekeeper then was a Mrs Cameron, though only he is listed as an elector in 1883. Thomas Spanswick, his one-time gardener, had joined the staff of *The Garden* as postal clerk.

From the same letter to Caroline Hole it emerges that William Robinson was now busy designing the Hole garden at Caunton.

Pray make my apologies to Mr Hole for making such deep forays into his purse for the improvements and garden changes. However, I am hopeful that, two or three seasons hence the harvest of beauty will be richer than you anticipate!

He spent a week at a time at Caunton and hoped for much from the rock garden, though 'Kindly save the alpine flowers from those dreadful hoofs,' he begged. Reynolds Hole was an inveterate rider to hounds.

Robinson at heart was a Pre-Raphaelite: nature and naturalness were his abiding theme; but whereas the Brotherhood continually looked back for inspiration, William Robinson continually looked forward. On the 23rd of May 1875 he was writing to Asa Gray about his plans for the future of *The Garden*.

I have improved it this year I think and am preparing something quite new in weekly journalism for the coming year—first-rate & original colour plates ...

He intended, he wrote, to make *The Garden* 'a richly illustrated magazine (in colour I mean ... I feel the time has come to use colour in a weekly).' He started the experiment that same year by including nine coloured plates, and this was the 'improvement', or one of them. But 1876 saw the real start of coloured illustrations in a weekly magazine, when he published fifty-six.

In the following year he was able to report to Gray that 'the experiment has succeeded admirably.'

The enterprising editor of *The Garden* also thought the time had come to have coloured illustrations in *Alpine Flowers* and he was 'now busy getting out a second vol. of *coloured plates* of the important genera to accompany Vol 1 and same size.' He told Gray he had a good man at York drawing the alpines from living plants in the Backhouse collection, 'and I believe we shall have something that will interest your Boston people who seem to know so much about good gardening.'

The good man was Henry Noel Humphreys who had illustrated Jane Loudon's *British Wild Flowers* and drew for several botanical periodicals. But alas, the companion volume never appeared. Instead, his exquisite coloured plates were used in *The Garden* in the feature 'Garden Flora', interspersed with coloured plates of herbaceous and other plants.

The illustrations for the herbaceous plants were likewise a compromise, for he had announced the preparation of 'a Serial Magazine, to be called The Garden Flora, planned to illustrate in colour the best of the newer flowers and fruit.' However, in collecting the material for it the idea arose of incorporating it with *The Garden*. This was done in 1876, each weekly issue containing a coloured plate of some new or rare flower or fruit likely to prove of permanent garden value. He turned another honest penny by selling the plates loose 'For Screens and Scrapbooks'. They could be purchased by the dozen, twenty-five, fifty and one hundred.

The artists were a distinguished lot. Besides Noel Humphreys they included Mrs Edward Whymper, wife of the alpinist and wood engraver; Frederick William Burbidge who started as a Kew gardener and became curator of Trinity College garden, Dublin, writing among other books *The Art of Botanical Drawing*; Mary Elizabeth Duffield, author of *The Art of Flower Painting*, and Mrs G. F. Wilson, wife of the candlemaker who created Wisley.

Bringing out *The Garden* was 'a long & severe but successful struggle'. It was certainly successful and in many ways, running under its own banner for more than half a century before amalgamating with *Homes and Gardens* in 1927. William Robinson had set its feet upon the right path. He had introduced a series of monographs of the more important genera of hardy plants; the correspondence columns were valuable for reader-participation; he travelled up and down the country and abroad, visiting more gardens, seeing new plants and making new contacts. In London he was at his desk at six in the morning dictating notes to his shorthand writer Rowland I. Jones who was there till eight o'clock—though not working every minute. 'I have pleasant memories of participating in the excellent porridge we had from time to time,' he recalled in a letter of the 14th of July 1933, congratulating his old employer on his ninety-fifth birthday. There was another happy memory, of 'the morning of my marriage 22nd July 1882' when 'you were kind enough to take me to Covent Garden and there purchased some flowers.'

13
Aspersions and Asparagus

Success breeds success. In March 1879 William Robinson launched a new magazine. This was *Gardening Illustrated*, though William always referred to it as 'Gardening'. To him this was sufficient title, the ultimate in its subject. The public took to it instantly. On the 11th of October its editor was able to announce that the weekly issue was now larger than that of the whole of the horticultural press of the United Kingdom combined.

By the middle of May 1881 nearly a million and a half copies had been issued during the previous six months. It was a staggering figure and William had no hesitation in declaring it 'no doubt by far the largest number of any journal devoted to gardening or rural economy ever published in a similar time.'

Success also breeds jealousy, and this reiteration was something the editor of *The Gardener's Magazine* could not stomach, for James Shirley Hibberd advertised his own periodical as having the 'Largest Circulation of any Horticultural Journal'. The result of his ire was faithfully reported by 'W.R.' in the August 20 issue.

> I have received a letter from Mr Hibberd's publishers, or rather their legal advisers, in which they ask 'what steps I propose to take to remedy the prejudicial effect' presumably of what appeared in these columns as regards the circulation of GARDENING a few weeks ago. But the statement is true, and within the mark. . . . Even the public must know as well as those who have the proofs, that for every copy of their magazine sold, or any other on horticulture that now exists, there are seven of *Gardening*.

Early in spring the weekly circulation had topped the 30,000 mark, as we know from another paragraph in the same issue when the editor had the pleasure of presenting his readers with a coloured plate of roses, drawn life-size by Alfred Parsons. 'It was our intention to have presented this plate with GARDENING early in Spring, but at that time only 30,000 of the plates were ready, and these not being sufficient for our then issue, we had no alternative but to offer the plate in limited

[125]

numbers with our index, and wait till a number of plates sufficient for our weekly issue could be got ready.'

How Shirley Hibberd must have squirmed! He has been described by Walter Page Wright, the prolific writer of gardening books and founder and editor of *Popular Gardening*, as an extremely pugnacious and dogmatic man with no respect for the feelings or opinions of others, though at the same time very witty. Pugnaceous, dogmatic, self-opinionated people very often are witty and always at the expense of others. But in William Robinson he had met his match. Hibberd criticized his opponent for introducing a personal element into horticultural journalism. Replied the editor of *Gardening Illustrated*, 'It is Mr Hibberd who ... has introduced the personal element. Many instances could be given of offensive and silly personalities of his—aimless, too, so far as the public are concerned. Poor Andrew Murray, secretary at the time of the Horticultural Society, was spoken of as the "whiteybrown" man by Mr Hibberd, who proposed to erect a statue of mud to Mr Murray at South Kensington.'

There were other offences of which Mr Hibberd was guilty. He had also misleadingly reported the giving of prizes for asparagus at the Bath and West of England Show. This, the first exhibition of that delicacy, had been instituted by William Robinson with the aim of improving its culture throughout Britain, and he proposed to donate a series of annual prizes extending over seven years. They were to be given in London, Dublin, Edinburgh, and the north, south, and west of England in different years. Announcing the competition in the March 12 issue of 1881, the editor of *Gardening Illustrated* pointed out that 'Our Markets are full of Asparagus in spring grown in other countries, sometimes hundreds of miles from London. It is a vegetable which perhaps more than any other loses quality every day after it is cut. This is one reason why it should be grown in our own country.' The soil and climate were admirably suited for it. Yet 'not only do we not supply our own market, but many possessing estates cannot get a good dish without sending to Covent Garden for it.'

It was typical of William Robinson that he should see a thing not done that could be done with benefit to everybody, from the highest to the poorest, 'for every farmer's garden and every cottage garden might grow it well.'

The competition caused a stir, resulting in more prize money being added to the original hundred guineas. And although the aim and object was to encourage home production at the expense of the French growers, a further ten pounds came from A. Godefroy-Lebeuf of Argenteuil, France's leading asparagus grower.

Aspersions and Asparagus

The results of the seven years' competition were embodied in *Asparagus Culture: the Best Methods employed in England and France*, written jointly by James Barnes and William Robinson, with a translation of M. Godefroy-Lebeuf's Essay on Asparagus. It was published by George Routledge and Sons in America and England, and formed one volume of 'Robinson's Country Series'.

The financial rewards came pouring in, and not only from the successful *Gardening Illustrated* but from his books. In 1878 *Hardy Flowers* went into its third edition, *Parks and Gardens of Paris* a second edition. The rival publication, *The Gardener's Magazine*, had more than a word of praise for the latter. 'Paris is the best known of any city in the world, and has been described a thousand times, but this book contains quite a new and fresh revelation of its rural aspect and the results of its municipal economy. Its object is evidently to institute comparisons, and to establish conclusion with the strictest impartiality.' Perhaps at this moment Shirley Hibberd was on holiday from his editorial chair.

In this same year, adding to Robinson's journalistic triumphs, a new paper made its début at 37 Southampton Street. This was *La Semaine Française*, a weekly journal and review, in French, for 'general and family reading'. It dealt with 'Paris—Society, Life, Improvements, Institutions', as described in the English advertisement in *Gardening Illustrated*, one in the French language adding *'Politique, Litérature, Sciences, Arts, Variétés, Nouvelles, et Notes.'* The press received the new weekly with acclaim. It ran until December 1883.

Robinson was very proud of the first coloured plate in *Gardening Illustrated*. The two roses depicted were Maréchal Niel and La France. The first was the great rose of the period introduced by Pradel fourteen years earlier. A climbing noisette with soft golden-yellow flowers, tea-scented, it was grown on sheltered walls outdoors; and in the cool greenhouse trained under the roof for house decoration, bouquets and buttonholes. La France, younger at eleven years old, was bred by Guillot and was the first of the hybrid teas. It was loved for its large cupped flowers of silvery-pink petals with a rose-pink reverse. Alas, it is rarely seen nowadays.

Gardening Illustrated despite its modest cost of one penny was a more sophisticated and more technical paper than *The Garden*. Its policy was to provide the very best practical information, and its scope was wide: flowers, fruit, vegetables, town and suburban gardening, villa gardening, the cottage garden, window gardening, with a calendar of work to be done in the garden each week. A useful 'Notes and Queries' feature became popular. Readers' queries, numbered for reference, were asked one week and usually answered the next.

It is interesting to look back to old volumes of the paper. Here you see reflected the flower fashions of the day. The multitudinous ways in which flowering and other plants were used indoors takes one's breath away. 'How Vines are Grown for Table' is an example. A single stem but with off-shoots trained in a circle around it and bearing—in the illustration—a dozen bunches of grapes! Peaches and oranges were other fruits making an orchard of the table, 'all of which are specially ornamental and interesting when laden with their delicately-tinted luscious fruit and fresh green foliage.' Judicious pinching during the summer kept them dwarf and symmetrical.

The receptacles, too, were varied: vases and plant-stands of all kinds; tazzas and epergnes for 'Table bouquets'. Baskets, both hanging and for the table, while a bay window was the scene of a set piece combining a miniature garden with an aquarium complete with fountain.

There was also the miniature air-filled greenhouse invented accidentally by Nathaniel Ward who in 1829 found a fern and grass flourishing on some mould containing the pupa of a moth he had placed in a covered glass bottle. The Wardian case, as it was called, did not require to be watered and was invaluable for transporting plants on long voyages. They are still in use. In Victorian times no lady's drawing-room was complete without one.

Personal decoration dictated a 'coat flower' for the man, and for his lady going to a ball or rout a flower spray for her hair, usually in a tasteful crescent ending just under the chin.

Nor did William Robinson neglect the younger members of the family. Articles on children's gardens appeared from time to time and even took care of gardens for babies. Wrote one contributor: 'When our babies are too young to know what it means, their tree-loving papa has planted for each a fruit tree—Cherry, Apple or Pear—and the spot around it is called the garden of the baby to whom the tree belongs. It is a treasured spot in their eyes, and at the age of two I have seen the little one out with a few peas, or seed of Morning Glory or anything else that was at hand to plant in "mine gardy". As they grow older, this becomes a sort of experimental ground; cuttings are planted out, roses set out, and each tries to outvie the other.' In this way the children learnt the names of the flowers they grew and earned pocket money by selling their harvest of fruit.

Another writer dismissed this sort of gardening. 'It is desirable on many accounts that children should cultivate flowers rather than fruit or vegetables. Most children are fond of flowers, and all can be taught to love them, and the commoner and hardier sorts at least do not tax the energies so heavily in cultivation as either fruits or vegetables.' Children, he added, 'must be taught to use the products of their little garden as a means of conferring happiness on others.'

There was one little piece that must have especially appealed to young gardeners. 'There is a time in the life of every child when he or she must have a garden to take care of—to own. . . . The parent who is unwilling to aid its development neglects a duty. Better encourage gardening in a willing pupil than constrain a child to practise from two to four hours a day upon the piano.'

With *Gardening Illustrated* an assured success Robinson could now embark on various investments. One was bearing the expense of publishing C. W. Shaw's *The London Market Gardens*. It was a sensible practical book of use to all gardeners having even a small plot of ground, teaching them how to make the most of it, not only for their own table use but with fruit, flowers and vegetables to sell. The press gave it a handsome accolade.

Another useful work emanating from 37 Southampton Street in 1880 was *The Orchardist* by J. Scott, claimed as 'The most complete Work on Fruit in the English language.'

He never missed an opportunity of making an honest penny. He turned bookseller, devoting part of 37 Southampton Street to a mail order business but storing the books at his warehouse in North Row, Covent Garden Market. 'All New Gardening Books as published' could be obtained and by 1879 he was listing fifty-five titles. The authors were the élite of horticulture. Here was William Paul's *Rose Garden* and *Roses in Pots*; Charles Baltet's *Grafting and Budding*; Mrs Loudon's *Ladies' Companion to the Flower Garden*; John Lindley's *Botany School* and Asa Gray's *Botany for Young People*, with, of course, Robinson's own books.

In 1880 he added *God's Acre Beautiful: or the Cemeteries of the Future*. This was first published at *The Garden* office, subsequently by John Murray, and a cheap edition by Cassell. Later editions were illustrated by photographs of ancient cinerary urns sent to him from Rome by the distinguished surgeon Sir Henry Thompson, himself the author of a book on cremation, who was one of the founders of the Cremation Society and of the company which erected the crematorium at Golders Green.

The subject had interested William Robinson as long ago as 1863 when he had seen the garden-like Dean Cemetery in Edinburgh. Then in Paris he had witnessed the horrors of the *fosse commune*, the long trench where the poor were buried: the rows of coffins packed close together like bricks, the bones dug up after a short lapse of time and the ground prepared for another crop, the wooden crosses sent to the hospitals as fuel and the headstones broken up to make hardcore for a new road. In America he had seen beautiful cemeteries, some as large as national parks and as full of trees and flowers as a choice garden. 'The Americans,' he declared, 'are the only people to bury their dead decently and beautifully.'

The burying of paupers in London rivalled Paris as an abomination and disgrace. It had been found that seven acres could contain 133,500 graves and each grave ten coffins, thus accommodating 1,335,000 dead.

Robinson's book pleaded for cemeteries that would be permanent, unpolluted and inviolate, in a word urn-burial or cremation. He visualized soft green undisturbed lawns; stately and beautiful trees in many forms; a background of surrounding groves; no hideous vistas of crowded stones; and the certainty that any monuments would remain. In old Roman cemeteries beautiful tombs could still be seen, the urns within them in as good order as when placed there two thousand years ago. It was typical of William Robinson that he should add that the open central lawns of the rest-garden 'should always be preserved from the follies of the geometrical and stone gardeners', so as to secure freedom of view and air, and a resting-place for the eye.

He was present at the first cremation in England. On the evening of Sunday the 8th of October 1882 the body of a Mrs Hanham was cremated by her husband, Captain Hanham, at Manston House, Dorset. It was a curious occasion, for she had died six years before, in July 1876, her body placed in a wooden shell encased in lead and later laid in a specially built mausoleum until the cremation she had begged for could take place. In 1874 the Cremation Society had held its first meeting and it was formally constituted on the 29th of April that year. William Robinson was a member of the provisional council, and when *God's Acre Beautiful* was published he sent a copy to Lord Russel Gower, begging that something be done to legalize cremation. Back came the reply that nothing could be done while Parliament and Harcourt blocked the way. Sir William Harcourt was Home Secretary in Gladstone's Administration in April 1880 and a Privy Councillor. It was not until 1884 that the legality of cremation was established.

The original crematorium was at St John's Woking and was first used in 1885. William Robinson is listed as donating twenty-one pounds to the building fund. He was one of the first directors of the London company when it was formed in 1900 with Martin Ridley Smith and J. C. Swinburne-Hanham, and when Golders Green was to be opened it was William Robinson who laid out the grounds.

God's Acre Beautiful was well received by the press and must have been a strong influence in furthering the cause of cremation.

Meanwhile in October 1880 a quarrel blew up over a leading article in *Gardening Illustrated*. It was on 'Hardy Flowers: their Uses and Culture' and was woven around the Robinson theme of the permanent planting of the mixed border, and was addressed to 'those who hold that the flower garden, or terrace garden, or parterre, or whatever they like to call it, is not a proper place for hardy flowers.' Robinson had a hatred of terraces—not all of them ('the beautiful terrace gardens are those that are built where the nature of the ground requires them', as at Arundel and Hadham) but sham ones as at Sydenham, which aped Versailles. If terrace there was or had to be, then 'the ugliest and most needless terrace in England may be adorned in the most beautiful way with hardy plants alone.' People, he added, were beginning to see the folly of the 'bedding-out' system.

No so David Thomson, editor of the sixpenny monthly *The Gardener*. Thomson was gardener to the Duke of Buccleuch at Drumlanrig in Dumfriesshire and enjoyed a great reputation—'in the forefront of British horticulture', H. R. Fletcher has described him. Nevertheless, as the editor of *Gardening Illustrated* wrote, 'Mr David Thomson is extremely angry with us as regards the vexed question of the flower garden, forgetting his dignity and resorting to personal deprecation to help him out in an argument on the cost of hardy *versus* tender flowers! Part of his argument is that we have no "charge of a garden establishment".'

This was perfectly true, and although Robinson's retort was a tart 'Not likely, having so much on hand', the rebuke hit home and he was quick to add, 'but we are seeking a good man to take charge of one for us, and'—he could not resist poking fun at Drumlanrig's gardener—'if Mr Thomson's ideas on the flower garden were as advanced as those he holds on the fruit garden, we should be happy to consider him among likely candidates for the place.' A neat hook to the left.

Thomson's claim as a flower gardener depended on 'geometrical bedding-out only', and on this ground William Robinson mentally dismissed him.

The most likely practical gardening correspondent was John Cornhill, a florist of Bayfleet, Surrey, who became a regular contributor on all matters horticultural. He and Robinson were old friends: they had been in Paris together at the time of the 1867 Exhibition, and one of his first articles was on lantanas and their culture, in which he referred to their use in Continental gardens. Cornhill had been a gardener in France for a number of years. He liked living as a French peasant and when he returned to England he continued to look like one by wearing the blue smock and beret. Settling at Byfleet his cousin Lizzie Towers came to look after him. He managed to run his market garden so as to be self-supporting, though he and Lizzie never had more than just enough to live on. The income from the paragraphs and articles he wrote for *Gardening Illustrated* was therefore welcome. He was well educated—curiously, for he spoke with a strong country accent and it was supposed that his origins were humble. For all that he was widely read and well able to express himself in good plain English. He was also an eccentric. At the foot of his garden was an earth closet, on the walls of which he pasted snippets from the newspapers. On Sunday mornings on his way to church the local vicar would sometimes wave a hand to John and with a cheerful 'Call of nature!' dive into the closet where, reading the snippets, he got many a note for his sermons.

In 1881 Robinson brought out *The Garden Annual, Almanac and Address Book*. This was the second new publication in two years. But he now had an able lieutenant in William Goldring whom he had appointed assistant editor of *The Garden* when *Gardening Illustrated* was launched. Goldring had spent four years at Kew, his keen interest in hardy plants bringing swift promotion, for he was soon put in charge of the herbaceous department. Robinson now sent him back to Kew as the best person to compile a complete list of the hardy plants in the herbarium. This he was going to publish in *The Garden*. In the following year he sent Henry George Moon, then 'a very competent young man' who had recently joined the art department, to draw the new plants which had arrived at Kew and which were likely to be of permanent and high value for English gardens.

The list of hardy flowers was also published in *Gardening Illustrated*, a series of selections omitting only very new or rare species. Robinson made no apology for using the list twice. So many of the errors and disappointments regarding hardy flowers had arisen from a bad or careless selection of plants.

He began with the hardy herbaceous division—vigorous plants for borders, beds or groups, which could be grown in any soil. The English name, botanical name, colour of flower, and height were given in four columns, and side by side with these were notes on culture. The advice he gave is quite as applicable today as when it was written a century ago. I quote a few examples.

In planting, plant in groups, and not in the old dotting way. Never repeat the same plant along the border at intervals, as used to be done with favourites.

Do not be particular to graduate the plants from back to front, as is generally done, but occasionally let a bold and sturdy plant come towards the edge, and, on the other hand, let a little carpet of a dwarf plant pass in here and there to the back, so as to give a broken and beautiful instead of a monotonous surface.

The border should remain for years without any digging in the usual sense. All digging operations should be confined to changes and to the filling up of blanks with good plants.

When the plants are old and have got rather too thick, never hesitate to move them on a wet day in the middle of August or July, as well as in the middle of winter. Take them up and put a fresh bold group in fresh ground; they will have plenty of root by the winter.

Do not pay much attention to labelling; if a plant is not worth knowing it is not worth growing.

These wise ways were all revolutionary, but most typical of William Robinson was his plea that in garden-making 'The aim should be never to rest till the garden is a reflex of Nature in her fairest moods.'

14

A Window on a Wealth of Plants

In March 1882 William Robinson launched another new periodical, this time *Farm and Home*, a weekly devoted to practical agriculture and housekeeping, costing one penny. He at once appointed an editor, and this was D. E. Thomas whom he promoted from *Gardening Illustrated*. Thomas was with Robinson for more than thirty years, as a letter from his widow tells us when on the Grand Old Man's ninety-fifth birthday she wrote to congratulate him.

He now had capable men in charge of the editorial desks and could lean on his laurels. There was reason to do so, for overwork had somewhat taken its toll. At the end of 1882 he visited Smedley's hydropathic establishment at Matlock Bridge and derived much benefit from the treatment. A sea voyage was recommended but he was torn between the Mediterranean and exploring the gardens of Egypt. Richard Owen was cautious about Egypt: for 'pthysical or acute affections' it was 'hazardous', 'too exciting', with which the Cairene doctors concurred, and he had seen an instance of this truth in the death of a young man, son of an artist friend, whose cortege he had followed to his Egyptian grave.

> If, however, you go to Cairo, the Gardens of the Kasr-el-Nil Palace on the Libyan bank of the Nile are best worth your notice; and I cannot imagine there won't be any difficulty of admission—but I don't know the present Khedive as I did his father. Of the average gardens, in or about the Town, that behind Shepherd's Hotel is an example. The 'Hotel du Nil' I would recommend were it not for the approach and entry, which is from one of the narrow streets in the old Town; but it has—or had—a good garden & it was like a change on the Stage to contrast its quietude and space with the crowded turmoil one left behind. It was always chosen by Continentals in preference to the 'British' '*Shepherds*'. The only Resident at Cairo that I could have given a friend's introduction to, I came upon at our *Station* a few days since—to mutual surprise. He congratulated himself on his

escape from his charming residence & garden a little way out of Cairo.

Certainly he would be seeing both Alexandria and Cairo at an exciting period, for these were the days of the riots against Europeans. The British had entered Cairo on the 14th of September (1882) following their victory at Tel-el-Kebir the day before, and Owen's letter was written only ten days later. For himself, he added, he would vote for Mentone or thereabouts.

But Robinson decided on Egypt, and he went armed with letters of introduction from Philip Henry Wodehouse Currie of the Foreign Office to whom he was to dedicate his next book. Currie was Under-Secretary-of-State and had already had a distinguished career. Knowing the Near East well he was full of good advice about hotels, routes and steamer services, adding, 'If you have time to send me a line occasionally, I shall be so glad to hear of your proceedings & if you wish for any more letters I will send them to you.' He enclosed four: to diplomatic men at Constantinople, Cairo, Madrid and Beyrout.

It was a much longer trip than he had originally thought of, for early in February 1883 John Murray junior in writing to thank him for a copy of the new edition of *God's Acre Beautiful* hoped he would 'derive much pleasure & benefit from your trip to Madeira', and at the same time Alfred Parsons was asking 'Have you given up the Madeira idea?'

No, he had not: he was making Madeira his first port of call. He left in the middle of February.

A letter came from Gertrude Jekyll dated the 5th of that month. The subject was boots. But not her pair made famous by William Nicholson in his painting.

> Your french boots have come & I send them up today—marking the parcel *Boots* outside for fear your people in your possible absence might think they were Flowers Perishable and put them in water—though they would stand it better than some of their kind—Don't be frightened at their new pale complexion—a few greasings and wettings will cure that.
>
> I hope they will be right though I see the heels are a good $\frac{1}{8}''$ higher than you ordered—The pattern shoe & a box of grease are enclosed with them.

'Robinson's Country Series' of books was launched in that year with a preliminary eight titles on such subjects as *Fruit Culture for Profit* by E. Hobday of the Ramsay Abbey gardens, Huntingdonshire; *The Grape Vine* by John Simpson of the Wortley Hall garden, Sheffield; *The Apple* by James Groom, and *The Potato* by R. Fremlin. Some of these were reprinted from *The Garden* but with the matter revised, considerably enlarged and brought up to date. Robinson's own *Mushroom Culture* was one of the series.

His output of journals and books was monumental. In December 1883 a letter came from Gertrude Jekyll who was holidaying in Capri, thanking him for sending *Woods and Forests*. This, a weekly illustrated journal of forestry, ornamental planting and estate management, costing a modest twopence, was the latest production from 37 Southampton Street and to her it seemed 'all that can be wished in such a paper'. Unfortunately the public did not share her enthusiasm. The paper was absorbed by *The Garden* after only ninety-one issues.

They were corresponding regularly. His own trip had done him a world of good and he was now able to walk for miles, rising early in the morning. She was glad to hear of those big walks and great doses of early fresh air, confiding that sometimes at home she made an early start on a winter's morning so as to have a clear day's gardening, and always wondered at the beauty of it. She was revelling in Capri, high up in the sun and wind, with clean fresh sea all around, no business letters to write and no acknowledgements. One day was like another 'except for its varied beauties, & the perfectly free & simple ways of living I keenly enjoy.'

She was staying out of England until the end of January, she told him, so as to escape 'the horrors of the English Christmas, the sham festiveness & general *festering*', because 'to do it well or even inoffensively is not in the genius of the nation!' She would be remaining in Capri till the 12th of January, returning home in one of the big ships of the Orient Line from Australia, as she was so bad a railway traveller, and 'soon after I would claim your visit.'

William Robinson was no stranger to Munstead, the Jekyll home near Godalming, Surrey, where Gertrude lived with her mother. He had first visited them in 1880 when he was taken there by Canon Hole. Since then he had advised on plants for her garden, and had Woolson the nurseryman despatch a consignment. Despite a long delay on the journey they had arrived in capital condition. 'My mother asks if you will come and help plant them,' Gertrude had written, and she added, 'That would be very nice.'

A lawn was the next project. It had done well, evoking a delighted 'You should see your new lawn,' from Gertrude.

Professor Richard Owen began contributing a series on birds, which appeared in *The Garden* from April 1883 onwards. When Robinson sent him a copy of *Woods and Forests* he wondered how anyone could take the strain of editing two such periodicals as this and *The Garden*. But

A Window on a Wealth of Plants

Robinson had not only shifted this editorial burden to the shoulders of William Goldring, he was about to give Goldring further charge as assistant editor of *Woods and Forests*. Later Goldring became its editor. It was a kind of journalistic musical chairs.

Robinson gives credit to Goldring for his valuable help in the preparation of the second part of his next work. This was *The English Flower Garden* which became the most widely read and influential gardening book ever written. It was published by John Murray in 1883.

William Robinson set out with the definite object of changing people's minds about the style of gardening then existing. In his preface he claimed that in the various books he had written, and in journals founded by him, a good deal had been done to disturb people's opinions about the flower garden. But while many would like to make changes, little help of a positive character was to be had from books. *The English Flower Garden* was an attempt 'as far as possible within the limits of a volume not beyond the means of every amateur and gardener'—its price was 15s—'to supply the want.'

That the book fulfilled that want was evident: it ran through fifteen editions in his time. Besides these there were nine reprints—one each of the fifth edition and the sixth, four of the eighth, and one respectively of the tenth, eleventh and twelfth.

Hitherto he had dealt mainly with the flower garden from special points of view, describing various features that add to the beauty of a garden—rock gardens (*Alpine Flowers*), plants of fine form (*The Subtropical Garden*), those we may grow without care in any rough or out-of-the-way places (*The Wild Garden*), and the many beautiful plants of the northern countries (*Hardy Flowers*). Now he was presenting 'A book on the convenient and simple plan of a Dictionary, embracing all the plants, both hardy and half-hardy, annual and bulbous, suitable in any way for the British flower garden' and this seemed likely to best meet the needs of the time. His whole aim was to make the flower garden a reflex of the world of beautiful plant-life, instead of the poor formal array it had long been.

It was illustrated with 1,280 fine engravings, many by H. Hyde who had helped select the pictures, Alfred Parsons having drawn many of the originals. With it William Robinson opened the window wide on the abounding wealth of flowers ready to beautify the English garden.

Thanks to plant hunters like David Douglas, Robert Fortune and John Gould Veitch a flood of new plants had been coming into England, though few people knew about them and there still existed the 'prosaic stereotyped garden of half a dozen kinds of plants'. But here they were now in *The English Flower Garden*.

[137]

But the book was not only a valuable descriptive catalogue. In the first part, occupying more than a hundred pages, William Robinson declared his thoughts on the English flower garden. It was more than criticism of bad taste in garden planning and layout, more than praise for what he had found that was good: it was a complete philosophy based on the principle that Nature is law and life is law. True taste would arise from it. Hence Nature, a reluctant pupil for geometers, would take her revenge on the classical garden which relied on man to keep boxwood trimmed, yew shaped, statues and stonework protected from decay.

We must not forget that it was William Robinson who was responsible for sweeping away the carpet-bedding that robbed plants of their dignity by treating them merely as pieces in a mosaic. Nor must we forget that it was he who—having a whole new range of plants to add to the existing ones which had been coming into this country since the seventeenth century—it was Robinson who emphasized the need for their artistic arrangement. 'At present the rule is, no thought; no arrangement; no bold good grouping; no little pictures made with living colours (by which he did *not* mean parterre patterns); no variety; no contrast' but mere repetition.

He condemned the choke-muddle shrubbery where the poor flowering shrubs dwindled and killed each other, supporting a few ill-grown and ill-chosen plants disintegrating in summer to wide patches of bare earth in which, in better hands, 'pretty green things might crowd'.

'It is disheartening,' he wrote, 'to see how little pleasure men get out of their gardens, and how near to a desert they make them in this country of verdure and fertility.' Yet the smallest garden could be as pretty as a picture. Even small suburban gardens could refresh us with their brightness and pleasant variety. In the larger garden the opportunities were proportionately greater and seldom used. They were stereotyped at the very seasons when they ought to be full of delightful change.

He discussed the great gardens of places like Thoresby in Nottinghamshire and Highclere, Hampshire, then turned to the smaller gardens that were now far more numerous, for this was the age of Victorian middle-class affluence, the small property rather than the magnificence of the stately home, though still with its stables, kitchen garden and flower garden.

One of these was Pendell Court, of which he wrote: 'It is a great pleasure to see a beautiful old house, made to live in, with nothing to keep one away from the door but the pleasant Grass. From a gardening

15 A fine etching of William Robinson in middle life
by Francis Dodd

standpoint there are three distinct views of it which are good; first that of the lawn in front of the house, which, when we saw it, was a flowery meadow yet uncut, and no beds or other impediments between the point of view and the house, with a group of some fine trees on either hand. It was a poem in building and in lawn. Quite on the other side a border of flowers and a wall of climbers ran from the house, a shower of white climbing Roses is seen falling from the wall, and a quaint gable and a few windows and glistening rich Ivy form such a picture, that one regrets to know it is old and rare. Another view of the house from across the water, showing its west end, is also very beautiful. There is a wild Rose bush on the right and a tuft of Flag leaves on the left; before the beholder, the water and its Lilies; then a smooth, gently rising lawn creeping up to the windows, which on this side are all wreathed with lovely white climbing Roses.'

A Window on a Wealth of Plants

To William Robinson this was garden art near perfection.

He brought his friend Robert Marnock into a discussion on the flower garden. Marnock had retired in 1879 but it was still as the leader of his profession that he looked back, modestly, over his forty years of creating beautiful gardens. He took a moderate view of garden embellishment, agreeing with Robinson that 'the excessive use of artificial decoration does very often vulgarise many an otherwise fair garden scene' but adding, 'Though this be true, it is not . . . necessary to be driven to the other extreme and renounce all artificial accompaniment, but to use sparingly and with a delicate hand whatever is good.'

William Robinson was now forty-five and a formidable figure in the world of horticulture. He was able to attract all the leading writers and among the seventy authorities whose contributions were embodied in the book were Peter Barr, F. W. Burbidge, the Rev. Harpur-Crewe, the Rev. C. Wolley-Dod and Canon Ellacombe, with H. J. Elwes of tree and lily fame, Max Leichtlin, Gertrude Jekyll, George Maw, faithfuls like Dean Hole and Robert Marnock, and many others, who not only contributed articles on hardy plants, their care, culture and ways of best displaying them in rock garden, bed or border, but also wrote special descriptions for the dictionary part of the book, which was subtitled 'Flowers of the Open Air'. Thus although he was not the sole author of this unique garden catalogue, William Robinson was instrumental in gathering together authoritative descriptions of all the plants worth growing in an English garden. And not only English, for the book was to go far and wide, most importantly to America. *The English Flower Garden* became the gardener's bible there as well as in the country of its origin.

Subsequent editions made the book even more popular, for the little chapters on such subjects as 'Spring Flowers' which had occupied scarcely more than two pages became 'Spring Gardens' occupying nearly fourteen, this in the tenth edition in which Robinson's writing took a vast step forward in style and authority. Part I of the fifteenth edition, which was published two years before his death, ran to 286 pages, the whole book to 720 pages instead of the original 427. Again the book had increased in stature and now covered hardy flowering plants and shrubs, roses, bulbous plants, aquatic plants, tree and soft fruits, climbing plants and alpines.

From the time of the second edition (1889) he was writing from Sussex where a few years previously he had bought an estate. Here at last he had 'charge of a garden establishment'—remembering the jibe levelled at him by David Thomson; and his floral experiences there gave him much. Working with a garden that was his, he was able to put into practice his theories and philosophy. Some dearly held ideas floundered and were cast out, and eventually he wrote that 'The first editions of this book were burdened with much about the ways of flower gardening at the time; many thousands of plants set out in May or early June in formal and geometrical array, the result a bad carpet.' (He had, however, included designs which he considered would make 'good' carpets.) 'Experience has taught me to throw overboard all tender plants and devote the book to hardy plants only, that may be planted in the open air on every fine day in the fall or winter.'

So overboard went 'tropical weeds that give a little showy colour for a few months', plants that never flower in cold districts, coarse herbs that rob the ground and give little return in beauty, 'palms never at home in look in our clime'. He ended by stating: 'This is not a theory but a record of what took place in my garden for many years past.'

And so vanished the preposterous *Musa ensete*, the Abyssinian Banana, and other horrors. The plants that remained were indeed the English flower garden.

15

'At last, a garden of my own . . .'

In 1883 William Robinson found himself to be a wealthy man. The financial rewards from his books and periodicals had been mounting up and he had put much of his money into City bricks and mortar. It was a propitious time to do so, for property was rising in value and if one had the right advisers one could buy cheap and sell at a profit.

William Robinson had the right advisers.

But for some months he had been looking for a different kind of property. All his life he had lived in the aura of great gardens. Lived vicariously, at first as a garden servant and then as a garden visitor. Through these gardens he had evolved his ideas of landscaping and planting, but it was high time that William Robinson who wrote about gardens and gardening should have a garden of his own. It was ridiculous that he possessed no such thing! As incongruous as a violinist without a fiddle, a carpenter without a saw. The advice he had given other people about their vegetables and fruit-growing, their woodland gardens and mixed borders, was, however sound, a second-hand affair. Never could he back up a recommendation with his personal experience: 'I've tried it out at my own place . . .' He could only quote what he had seen done successfully at Dalkeith Park or Berry Hill or Bicton.

Besides, he wanted a home.

He had got so far as to engage an architect to do some plans. It need not be anything grand but must be well built and with some originality. In December he wrote excitedly to Gertrude Jekyll, who replied: 'Your architect has fine vigorous wholesome notions—I should like to talk to him,' adding, 'It will interest me extremely to see your house plans—I always think no house, however small, should have a mean or *poky* place to first come into—My ideal house, after an enclosed porch would have a good size habitable hall or room. If space or means could not allow it as an extra sitting room it would be the place to dine in & the stairs would rise from it.'

She was at odds with him on one point—designing a house before one knew where one was going to put it. 'I can never satisfactorily imagine a house without knowing the particular site. A house must grow up between the ground on one side & its master on the other & must marry both. A house planned in air would be as soulless as an Aldershot hut.'

He set about looking for a site, first seeing how he could sell his City property. He consulted George John Rhodes who dealt in property investments for the Standard Life Assurance Company, in August 1884 offering him what he owned in the City. Rhodes wrote back that Robinson's price was too much. He made a counter-offer of some freehold property at Hertford which he could exchange, if the county would suit.

Robinson was not interested in the Hertford offer. He continued his search, and it is curious that in August of the previous year, 1883, Messrs Driver & Company, the land agents and auctioneers, offered for sale by auction the very property in Sussex which he was eventually to buy. A printed prospectus describes the valuable freehold residential estate, with other properties known as Gravetye Manor and Moatlands, containing together about 360 acres. Moatlands was described as 'a beautiful residential site', for the house was only 'the remains of a Residence' which of course could be added to or demolished and a new house built on the same site, which commanded almost bird's-eye views over picturesque countryside. He did not buy Gravetye until 1885.

Meanwhile he was busy with an echo of his Paris days. His old friend Henry Vilmorin was writing a book on the vegetable garden and had asked him to read the proofs. When after a lapse of time none came, Robinson wrote anxiously: Was he too busy in field and office to bother with pen and paper? His guess was perfectly right, replied Vilmorin, and as yet he had sent nothing to the translator, though yesterday he had been taken again by his old complaint and was now laid up. This would give him full time with his amanuensis and he would now send the whole batch at once instead of part by part.

If William Robinson was a Francophile, Henry Vilmorin (who had long ago adopted the English form of his Christian name and had dropped the 'de') was an Anglophile, in the following September writing that he was bringing his son Philippe to enter the King's School, Canterbury. He hoped also to 'bring you a good deal of material for Plantes Potagères, with some additions in the way of new articles.'

The Vegetable Garden, as its English translation is entitled, was published in 1885 and at once became a gardening classic. It was the first work in any language in which, as Robinson said in his preface, were 'classified, described and illustrated . . . the most important of all plants to the human race.'

John Murray published it and William Clowes printed it. The translator was W. Miller, author of a *Dictionary of Plant Names* which

Robinson had borne the cost of publishing. But it was very much 'under the direction of W. Robinson, Editor of "The Garden" ', and in a letter to Murray we have the first demonstration of his passion for perfection. The paper must be beautiful; the type-faces must be beautiful. As for 'Ink for vegetable garden!' as he exclaimed, 'I hope to send for your inspection an old Italian book I bought a few days ago—printed at Bergamo about 300 years ago. If Captain Clowes can get us about the same colour & beauty of inking we will give him a whole series to do!' He referred to William Charles Knight Clowes of the third generation of this famous family of printers, dubbed 'Captain' when he raised No. 6 Company, the 7th Surrey Volunteer Rifles, which used to drill in the yard of the printing works at Duke Street.

From time to time the editorial chair was vacated for a tour of gardens—and a visit from William Robinson was now sought-after. In October he went to Bristol to see Berkeley Castle and was begged to break his journey at Higham Court, near Gloucester, where his host was Thomas Gambier-Parry, the philanthropist and fresco painter.

Higham Court was a mansion designed by Inigo Jones. There was an extensive park and well laid-out pleasure grounds, also a pinetum—which Gambier-Parry wrote to say was a wreck following severe spring frosts and violent storms. Conifers were in the family, so to speak. 'You must go and see my brother-in-law,' advised Gambier-Parry. This was Henry William Clinton-Baker who had continued the cultivation of the pinetum established by his grandfather at Bayfordbury in Hertfordshire. In 1948 Bayfordbury was taken over by the John Innes Institute.

In return for a delightful visit to Higham Court Robinson sent some of his books for the family.

He was sending irises in July 1885 to Ruskin, who acknowledged them gratefully and raised a query about lilies. 'I have been puzzled by the difference between the orange lilies in my greenhouse and the wild one of Italy, which I am going to call *Lilium "Fervidum"*. The petals of this last have an array of artifices for enhancing by roughness & furrowing, their force of colour which will take me all I can to describe, while my tame lilies are as smooth as leather.—would you please tell me if this is specific difference or merely mountain breeding against artificial?'

Another Pre-Raphaelite with whom Robinson was corresponding was Edward Burne-Jones, as well as with their opponent Charles Kingsley who scathingly described the circle as 'petrified Cyclops painting their petrified brothers.'

A letter came from his mother, from Dean Cottage, Carlow, where she lived in Ireland. Her writing was clear and well-formed, even stylish.

My dear William,

It is a long time since I wrote you a line. I got your last letter—it is singular there is no letter from the Cape. they could not have got your money. I am glad to hear you have a hope of getting out of London—it must be hard for you to stand it: the weather has been very bad here. I am very weak but a little better—as you are so kind to send me any thing. I would like a little fruit lemmons and oranges and a few grapes it was a pity that last was all unfit for use—and the first you sent came in perfect preservation. but if you are very busy dont mind them. will you tell me what did the Irish landlords call on you for. have you disposed of your property in the City?

with kind love and many thanks for all your kindness

your aff Mother

Catherine Robinson

pleas send some envelopes.

There is much of interest in this letter. It tells us that he kept in touch with his mother and that some married member of the family was in South Africa, his sister perhaps, although we know from a letter written by the Belfast nephew William Robinson to his uncle's nurse after his death that this sister died in Ireland in 1913. His letter also tells us of a picture by Herbert A. Oliver which William Robinson gave to his sister when, presumably, she visited him at Gravetye. The visit of the Irish landlords must refer to a delegation from the National Land League, formed with the object of securing the ownership of land in Ireland for the occupiers. This was a preliminary to the Home Rule Bill, brought in and rejected in 1886. The landlords were obviously seeking William Robinson's support in their agitation.

What interests us most is that William Robinson is tired of London and looking forward to escaping from it, thanks to his property in the City.

He escaped in 1885. In July of that year he was reading *The Times* when an advertisement under 'Properties for Sale' caught his attention. Edmund Robins & Hine of Pall Mall would be auctioning on Friday July 17th 'a singularly attractive and highly valuable residential property, distinguished (since XVI century) and known as Gravetye Manor Estate, comprising a grand old-fashioned and picturesque Elizabethan mansion, affording ample accommodation for a family of distinction; with suitable stabling, kitchen gardens, and usual adjuncts.' The pleasure grounds and park lands were of an undulating character, 'rich in verdure, and naturally picturesque and beautiful.' There were two large lakes with islands, a newly erected bailiff's residence, farm buildings and other appurtenances. Altogether the estate comprised an unbroken area of about 360 acres of rich succulent pasture and park-like lands, well timbered and watered. There was good shooting, fishing and hunting.

He went down to Sussex to see it.

There was everything wrong with it that could be. Typical of the garden was the dreadful 'rock work' against the house, with upstanding stones like some decrepit burial ground; typical of the house the reflecting lights in the roof of the basement kitchen which allowed the wet to get in and saturated the ceiling. The plantation near the house was mixed and muddled. The view of the fields south of the house was obscured by an old road, pathways and clumps of rhododendrons. In the whole landscape there was not a graceful or a sweeping line to please the eye.

But the house was beautiful. It was stone-built with mullioned and transomed windows. The tall chimneys extended their vertical lines and were perfectly complemented on the south side by four gabled dormers. He was much struck by its dignity, even seen through a veil, as it were, of neglect.

It had been built in 1598 by Richard Infield for his bride Katherine Compton. His business was extracting iron from the sandstone rocks found on the estate, and not far away was the furnace for casting the iron. In 1763 twelve-pounder guns were being made for Woolwich. When the iron industry left Sussex Gravetye drifted into the hands of farmers, and so it remained almost up to the 1880s. Some attempts had been made to bring the place up to date: a new kitchen wing had been added. In the garden was evidence of planning and planting, though in the worst taste; and throughout the estate every field, every wood, every cottage, every farmhouse, every road, and every fence would have to be overhauled. The roads which had sufficed for Tudor days, when transport was only by horses, were in no fit state for modern use. Sad neglect hung over everything, from rusting hinge to cracked and broken tree bough.

When, having toured the domain, through the woods and by field and lakeside, he came back to the house, he thought again how beautiful it was and what could be done with garden and landscape to make them a perfect setting.

His bid was accepted. Possession was immediate. He took up

residence in the following month. Not, however, in the manor house itself but in what was known as Moat Farm House, later to be called Mead Cottage, then Moat Cottage, and finally, today, 'The Moat'. He was to live here for four years while major improvements, restoration and repairs went on in the big house.

Viscountess Wolseley, the redoubtable lady who in 1902 was to establish the first school of gardening for women, referred to it as 'the little old-world manor house' and 'the small grey stone Elizabethan house', but then Frances Garnet Wolseley was perhaps comparing its proportions with more ducal residences. It was certainly large for a single man, with its fourteen or so bedrooms and various reception rooms, not 'counting servants' quarters and a plethora of domestic offices.

The size of the place did not worry him. He had two thoughts about it. Anything smaller, unless it were a farm house, would not have commanded such an acreage of land, and he was hungry for land; and the beauty of the garden he would create here—already taking shape and colour in his mind—was matched by the beauty of an existing house.

His second thought was that he would marry. The house then would afford 'ample accommodation for a family'.

Meanwhile he surveyed his domain: the fields, the woods and roads, the seven acres of lake. 'Fate,' he wrote, 'gave me a piece of land in which all had to be done.' 'All' did not refer only to repairs but to a remodelling of the entire landscape, to the removal of trees and the planting of others, to the uprooting of hedges in favour of a well-placed covert. He had spent nearly half a lifetime writing about formalities and informalities in relation to garden design, and he saw now that before he could tackle anything on the grand scale 'the real work of the landscape gardener only begins when the garden itself is completed.'

So it was that on the 24th of August 1885 he took his first steps to create his garden, a place of such flowery beauty that it was to become known and loved by the whole world of gardeners.

He was still a busy editor at Southampton Street, each morning travelling by the seven o'clock train to Victoria, each evening alighting at Three Bridges station, often to throw his despatch case into the carriage and run the miles home across the fields, there to see what progress had been made during the day.

The sloping ground around the house made terracing necessary, he decided.

We remember that in past days he condemned terracing unless the ground sloped so steeply that a garden could be created only by making it on a series of plateaux. Today, part of the charm of Gravetye's garden is the ascending and descending to and from one level to another. The house stands half-way up a gentle hillside, and it was Robinson's genius to use slopes and levels irregularly so that all looked natural. He had a bonus in that the house could be seen not only from all different angles but from all these levels, now looking down upon its beautiful Horsham stone roof from which sprang the tall chimneys; now from below looking up to see it riding against the sky like some noble ship.

His first work was to raise the level of the east end of the garden and remove the broad spruce hedges there, together with a rosery, fernery and rockery. This clearance and levelling gave him what he called the Playground, and it is interesting that he called it this at such an early date. For here children were to play: gardeners' children, neighbours' children, children from the village school, and the little girl he named Iris because it was in 'Iris time' (the *stylosa* species) that she was born.

Side by side with improvements in the garden, under the skilful direction of Fuller the garden-work foreman aided by a gang of men, went improvements to the interior and exterior of the house. He razed the existing hall and built a new one, work completed in 1886, and he began now to think of planting part of the garden. His first book on plants had been *Alpine Flowers*: his first plantings were of these mountain gems. The retaining wall above the playground, holding the slope which he later devoted to heathers, was specially prepared for the reception of alpines and their long roots straggling about to find soil and moisture. Many were planted as seeds in the chinks of the wall as it was being built, others as small seedlings carefully inserted. Walls, he wrote in *The English Flower Garden*, were the easiest way to enjoyment of the most interesting and charming of the mountain flowers. This observation was made when he had established the Gravetye garden and had three different kinds of walls thick-set with plants; though even in 1883 before he bought Gravetye he was writing in the first edition of this book about the 'fixing of alpine flowers on old walls, ruins, &c.' as one of the most interesting ways of cultivating these plants. 'They root themselves wherever they get a chance; but when man assists them, then the old wall becomes the most beautiful of gardens.' He cited the Colosseum in Rome, once so rich in flowers that Dr Richard Deakin wrote a flora of it; now, alas, as Robinson mourned and those who followed him, cleared of its plants and made in consequence much less beautiful than when it wore its garlands.

Next at Gravetye came the planting of tea roses and tufted pansies, with the transplanting of young yew trees to make a picturesque group where he would build a summer house.

Old mare & Carter with which we commenced.

16 (a) and (b) Robinson made a photographic record of Gravetye from the first days of his ownership. The captions are in his handwriting.

Making the Play-ground above House (Autumn 1885) Showing also portion of large Spruce Hedges removed, & part of old Kitchen Garden. — Fuller (Garden work Foreman) & some of his men.

New after building of new hall

17 A photographic record of Gravetye

There came the day, surprisingly soon, when he looked round the place, rough and unfinished as it was, and knew that it wore a different look. Something of himself was there now, in place of what had been a spiritless emptiness. A reflection of him, as if the plants were his in the way they were growing. It seemed the very air breathed to his presence.

He stood exulting. Yet with no mere pride of possession, but in dedication. He would make this garden and the landscape around it *supremely* beautiful. Everything should be done to get all the beauty possible out of it and into it. And there should not be a false note anywhere. Beauty would be his tool.

And this was his to do. For he had come into his kingdom.

[150]

16
The Making of Gravetye

He never lost touch with France, and when the news reached his old friend Edouard André that he was, at last, planting a garden of his own, there arrived at Gravetye a box of autumn-flowering cyclamen.

André's letter was dated the 22nd of February 1886.

Mon chèr Robinson
Je vous fais envoyer une caisse de 400 cyclamens. Veuillez les faire planter *sous bois*, en bordure des allées, où ils fleurisont cet automne.
  Ces jolies fleurettes, vous rappeleront
  Votre dévoué ami,
    Ed. André.

He planted the corms on the 2nd of March, on each side of the south end of Smugglers' Lane. This was a very old road reputedly running from the Sussex coast. In most parts it is obliterated by modern buildings, but on the Gravetye estate the straight lines of its route can be picked up intermittently, where, for instance, it crosses the rough road leading down to the Moat. Robinson was proud of possessing such an ancient highway and preserved it from landsliding by retaining it with stone. The sides were steep, evidence of its age, or rather the road through the years had sunk and the banks probably kept high purposely for protection in bad weather. The name of the road, however, is undoubtedly sheer romance, for what self-respecting band of smugglers would time after time use the same predictable route? This would be to land themselves and their contraband straight into the hands of the waiting excisemen.

Though planted with care the cyclamen corms produced no flowers. A sad note written in March 1888 says, 'They did not seem to take well to the soil.' Neither did the Moccasin Flowers (*Cypripedium spectabile*) sent him in 1886 by 'Mr Elliot of Philadelphia'. Despite the care also with which he 'Planted small groups in bog moss in pond (old pit) in Bushy Wood', he 'Never could find a trace of the plants since.' Strange, for he had seen the orchid growing in just this sort of habitat in America, in 'open boggy woods, moist meadows, and also in peaty bogs'. But even great gardeners can have their failures. 'Much worried by floods and the soil too dry' were the reasons for the trilliums not prospering, the White Wood Lily sent him by another Elliott —J.W. of Pittsburgh, Pa., and also planted in Smugglers' Lane; while 'The soil again a nuisance' spelt the fate of the Winter Aconites he scattered by the 'dick' or dyke above the crossroads near the farm, along the sides of the drive, and among the firs above the house. They 'never did any good'.

These notes and correspondence with Kew in 1887 show how he began building up his garden. He wrote to George Nicholson who was Kew's curator from 1886:

> I should like to grow any new promising flowering shrubs of the hardier sort on my rather loamy cool soil. You know all that is good in that way & I am sure would be willing to help me with the names of some likely kinds. It might interest you to see them grown on a very different soil to yours. I am not seeking rarities or curiosities at all but beautiful things likely to add to the charm of our gardens & to be worth figuring from a gardener's point of view.

George Nicholson was later to publish (1894–1902) a *Hand-list of Trees and Shrubs*, and at this moment was producing his valuable *Dictionary of Gardening* (1884–8). He sent his correspondent '32 small plants', and later in April of the same year 'a set of young trees' for which Robinson thanked him and Kew heartily, saying that he hoped now to do some planting every year 'as long as I do anything'. To plant and make known good flowering trees and shrubs would be useful work and pleasant, and he decided that to make a fair test he would plant in groups or a minimum of three. This was how he had planted the tea roses, in bold masses, their colour at the end of September in his first year of planting being more showy than even the bedding-out in the best London parks, while infinitely more beautiful.

But trees were almost his first thought. The stately oaks and pines of his beloved California had inspired him; and recalling his early days in Ireland, the beautiful River Barrow where people were happy in having gardens on its banks, he saw that a knowledge of trees and shrubs could be applied there effectively, 'and all matters such as composition, breadth, repose, and the many things which have to be considered and to which the term "landscape gardening" is truly applicable.'

> Even in places of only moderate extent the planting of trees from all the northern countries of the world deserves much thought, and

without a knowledge of them it is hopeless to expect the best results. The noblest trees we know were unknown to us until recent times. They are now coming into use not merely as ornamental things but as forest trees, and in view of their value no one should attempt to practise the art of landscape gardening or planting, without knowing them both in the wild and in the cultivated state. In planting such trees in the many conditions of our country of river, estuary or lake, or even in ground without these advantages, we have almost the same problems to consider as landscape painters often have as regards composition and other effects.

There were several Wellingtonias about the place, the Big Tree of California, and despite his admiration for their native land he cut them all down as being ugly and unsuited to the English climate; also many spruces, because these rarely did well in this part of England. To the south-east of the house were groups and belts of Scots Pines forming with a number of other trees part of the usual 'mixed' plantation. He could see that the pines would give, in time, the best effect, and 'freed' them by removing the others. The result the first year was good, he reported, 'but the true effect I sought can be seen when the trees get old.' He was right. Nearly a century later the Scotch Firs, as he called them, are in good heart and magnificent against the skyline.

He was prodigal with his trees. He planted handsome hollies—gold, silver, and fine green kinds—to shut out the view of the new kitchen garden from the pleasure ground (alias the bowling green, alias the playground). Well-grown specimens were brought from Waterer's of Knaphill by road in his own and the nurseryman's wagons, which met and exchanged horses at Ockley, this to avoid injury to the trees from several changes by rail. By the time he finished landscaping the Gravetye estate, William Robinson had planted some hundreds of thousands of trees.

Fruit trees came into the picture. He dealt first with apples, and these were planted on the site of the old kitchen garden sloping towards the drive. He chose high quality kinds, not merely the most popular, and a dozen of each so as to secure a good 'gathering'. There were eighteen different varieties: Ribston Pippin, Claygate Pearmain, Blenheim Orange, Cox's Orange Pippin, Lane's Prince Albert, Bramley Seedling, Dominic, French Crab (now Winter Greening), Sturmer Pippin, Stone's (also called Loddington), Forge (an old Sussex variety round about Crawley), Allen's Everlasting, Ord's Apple, Irish Peach, Lodgemore Nonpareil, Sam Young, Reinette Grise, and the Kerry Pippin.

[153]

The Making of Gravetye

Frank Lloyd Wright, the great American architect of our own day, believed that a house should seem to grow out of the ground on which it stands. William Robinson believed the same thing of a garden. It 'should grow out of its own site', he declared, 'if we are to have the best of it. One should think of the spot and what can best be done in it, instead of following set models.' He thought his experience in forming his own flower garden might be of use to others. The things he had to consider were—

1. His favourite flowers.   3. Soil.
2. Climate.   4. Season of enjoyment.

The first question was: What do we care to grow? He pointed out that we can rarely succeed with numerous plants on the same spot of ground. Botanical and other gardens attempting large collections were kept up only by ceaseless additions. And even the growing of a mere few groups of favourite plants often depended on the soil and situation. The soil at Gravetye was cool, the climate cool, the situation high and somewhat retarding for a southern county. The seasons of greatest enjoyment were summer and early autumn. There was to be no specially set-out 'Spring Garden': spring flowers were planted in the grass to naturalize.

The antiquity of the house prevented him from indulging in any extravagance of colour or mere collections of flowers. The simple form and colour of the house were so beautiful in themselves that everything about the garden must be done in relation to them. He decided, after considering all the circumstances, and not forgetting the great range of hardy plants, to restrict his choice mainly to a few kinds of flowers: roses, carnations, pansies, and starworts (by which he meant Michaelmas Daisies), and in each case to special and favourite varieties of these plants.

These were the inhabitants of the series of beds he began to lay out in March 1886 on the grass in the West Garden which also went by the name of the Flower Garden.

To William Robinson the most beautiful of all were the tea roses. 'I wished to gratify my own taste for these things,' he wrote, 'and at the same time do something to make them better known.' He thought that these lovely roses had been much neglected and resolved to grow masses of them. The use of the misleading term 'Hybrid Perpetual' had cast dust in the eyes of rose growers, who paid much attention to the red roses and almost wholly disregarded the supremely beautiful tea and China roses as flower-garden plants. They were frequently grown as pot plants, but, as their champion declared, 'The most beautiful roses we have deserve the best place in the flower garden.'

So he planted a large collection of them, and of some seventy sorts none was lost from the winter's cold. In the spring of 1886 after a three months' frost, men were skating on thick ice on the lake on St Patrick's Day. The next two springs were also severe, that of 1888 being followed by a summer worse than winter in its dullness, cold, wind, and rain. But even in that year the tea roses were lovely, though sometimes the buds rotted with cold and could not open. In the fine summer of 1887 some of the kinds—Marie van Houtte and Anna Olivier were two—flowered for four months on end. 'Thus,' Robinson wrote, 'we were able to prove several things of importance in flower gardening: (1) The hardiness, in South England at least, of the most beautiful class of roses; (2) Their surpassing beauty as flower garden plants in long given bloom, graceful form and foliage, loveliness and tenderness of colour, such as no other Roses show; (3) to add to the number of these flowers by growing a number of kinds and finding new and distinct ones not hitherto grown in our gardens or nurseries.'

His first planting of carnations was lost to rabbits. The estate was overrun with them when he came to Gravetye—fields half bare, in Bushy Wood six acres of underwood eaten clean down. Over a thousand were killed during three months of the autumn and winter. To keep them out of the garden he erected not only an iron and wire rabbit-proof fence, concealed in various ways so as not to be visible, but barriers provided by a sunk fence and water. In the autumn of 1887 he did a second planting, of about 2,000 carnations. The reason for growing so many was to show the value of the self-coloured kinds for the flower garden, as compared with the carnations grown by florists. He collected the best from every source and their effect from the first was good, the healthy rosettes being very pretty in colour; and although the dull rainy season of 1888 suited them so badly that the flower buds rotted away, towards its close there was a lovely show of varied bloom lasting until late in October. One variety, the Comtesse de Paris, flowered into mid-November. Robinson's comment was that a race with such qualities would be splendid for the English flower garden, far handsomer than the old cloves and the few kinds hitherto grown out-of-doors. At Gravetye they proved to be the most precious of late summer and autumn flowers. In bold groups among the tea roses, and intergrouped here and there with other things, there was splendid colour, such as no bedding plants gave that dismal year. In fragrance, colour of foliage, association, and value for cutting, they were far ahead of all the other flowers, except only the rose at its best, and out of the 2,000 plants not one perished from cold.

[155]

The Michaelmas Daisies were a wonderful sight in the autumn, and Robinson reminded his readers that some years previously they were never seen except here and there in 'bundles' in botanic gardens. Like the lilies, before the practice of growing them among shrubs, they were 'lost'. (Although introduced from Virginia into England by the younger John Tradescant in 1633, it was not until the Royal Horticultural Society's conference upon them in 1891 that Michaelmas Daisies were brought prominently into public favour.) As soon as the heavy groundwork all round the house allowed the planting of shrubs, Robinson dotted a number of the best starworts among the rhododendrons. The result was charming, picturesque and natural in the best sense, their graceful spires brushed by the winds and lighting the dying year with loveliness of colour.

The pansies he planted were his favourite tufted kind, such favourites that he used them on his bookplate. He explained the term. 'I call these Tufted Pansies (instead of Violas as they have been called) to avoid confusion by giving the Latin name of the whole genus to a section of varieties. They are simply Pansies more tufted, closer and hardier than the older and larger florists' Pansies.'

These crosses of *Viola tricolor* with some of the alpine violas like *cornuta*

18 Among his Tufted Pansies

for the beauty of their simple blues, lilacs, whites and yellows, were so superior to the striped, bizarre and wiry kinds that he considered they deserved a place with the roses and carnations. They were early in bloom and continued through summer into autumn. In the wet cold season of 1888 they were profusely in flower—'little clouds of delightful colour'—when other plants were half dead with cold.

Mrs Fryer, whose grandparents, named Du Croz, were Robinson's neighbours at Courtlands until 1906, remembers when they were going round the garden one day and came upon Boy, his little fox terrier, lying on these beloved pansies. All Robinson said—in a most reproachful voice—was 'Oh! Boy ...' and the dog sheepishly got up and joined them. What always impressed her was his 'gentleness of manner and of outlook'. She particularly recalls his quiet voice, a soft Irish voice as it has often been described.

He planted the pansies in colonies and bold groups, far preferring them to the 'ordinary English kinds and the showy and often ugly French race' because they reminded him of the blue violas waving their thousands of flowers above the densely matted turf of the Alps in early summer.

When planning a bed he seldom adopted a colour scheme, for all his plants were so good in themselves that there was colour enough without the geometric monotony of a pattern. He found he got more 'strength of colour' than in bedding-out, with colour interest even in winter. There was the good blue-grey rosette of the carnations and the ever-lovely leaves of the tea roses growing above carpets of mossy rockfoil and green and grey stonecrops.

This is interesting for his use of what we today would call ground-cover. He found many small alpines, particularly the stonecrops, most useful in 'carpeting' the surface, and in this way, he wrote, while themselves beautiful, they added to the charm of other flowers. They were especially useful in 'holding groups together', as when the ground beneath a group of delicate tea roses was surfaced with these dwarf and hardy plants. With no rocks in the place many of the vigorous alpine flowers thus found a home. And many of them were not only pretty in colour even in winter, they were also useful in helping to get light and shade in the beds. 'So cool and refreshing are they at all times that they were found useful as a "relief" by having a piece of ground merely surfaced with one or more kinds, and left to form a little lawn between the flowers.'

The beds, whether in grass or gravel, were large and simple in form. He found it impossible to do good work in the small beds so commonly seen. If the bed was to be well planted it was essential that it should be large enough for grouping and the forming of bold and picturesque masses. The shape and positioning of the bed could best be arranged on the spot and according to the ground. One of his objectives was to find which plants could be used near the house, to get the best effect, and here he was back to his old principle—that it is only by the use of hardy plants that the most beautiful effects and garden pictures can be got.

By his plan of planting almost everything in groups, varying their shapes and sizes, holding some apart and some together by underplanting, and by having 'spaces of repose' around, letting other groups merge into one another, all set pattern was destroyed so that it was impossible for the eye to take in the arrangement or contents of any single bed from one standpoint. The arrangement of a geometric garden could be seen at a glance: here it was necessary to walk round each bed to acquaint oneself with its contents.

As to the setting for the garden: 'My friend Mr Marnock, the landscape gardener, thought the best thing to do was to make most of the fields into a park.' Marnock left his one-time foreman to chew over this suggestion, but 'After some consideration I came to think that the divisions of fields necessary for the working of the place as a farm was the best and prettiest way,' Robinson wrote. 'The divisions and copses or "shaws" have much use as shelter, and for a place of its size I feel sure its present plan as a manor is far better than any approach to the more pretentious park.'

At the same time as improvements to the garden were being done—some of it real earth-moving operations involving up to thirty men—the work went on of redesigning and refurbishing the interior of Gravetye Manor. He was still living in Moat Cottage and making this old house prettier and more comfortable, in 1888 adding an attractive porch designed by Alfred Parsons, of oak framing and rafters with two strong oak seats along its walls.

The Moat was even older than the manor house but mainly in a good state of preservation. He was careful in his work of restoration to retain its character of oak framing, wattle and daub; and when he rebuilt the south end, which was in a dangerous condition, it was with stone quarried on the estate and with his own felled oak that the repairs were made. The roof was stripped off, the rafters made good and the Horsham slabs relaid. It emerged as a gem of a house and he surrounded it with flowers. In spring it stood in a sea of pink apple blossom.

In June that year an unpleasant incident forced him to take seven local men to court. The nuisance had been building up since his first

19 Children blackberrying at Mill Place

days at Gravetye. It concerned the sacred matter of rights of way. As he related: 'When I went to Gravetye every field in the place and even the garden round the house had rights of way, or reputed rights of way! People passed under the windows, and any garden made round the house was crossed by gangs of men with dogs betimes!'

Particularly in dispute was a footpath he had made in 1885 (the year he bought Gravetye) solely for his own convenience. He discontinued using it the following year, absorbing part of it in the pleasure garden he was laying out with valuable shrubs and plants. Soon he forgot it had ever existed. But not the men of West Hoathly, seven of whom 'alleged untruly' that there was a public right of way over the said footpath. Things came to a head a few days before the 9th of June 'when in pretended exercise of such alleged right they passed over the alleged site or thereabouts, and so over Warren Field . . . and destroyed some of the shrubs and ornamental plants and committed other injuries to my property, notwithstanding the remonstrances of my men.'

His solicitors took proceedings and a writ was issued: it was not defended, and judgment was given in favour of the owner of Gravetye who was also awarded costs.

He was still at the Moat in September 1889 when Dean Hole visited him, writing to his wife that he had spent a delightful day with Robinson and recommending her to see the garden before its beauty was gone.

Robinson had now bought in the Mill Place estate, and Hole exclaimed to his Caroline, 'Think of Robinson, the working gardener, Lord of the manor of Gravetye and 700 acres of land!' He thought that the manor house would ultimately be one of the most attractive abodes in the country.

Two months later both men were greatly saddened by the death of Robert Marnock on the 15th of November. Dean Hole called him the most successful landscape gardener of his time. Robinson, who thought of him as his great teacher in so many ways and also as one of his best and dearest friends, wrote his obituary in *The Garden*. He stressed how Marnock's work differed from what was often called 'landscape architecture' in Britain and other countries, and explained the sources of its inspiration.

> It was the result of a keen love of Nature. To the last he never, even when travelling in a railway carriage or other conveyance, ceased to look keenly at earth and sky. If only a hedgerow, there was for him a lesson in it. One April day, in 1887, we went with him out of a London fog into a large Oak Wood in Sussex, the first Spring after the underwood was cut. The lichened stems rose out of many acres of primrose and Ladies' Smock. He was happy as a child in it, and said, 'What is all our gardening to this?'

He had lived to be nearly ninety, and only ceased work a few years before, and until recently was still helping old clients and friends, despite the fact that for some time he had been 'feeling his age'. He was cremated at Woking and his ashes buried in his wife's grave at Kensal Green, only a step from another famous gardener, J. C. Loudon.

Dean Hole recalled how only the year before, 'Three friends, three famous friends—Mr Robert Marnock aforesaid, Mr William Robinson, and Mr William Ingram, who had established at Belvoir the most beautiful spring garden in Europe—came to give me not advice merely, but personal, practical help.' This was for the laying out and planting of his garden at Rochester, to which diocese he had newly been appointed.

The alterations to the manor house were nearing completion. In 1885 Robinson had built a new hall: the panelling of this was finished in November 1890 and 'very well done'. He had taken great pains to keep it as simple as possible and free from too much carving and decoration.

20 The New Hall, Gravetye, and as it is today

Even the chimneypiece was not carved elaborately, and spaces for pictures were left above the fireplace.

It was the pictures in the house that intrigued Frances Wolseley when she first visited Gravetye with her mother in the spring of this year, the flower paintings by Fantin-Latour that hung upon the pannelled walls of the great parlour, the Corots and paintings by Moon.

She was eighteen and when her schoolroom days were drawing to a close Lady Wolseley decided that her daughter should have some solid hobby. As she had always loved flowers the home garden at Ranger's House, Greenwich Park, was given over to her. She took to her duties wholeheartedly, subscribing to *Gardening Illustrated* and being delighted when one or two of her queries, asked through its columns, were answered by the Editor himself. A personal correspondence followed between them, and seeing how anxious she was to learn Robinson invited Frances and her mother to spend the day at Gravetye.

It was a day of sunshine, and here beneath apple trees in full blossom, as Frances recollected many years later, were carpets of dancing daffodils, and 'this was the first lesson I learnt, for in those days it was a novelty to combine bulb-growing with fruit culture.'

To her we owe the first description we have of William Robinson. He was 'a six-foot tall, black bearded, keen-faced man' who showed them round the many surprise gardens he was laying out. When their tour of the garden ended, Frances and her mother were handed over to the care of a rather austere elderly housekeeper. Lady Wolseley was so interested in the pictures and other beautiful things in the house that she turned to the housekeeper to inquire ('furtively', Frances wrote) if there were a Mrs William Robinson? The housekeeper looked sternly at her and replied, 'Mr William Robinson has not married. If he did so, the lady would have to be as lovely as a flower.' And, added Frances, there seemed no likelihood in her imagination of his being successful in finding anyone so perfect.

17
Planning and Planting

William Robinson was not content with 700 acres. The notebook on which he based his story of the making of Gravetye records his acquisitions year by year. But these acquisitions were all part of a plan. In 1888 he bought eighty-six acres originally belonging to the estate and long wished-for to allow the construction of a good and easy road to the house. In April 1889 he completed the purchase of the Mill Place estate, where arose a tributary of the River Medway, giving him land better than any other part of Gravetye. Stone Farm was bought in 1890 for the sake of securing a fine group of rocks. He had no use for the rest of the farm and promptly sold it to a neighbour. Some oak trees concealed the rocks. He removed them, thus continuing the line of rocks in the next field, and this made an unusual feature visible from many parts of the estate. 'The effect of the fine wreath of rocks over the level meadows by the stream is good,' he wrote. The following year saw Crow Fields Farm added, purchased from the Vicar of Portslade. He threw its fields together, simplifying the outline of the whole and obliterating a lane in the process. In 1892 he bought Old Coombe Farm and got himself a road to West Hoathly railway station. It all added up to 1,100 acres.

All this entailed considerable earth-moving by horses, men and monkey-wrenches. The new upper drive to the house, for instance, took eight months of very heavy labour: felling trees, filling hollows, removing many thousand loads of earth to get good vistas and an easy gradient, closing old and useless roads, in all making the approach to the house simple as well as beautiful and easy. With sight-lines and gradients perfected, only now began the surfacing of the whole length. This was dug out to sixteen inches deep and one foot of sandstone put in. The sandstone was dug from a quarry beside the drive and from another in Warren's Wood nearby. Next, six inches of flint and two inches of hoggan,[1] both brought from Croydon, were put on and carefully set and rolled. Twenty-two gulleys, grates and drain pipes were put along the road, and many along the side entrances to it, such

[1]Screened or sifted gravel.

as up-hill from the stable towards the Moat, to divert the rain water which rushed down the hillside.

As soon as the basic work on a project was completed he had the ground and surroundings planted according to carefully prepared plans of landscaping. The open ground along the drive, for example, was planted with dwarf or low native shrubs: heather, gorse, brier, bramble, broom, sloe, cherry, plum, dogwood, spindle trees and barberry. The drive was fenced with his own split-oak posts and rails, handsomely and well made by A. Brazier who was 'an excellent type of the Sussex woodman'.

7 A. Brazier, his Estate Carpenter

Robinson was pleased with his new road. The views resulting from cutting away a few plantations were wide and fine, and the feeling of air and the views gave one a quite different impression from the old roads through the hollows and woods.

Nothing, from making a road to forming a fence, was done without considering its effect on the landscape from every viewpoint. The fields, small in this old forest district, in being enlarged were given good boundaries, often woodland boundaries because of the number of woods and shaws on the estate. Any straight hard common fences which cut up the country like a chessboard were removed in favour of more picturesque dividing lines, usually following the natural curves of the bosom-like hills. The trees in the woods were left to be dealt with as timber, but those in open fields were carefully considered as regards effect. Those confusing a line or obscuring the view he wanted were removed. Any planting done was in masses which worked in with the other masses of wood. He could not abide a spotty effect.

When William Robinson died he bequeathed to the nation one of the finest collections of trees we possess. Seen from afar you can tell where Gravetye lies, for in no other woodland around is there such beauty of grouping, such contrasts of leaf-colour gorgeous in autumn and lovely in a different way with the tender greens of spring. The variety of the trees astonishes Kenneth Most, the head forester who now looks after them. He has been with the Forestry Commission for more than forty years and has never seen anything like the variety of trees at Gravetye.

William Robinson was now planting them, over 500 acres of woodland; and he planted with a lavish hand, such items as 1,000 *Acer saccharinum*, the Silver Maple, 100 *Liquidambar styraciflua* to make flaming autumn colour, 5,000 hollies, 1,000 Cedars of Lebanon for the 'ground above the stable to form part of the wood of hardy pines', 1,000 Riga Pines planted 'in same wood near the pit hole where we dug stones for the stable walls', 1,000 Austrian Pines 'to fill gaps made by rabbits', and 'a few thousand' Larch trees planted among the Corsican Pines near Birch Farm.

Other interesting trees came from Frederick Law Olmstead, the great American garden designer who with an engineer's training and an eye for the beauty of landscape became interested in ornamental grounds both of private estates and public places. He sent thirty-eight different kinds of American trees. There were many nuts including hickories, the Chinkuapin Chestnut and the Mocker-nut; oaks, the Stagger-bush, Persimmon and Pawpaw, Sassafras and Scarlet Maple, Yellow Root and Yellow-wood, the Wisconsin Weeping Willow and others.

Willows, both for beauty and use, gave Robinson the greatest pleasure. In 1887 he had planted a moist slope in Warren's Wood with the Cardinal Willow (*Salix fragilis decipiens*), and ever since had delighted in the young trees with their polished red twigs. The spectacle created by these red willows under various lights was the most beautiful thing in the woods; and in summer, when the delicate silvery leaves partly hid the red of the stems, the effect against the sky was exquisite.

He had been planting willows ever since.

The White Willow (*Salix alba*) was not so effective in winter as the red and yellow willows, but in summer it assumed its full beauty in great billowing silvery clouds. Robinson hoped that 'Country gentlemen might therefore take the tree Willows under their care, and plant them in colonies here and there, by water, or in wet, marshy, and often useless places. A marshy place planted with underwood formed of the

[165]

Yellow or Red Willow would be charmingly picturesque and as useful, if not more so, than some other underwoods.' There was no difficulty in getting any of these willows by the thousand, he pointed out, and an interesting thing about some of them was their usefulness for tying, often now forgotten. 'There used to be many things done in gardens in which these willow shoots were used for tying and packing, and now we notice wire, tarred twine, and other manufactured articles used instead—a mistake.' All in all, 'In the whole range of planting I know nothing which gives more satisfactory results than these forms of our native Willow,' he declared.

Between 1889 and 1890 William Robinson planted some 120,000 trees of all kinds, including 10,000 of the little-known Calabrian Pine.

He was also busy with shrubs, making a decorative feature of the Rocks by planting 4,000 kalmias and alpine rhododendrons. The Rocks became a favourite retreat. It was a pleasant walk to them and he often spent all Sunday sitting there and writing. He paid Owen Miles, one of the West Hoathly boys, a shilling to carry his books and papers.

He was the fortunate possessor of two lakes, and it was his habit to swim in the Upper Lake before breakfast and going off to London. In 1893 he connected the Lower Lake with the pleasure garden. Previously they had been cut off from each other by a sunk fence. He now made a walk from the upper lake to the lower, so that it was easily accessible from the garden and house, and here he built a boathouse 'all of our own silvery Oak, untouched in any way by paint or varnish', and here planted a collection of daffodils in masses and groups, choosing good trumpets such as *princeps* and *maximus*, thinking they would look very beautiful in the spring under the grove of oaks running by the water.

He had been planting daffodils from the beginning, the common English sorts by the lower end of the lake, Poets on the lawn near the oaks on the way down to Smugglers' Lane, the Tenby daffodil on the slope of his sweetbriar meadow where it reached the water. All were planted in natural-looking colonies, the centre closely massed, tapering outward to fringes and groups. The wild tulip, *Tulipa sylvestris*, sent to him from Touraine by Edouard André, also found a home here. He planted these bulbs in one large colony near the oaks. Thousands of bulbs of the Star Narcissus (*Narcissus incomparabilis*) and its varieties were planted on both sides of the drive and on the grass slope above the farmyard.

In 1893, having completed building work, road-making and other estate improvements, and intending now to devote the land to his herd of Sussex cattle, Robinson sold his horses, most of them bred on the

Planning and Planting

21 View from edge of lower lake. The lake was drained following a
tragic suicide, but now again reflects the beautiful old manor house

estate, and with them his Southdown sheep. The flock contained some
of the best Southdown blood obtainable, having been bought from the
most noted breeders regardless of cost; and just as he had abolished
purely utilitarian field names such as 'Eleven Acres', adopting the more
picturesque Beeches, Birchfalls, Bushy Mead and Dean Pasture, so he
now gave charming names to his cows: Gravetye Meadow Sweet,
Gravetye Columbine, Gravetye Bramble, Gravetye Bluebell, Gravetye
Marguerite were some of them. They were of a beautiful dark red
colour, and the way the cows, calves and bullocks grouped themselves
in the fields was a constant source of pleasure to him.

There were highlights, details, lovingly planned and brought into
being. At the side of the West Garden, variously called the Pleasure
Garden and the Rose Garden, he had a tank built for special water
lilies. A large collection of new finely coloured kinds raised in France
was sent to him by Maurice de Vilmorin, and by Joseph
Latour-Marliac the famous horticulturist of Temple-sur-Lot who
specialized in hybrid nymphaeas. One was named in his honour
Nymphaea marliacea, though the specific epithet is now used as a group
name, the colours of the blooms ranging from snow-white through soft

yellow to a glowing rose. Another bore the name *Nymphaea robinsonii.*

Wrote Robinson, 'We owe a deep dept of gratitude to M. Latour-Marliac who has given us an addition to our hardy garden plants which cannot be over-estimated. He has added the large and noble forms and the soft lovely colours of the Eastern water-lilies to the garden water of every northern country.' The splendid beauty of these plants, he believed, must lead people to think of the true and artistic ways of adorning garden waters, adding, 'Even the wretched formless duck-pond which disfigures so many country seats will at length begin to have a reason to be.' The Lower Lake became jewelled with these lovely flowers, and in 1895 he wrote that four different landscape painters 'painted our water lily pond in the summer and autumn—Mark Fisher, Alfred Parsons, H. A. Olivier and H. G. Moon. Mr Fisher found plenty of other pictures about the place and painted some of them. This was gratifying to me as proving that the garden can be made artistic and beautiful to those best fitted to judge.'

He had to use persuasion to get Mark Fisher to come, even into a district remarkable for its natural beauty—to which invitation Fisher had retorted, 'There are too many gentlemen's places there to suit my work', referring to the hardness and ugliness of the surroundings of most country seats: the iron-bound pudding-clumps of trees, railings, capricious clippings and shearings, bad colours and absence of fine and true form, with, almost certainly, an ugly house in the midst of it all.

It was not the first time artists had visited Gravetye, for early in the summer of 1891 Henry Moon came with his friend William E. Norton, an American trained in Paris. 'It was in Apple-blossom time,' Robinson recalled, 'and charmed by their sketches of the Apple-trees and the Narcissus mead, I asked them to stay and watch the beauty of the year on one spot of English ground.' This they did, 'from Daffodil time to the fall' (He sometimes liked to use the American term for autumn) 'and even into Winter, when the colour in Sussex woods is so beautiful.'

The summer of 1891 was wet and stormy, and often the artists, though hardy men, were driven off the fields by heavy rainstorms, which 'also drove away the pictures'. There were, however, enough pictures to stage a notable exhibition in London, held at the gallery of Stephen T. Gooden, 57 Pall Mall, in the first week of November.

The catalogue, listing sixty-eight pictures, was entitled 'A Story of the Year Round an Old Country House; in Woodland, Field, and Garden', and was prefaced by an introduction by 'W.R.' himself. In it he made critical reference to the currently fashionable school of landscape gardening directly opposed to his own 'natural' principles, writing, 'One thing may perhaps be said with profit in a day when there is so much talk of "idealising" things. Those who hold such views of the landscape art will find no encouragement here. The aim was, as it always should be, to get as near the visible beauty of things as it is possible for the artist to go—not always far. Clear and loving eyes see enough of the divine beauty of sky, sea, field and tree, ever to wish for more than getting as near a faithful record of that beauty as the winged minutes and ceaseless changes in sky and land allow to human effort.'

Thus William Robinson who was to cross swords violently with Reginald Blomfield, an ambitious young architect who was co-author of *The Formal Garden in England*. The book called forth Robinson's scathing reply in his own *Garden Design* published by John Murray in 1892. He continued the argument at length in 1907 in *The Garden Beautiful*, though concentrating more on woods and landscape.

He was increasingly interested in landscape and was delighted when an artist could faithfully capture the feel and flavour of a flowery meadow, a hillside or valley. He greatly admired painters like Crome, Corot and Turner because they sought not only the natural but also the beautiful, 'selecting views and waiting for the light that suits the chosen subject best, working always from a faithful study of nature and from stores of knowledge gathered from her.' A newspaper critic of the Moon and Norton exhibition wrote, 'We should have said they were handicapped by looking at nature through Corot's eyes'. A handwritten comment in the margin of the cutting was 'Rubbish W.R.'

He himself had other Moon pictures, painted on different occasions; for Henry Moon was an early visitor to Gravetye: he had joined the art department of *The Garden* about 1880. Robinson hung several in his dining-room with Hugo König's 'Fishing Village, Holland'. Some were characteristically labelled not with the month but florally by the season: 'Crocus time north of the House', 'Pansy and Carnation time, Gravetye', 'Pansy time, little front garden', and so on. By 1895 the list of pictures hung on the walls of Gravetye was impressive. Several were by Fantin-Latour, three by Cazin, and on the stairs hung two Corots and 'Various Flowers' by Jan van Huysum, finest of the Dutch eighteenth-century flower painters. There was de Wint's 'Group of Rocks' and his watercolour of 'Rainy day in Lincolnshire', a David Cox watercolour of a shipwreck, and more Fantin-Latour pictures gracing the drawing-room. There was also a fine painting, 'Mon Jardinier' by Carolus-Duran, otherwise Charles Emile Auguste Durand. Robinson had bought it in 1894, greatly pleasing the artist who told him it was one of his favourite works. Robinson wondered if he could not have Durand paint his own portrait. But could he make such a good job of it as he had of his gardener? There was an alternative, as a letter from Alfred Parsons tells us.

> I think you are very wise to get your portrait done by Fantin. There is a fine portrait done by him in the front room at the Academy. . . .

Robinson had meanwhile received assurance from Durand. *'Quant à votre portrait, vous pouvez être tranquille, il sera aussi bien que "Mon Jardinier".'* So it was arranged, and in 1894 William Robinson was in Paris sitting in the Durand atelier. The result was a rather grim study set in a shadowy background, his eyes lacking the Irish twinkle that was the real look of William Robinson.

Carolus-Duran was then fifty-seven and approaching the height of his distinguished career. He was to become co-founder of the Société Nationale des Beaux-Arts and its president; a member of the Institute, Director of L'Ecole Française at Rome, and finally Grand Officer of the Légion d'Honneur.

Paris was not the only place William Robinson visited in these years. In the spring of 1891 he was in Greece, as he tells us in the third edition of *The English Flower Garden*, delighting in the acres of the blue Greek anemone on the mountains, and, in the King's garden at Athens, charmed with the masses of violets in sheets over the beds. This visit was by special arrangement, the King having expressed his pleasure that William Robinson should see his garden. He also met the redoubtable Mrs Mary Anne Robb who was plant-hunting in Turkey, whence she introduced *Euphorbia robbiae*, nicknamed 'Mrs Robb's Bonnet' because it was in her hat-box that rooted plants of it travelled home to Liphook in Hampshire.

In 1892 there was a sad visit to Ireland for the funeral of his mother. Catherine Robinson, described as 'Widow' and also as 'Farmer', died on the 27th of April, aged seventy-four, either at her home, Dean Cottage, as stated in the letters of administration, or, as given in the Register of Deaths, at Browne's Hill nearby, the home of her brother Thomas Farrell. The former is likely to be correct because William Robinson himself was the executor to whom the letters of administration were granted in May, for she had left no will and her effects amounted to only £175. On the other hand, the only person present when she died was her brother who, however, did not register her death until July. She had suffered from pulmonary tuberculosis for twenty years.

It is curious that Thomas signs his name 'X his mark'. But this can be explained. In a family of boys and girls it was sometimes the girls who

22 The portrait of Robinson by Carolus-Duran, painted in Paris in 1894. Its last known owner was Robinson's cousin Sarah Handfield Robinson of Surrey

were given more years of education, while their brothers worked on the land. Browne's Hill, though Thomas's address, was the 'great house' of the district, the owners being the Browne-Clayton family. Thomas Farrell must have been an employee living in one of the estate cottages. Dean Cottage also belonged to the Browne-Claytons, though Catherine had a 'tenant's interest' in it.

This interest was advertised for sale by auction, three insertions appearing in *The Carlow Sentinel* in May and June, and from it we learn that Dean Cottage stands on five acres of ground with a nice garden, the house having two sitting-rooms, three bedrooms, a kitchen, pantry and out-offices.

In January 1893 Robinson was writing to Lady Wolseley from 63 Lincoln's Inn Fields, his London home address at this time, thanking her for a letter and hoping to see her in Ireland in the spring. He promised to send her some copies of his new little paper *Cottage Gardening*. Oddly it was published by Cassell and not the ubiquitous '37 Southampton Street', the first number having appeared on the 12th of October 1892.

[171]

Planning and Planting

A weekly cheap enough to appeal to the pocket of any cottager (its price was one halfpenny) it was both practical and imaginative, dealing not only with such matters as the use of Good King Henry ('one of the best vegetables for a poor man's garden') but urging the growing again of the old garden tulips, beautiful and richly-coloured, that once were a feature of the cottager's garden. The paper was well illustrated and after a trial year launched into a coloured plate, increasing to two.

Depicted in his opening leader was 'An English Cottage Garden', engraved from a picture by Alfred Parsons who had sat down to paint it when they were walking together in Oxfordshire. The cottage was a modest one, but the handsome Monthly Rose against the wall and the border of rich pansies below made a little picture of the place. It inspired what he called a startling contrast.

'Among the many differences between England and other countries, there is none more striking than is afforded by the appearance of the cottages. In England we have the cottage garden, pretty enough to warm the heart under the greyest skies, but on crossing into Northern France or Belgium the contrast is startling, the little houses standing in bare and ugly surroundings.' Whatever caused the difference, 'the fact remains that in England alone we have the delightful cottage garden.'

He set up a two-way answering service for gardening queries. For while 'the queries sent us will be answered by contributors specially qualified to deal with them', the editorial aim was also 'to get our readers to help one another'. And no one was better able to help a small gardener than another owner of a small garden who had gained experience in dealing with the many difficulties that had to be faced.

By this combination of professional expertise and reader-participation added to a wealth of special articles the Editor (modestly 'W.R.') hoped to ensure success for his new journal. Alas, *Cottage Gardening* ran for only six years, until 1898.

Spring in Ireland took him to Narrow Water House near Newry, Co. Down, childhood home of Jane Hall who married his old employer, the Revd. Sir Hunt Johnson-Walsh, as his second wife. It was March and the picturesque view across the park to the bay and the mountains that guard it was broken by a mound covered with daffodils. These, he wrote, were the double kind so common in Ireland and were spread over the mound in clouds, here and there massed close. The effect 'was not only good as a picture but as a lesson in the planting in the wild garden of such flowers ... in masses and bold groups, running out here and there into smaller ones.'

Planning and Planting

This he wrote in 1894 in the 'Forewords' to the new edition (the fourth) of *The Wild Garden*. The original edition was published before he moved into Gravetye, and since then—or as he expressed it more lyrically, 'The wild rose has given her petals to the wind for over twenty summers since this book with its solitary wood cut first saw the light'—his years of gardening had proved that the book deserved to live, and that the ideas in it regarding soil and other elements affecting plants in different localities could be useful in making what he called 'open air' gardens more artistic and delightful. His use of the term 'open air' here shows how very much in those days gardens still depended upon glasshouses for raising the plants that would indeed, eventually, find their way outdoors.

The years at Gravetye had taught him something else. It was an influence deriving from his sojourns in the Alps and the mountains of North America, Greece and Asia Minor. Following the breathtaking sight of the blue Appenine anemone on the hills of Greece he 'planted several thousand roots in grass' at Gravetye, putting them in meadows around the house in light broken groups and masses, and there they flowered and increased every year without the slightest attention, disappearing before the grass had to be mown in summer.

So from woodland wild gardens planted with 'perfectly hardy exotic plants' his ideas went in a new direction: he now concentrated on what became known as the Alpine Meadow. 'The best thing I have learnt from my own wild gardening is that we may grow without care many lovely early bulbs in the turf of meadows, i.e. fields mown for hay, without in the least interfering with the use of the fields.' He listed fourteen kinds of bulbs he grew in this way: the blue anemones, crocuses, snowdrops, daffodils, Snowflakes, grape hyacinths, dog's-tooth violets, Stars of Bethlehem, fritillaries, St Bruno's Lilies, Snow Glories, wild hyacinths, scillas and wild tulips.

His Alpine Meadow is still a glory of the spring at Gravetye.

18
A Fireproof House and a
Fumiste from Paris

In the midst of all these plantings and journeyings his other activities went on merrily, both indoors and out: the perfecting of the garden and the transformation of the house. The kitchen wing was reroofed with stone. Floors, ceilings and even walls were rebuilt. Sensitive to the dangers of fire, he removed all the matchboarding in the top rooms, and plastered the walls. He ripped up the old wooden floors downstairs and laid new bases of reinforced concrete. The stairs to the kitchen and basement were all of wood and in the dry air would soon become combustible as tinder: these were replaced by stone or brick. Various rooms were separated from a passage by a partition made of deal boards, the centre filled up with sawdust and all painted over. The partitioning had to go and was replaced with stock brick.

Despite these precautions his architects and builders told him he could not make the house fireproof. 'But I did,' Robinson boasted, 'and after many years work I gave up insuring the house!' His accountant, David Tyrrell of J. H. Hugill and Co., Leadenhall Street, was so distressed that he had to give way and insure at least the contents of the house including his now valuable collection of pictures. Tyrrell used to visit Gravetye at regular intervals, either to write up the estate books or to check them.

Robinson never forgot the gimcrack state of the partition walls, or forgave the builders who had thus constructed them. He was scathing on the subject to his architect friend Mervyn Macartney who looked after cathedrals and was to build him the 'very happy looking small house' called Holms Cottage. 'Your brethren build houses to burn,' he declared. At which Macartney 'looked askance'.

Finally came the fireplaces. They all smoked, and with a strong prejudice against coal as fuel and with a desire to have wood fires, he asked his architect George Devey who had built the new hall, to reconstruct the fireplace and chimney there. Devey failed to make the chimney draw and Robinson's comment was, 'Our architects appear to have no principle to guide them in making fires of this class.' However,

A Fireproof House and a Fumiste from Paris

'Having noticed the good way in which fireplaces for burning wood in France acted, I found a "fumiste", M. Pichon, in the rue de Seine, Paris, and got him to come over to see if there were any means of getting the fireplaces to work well.'

Pichon solved the problem by advising a totally different way of forming the fireplace, by the introduction of air from outside. Carried in small-bore piping, the air was passed beneath the fire and then around it, and then across to the front, discharging into the chimney inside the breast of the mantelpiece.

They began by experimenting on the Moat, and after some difficulty—due to arguments with the English workmen who could not see how such a contraption could work—a very bad chimney was made smokeless in all weathers. The French fireplace acted like a charm, and a room he was often driven out of by smoke became a very pleasant one.

From this triumph Robinson went on to repeat the pattern in all the rooms of the big house, making the aperture of the chimney fourteen inches by fourteen inches, and building the hearth ten inches above floor level. The beautiful iron firebacks were a feature, most of them old French ones, at least one from the Louvre of the Louis XIII period.

So much for the warming of the living-room and bedrooms, but he was shy of tackling the cooking problem, seeing that all the houses round about had long ago abandoned wood-fire cookery in favour of coal and the kitchen range. He was delighted when at last a neighbour, Dr Cruikshank, told him how well the Norwegian people cooked with wood, the fuel used being the common birch, wild in that country. 'So,' he related, 'I got one of their cooking ranges and it has cooked well for me ever since; though I might have got a better choice in large cities like Vienna or 'Buda Pesth.' In one large house there he had seen the cooking for over thirty persons done with success where nothing but wood was used.

From these experiments and successes came two books: *My Wood Fires and their Story*, published in 1917 by Country Life in London and by George Newnes; and in New York by Charles Scribner's Sons. *Wood Fires for the Country House and Cottage*, published by John Murray, took a wider view of the subject and made a plea for a pure-air campaign to rid London of its grime and pollution. He related the following story: 'My friend, the late Maurice de Vilmorin, known to us for many introductions of trees and shrubs came one summer evening with his son to London. The next morning the boy looked out into the Haymarket and asked, "But, Father, where is the fog?"' Robinson cited the loss of revenue to London from the numbers of people who fled to seashore towns and abroad; the keeping away of visitors to the capital; the cost of bringing unpolluted water, and the death toll of the self-inflicted plague of soot and fog.

Above the new hall he had built in 1885 was his bedroom, and this he turned into a book room—he never called it his library. When Gravetye was fully staffed May Henley was the tweeny at fourteen years of age; but her duties also included dusting the books—mounting a tall ladder and clapping them together two by two, then going over them with a duster. She was very small and the task was almost too much for her. 'It made me cry—it was such hard work,' she recalled.

The shelving and backing were all of native oak of good quality. Everything used or looked at by William Robinson had to be as near perfection as possible. He made a new dairy out of some cellars at the north end of the kitchen wing. For the floor hand-made tiles from Caen were used, 'harder and better in colour than any English tiles we could find.' Perfection was not for mere pretty-pretty but the practical.

He built the dairy in 1896 and a year later decided to give up farming. In the dozen years since he had come to Gravetye there had been continual heavy losses and he now resolved 'to give up every kind of farming on my account and let the farms.' Personal attention was needed, 'which in my own case would not have been skilled attention'. Farming, he realized, was often supposed to be a simple matter but was really a complex business demanding good and early training, much and varied experience, and natural ability and love for the work.

The various farms he let without much difficulty, the stock 'live and dead' sold—from hoes and turnip picks, hay rakes and implements of all kinds to his valuable herd of pure-bred Sussex cattle: the cows Harmony, Beauty, Stormy, Brandy and others, the bull Gravetye Bullfinch (the horses and sheep he had already sold). But he could still see cattle in the meadows and hear the plodding of horses' hooves, even although they no longer belonged to him.

Building work extended to the garden, to a fantastic wall of stone quarried on the estate that could have withstood a battering ram: its foundations were eight feet deep and outside buttresses were added to give it further strength if this were needed, though it was the hardest and best stone in the district. The wall enclosed his orchard-cum-kitchen garden, or as he preferred to call it his fruit garden. It took two years to build. The foundation stone was laid on the 28th of July 1898: it was not completed until the middle of July 1900. In shape it was an immense broad oval, which suited the lie of the land, as the usual rectangular plan would have led into awkward angles and levels; in size over an acre. He planted his first peaches against the wall so far as it was

[176]

built in the late autumn of the first year. Later, in 1905, he built a glasshouse for them, sixty feet long.

Always he preferred trees, shrubs and even clematis grown on their own roots, and this applied to the fruit trees in the New Orchard, which was the sloping field near the house. These were nearly all apples and were procured with much difficulty. After searching England and Europe he got most of them from Capel, near Dorking, from a nurseryman named Sheppard, the only one he could persuade to propagate trees on their own roots. He also propagated his own, and these were planted at the same time. 'If this orchard succeeds, it will be an interesting proof of trees grown on their own roots,' he wrote. 'It is certainly the first orchard in the County of Sussex planted on its own roots—or in England.' Similarly, in 1893, 'Planted large bed on south lawn with Lilacs on their own roots. Having suffered so much from the grafted kind I made special effort to get the plants on their own roots of the kind obtainable in that way, either in French or English nurseries.' He cut off the graft roots of any clematis grown on *viticella* and let the plant have its way on its own roots, describing the process thus: 'We wash out the roots clean, and then are seen two "rings" of rootlets, one clear above the other, the first being the effort of the plant to free itself, the other, the lower one, the stock on which it is grafted. We cut the lower one clean off.' Rhododendrons received the same treatment. Despite the fact that in Devon, Cornwall and the West of Scotland species rhododendrons were growing happily from seed sent from the Himalaya by Joseph Hooker in 1850, it was still generally believed that none but *Rhododendron ponticum* was hardy. Robinson found otherwise. In 1899 he began to plant rhododendrons on their own roots in the large beds on the east side of the house. 'In this way,' he noted, 'hope to get over the usual result of growing all kinds of Rhododendrons on the pontic kind, & mainly prove that the finer and hardier forms may be grown in ordinary soil in a better way than is usual when they are grafted.'

He succeeded: some of the rhododendrons he planted are still there.

The next piece of building was also of stone but a much smaller edifice. It came about because this man, though he filled every minute of the day, working and planning, was often lonely. Ideal would have been a boy about the place, whistling and demanding, even noisy and getting into mischief. He bought himself a dog and gave it that name. Boy, the fox terrier aforementioned, was a duplicate of Edward VII's favourite and of the famous dog listening to 'His Master's Voice' on the gramophone. He built Boy a charming stone kennel in the corner of the courtyard looking to the front entrance of the house. Boy was succeeded by Bobbie, an Airedale.

He was still acquiring land and still writing books. In 1900 he 'simplified' two fields by removing a belt of trees and making them into one. This was land by Vowel's Lane, which he bought from H. Longley of Selsfield, and it completed the estate up to the line of the road from Kingscote Station to Turner's Hill, thus giving a long and good front to the estate from this side, with the advantage that he could make a new entrance from Vowel's Lane, the main road, at any point he might wish.

8 Boy, his Dog

He had a genius for creating new features, and in this year also he built the summer house in the south-west corner of the West Garden, from the design by Ernest George who was to be knighted in 1911. George had been in partnership with Harold Peto and was famous for his elaborate domestic architecture. His office became a fashionable training ground for young architects.

The sides of the summer house were of Gravetye stone quarried from the Beeches, with plate-glass windows, the framing and roof of Gravetye oak. Previously he had thinned out a group of yew trees there, reducing them to three to give a better effect and stripping their boles in a process he called umbrella-ing. The removal of their lower branches gave him a clear view of the garden, while leaving the upper branches to cast a welcome shade, for there were no other trees nearby. Under the yews he placed the stone table Holland and Hannen made for him of 'best brown Portland stone'. There is a photograph of H. G. Moon

[178]

sitting there. The summer house was to become Robinson's favourite retreat in later years.

Mark Fisher was one day sketching the West Garden and pointed to the yew hedge dividing it from the Alpine Meadow below. 'Why don't you give me a free line there instead of a hard, black one?' he asked. The remark struck Robinson forcibly. 'Next Autumn,' he wrote, 'I took away the hedge of Yews and planted the noble rose Bouquet d'Or, mixed with the claret-coloured Clematis and both have formed a charming dividing line for years. The lesson I never forgot; we abolished the shears and clipped no more.'

He had always abhorred the practice of clipping shrubs and, with only certain exceptions, hedges. Topiary was of course anathema to him. 'We have such riches now,' he wrote, 'in the lovely climbing shrubs from parts of the world hitherto not much explored for plants and varied Evergreens, that to anyone who studies our wealth in this way, the forming of dividing lines and shelters should be easy without the aid of the shears. Without naming the most grotesque examples of tree mutilation in England, it is clear that much beauty is lost in our gardens by the stupid and ignorant practice of cutting trees into unnatural shapes. And it is not only in its ugliness, but also in the waste of labour it entails—in many cases acres of Laurels are cut into hard level plateaux every year—that some of the worst results of the practice are seen in important public gardens as well as in private places.'

The English Flower Garden had meanwhile been running through several editions. In June 1900 the eighth edition came out and was reprinted six months later. The sixth edition of *Hardy Flowers* also appeared this year. Previously *The Wild Garden* had reached its fifth edition, this in 1895 when he had given Donald McDonald's *Sweet-scented Flowers and Fragrant Leaves* a good send-off by writing the introduction. He was also looking after his various journals, including of course *The Garden*.

But the time came when he felt he must vacate that editorial chair. Early in December 1898 he was replying to an invitation from Charles Sprague Sargent to visit America, to see what had been accomplished there since 1870. 'It would give me enormous pleasure to go again,' Robinson wrote, '... but I have no partners or anybody to take my place so do not see my way easily', though he thought it ought to come off some day.

'Some day' came very soon. He released himself from the chair of *The Garden* the following year, and Gertrude Jekyll and E. T. Cook succeeded him as joint editors.

He wrote his farewell in the leader of the December 30th issue.

A Fireproof House and a Fumiste from Paris

It is with much regret that I now bid good-bye to the readers and contributors of 'The Garden' which with the new year passes into other hands. Ever since its first year the paper has had the sympathy and support of garden lovers blest with fullest opportunites of practising the art; and not even the fierce competition of the cheaper press has lessened their number. From what I know of those who are to have the care of its columns in the days to come, its readers will have good reason to give it the same support as they have given during the many happy and busy years it has been in my hands. The new directors are able and willing to do full justice to 'The Garden', and to give more time and thought to the business work of the paper than the growing needs of the 'English Flower Garden' and other cares have of late allowed me to do.

The first volume of 'The Garden' was dedicated to the memory of a man, J. C. Loudon, who left us a precious possession of books worthy of the art. The 56th volume is dedicated to that of Henry de Vilmorin, one lately among us in the prime of life, and his great loss calls to mind that of many others who have written in its pages or in some way aided and encouraged it: Robert Marnock, J. C. Niven, James Veitch, James McNab, Noel Humphreys, Anthony Waterer, Stuart Low, Frank Miles, David Moore, James Backhouse, J. F. Meston, Richard Gilbert, the Rev. H. T. Ellacombe, J. McHutcheon, and T. W. Girdlestone.

To these and to many more of the long-lived race of good gardeners who are still alive—among them being Miss Jekyll and Mr E. T. Cook, who will now edit the paper—I owe a deep debt of gratitude.
December 29, 1899   W.R.

It was E. T. Cook, author of *Gardening for Beginners* and other books, who persuaded Gertrude Jekyll to become joint editor with him, though she remained in this post for only a year.

They took up their work of *The Garden* 'remembering the long labour and wealth of solid material that have gone to its making; ever mindful of the clear purport of its teaching, that had won it honour from the beginning; looking forward with good courage to gaining for it an ever-widening field of usefulness, and working onward with the determination to build well and soundly upon a firm foundation.'

They recalled the long battle waged by their great predecessor against the bedding system, the 'wearisome monotony of its all-prevailing practice' being almost the only expression of gardening existing throughout the country, 'a bondage of fashion, spreading from end to end of the land that had even ... driven the good old border flowers out of the little cottage plot', adding, 'There can be no doubt

23 Charles Sprague Sargent of the Arnold Arboretum, to whom Robinson dedicated the sixty-fifth volume of *The Garden*. (Royal Botanic Gardens, Kew)

that it is mainly owing to his work and influence that our gardens have regained their ancient and most precious character of peace and beauty, and power of giving happiness.' The wholesome change had been wrought not only in private gardens great and small but at Kew itself where 'the intentional pictorial treatment of tree and shrub and flower adds a new and vast range of instructive teaching to an already magnificent scientific establishment', and following this good example the curators of botanic gardens throughout the kingdom were now vieing with each other in adding beauty to scientific efficiency, while the great improvement in the treatment of flowers in the London parks was traceable to the same good influence, the beautiful grouping of plants, especially as in Regent's Park, having become an important means of popular instruction, both in the making of good acquaintance with ornamental vegetation and in the enjoyment of one of the best and purest of human pleasures.

In the same issue, that of 6 January 1900, Dean Hole who had given *The Garden* its name wrote a page-long eulogy in his own lively style, punctuated with scholarly reference, metaphor and humour. He gave a fair and impartial appraisal of his friend's work, deftly throwing a spotlight of appreciation on all the details that expressed his genius in creating a garden as a thing of beauty and as a joy for ever, rather than

[181]

merely the kind 'supplying pretty bouquets, tender peas, new potatoes, and a clean promenade on Sunday.' Where, asked the Dean, could we find a new editor for *The Garden*? Most gracefully then he introduced Miss Jekyll and Mr Cook, her able and energetic co-editor.

There also appeared in this issue an article by 'W.R.' on the large blue Wood Anemone which bore his name in the specific epithet: *Anemone robinsoniana*. It has now been relegated to a varietal form, thus *Anemone nemorosa* 'Robinsoniana'.

9 *Anemone nemorosa* 'Robinsoniana'

With more time to spare for new improvements at Gravetye, Robinson went on a fresh spree of tree-planting: Silver and Russian Fir and Northern Spruce at the south end of the paddock on awkward and almost useless slopes, with broom and furze sown among them; in Warren's Wood renewing the underwood with tall saplings of maples, sycamore, oak, acacia and poplar; in the higher corner of the Bushy Field a colony of Sitka Spruce.

He began to consider the rides through his woods, how he could change them into more airy and roomy ways. He studied the line of each for its beauty as well as for the convenience of shooters and any light carting. Then, beginning with the pine wood above the house, he drove men and machines on through Warren's Wood until all the rides intersected. In this way he made access from one wood to the next easy and without gates.

He loved his woods. As he wrote: 'No work ever gave me more pleasure or greater satisfaction.'

These woods with his plantings of hundreds of thousands of trees were to become, on his death, part of the nation's heritage.

19
The Coming of a Friend

The next ten years were to be a wonderful decade. Or so he planned.

They were certainly varied. They began with the passing of John Ruskin, that social reformer and friend of the Pre-Raphaelites, accepted in his time as the greatest authority on art in England, who in his love of nature found a kindred spirit in William Robinson. They ended in a tragedy out of which was to be born a new William Robinson.

The leader in the February 3, 1900 issue of *The Garden* was devoted to an appreciation of Ruskin which the two new editors asked the ex-editor to write, as one of 'the favoured few' who had known him personally. In his later years Ruskin's brain had collapsed in attacks of brain fever. He gave up the idea of the Pre-Raphaelite dream. Robinson never did. But his admiration for Ruskin's work never dimmed, these writings and teaching which had awakened men's minds to a comprehension of the ethical relation of art to the simple needs and experience of daily life. Ruskin, wrote Robinson, had made clear to us what in nature was most wonderful and lovely, and what in the best of man's work was true and honest, good and beautiful.

Besides collecting pictures Robinson collected furniture, again with an unerring eye for the best and finest. In December a letter came from the Prince of Wales thanking him for lending an old oak manor-house table and old oak sideboard to the British Pavilion at the 1900 Paris Exhibition. The pavilion, designed by the rising young architect Edwin Lutyens, was visited by more than 600,000 people and Robinson's contribution 'formed the most attractive feature of the British Section, exciting universal admiration.'

He was always generous with gifts of plants and books, and in 1901 he gave William Jackson Bean, Kew's assistant curator, the eight volumes of Loudon's *Arboretum et Fruticetum Britannicum*, a work as invaluable today as it was then for its wealth of information on trees and shrubs and their history and the gardens in which they were to be found growing in the last century. W. J. Bean, who was to become the shrub authority of his own day and thereafter, was naturally delighted to have the books. 'They are beautifully bound and I am so glad to have the Gravetye book plate inside the cover to remind me of the giver.'

Robinson's habit when giving books was to label them with the season rather than the month, thus 'Crocus time', 'Rose time'. Christmas was 'Hollyberry time'.

In January 1902 an invitation came from Lady Wolseley. Again he had to send his regrets, explaining that he was in Paris buying fruit trees. It was probably on this visit to his beloved city that, with the fruit garden completed and ready for occupants he brought back also a French fruit expert to plant and train them. He was there for fifteen years. Gardeners now retired who were at Gravetye remember talk of his wonderful skills and the meticulous care he put into the task. His work lived on in cordon, espalier and pyramid, and they saw how if a side branch had died he had made a graft to fill up the gap; and how sometimes a top would be grafted on to the bottom, making a loop, thus containing the strength of the tree by reducing apical dominance. He had made full use of the walls, cordon-training even gooseberries and raspberries as well as apricots and apples. There it all was for Percy Picton and the brothers Bob and Ernest Snashfold, three of his successors, to continue his work. Some of the pear trees were twenty to twenty-five feet high. The Frenchman had trained them in whorls or pyramids, and the tradition he founded went on. Bob and his brother remember winding wire round them to keep their shape, so that the sap would be fed equally to all the branches, and so produce uniform fruit. And, as he did, they tied the main boughs with willow wands instead of string, in five-foot lengths.

'The lawn,' William Robinson once declared, 'is the heart of the garden, and the happiest thing in it.' But in 1902 in reorganizing the West Garden he removed the lawn which, apart from corner and side beds, occupied the entire space. He now threw (as he put it) the whole thing into forty-six rectangular beds, edging them with York stone and paving the paths between with old London pavements. Two years previously he had erected a pergola on the west and north sides to give some shade on hot days, and planted it with wistarias, roses and vines. He now paved this with old stones from the recently demolished Christ's Hospital in Newgate Street. This was the Blue Coat School founded in 1553 by Edward VI, the original buildings being those of the Grey Friars' monastery.

The London, Brighton and South Coast Railway line ran through

24 The West Garden, Gravetye

the Gravetye estate, and not content with planting his garden and woodlands Robinson planted its embankments. He had begun this in 1889, sowing seeds of furze, broom and acacia. He now planted trees in the Railway Shaw, the slips over the railway on the north side, using some of the tall saplings he had bought from nurseries at Oudenbosch in Holland to replant some of the woods. They were of oak, ash, beech, Canadian and Black Italian poplars, wild cherry, white willow, Norway maple, sycamore and abele. In the following year, 1903, he planted alpine laburnums, and sowed several pounds of cornflower seed—these between West Hoathly and Kingscote in the hope of naturalizing it. Finally he scattered thousands of bluebell bulbs, so many that when part of the line which had been dismantled was reinstated under private enterprise it was nicknamed the Bluebell Line.

At sixty-five William Robinson was in business with a new monthly, *Flora and Sylva*, a lush and handsome production of quarto pages, the paper unbleached Arnold, the bound volumes vellum-backed. Almost a gift at a guinea a copy, it was richly illustrated with coloured plates

[185]

and engravings from drawings and photographs by Maurice L. de Vilmorin, H. G. Moon and others. Its contributors included Lord Redesdale on hardy bamboos; Miss Fanny Currey of Lismore in Ireland discussing new daffodils such as the noble King Alfred which she described 'as if hammered out of pure gold'; the great American lily-breeder Carl Purdy on a revision of the genus *Calochortus*, which belongs to the lily family; George Nicholson of Kew writing on magnolias and illustrating his article with a superb painting of *Magnolia rustica flore rubra* flowering at Gravetye. Other contributors were W. J. Bean, the Revd. Charles Wolley-Dod, G. Reuthe, and Charles H. Shinn, head forest ranger in the United States with an article on the Sugar Pine. Not least was a series by William Robinson himself on 'The Garden Beautiful', sub-titled 'Home Woods and Home Landscape'. It became the book of that name published by John Murray in 1907.

He had spring in mind when in 1904 he planted more than 50,000 daffodils of various sorts in the pasture woods and orchards. In that year there was another sad passing of a friend when Dean Hole died. He was a special link with the past, giving a callow young man from Ireland the impression that he was accepted by that wise and kindly man almost as an equal. In October of the next year H. G. Moon followed him: he had been in failing health for some time, but his death was sadly premature—he was only forty-eight. Since joining the art department of *The Garden* there was hardly a Robinson publication which did not feature some Moon drawings or paintings. His greatest achievement was perhaps the illustrations he did for *Reichenbachia*, a magnificent work on orchids which came out in 1886 and continued until 1890. It was written by Frederick K. Sander, Moon's illustrious father-in-law.

It was curious that *Flora and Sylva*, which Robinson had seen as one of his best productions, should also end its life in this year. He pondered the reasons for its failure. Too costly a production to meet the limited demand? A periodical too diverse in its choice of subjects? These seemed to supply the answers. But he sought the advice of E. A. Bowles, that great gardener of Myddelton House, Enfield, a bibliophile with an extensive collection of gardening books, asking if he would come to luncheon some day and talk about the future of *Flora*.

It was never revived and this was the last time William Robinson ventured into the world of magazines.

Incidentally its editor wrote from 63 Lincoln's Inn Fields, as the address of *Gardening Illustrated*, *Farm and Home*, and *Flora and Sylva*.

Though he had relinquished the editorship of *The Garden* Robinson was still its proprietor, and the paper now had its offices in Tavistock

Street. But in 1906 he called in Edwin Lutyens to give him a design for new offices for it in Kingsway. Discussions with 'my cantankerous old friend', as Lutyens called him, were finally settled in time for the already successful young architect to go off on the steam yacht *Miranda*, joining a party of friends which included Sir Herbert Jekyll and his wife and children.

Robinson was sixty-eight at this time, Lutyens, a pupil of Ernest George, thirty-seven. Each held strongly to his own ideas and was impatient of the other: Robinson the champion of the naturalistic in garden design, Lutyens requiring geometry and thus defining his guiding principle: 'A garden scheme should have a backbone, a central idea beautifully phrased. Every wall, path, stone, and flower should have its relationship to the central idea.'

Two gardens typical of Lutyens formalism are those of Great Dixter where he even made architectural features of the hedges; and Le Bois des Moutiers at Varengeville-sur-Mer, home of the Mallet banking family, where having designed the house under the influence of *Art nouveau* modernism Lutyens laid out formal gardens each side of a central approach to the house between twin herbaceous borders now planted in Burne-Jones colours. Lutyens would have approved of this, and that every plant throughout the garden should be chosen for its colour; for while he declared—rightly, William Robinson would have said—that 'the true ornament of a garden lies surely in its flowers and plants', Lutyens saw flowers and plants merely as pigments, for he added: 'No artist has so wide a palette as the garden designer ...'

It is a beautiful piece of juxtaposition that the woods beyond the back of the house are planted to the ideas of William Robinson, work begun by the grandfather of Robert Mallet, the present owner, who carries on the Robinson tradition according to *The Wild Garden*. It is the only garden in France deriving its influence directly from him.

Lutyens, incidentally, never had a garden of his own. Neither, for a long time, did Reginald Blomfield (in Robinson's eyes the worse culprit in the matter of formal garden design), and it is fascinating that when he did come to possess a garden he completely reversed his ideas. He saw that the needs of the place dictated its style and ended with a delightfully free garden with not a straight line in it. Robinson was accused in his lifetime of making a similar *volte face*, both in the little South Garden where he had square beds—causing a young lady visitor to exclaim in surprise, 'Oh, why *you* have a formal garden!'—and in the West Garden with its forty-six beds laid out in a design that was entirely rectangular. He parried the challenge. The difference, he pointed out, between himself and the formalists was not the shape of the beds. What he objected to was 'where the plants of a garden are rigidly set out in geometrical designs, as in carpet gardening and bedding out'. Kew had made vast improvements in recent years, he wrote in *The Garden Beautiful*, but it had not emancipated itself from this ugly way of flower planting, as could be seen in front of the Palm House—purple beet marshalled in a pattern and the whole laid out in imitation of the worst possible pattern of carpet; and he added that 'we shall never see beautiful flower gardens again until natural ways of grouping flowers and variety of true form come back to us.'

A new entrance to Gravetye Manor from Vowel's Lane was open to the road. There were gates at the end of the long drive, but somehow they did not clearly mark the way to the house and in 1906 Robinson erected noble stone piers supporting wrought-iron gates designed by Ernest George and incorporating the initials *W.R.* He also formed a forecourt, sweeping away the bushes and other plants which were too close to the house. In the following year Robinson bought Blacklands Farm and its woods as a good addition to the estate, and this brought it to over a thousand acres in extent.

The work of only one more year is recorded in Robinson's *Gravetye Manor*, and the last two years are sketchy compared with the elaborate and sometimes lyrical descriptions of work done at the start of his ownership. The book ends in 1908, although various chapters on his heath garden, woodland garden and other Gravetye facets are appended. His notes for the book go on until 1911 when he instals electricity throughout the house and stables.

And that is all.

It is as if some dead hand descended to halt his endeavours, and this is exactly what happened.

Yet to his friends and acquaintances his life appeared to go on much as before. On the 5th of August he wrote to E. A. Bowles that he was going to France with Mr Sargent of Boston early in September. This of course was Charles Sprague Sargent of the Arnold Arboretum, who had come to England to discuss with Harry Veitch the prospects of a new expedition to China. William Purdom was engaged as the plant hunter.

Then almost a year later Robinson was again writing to Bowles but this time about a misfortune that had befallen him. His letter is dated 21.8.09.

I think it is about a month since you were here and I fell away. I regret to say I am in the same room still. I am feeling quite well but the power to move comes very slowly back.

[188]

The Coming of a Friend

It is known by those who remember the incident that William Robinson was on his way to evening church service at West Hoathly when he slipped on a stile and fell away from it, injuring his back. He could not move and lay there while Bowles went back to the house for help. Some of his men arrived with a door as stretcher. They carried him home and brought a bed down from upstairs.

25 An unusual photograph of Robinson standing on his own two feet. It was taken in the garden of his neighbour William Harris

A nurse from Westminster Hospital was summoned to look after him, one of several that came and went. Nothing any of them did pleased him. They were too young, or too fussy, or too dictatorial, in some way irritatingly wrong or not right. He sent them packing.

In October he was writing more cheerfully to Bowles, 'I have had a great expert down from London who tells me that every sign and test promises well, but still I am in the same old room, where I shall be very pleased to see you on the 23^d. Take a fairly early train so as to get here by one....'

The last of these nurses was Mary Gilpin, also from Westminster, who agreed to come for a month, no longer. It was not his reputation as a fractious patient that discouraged her: this was not the sort of thing to deter a person like Mary Gilpin. It was the fact that London was her life. She had just come from nursing Clara Butt through an illness at her home at North Stoke, a village in Oxfordshire, and was glad to get back. Although born and brought up in the country she had gone to live with an aunt in Bournemouth while still in her teens. The country and gardens meant nothing to her, although an eighteenth-century relative was the Revd. William Gilpin, a man of the trees and author of *Forest Scenery*.

So Gravetye might seem an unlikely destination, and her patient to whom gardens were his world someone with whom any accord was also unlikely.

But to Nurse Gilpin a patient was a patient. She undertook the job because nobody else would go, and from the moment the noble wrought-iron gates clanged behind her she felt imprisoned and vowed to herself that she would not stay more than the month.

She broke her vow. Her patient insisted that she was the only nurse he could bear to have near him. She must stay. Clearly he needed her help a little while longer. She promised to stay for another month—reluctantly. She used to look at the big gates at the end of the forecourt and say to herself, 'There lies my freedom.'

She took a daily walk and the bleak early days of the year did nothing to help. Had it only been summer she might have enjoyed the gardens and the woods. Her patient surprised her by asking if she had noticed the Algerian irises which would now be in flower. He told her where to look—in the long narrow border nearly under his very window! And the snowdrops: how many different kinds could she make out? He made her go and pick some with their leaves, so that he could show her. It was a lesson in observation she found she enjoyed.

The end of the two months drew close and she asked if he had made arrangements for another nurse to take over. He had not, and roundly told her so. He would increase her salary, he said, tempting her. As if that were the end of the matter. She wrote to the hospital to ask when they were sending someone else, and was promptly told that she ought to stay.

The doctors had been hoping that the spinal injury would heal itself. They now knew that the damage was superimposed on something else. He was suffering from what, even today, is euphemistically called a social disease. Then, the names syphilis and gonorrhoea were scarcely breathed aloud, even if people knew them, and even veiled by the doctor as long as he could. A doctor might, with a carefully jocular look, accuse his patient of having been 'fond of the ladies!'—and so make the victim feel less of a social outcast—before taking the conversation into more serious vein. It was a deadly serious subject, for until present

[190]

times there was no certain cure for venereal diseases.

How had it happened . . . ? It was of long duration, he was told, and it was probably the recent injury to his spine that had caused the syphilitic condition to manifest itself in a flare-up characteristic of the end of the latent stage of the disease, as was the sudden paralysis. It was possible that he might be paralysed to the end of his days.

William Robinson had been a fighter all his life for the things he believed in. To be told that this was a battle he could never win made him furious. He shouted his specialist out of the room and lay in a ferment, brooding on how he could defeat them all.

His frustration was terrible. Never to work in his garden again, or even walk in it . . . Never to swim in the lake . . . Never to run from the station (as he still had done), gleefully arriving at the house before the horse and trap.

Were there no warnings of the oncoming disaster? Truthfully he supposed there had been, but he had told himself that the signs could be misread or mean a dozen things.

The doom the doctors had spelt out came over him in waves of horror. Perhaps, he thought, he ought to feel disgraced, but all he could feel was outraged anger.

The days dragged on, but gradually he was able to be helped out of bed and into a chair. One afternoon as he sat looking out of the window Nurse Gilpin asked if he did not consider himself to be a lucky man. *Lucky!* The question shocked him: was she making cruel fun of him? He eyed her sharply, but her gaze was honest and clear.

'Yes. You are looking out at your garden . . . some people are blind. This morning you heard a bird singing, you told me . . . some people can't hear that. And you have all this . . .' Her arms spread in a gesture that embraced all of Gravetye—the beautiful old house and all that surrounded it. 'Some people have *nothing*.'

'Then they haven't worked as I worked,' he retorted.

She told him he could still work: he could sit and write another book. 'What about this place? From what you've told me, it would make a lovely story.'

Gravetye Manor, or Twenty Years' Work round an Old Manor was published by John Murray in 1911. He gave a copy to his nurse, inscribing it

Mary Gilpin
From the author
Souvenir Gravetye Xmas 1911

20

Home Landscape

They were changed days. Mary Gilpin had come to a house whose rooms, all but the few occupied, were covered with dust sheets, as if, she felt, each piece of furniture were a dead thing wrapped in a shroud.

The next stage to sitting up in a chair was being wheeled in a wheelchair, and before then she asked her employer if she might remove the dust sheets and make the house more cheerful by putting flowers in the rooms. In some surprise he assured her she could. He had not realized, living in one room for so many weeks, that everything had been put in store, as it were; and when she brought him a bowl of flowers for his room he saw what a pretty touch she had in arranging them. He approved, and this was praise indeed from William Robinson who had an artist's way with flowers. He liked them arranged in bronze vases.

Under her guidance Gravetye came alive again. It had always looked attractive because of his good taste in furnishing it with just the right pieces and pictures. Mary Gilpin added something more. There were servants enough to run the house but until her coming there was no one to make it a home.

By spring he was able to go for little jaunts on the paved paths in the West Garden. His coachman or one of the gardeners wheeled him, but steps demanded two men to hoist him and his chair up or down. He had them made into ramps.

He began to notice that all was not well. There were weeds in the borders and a general untidiness. Only a few acres of garden and a dozen men to care for them! He had the men arraigned before him and demanded an explanation, but having exploded his wrath he knew the reason without having asked for it.

They lacked his guiding hand and eagle eye. There was nothing for it but to engage a sound man with whom he could confer and who would see that his orders were carried out faithfully.

Ernest Markham came to Gravetye in the spring of 1910. Though only twenty-nine he was already a gardener of wide experience, latterly head gardener to Lady Chichester at Arlington Court in Devon and then in charge at Bishopsgate, Surrey, Lady Marcus Beresford's lovely place. It was love at first sight when he saw Gravetye, appreciating not only the way the gardens were laid out but the wealth of plants in them. Markham had an extensive knowledge of plants and studied them from all points of view, interested not only in their culture but in their habits and history.

William Robinson was seventy-one when Markham came to Gravetye, thinking that with someone of that age who was an invalid he would not be there for many years. As it was, he was to remain at Gravetye for the rest of his life.

Although a disciplinarian, which showed in his smart appearance and brisk walk, he was modest and unassuming. He won the respect of the men in working hours and their friendship off-duty—he was a fine cricketer.

Hardy plants, trees and shrubs were his speciality, but with William Robinson as his mentor and Gravetye as the supreme demonstration of William Robinson's principles of garden planning and planting he was to become an expert in many other directions.

We remember Sarah Robinson of Bloomfield who befriended Catherine Robinson and her young family. Her grandson William Haslett, a distinguished doctor, later knighted, was William Robinson's cousin. Sarah was very fond of the boy she called 'My own Willie'. She sent him books to amuse him in the long winter evenings and followed his proficiency in reading and arithmetic with great pride. He always wanted to be a doctor and even as a boy earned the nickname 'Doctor William'. About the year 1890 he left Ireland for London to complete his medical training. He had an introduction to his older cousin William and called on him at *The Garden* offices. But both were too busy to build up a friendship at that time: only about three years later, in 1893, when he was twenty-eight, William Haslett had not only qualified as a doctor but become medical superintendent of a nursing home. We do not know if they saw anything of each other in the interim but certainly Haslett started visiting Gravetye from April 1911, and it must have been some comfort to Robinson that he could admit to him the difficulties of his illness, a subject he could not discuss openly. The two became close friends and saw each other regularly. Naturally it was easier for Haslett to visit Gravetye than for Robinson to come to London, but from March 1912 he sometimes did, in 1916 arriving in a car with his 'nurse and 2 men'. Haslett lived at Halliford House, the private mental nursing home at Upper Halliford, Middlesex, of which he was still medical superintendent.

This was nothing to the adventurous journey Robinson undertook in

26 At Moat Cottage with his nurse Mary Gilpin and Miriam Markham, wife of his head gardener

1911. We know from both Gilpin and Haslett sources that he went to France and Switzerland more than once with his nurse. Perhaps this was one of these occasions.

A letter from Vernon Lushington in that year reveals that he and Robinson were travelling companions on previous jaunts abroad.

> Your invitation is delightful,—most delightful it seems to me with memories of the past, & pleasant pictures, incidents and conversations to come. But—alas—you will be sorry to hear that my health, which has served me so well 75 years & more, has quite broken down this year.
>
> Besides suffering 6 months facial Neuritis (Bell's Palsy as they call it)—I am now quite a cripple from *Arthritis*,—the malady you used to denounce so as brought upon us by our vices and those of our forefathers.—Otherwise I think I am quite well, except that my hearing is impaired.
>
> I am off to *Wales, Llandrindod Wells*, tomorrow morning, in the vain hope to get a little better.
>
> So you see my dear Friend, I am in no case to go a-touring with you, which w^d. have been so great a pleasure. But do go, with another mate & come back and tell me of it.—
>
> Always, with affectionate regards, yours
>   Vernon Lushington

It was perhaps a hard-earned holiday for the author of *Gravetye Manor*, or a celebration of its publication, but for poor Vernon Lushington his travelling days were over: he died at the end of January the following year.

The Robinson pen was still busy. In 1912 John Murray published his book on clematis and their culture at Gravetye. Romantically Robinson entitled it *The Virgin's Bower* but seems to have tired of this appelation, for in the proof copy he uses the generic name, clematis, deleting with positive pencil strokes such names as 'the European Virgin's Bower' in favour of 'the Indian Mountain Clematis'.

The book was the outcome not only of the pleasure he had from the cultivation of these lovely climbers, but from regret at seeing 'even large gardens desolate so far as they are concerned'. Once more he wrote in order to popularize, and so bring to others the pleasure he himself enjoyed. The book although small was a mine of information about the habits of clematis, and from it Ernest Markham learnt a lot, in 1935 writing a book of his own about them. He became a leading authority on the genus, and breeder of many new varieties.

Relieved and glad though he was to find a suitable head gardener, the handing over of even some responsibility was a sad relinquishment to Robinson, a portent of things to come. The uncertainty of what turn his illness might take, and his age—he was now seventy-three—told him that he must make his will. He named as trustee his friend Cecil G. Harris of Moatlands next door, but writing to him that he still hoped for a long life.

To the Harris family Gravetye was a second home. They went down there on Sundays, and if there were special visitors (he had visitors most weekends) there would be special cakes for tea. The three Harris children—Audrey, Rhoda and William—adopted the Gravetye garden and woods as their playground, much preferring them to their own, and when they were old enough Robinson allowed them to swim in the lake, the only people to whom he gave this privilege. Audrey, who married Edward Malan, recalled how 'We used to swim there at night in the moonlight, and when the magnolias were in bloom it was magical.' Gravetye was 'part of life for us children.'

William Robinson loved children, and they loved him. He would sometimes even refer to flowers as earth-children.

In 1911 the National Insurance Act was passed, requiring employers to pay contributions for their employees. William Robinson refused to do so for six of his employees, these being his house servants. He was summonsed for resisting. Not fit enough to appear in person at the East Grinstead Petty Sessions on Monday the 23rd of February 1914 he stated his case through his barrister, Mr Inskip. His plea was that having a conscientious objection to the Act, he felt he could not consistently comply with it until compelled to do so; he had always provided for his servants in cases of illness, and he claimed the right to continue to do so: the best relations existed between him and his servants, whom he had always treated liberally, so that it was no question of money that influenced him in resisting what he considered to be a bad Act.

A heavy fine was imposed. He remained adamant, whereupon the Bench (doubtless feeling this would hurt him more) sent bailiffs to sequester one of his pictures. They chose one hanging in the hall. Robinson refused to let the men take it away but suffered the label they stuck upon it, which read *Property of H.M. Government.* At first regarding this as a great joke he let it be known what was happening and had an amused letter back from H. Vertens, only hoping 'that when they seize a picture, it won't be a Fantin.'

[196]

27 With the Harris family and Ernest Markham

At the same time, Robinson circulated a sixteen-page pamphlet on 'Civil War and Party Lawyers', setting out his 'honestly felt opinion of the acts of our fatuous Government and some of its members'.

Among the commiserators was Rudyard Kipling, his near neighbour at Bateman's, Burwash, who wrote

> I sympathize with you and I thank you for your pamphlet all of which is undeniably true *but* when a country has revoked its Constitution it is only a question of time when it will break up in revolution—and our time seems to be coming rather quickly.
>
> Most sincerely
> Rudyard Kipling

Amy Paget was equally forthright. She called the Cabinet 'callous brutes'. Her brother had been 'ordered to do most painful things': the whole situation was enough to crush the heart out of a brave race.

Robinson had something on his side. As he asked in his pamphlet denouncing the measure: 'Save for the hosts of officials, is there anyone who really benefits from its infliction? Certainly not the poor consumptives seeking in vain for the first-class sanatorium. What of the casual labourer? How does he fare who often on the Monday morning has to stamp his card before he can get a few hours' work? And the domestic servant, whose poll-tax on her few shillings a week is little less than that of the well-paid artizan? Let those who think of the Act's results go to the Hampstead Workhouse and see it full of servants sent there by their mistresses, who, had it not been for the Act, would have been cared for at home.'

There was more.

Meanwhile in this same year, 1914, a tragedy struck the horticultural world. The firm of James Veitch & Son ceased to be. This, the greatest of all nurseries, made the fame and fortune of five generations of the family. They employed not only remarkable plant hunters who collected in South and North America, Japan and China, but also remarkable cultivators who grew the new plants and developed varieties from them. Sir Harry Veitch was the last to run the business and rather than allow the name to be used by anyone else he dissolved the company, though the branch at Exeter carried on as Veitch.

The enormous stocks of plants were sold and dispersed. William Robinson bought all the Veitch clematis and from then on they became one of Gravetye's most beautiful features. He had grown clematis for many years, but now they flowered from May through September, and that difficult flower-month, August, was made memorable by an avalanche of bloom.

He had recently been visiting Nymans, the splendid garden founded by Ludwig Messel which now belongs to the National Trust. Alfred Parsons who was painting there wrote that 'Messel tells me you are well and found plenty to interest you here.' Ludwig Messel's granddaughter, the Countess of Rosse, was writing a garden flora of Nymans, to which Robinson was contributing one of his famous forewords, summing up his admiration for Messel and the garden he made.

Another foreword he wrote at this time was to a book on climbing plants by William Watson, curator of Kew Gardens who had succeeded George Nicholson. 'After the gift of trees of the earth-mother,' Robinson wrote, 'the greatest for the gardener are the climbers that adorn them with infinite grace.' In many large gardens they were rarely grown: he hoped to encourage them.

A charming letter came in December from Sydney Spalding, a friend of long standing. They first met at the firm's London office in Drury Lane, just round the corner from Southampton Street, when Robinson the connoisseur was hunting for hand-made paper. Spalding & Hodge Ltd advertised *Papier de Luxe*, which was just the thing to catch his eye. Business relations developed into friendship and Robinson became godfather to Sydney Spalding's daughter Rosemary.

The December letter read:

28 The magnificent pergola running from the forecourt to the stables

My dear Robinson,

I hope that you have survived the great festival of Xmas. For us the situation has been saved by the happy little child in our midst who has helped us to live again in the long ago. We all thought of you at Gravetye & drank your health at dinner—Perhaps the past does not speak to you in the same way as it does to us and yet you have a great past to look back on; the revolution of gardening. A revolution that will make its mark for all time. I do not suppose you realise this perhaps so clearly as those of us who have been the interested & silent witnesses of your work. That you may long be spared to continue to guide the great work is the hope of yours always sincerely,

    Sydney Spalding

His firm had an office in Paris at 106 rue Lafayette and he was there at the time of the signing of the Armistice ending the 1914–18 war. His letter dated November 15 is worth quoting.

Home Landscape

My dear Robinson

I got here on Oct 31 & seem likely to be here till the end of the month. Paris seemed extraordinarily indifferent to the events happening during the Saturday & Sunday of the Armistice negotiations. I got to the office at 10.30 on Monday morning & saw no sign anywhere of excitement—Suddenly at 11 the bell of the Church close by rang out. I went down into the street & bells rang & guns fired & there was a general stir amongst the people. Soon flags began to appear at the windows & by 1 o'clock Paris was gay with flags & crowds began to fill the streets. On Tuesday night I watched the crowd from the steps of the Opera house but the Republic lacks a rallying centre—They have no King. I would have rather witnessed the scene outside Buckingham Palace in London than any Sight in Europe.

I heard an interesting thing from a Pressman of the U.S.A. Associated Press who was present at the actual signing of the Armistice on Monday. He says Foch did not himself speak to the delegates but instructed one of his generals to present the Armistice terms for their signature, he standing a silent witness. Erzberger[1] said that altho they now had authority to sign he desired to say that such terms were impossible of fulfilment because Germany was in the last stages of absolute starvation. To this Foch's general replied "No discussion". Then Erzberger tried to obtain some modification of certain points & again the general said "No discussion". Whereupon Erzberger signed & motioned to two of the generals with him to sign which they did weeping.

I hope all is well with you—& that I shall see you again before long, & have a talk over all the wonderful happenings that have taken place since I saw you last

Yours very sincerely
Sydney Spalding

The year of the outbreak of World War I saw the publication by Murray of another of William Robinson's lush folio volumes. Illustrated by superb photographs taken by George Champion at different seasons of the year, it was even more magnificent than *Gravetye Manor* but was on the same subject, this time the *Home Landscapes* of the

---

[1] Matthias Erzberger was Propaganda Minister and signed for 'Peace without annexation'. After the war he wrote *The League of Nations, the way to World Peace*. He was assassinated in 1921.

estate. Surprisingly, since it would have seemed to appeal to a limited public, it went into a second edition in 1920.

The aim of the book, as he explained in the Preface, was to show the value and the meaning of landscape gardening around the country house.

'This art,' he wrote, 'is a purely English one—we were the first to depart from the builder and decorator's way with a garden. The proof is that when we see in France or Germany' (he had spent six weeks of September and October 1900 in these countries) 'ground bearing trees in their true forms it is usually called an English Garden, the most sincere compliment ever paid to us. The effect in our islands of this change from the old idea of gardens laid out in geometrical ways was vast in the gain of picturesque beauty. The landscape art is a precious possession for us and for others in our Colonies and in other countries, and one we should take care of for ever.'

His first idea was to travel throughout Britain to describe examples of picturesque design and planting and so show the noble gain to our islands. 'But having met with an infirmity which prevented me from getting about the world in a free way, I turned my thoughts to what was done in my own place to illustrate the theme.'

He had not done so badly, however, travelling as he had about Europe.

During the war Gravetye was a haven of peace for many people. They came for the weekend or just for the day. Mrs Malan recalls a typical Sunday afternoon when 'We used to sit with Mr Robinson all over the garden. Everyone would be in attendance—Markham, a gardener, Nurse Gilpin. He would take us round the rose garden and show us anything special that was out.'

One of the visitors was Gertrude Jekyll, who often stayed at Gravetye. 'She was a dear old thing with bird's-nest hair and lilac-coloured flouncy flowing dresses.' Reginald Farrer came before he went off to Kansu with William Purdom; Ellen Willmott, Lilian Braithwaite, J. C. Swinburne-Hanham; Clementine Spencer Churchill, Harry J. Veitch, Augustine Henry, Harold Peto, Frank Crisp, Vicary Gibbs—indeed, a never-ending flow of visitors.

Lady Wolseley was there on the 15th of July, 1914. Her husband had died in March the previous year and Frances was now Viscountess, a peeress in her own right, in this same year receiving the Freedom of the City of London for her work in founding the Glynde School of Gardening for Women, which during the war did wonderful work in supplying highly trained lady gardeners to fill the place of men called up for the forces, supplying vegetables and fruit, too, to augment market supplies. The lady gardeners several times visited Gravetye to hear lectures by William Robinson on fruit-growing and the care of produce. These talks were delightful, given as they followed him in his chair or grouped round him in one orchard or another, or in the famous eliptical Fruit Garden which also grew vegetables.

In December 1916 Charles Sprague Sargent was congratulating Robinson on the award from the Massachusetts Horticultural Society of the George Robert White Medal of Honor. It was given for his educational work in horticultural literature. 'I do not suppose you care very much about such things,' Sargent wrote, 'but as awards go this is the best thing in the United States in its way.' He was delighted that it was at his suggestion the medal was sent.

Alas! the medal never arrived. They both concluded that the ship bearing it had been sunk by enemy action.

In 1897 there had been another mishap concerning a medal. Among some correspondence belonging to Sir Frederick Moore and his father was part of a letter from J. T. Bennett-Poë, a member of the R.H.S. Council, in which he stated that William Robinson had refused the offer of a Victoria Medal of Honour. On my seeking confirmation of this, the following reply came from Mr John Cowell, secretary of the Society:

> The only statement that has come to light suggesting that a VMH was offered to William Robinson was in the *Journal of Horticulture*, 8 July 1897, p. 18, where his name appears in a list of the original sixty recipients; but this list was published in error, as was acknowledged in the issue of 15 July, p. 42: 'In response to our application a list was obligingly supplied to us shortly before going to press, but in his haste to supply it to us in time the Secretary made use of an old printed list of many names, some of which were erased, and others were added in writing, and unfortunately the explanation as to which of the erasures and additions were to stand and which to be ignored was misunderstood.'
>
> In fact seventeen names appeared by error on that list, so it must have been a comparatively early draft, and there is no evidence that all seventeen were actually offered the VMH.

Sometimes there was sad news, for beyond Gravetye's peaceful bounds the war raged on in horrible slaughter. In November 1917 the Countess of Strathmore wrote from St Paul's Walden Bury where her daughter, now Queen Elizabeth the Queen Mother, spent her childhood. Part of it was a gardening letter, asking where she could buy a special clematis

29 With Mary Gilpin at the South Porch

'called *C*. Heracleifolia *sweet scented*' which she had read about in *The Garden*, and she recalled how in 1916 he had been very kind in helping her with her garden in the Grampians (it was in Glen Clova), where, inspired by *The Wild Garden*, she was making a collection of British wild roses.

She had not thanked him for his help and said he must think her ungrateful, 'but just at the time you sent me the lovely photograph of your daffodils in y^r. wild garden & the *delightful* book—I was overwhelmed by the loss of a darling boy of mine, killed in action in France—& I am afraid I thought of nothing else for the time.' She went on, 'However, I have experienced *three* times now the greatest sorrow a woman can have the loss of her children & the *only* thing that does *comfort*, is gardening.'

It was the same, indeed, for William Robinson. Whatever life had denied him he still had his garden. He lived for it, planning it, sharing it, writing about it.

Gravetye sang in him. A theme with never-ending variations. This time it was *My Wood Fires and their Story*, a book that was as strictly practical as its all-embracing subtitle declares:

SHOWING THE BEAUTY AND USE OF THE WOOD FIRE: OF THE WAY TO SECURE GOOD DRAUGHT AND COMBUSTION: OF THE NATIVE WOODS BEST FOR FUEL: OF THE ABOLITION OF THE FENDER: AND OF THE ECONOMY AND VALUE OF WOOD AS FUEL.

The book is as relevant today as when he wrote it, and as timely for a world largely dependent upon oil and coal for fuel. William Robinson knew how tenuous is our possession of these. He wrote: 'However rich in coal or oil a land may be such gifts are exhaustible, whereas the earth-mother bears her sylvan children for ever.'

21

Iris Time

Arthur Kilpin Bulley, whose forty-three enchanting acres became the Liverpool University Botanic Gardens, was a regular visitor at Gravetye, like most of the great gardeners of the day. In 1918 he was perturbed to hear that Robinson was giving up journalism—'both glad and sorry,' he wrote. 'Glad because you are now too old to have to worry with the innumerable small chores which newspaper owning must bring. Sorry because your successor isn't likely to make the reading matter as interesting to me as you have done.' He added what had become a family joke: 'Tell nurse, that if I don't find Gentiana Farreri in good form, she will have to die.'

This wonderful gentian was one of Farrer's finds in Kansu in 1915.

'Add my voice to the chorus of regret on your retirement,' wrote H. Mansfield who had made successful improvements to his garden at Moulton Grange, Northampton, 'on what I might venture to call "Robinsonian" lines.'

Another tribute came from Sir Herbert Maxwell, the distinguished Scottish writer on gardens.

> It is grievous to hear that you are giving up Gardening Illustrated—the hebdomadal refreshment of hundreds of readers. But one must not grudge you repose after these long years of work. Few writers have tackled any subject with such sweeping results as you have accomplished. I look back to the early seventies when your precepts were first taking effect, and I marvel at the change that has come over British gardens. You must surely feel gratified that it is owing to your books and the original *Garden* that, for every amateur who took an intelligent interest in horticulture fifty years ago there are now hundreds. . . .

His claims for Robinson's readership were modest. *Gardening Illustrated* had a circulation equal to that of the great dailies, and of course he influenced a whole nation.

Alfred Parsons wrote that for some weeks past he had noticed a change in *Gardening* and that 'Mrs Berkeley here a few days ago, told me you had given it up.'

It was not quite true that Robinson had parted with his papers. This did not happen until the end of December 1918. What was un-comfortably true was that *Gardening Illustrated* was certainly not what it used to be. Reginald Farrer had sent a stinging complaint, but his letter, written from Lanchow on New Year's Day 1915 has solved what has been a mystery concerning William Robinson's part in 'The Crispian Row'.

It has always been laid at Robinson's door that he was responsible for vilifying E. A. Bowles during this astonishing horticultural scandal. In the preface to Bowles's book *My Garden in Spring* Farrer poured invective upon 'the very rich' who were 'out to purchase the glories of the Alps at so much a yard'. The unmistakable target was Sir Frank Crisp who had reproduced in four acres of his garden at Friar Park an exact model of the Matterhorn complete with a 'floral carpet' of 4,000 alpines and a tin chamois. Crisp in a furious reply tacitly labelled Bowles as the author of the attack, and this was distributed in pamphlet form at the 1914 Chelsea Show—by none other than Ellen Willmott who stood at the gates handing them out from a bookmaker's large leather bag. It was reprinted in *Gardening Illustrated*.

But Robinson had nothing to do with this indiscretion, as we now know from Farrer's letter.

> I had always hoped to send Gravetye some token of my travels, in memory of our last talk. But now I fear, considering the astonishing behaviour of your Sub-Editor, you will feel my Poppy as a coal of fire! Let me only hope he may be better supervised in future, not single out my humble self for special outbursts of vulgar venom.

'Better supervision' certainly applied to Robinson as editor, for he could go up to town only infrequently, and he had trusted his journalists to run the paper properly.

The rumour about his retiral crystalized in *The Garden* issue of December 21 in a leader headed 'A Farewell (to Journalists only!)'. The same *Vale* was printed in the January 31, 1919 issue of *Gardening Illustrated*.

> From its birth to the present year it was my happy lot to pilot *The Garden* through fair-weather seas. It started without noise in the Press and without an advertisement. In a few weeks it was a success, and so went on for many years, meeting no enemies and many friends, until the Hun arose in his might to devastate the world. With over 50

volumes of the old GARDEN and forty of *Gardening Illustrated*, these both founded and edited by me, 35 years garden and woodland editor of the *Field* and three years *Flora and Sylva*, my journal work is now given up and I turn to my books. . . .

He went on to list those who had given him help and encouragement but who had now left their gardens for the Elysian Fields. Among them were his old friend Henry Vilmorin; C. M. Hovey of Boston, famous as a fruit breeder and editor of the *Gardener's Magazine* and the *Magazine of Horticulture*; Joseph Latour-Marliac, Dean Hole and David Moore.

He was looking back on sixty years of gardening friendships, and now, because change was the law of life, looked forward to 'the young to continue in the right way, never disheartened, and always in the hope that intelligent beings will never return to the Victorian way of degrading the flower garden. . . .'

Following the 'Farewell' came a fresh raft of letters regretting his departure. From Gerald W. Loder, the future Lord Wakehurst whose estate of that name is now Kew's 'country garden': 'I hope it is some consolation to you to feel that your work rests on foundations which are secure and cannot be upset.'

From Charles Sargent: 'How much you have accomplished . . . and with what satisfaction you can look back to all the years of useful labour which you have devoted to the horticultural press!'

From George H. Barr: 'Please add my congratulations to the many I know you have received on all the work you have done for horticulture. Surely no man deserved more the quiet & repose of retirement . . .'

Again there were many more appreciations of a long life well spent.

There was sad news of William Goldring, his death on the 26th of February 1919. Goldring had been his assistant editor on *The Garden* and editor of *Woods and Forests*, and it was during these years that he and Goldring had designed gardens together. In 1886 he had left journalism to devote his whole time to the art in which he earned world-wide recognition as a leading landscape gardener.

The following January brought news of Alfred Parsons's death at the age of seventy-two. He was, said *The Gardeners' Chronicle*, one of the few artists who painted a flower just as a gardener sees it, for he had not only the artist's but the gardener's instinct and passion.

To William Robinson he once described how he painted. He had two maxims. One was that he must feel 'some truth or underlying principle, which causes that beauty'. The other applied to landscape painting. 'I put flowers in a foreground because they are lovely and add to the sentiment of the place, and not to teach the flora of the district.'

Like Goldring, Alfred Parsons designed gardens with skill and success, as well as being a fine painter.

It would seem that his world was shrinking, life closing in on him. He was of an age when most men are content to sit by the fireside and dream back over the years. As always, William Robinson dreamed forward. In 1922 his world expanded by reason of the small miracle of a half-track vehicle made for him by Citroën, yellow in colour and with eight gears. Its inspiration was the caterpillar wheels of the tank, used with success in the recent war. In it he was able to tour the whole of his

30 The famous Citroën half-track. In it Robinson could tour his whole estate

estate. He had made walks round the lakes, wide enough and firm enough for his wheeled chair, but now with William Farrant his chauffeur at the wheel he could travel anywhere—across fields, along the woodland rides, and mount even small hills. In July he wrote to E. A. Bowles confirming dates for a visit from him, adding in a postscript: 'I have a citroen motor coming & hope it will be ready by the time you come & so let us see the woods as they should be.'

His world was expanding in another way. It began to happen on the 28th of November 1921, a month remarkable for being unusually warm and dry, as indeed was the whole year. Nurse Gilpin's thoughts were not entirely on her patient as she wheeled him along the level stretch of paving by the house on the west side. Her sister Ruth was expecting a baby, her fifth child, and things at home were difficult because her husband was never in good health: he had been gassed in the war and had pulmonary tuberculosis. Suddenly they heard an excited shout behind them. It was Annie the parlourmaid, who was normally rather withdrawn but at this moment was running to meet them and waving a telegram. It announced the arrival of a little girl.

William Robinson was looking at a flood of flowers that had opened to the bright sunshine. They grew against the wall among rushy leaves and were irises of a most delicate and exquisite mauve, an annual wonder that such tender petals should brave the winter. 'Tell your sister to name her Iris,' he said.

The parents of the baby asked each other, 'Why not?' And thus she was christened.

In 1923 the unexpected happened. A small child arrived to live at Gravetye—Iris, aged two years and one day. Her mother's sister Nellie brought her to London, there to be met by Aunt Mary and borne off to Sussex.

She came on William Robinson's invitation when it became impossible for Ruth Poynter to nurse her husband and look after five children. Robinson had inquired what was happening to his nurse's sister, and on hearing that the four elder children were being dispersed to various relatives and that it was not certain whether Ruth could or should keep Iris, he decided gruffly, 'She had better come here.' This was a tremendous decision for an eighty-five-year-old bachelor to make and Mary Gilpin was quick to assure him that the child even if seen would not be heard. He had no doubt of it. Nurse Gilpin made rules that were always kept by those for whom she made them. They had to. She was a strict disciplinarian and rather old-fashioned—everything had to be meticulous and nothing slipshod. She was a serious person who took life seriously, but all this was relieved by her happy nature and charming smile. She did not, however, tolerate lapses or broken rules.

Iris and the man who became 'Robbie' broke them.

At two years old the world holds a thousand surprises. There is a surprise, for instance, round the corner at the end of every corridor. A half-open door must be explored to see what is round it. And provided one wasn't *seen* or *heard* . . .

The bedrooms were given the names of flowers and trees. There was the Rose Room, the Pansy Room, Gean, Birch. 'Once I got past Birch I could make a noise!' Iris recalls. Elm was the bedroom of Annie and her housemaid sister Connie. Cedar was Nurse Gilpin's where Iris also slept, next door to Mr Robinson's which is now called Bay and in his day was the Old Oak Room. Nurse Gilpin, in case of need, was able to reach her patient quickly by a communicating door. His room, with Ash and Birch, were the only bedrooms panelled, and his fireplace bore the date when the house was built: *Ano. Do. 1598.* As with the other rooms the fireplace was open for burning logs. It had a bender from which swung a copper kettle for morning tea.

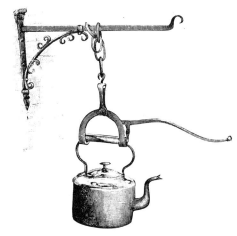

10 A Bender

Part of the Gilpin rule was that during this early tea-time Iris had to go into his room to wish him 'Good-morning!' He would be sitting in his dressing-gown in a big chair with a camel-hair rug over his knees. He had a passion for this light-tan colour, and Iris had a liking for knees. Being the baby of her family and full of winning ways she was accustomed to scrambling on to people's knees, and it was not long before the camel-hair rug became her favourite seat, whether in the morning or at any time of the day that Mr Robinson was wheeled about the garden in his chair.

At two the name and saying of 'Mister Robinson' was difficult, and after some garbled attempts Iris settled for 'Robbie'. Mr Robinson settled for it too, and when that disciplinarian Nurse Gilpin protested that her small niece was taking liberties, Robbie's very blue Irish eyes twinkled denial. 'I like it,' he told her. 'She amuses me.' It was her innocence that touched him, as with flowers and the birds that sang in his garden.

When visitors came he had her summoned so that he could show her off. When a photographer arrived to do an official portrait of the great man, Iris must be included. He began to teach her the names of the flowers; and when she was old enough, about four, he gave her a little space for her own garden, near the sundial at the house side of the West Front. She grew little low plants like pansies and daisies that she could tend herself. The gardeners were told not to interfere with it, and of course because it was thoroughly out of place and they were not allowed to touch so much as a leaf or stem within its small bounds, it can be imagined how they objected. But they objected with a forgiving smile, for Iris won their hearts. Unabashed she called the wife of the head gardener 'Big Markie' because Miriam was taller than her husband, and Ernest Markham himself 'Little Markie'.

And of course every gardener must have tools.

'We must get you a wheelbarrow,' Robbie declared.

'Red,' Iris stipulated.

'No. Red is a hateful colour. Green is the proper colour for a wheelbarrow.' And it was a green one he bought her; but a Sussex trug was specially made in miniature, and a set of small tools.

31 Two-year-old Iris plays pat-a-cake with 'Robbie'. She was one of his many small friends

One of the visitors to Gravetye in September 1926 was the Right Hon. Sir Guy Fleetwood Wilson who signed himself in Mary Gilpin's visitors' book as far back as September 1917. He was a very great man, much decorated, who had attained the highest posts in the Civil

Service, including being the Viceroy of India's *locum tenens*. He too was won over by Iris, and following his 1926 visit wrote to her aunt, 'I am so glad the dear little girl liked the chocolates.'

Iris did, and so did the next few visitors, for dressed up as a nurse she administered them as medicine.

Her frolics were ended at six o'clock when she was given supper and put to bed.

One morning very early she woke to find no Aunt Mary in the bedroom. Alarming sounds were coming from downstairs and these she tracked to the kitchen where an amazing sight met her eyes. Instead of the kitchen floor there was a lake. Aunt Mary was there looking very anxious. One of the outside men was hammering a pipe. There were cries of 'Taps—taps!' and someone dashed past her up the stairs. Discovered, she was being loudly told she should not be where she was when a voice called from above, 'Bring her up to me!' A four-year-old, cold and frightened now, was glad to creep into the warm bed beside him.

In the very early spring of 1923 a lovely little plant, *Campanula muralis*, the Wall Harebell, travelled from Gravetye across the Atlantic to the garden of Henry Ford and his wife Clara. There at Fair Lane, Dearborn, Michigan, they cut it up 'and made many little plants of it' for Clara's rock garden. She wrote thanking Robinson for it and adding, 'Have known you through your "English Flower Garden" for many years.'

The bearer of the plant was William Ormiston Roy, a son of Scottish-born Frank Roy who emigrated to Canada in 1869. Roy was a well-known horticulturist and William followed his father's footsteps, becoming recognized in Canada, the United States and Britain for his horticultural and landscaping achievements. He was also a supporter of the cremation movement and was instrumental in establishing Canada's first crematorium, the Mount Royal, in 1901. He became its superintendent and was president of The Cremation Association of America. The two interests of gardening and cremation brought William Robinson and the Roy family together.

Percy Picton was now one of Gravetye's eighteen gardeners and had to obey the strict order against smoking when at work. It was only when 'Billy', as they called their employer, was out that they dared have a smoke, even Markham sometimes getting out his pipe. The inevitable happened. One day Picton was pruning a large *Magnolia grandiflora* growing against the house. He was enjoying a pipe when he heard his master's car returning, and quickly put it out. But he had not realized

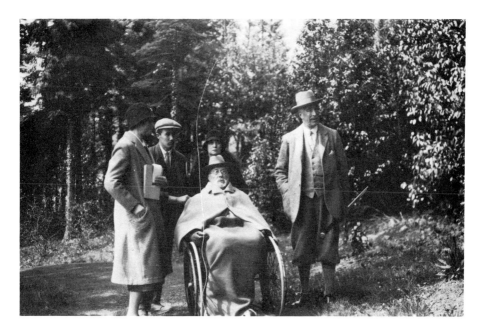

32 A visit from the Moores. Sir Frederick was curator of the Royal
Botanic Garden, Glasnevin, succeeding his father David Moore in
whose time William Robinson was an apprentice gardener. Percy
Picton, one of the gardeners, is with him

that the smoke had been blowing straight into an open window, making
the house smell strongly of the evil weed. He got a firm reprimand.

Picton has another interesting memory. He had just helped Mr
Robinson into the Citroën half-track one morning when two American
ladies arrived to see the garden. They had a piece of news for Mr
Robinson. Did he know that a place in the United States had been
named for him? The reason was that it had lovely gardens.

American visitors came, as many of them come today, well aware of
William Robinson's fame. Another at that time was J. Wilkinson Elliott
of Pennsylvania who was to write about him in his book *Adventures of a
Horticulturist*. He regarded Robinson as 'the greatest gardener and the
greatest writer about gardens that ever lived', and many times visited
Gravetye which to him was 'one of the most beautiful gardens in the
world'. Early visits were in the days when Robinson met him at
Kingscote Station, having walked the two miles to it, and again walked
to the station with him in the evening.

On the 9th of December 1923 the house was thrown into a state of grave
anxiety. Its master was critically ill. Dr Haslett was there, and at his
insistence after consultation with Robinson's own doctor, W. Evershed
Wallis, Cecil Rowntree who was a top surgeon of the day was brought

from London, and a second nurse engaged to help Mary Gilpin. She was Lilian Suddaby, a distant cousin of Elsie Suddaby the singer. Hurriedly a bedroom was prepared as a theatre. The operation, for a twisted gut, took place at midnight. Haslett had warned his cousin that unless he would submit to the knife his chance of survival was slender. The operation was successful.

William Haslett had married Norah Macan the previous year, and they now had a little girl, Mary, who was to be followed by four other children. One of Robinson's wedding presents was several flower paintings by H. G. Moon.

The name Ingwersen is almost synonymous with alpine plants, and gardeners know that the Ingwersen nursery is on the Gravetye estate. Founder of the firm was Danish-born Walter E. Th. Ingwersen who had much experience of rock gardening at Wisley, the Royal Horticultural Society's garden; at Stevenage under Clarence Elliott, and with Gavin Jones at Letchworth. He met William Robinson from time to time on gardening occasions, one day confiding that he was looking for some land to lease for a nursery of his own. Robinson told him, 'You can have Birch Farm if you like it.' Ingwersen was pleased with the house and a sloping field of six acres. The bargain was closed in 1926.

He found in Robinson a convivial friend, for here was the author of *Alpine Flowers for Gardens*, owner of a long retaining wall specially built to accommodate such plants, and who used them in every way possible. Robinson took a close interest in the Ingwersen alpine nursery and often went down to see what new plants were there. Some were of Ingwersen's own discovery on plant-hunting expeditions.

The nursery was to remain in Ingwersen hands, his sons Will and Paul eventually purchasing the property with extra acres in 1969. Will, who has many memories of 'W.R.', remembers him as a perfectionist both as regards people and plants. 'He did not suffer fools gladly and had to size you up before accepting you. But after he got to know you there was no barrier.' He illustrates this with the recollection of Robinson's finding him one day in his book room. 'Interested in books?' he barked. Will said he was very interested—and in plants. He was accepted.

The number of gardeners at Gravetye ranged between fourteen and eighteen. In 1925 young Robert Snashfold joined the staff as an apprentice, and two years later Harry Pattenden who had known Gravetye since he was seven, for his father was a woodman on the estate and tenant of the Home Farm. Bob helped with the glasshouses, of which there were five, none heated till February. Alpines were grown in glass frames below. Bill Grainger was one of the senior gardeners and on Bob's first day Markham pointed him out. 'You see that fellow in the green apron? Well, you go and hold on to his apron strings.'

In 1927 there was another newcomer, Miss Adeline Astbury. She was an innovation, for she was a typist.

She first saw her future employer as he was wheeled into the dining-room by his nurse. 'Well, here she is,' Miss Gilpin announced to him. 'What shall we do with her?' 'Give her some fruit,' was William Robinson's typical reply.

She was engaged to come on the afternoons of Tuesdays and Fridays and found Mr Robinson 'a most interesting man', not at all the ogre whom she was terrrified of meeting. 'He was talked of as "that funny old man living in the woods". But as I said to my father,' Miss Astbury related, '"Well, it'll be an adventure."' It was more than that: it began a close friendship with Mary Gilpin who was 'a wonderful person', and as for Mr Robinson himself—'He was full of energy, marvellous. He never said "I'm too tired to go on." There was nothing pretentious about him, and in winter when it was very cold he would make me sit on the hearth and toast myself.'

They worked in the dining-room at the long oak table and when work was over for the day they would go into the drawing-room for 'a proper tea'.

Sometimes there were visitors. Often his cousin Sarah Robinson would be there. She was a fresh-complexioned buxom countrywoman very fond of her Irish homeland. Blunt, downright and outspoken, her views and comments sometimes infuriated her listeners, but she was an excellent nurse, housekeeper and cook, being all these in the household of the Rolls family who lived at Caterham, Surrey. Arthur Rolls, the son of the house, often came with her. He shared Robinson's love for France and in this year was studying there. Arthur Rolls still treasures the letters his old friend wrote to him, and his memories of the Gravetye garden which was never without flowers; even liking the wintry months most when enchanting surprise blooms appeared charmingly arranged by Miss Gilpin in rooms filled with the scent of burning logs.

It was in 1927 that the National Gardens Scheme was started. Among the first gardens to be opened in support of its charity was Gravetye.

In December that year, after fifty-seven years of life, *The Garden* appeared for the last time. It merged—'with considerable reluct-ance'—with *Homes and Gardens*, whose directors declared no change of policy. The editor of *The Garden* was to be responsible for the large gardening section. It was, in fact, to be a merger of the home and the garden, a very proper amalgamation.

On Boxing Day Dr Haslett had a telephone call from Nurse Gilpin to say that his cousin was very ill and that Dr Wallis had called in a second nurse. The country was deep in snow, whole areas cut off by vast drifts, and Haslett was unable to get to Gravetye till the 5th of January.

A sudden change to much milder weather lifted everyone's spirits. The patient began to rally. But this, his second severe illness, had shaken William Robinson to the realization that he could not expect to live for many more years (though he was not going to admit this to anyone else!). He was all but ninety and was determined to attain his century. The 17th of January found him putting his signature to his last will. It was witnessed by Dr Wallis and Nurse Catherine Matheson.

At the same time he gave over full charge of the garden to Ernest Markham.

It was a lonely illness. He had lost his little play-mate. There was no sunny-voiced 'Good-morning, Robbie!', for Iris had left Gravetye in the autumn to go to school: she was approaching six. Robbie would fain have kept her but Mary Gilpin was family-minded and deemed it best that she return now to her own home.

Summer came, long days of hot rainless weather stretching gloriously from June till almost the end of July, the sun shining from clear skies ten to fifteen hours a day.

Sometimes from the shade of the yews by the summer house he would glance up to the playground and think how many times he had sat there in his chair, watching Mary Gilpin throwing a ball for her small niece to run after and retrieve. He told her one day, 'The place needs children.'

'Do you think so?' Her question was thoughtful. Iris had become so much a part of Gravetye. But perhaps she could find other children for him. 'Would you like me to arrange for some of the village school boys and girls to come and dance for you on your birthday?'

He smiled at the thought, recalling the parties he had given for Iris, with every neighbour's child near her age scooped up. 'That would be nice. Please do—but only small children. Will you arrange everything?'

In the eighteen years she had been with him Mary Gilpin had spread her talents from being only a good nurse to being a capable housekeeper and trusted companion. The house ran on oiled wheels, and it was due to Mary Gilpin that it was also a happy house. The staff respected and loved her. He could say the same thing himself.

His ninetieth birthday, on the 15th of July, began with an amethystine dawn that broke into a perfect day for the picnic, and at

33 The Playground shelter garlanded with 'Nellie Moser'. Gravetye had the finest collection of clematis in the kingdom

three o'clock he was ensconced in his chair under the shelter at the house end of the playground, which in May and June was garlanded by the big mauve-pink flowers of the Nellie Moser clematis. On the long garden table before him, already laid for the picnic tea, was his gramophone. He thought he heard a chattering, like a flock of roosting starlings, and turned to see a crocodile of small boys and girls coming down the steps.

Mary Gilpin had leagued up with their teachers, and everything was beautifully organized. The children ran races and they danced for him. When they were quite tired out there was a splendid tea with cakes galore and orangeade. Charlie Bonsey of the baker's shop in West Hoathly had made a tray of buns, and Mrs Theobald, the cook at Gravetye, a birthday cake covered with white icing and with little pink roses, ninety of them, round it. They all had a piece, and when they left he gave each child an apple, an orange, and a packet of sweets. There was also a more permanent present, a pottery mug and plate decorated with cherries. Many are the households in West Hoathly and afar where these birthday mugs are treasured.

He himself was the recipient of cards, letters and presents. One was from Iris, the usual silk handkerchief which had become a tradition.

It was just a pity that such delightful little girls had to grow up and go to school.

22

Grand Old Man

Relentless time was fast depleting the amazing circle of amateur master-gardeners who had raised horticulture to the heights in the nineteenth century and borne it triumphantly into the twentieth.

Of the few that remained was that proud beauty Miss Ellen Willmott of Warley Place in Essex, one-time owner of three gardens and employer of 104 gardeners. Rich as she was her resources could not stand the strain, and despite the sale of Treserve in France and Boccanegra in Italy she remained deeply in debt. Sir Frank Crisp, of whom much good can be said, arranged for a group of her friends to contribute towards the running costs of Warley Place. William Robinson was one of them. She never repaid him, as we know from a letter to E. A. Bowles in which he wrote: 'It is all very sad about the lady & her finances. Some eight or more years ago I lent her some money & never had a farthing of interest back. My solicitors think I should prosecute her, but for an old friend like that I cannot.'

In 1931 he accompanied Ellen Willmott to Chelsea. As he told Lady Moore, 'I had no idea of seeing the Chelsea Show but Miss Willmott begged of me to go, and I am going.'

Poor Ellen Willmott, she was near her end in everything, not only her financial resources but her life. She died three years later.

He did not go to Chelsea every year and it was probably on this visit when he was 'well over ninety' (in 1931 he was ninety-three) that it was remarked how 'fitting that the King should pay signal attention' to him, 'since that veteran of horticulture has done more than any other man to make the English flower garden what it is.'

Part of the signal attention was when the King told Nurse Gilpin to put Mr Robinson's hat on his head: it was a windy day and he feared the old man might catch cold, but poor Mary Gilpin did not know what to do because Queen Mary was following and was very strict on protocol. Perhaps she need not have worried, for Queen Mary visited Gravetye more than once.

His ninety-fourth birthday was marked by a charming gift of ninety-four double white peonies. They came from his Canadian friend Ormiston Roy and travelled across the Atlantic in a refrigerated ship. The parents of the peonies had been brought to England by Robinson himself in 1870 when he visited North America, making a brief incursion into Canada. His garden then was at Scarsdale Villas, but his next address—domicile as well as office—was Southampton Street where there was no garden. If he did not possess them by the time he moved to Gravetye he certainly grew double white peonies from the same stock. Bob Snashfold remembers that some of the birthday peonies had roots and that they were planted in the big border to the left as you went through the pergola from the front door.

34 On his ninety-fourth birthday ninety-four white peonies arrived from Canada, sent by his friend William Ormiston Roy

The early 'thirties were the depression years. Robinson felt keenly for those who were unemployed, and as Harry Pattenden recalls he took on three extra men. Harry remembers the sad end of the young gardener Dickie Langridge who lived on Turner's Hill. It was a cold November day and he had been seen walking about the village that morning. People wondered why he was not at work. Later his clothes were found neatly folded under a clump of bamboos by the Upper Lake. His body was recovered from the water but no one ever understood why he took his own life: he had no unhappy love affair and no other worries. It was immediately after this that Robinson got his men to empty the lake and mud it. Thereafter a massive planting operation took place. Bob

Snashfold tells how they blew up the dam to empty the lake and chased the trout into the Lower Lake. 'We planted a lot of azaleas after that, and at the fringes of where the lake had been we planted trees, moving hollies thirty feet high, about eighteen of them, one hundred yards to the top end. We made a sledge and cut off their lower boughs and dragged them. Then we planted different clematis up them.'

Markham was by now a recognized breeder of clematis and in 1931 was made an Associate of Honour of the Royal Horticultural Society, both for this and for his work in naming plants for them. One of Bob Snashfold's duties was to look after the clematis seedlings at night, keep them clean and put pea sticks for their support. There were between two and three thousand of them. It was Bob who raised 'Ernest Markham', a beautiful petunia-red, by crossing *C. viticella rubra grandiflora* with *jackmannii pallida*. He also bred *C. macropetala* var. 'Markhamii', a blue with a double centre, and helped Markham with his book on clematis, becoming as enthralled with the genus as were Markham and Robinson himself. At Gravetye was the finest collection in Europe.

Percy Picton, Harry Pattenden and his brother Jim, Bob Snashfold and his brother Ernest who was the fruit gardener, were some of the remarkable team of Gravetye gardeners whose memories of William Robinson are still fresh: how they used to see 'Billy' sitting in his chair exercising his arms with dumb-bells; how sometimes he would ask one of them, 'Push me round a little bit', and this was a pleasant change from everyday toil, for one learned a lot from Billy. 'He would point to a plant,' said Bob, 'and ask "What's that?" and if I didn't know he would tell me, and all about it—where its natural home was and who had introduced it into Britain. Next day he would ask me its name and if I had forgotten he would be cross. "What's the use of telling you the name of a plant if you don't remember it!" ' Bob also recalls that when going round the garden it was his habit to take a walking stick and, if he spotted a weed, to push it out with the ferule.

There was the big Austin car. The running-boards were screwed on with wing nuts, and these were unscrewed and the boards fitted to the back of the car to make a ramp for Mr Robinson's wheeled chair. It took three men to load and off-load him. One winter Miss Gilpin made him a woolly cap with ear-flaps that tied under his chin. She brought it out and asked him to put it on: it was a very cold day. He refused. 'Put it on,' she ordered him, and her word was law. But not this time! 'You won't go out unless you put it on,' warned his nurse. He put it on—and then flung it off. This happened five times, and Nurse Gilpin was as good as her word. 'Unload him!' she told the men, and he was duly unloaded and taken back to the house. As well as his own courage and determination it was Nurse Gilpin's care of him in matters like this that enabled him to be as hale and hearty as he was, and to live such a wonderfully full life.

It was quite a holiday when Mr Robinson took one or two of his gardeners with him when going to visit a friend's garden. As when they went to Coolhurst, the home of C. R. Scrase-Dickins, a successful grower of difficult plants who was to be awarded the V.M.H. in 1934. To the gardeners he was a great hand with azaleas, both North American and Indian. His White Indian Azalea, more than ten feet across and growing by a magnolia tree, was a sight to be seen. He also grew the wonderful Himalayan blue poppy *Meconopsis baileyi (betonicifolia)* and it was a triumphant day when they brought home seedlings of it and planted them at Gravetye. Ernest Markham wrote a note about it for the fifteenth edition of *The English Flower Garden*, published in 1933, half a century after its first appearance, describing how each plant attains a height of five feet, developing three or four leafy stems producing fifty large beautiful sky-blue flowers with golden stamens over several weeks.

Scrase-Dickins and three other friends of Robinson's had presented a useful small table to him when he was ninety.

Robinson declared that there were only ten minutes in the life of a pear when it was properly ripe. Markham was the judge of this perfection, and five of them in a punnet lined with vine leaves were always delivered punctually. Pears were Robinson's favourite fruit. Otherwise it was left to the under-gardeners to pick the dessert fruit and place it in the West Porch each morning. Raspberries had to be cut on the stalk with scissors. There was always an abundance of fruit in their seasons: apples, gooseberries, apricots, melons, nectarines, and peaches by the basket-load. An abundance of vegetables too, giving visitors the impression that Mr Robinson was very much a vegetarian. He tended that way, but the good table he always kept was varied with meats of every kind, game, and Gravetye's own trout from the lake. Mary Haslett has a fond memory of decorating the dining table with finger bowls filled with bright little flowers.

Barbara remembers the lift which got Uncle Rob upstairs. It was a constant marvel in its soaring upward and downward. The younger Rosemary thinks of him as an old man in a panama hat and white beard, sitting in a wheelchair with a rug over his knees. 'I remember tea out in a small rose garden where there would first be a teasure hunt for us. The nurses had hidden little trinkets around the garden—a necklace or a bracelet draped over a rose bush (Woolworth's of course but magical to us!). The only thing I remember about tea is red currants and red and white raspberries and cream.'

There was the huge sloping lawn that they used to roll down (the Alpine Meadow), and 'a very dark quiet secret lake surrounded by tall trees, with a neglected and shabby boat-house, and water lilies.' The highlights of their visits were to go to the bedroom with the bloodstains on the floor! The story was that some poor man was looking into a heavy wooden chest when the lid crashed down, leaving his head in the chest and the rest of him outside. The bloodstains are still there.

From their father, perhaps, the Haslett children gained the impression that Uncle Rob disliked Miss Gertrude Jekyll. Be that as it may, when the news came in December 1932 that she had died he did not hesitate about driving the thirty miles to Busbridge to attend her funeral. She was eighty-nine.

Agnes Jekyll, her sister-in-law, was appreciative of that 'long and unselfish expedition'.

> I must write at once to tell you how very touched we all were at your kindness and affection in coming here yesterday, and I am sure it would have pleased Gertrude very greatly to think that you were so near her in spirit.

She asked that he would allow her son Francis to pay him a short visit some day. 'It would give him the greatest pleasure to do so.'

Seven months later came the great celebration of his ninety-fifth birthday. The national press acclaimed the event. Typical were the headlines of the *London Evening News*:

HE CHANGED THE
FACE OF ENGLAND
GRAND OLD MAN OF THE NEW
GARDENING
Flowers His Life's Love

which could not have been better said. Letters of congratulation poured in. Again from Ormiston Roy, to crown the occasion, came a fantastic load of double white peonies, one bloom for each year of his age.

Old members of his staff of *The Garden* and *Gardening Illustrated* days, fellow-gardeners whether garden-owners or employees, admirers of his books whom he had never even met, close friends and friends he had not seen for years—all sent him their tributes. Charles H. Curtis, then managing editor of *The Gardeners' Chronicle*, recalled how 'In the days of my youth while the youngest of the small band of horticultural press men, I used to regard you as "a grave and reverend seigneur", but the years have passed, that little band is sadly depleted, indeed I fancy only you, John Fraser and myself remain. But the passing years have served only to increase my admiration for your genius as a journalist and gardener.' He added: 'You are the Grand Old Man—this does not seem very respectful—of the Horticultural World, so please accept my homage and congratulations . . .' He hoped he would have the pleasure of congratulating him on his 'one hundred not out'.

Another old journalist was J. H. Bentley. 'Forgive my reminding you of my existence. Many years ago I was with you for five years in Lincolns Inn Fields & had the pleasure of working under you upon *Flora & Sylva* and *The English Flower Garden*.' He asked if he might 'come once again to see you, myself, for one moment, for old time's sake it would complete the real delight of such a visit.'

The Spaldings sent a telegram with 'Love and all good wishes from all at Avenue House'; Ellen Willmott 'Millions of good wishes, thousands of congratulations from your old friend.' There was a cable from William Ormiston Roy and the Stewarts, Howard and Ella of Montreal, another from Shanghai from his one-time neighbours the Harpurs. John Nayler, J.P. of East Cowes, the manager of William Robinson's former publishing house and now retired, felt sure that his life must have been a happy one 'because of the great and beneficial work you have done for gardens all over the world. Your books will probably be quoted and utilised hundreds of years from now, when many of our so-called leading politicians are forgotten.'

France honoured him on this memorable birthday by placing his name on the Comité d'Honneur of the Franco-British Association of Horticulture. The accompanying letter referred to Robinson's international reputation, and the members of the Association looked forward to celebrating his century.

Ralph Hall Caine wrote a lengthy eulogy in memory of 'The Father of the English Garden'.

There was a birthday party. H. G. Spicer was there, chairman of the famous firm which vied with Spaldings in supplying William Robinson with fine papers for his books. It was thirty-eight years since they had first met, 'and what a wonderful period to review!' he exclaimed. 'In Gravetye you have a wonderful monument, and though it was beautiful when I first saw it, the beauty has grown and developed in mellowness and ceaseless change all through the years. I cannot think of it, or picture it, without you, or in some modern vandal's hands. So many spots on the earth are spoilt in an attempt to alter nature.'

The Hasletts were there: father, mother, Mary who was nine, Philip,

35 a) His ninety-sixth birthday visitors included his cousin William Haslett (second right), Norah Haslett (on his right) and their daughter May on William Robinson's right with Mary Gilpin

35 b) A posy from Mrs Godwin-King of Stonelands, West Hoathly. She was a regular visitor

seven, Rosemary, four, and Barbara who was just eighteen months old. Other relatives were Sarah Robinson and a younger William Robinson from Belfast who was a nephew. His neighbours were there and friends from farther away who dropped in knowing he would be at home.

The day was gorgeous with heat, tiring even the village children who had come again to dance for him on the playground. They made a special feature for the many guests who gathered at Gravetye to honour him on this day.

One who was not there was Jane Hennessy, an Irish cousin who lived in Lancashire. She wrote hoping Cook had made him a big cake and put on it as many candles as he had years! She had rheumatism and was not well enough this time to come to see him.

Iris, too, was far away, though she had not forgotten the birthday silk handkerchief; but now he had another little companion—Joan, the daughter of his chauffeur Sydney Terry. She was seven and every Sunday morning her father used to take her down to the kitchen, and Miss Gilpin would bring her into the drawing-room where Mr Robinson would be expecting her. He would ask her questions about what she was doing at school.

'In the spring I used to go into the wood near the flat where we lived above the garages and get either a bunch of primroses or bluebells and wild daffodils. He would have a little vase waiting.

'He called me his Little Canary because I wore a yellow twin-set—he gave me one every birthday or for Christmas and Easter. I had to open the parcel in front of him—he liked to see my excitement. He gave me a serviette ring with my name on it. He really loved children.

'Mr Markham had camellias and Mr Robinson used to pick one for me and I took it home and put it in a saucer, as he told me to do. He always told me to love flowers and everything that grows.'

Christmas was as usual that year. A cart went round distributing beef, six pounds to every man employed on the estate, and this was followed by Nurse Gilpin in the big Austin with a gift for every child.

Fittingly 1933 gave him an anniversary present of the fifteenth and last edition of *The English Flower Garden*, and as a final triumph the offer of a knighthood. Ramsay MacDonald was leader of the National Government, and as Ralph Hall Caine wrote in a letter of the 27th of December, 'I was telling the Prime Minister of your splendid life work. How rich it must seem to have earned the well deserved title or description "The Father of the English Flower Garden". We owe so much of the beauty and sweetness of England, the Orchard, and the

Thicket to you. England is the richer because you have passed along Life's way these 90 odd years. The things for which you stand are very close to the Prime Minister's heart and I shall be surprised if he does not find an early opportunity of sending you a word of greeting, official or personal.'

This was followed two days later by a note marked *Private*, again from Ralph Hall Caine, saying that he had received a very interesting and personal letter from the P.M. 'He says it is of course too late to consider any addition to this List, but that your name will receive attention in the next. Of course you will be personally consulted before anything is said or done.'

The offer came, and this was William Robinson's reply:

Hearty thanks to the Prime Minister for the great honour he wished to bestow on me, but owing to my great age, and infirmity, I feel I must leave life as I entered it . . .

The letter was handwritten by Nurse Gilpin and signed by Robinson with an indecipherable scrawl. His sight was failing.

So he ended as plain William Robinson, as he had begun. With the difference that, as Ella Stewart of Montreal said of him, 'He left the world more beautiful than he found it.'

William Robinson's last piece of writing was the foreword to his head gardener's *Clematis*, dated February 1935. The book was published in June, too late for him to see it.

He had been ill since February and Dr Anthony Chadwick had called in Cecil Rowntree, his surgeon. But nothing could be done.

Easter was in April, and during the school holidays Mrs Hester Cobbold took her grandchildren to Gravetye to see the wonderful garden. Poor Annie, the parlourmaid, told her that her master was very ill, and broke down when she said how dreadfully she was afraid he could not be here much longer.

The weather was sublime and Monday the 6th of May the finest day of the whole year with perfect sunshine, warmth and sparkling air. It was King George the Fifth's Jubilee Day, a good excuse for William Robinson to give the children of the village an extra treat: he provided the fireworks, remembering how much he had liked fireworks when he was a boy. He could not enjoy the display himself, for he was lying unconscious, but he had arranged it all beforehand.

All that week the perfect weather went on, the garden basking in its glory. Dorothy Arbuthnot was one of the large crowd who attended the open-air Thanksgiving Service held on the Sunday evening as the climax of the King's Jubilee. But it was of William Robinson they were thinking as they stood among the flowers in the Alpine Meadow he had created and looked up towards his house. 'The flowers on the terrace walls were exquisite,' Mrs Arbuthnot remembered.

He had passed from them that morning, at a very early hour, in the unsullied stillness of dawn when the night clouds were lifting and the birds were beginning to sing.

Epilogue

Immediately after the death of William Robinson the weather broke in storms of sleet and hail. The day of his funeral, Wednesday the 15th of May, was fine though cold, but it did not spoil memories of the grand old man who had lived at Gravetye for half a century. Nor did it make foolish the words of his favourite hymn, 'All things bright and beautiful', sung by the West Hoathly children as they lined the path to the church door from the lych gate he had presented in 1923. They knew the hymn well, for they had always sung it on his birthday.

Along this lane of children his coffin was borne, followed by his staff and tenants. On it was a single sheath of the pure white flowers from the ornamental pear tree in his garden, named for his friend Charles Sargent *Pyrus sargentii*.

The church was crowded, the choral service arranged by Mary Gilpin 'all so beautifully done', as Agnes Jekyll wrote, 'and as he would have himself wished it, with simplicity and beauty and the right feeling of countryside peace and tranquillity.'

Many of his friends went on to Golders Green for the committal service at the crematorium amid the unique and beautiful Garden of Rest he had designed, there joining other friends and those representing various organizations.

In his address, after referring to William Robinson's great work as leader of the horticultural revolution, the Revd. Herbert Trundle spoke of him as a man of marked courtesy, of distinguished presence, and great charm, who loved children and who took a great interest in the ways of birds and animals.

The press of the nation acknowledged his genius. A *New York Times* leader called him 'The World's Grand Old Man of Gardening' and said that 'As our modern American gardening is based largely upon the school which William Robinson founded, our debt to him is no less great than that of English gardeners.'

La Revue Horticole praised his work in creating good relations between French and English horticulturists, and recalled his two books, *Gleanings from French Gardens* and *Parks and Gardens of Paris* and his friendship with Henry Vilmorin, one result of which was the translation and adaptation of the celebrated and encyclopaedic *The Vegetable Garden*.

The Canadian papers lauded him, attracting the attention of a Montreal merchant who telephoned William Ormiston Roy to say he had been born in West Hoathly and knew Gravetye Manor well as a boy. To Ormiston Roy himself William Robinson was a hero, and 'like everyone else who simply worshipped him and his great monument, Gravetye Manor' he hoped his estate would become a national park.

The Times reminded its readers that William Robinson had begun his crusade in the days when it was customary for owners of country places to allow their gardens to be bare and dismal for nine months of the year so that they might enjoy a floral display during the other three, and that Robinson showed how it was possible to have a garden gay for eight months and charged with interest during the other four.

'Untold numbers of gardeners owe him a debt of gratitude,' it added, 'of which they are today barely conscious, for he, more than any other man, has shown them what a ceaseless store of delight can be found in tending a garden.'

Country Life had published some of his books. Now it recorded that 'In William Robinson the garden world has lost a figure who cannot be replaced until a practical gardener, skilled with his pen, of indomitable and pugnacious energy, evolves yet another complete system of gardening related to modern architecture—if such a thing is conceivable.' It recalled Gravetye 'where it was a delight and a privilege to share the old gentleman's sunny happiness in the matured beauty of his great garden', and where, despite the fact that for the last twenty-five years of his life he had been a cripple confined to a wheeled chair or a caterpillar wagonette, he continued to take as close an interest as ever in every plant, almost in every tree.

His own *Gardening Illustrated* devoted a page of obituary to its founder, with a photograph of his home seen from the heather garden, and one of the grand old man himself looking over the wall to his Alpine Meadow. Herbert Cowley had been editor now for twelve years and was probably the author of the article: it was someone who knew him well and who knew Gravetye. He wrote that the gardens at Gravetye Manor had never looked so beautiful—magnolias, camellias, azaleas and prunuses, all were in profusions of blossom over carpets of spring flowers. It had been said of William Robinson that gardening was at once his hobby and his religion. The fact was that he had no other hobby, and no other religion. It was difficult to convey to anyone the sense of holiness that he found in a garden.

The appreciations had started on the day of his death with a broadcast by the B.B.C. Lady Moore was one who heard it. She wrote to Mary Gilpin: 'When the wireless broadcaster began "All garden lovers will regret to hear ..." I knew that it was our old friend.' She hoped that the end of his long life was peace. 'For you, Mrs Matheson, and Annie, Sir Frederick and I feel great sympathy. We feel we are parting with three welcoming faces in you three, as well as an old friend.'

Mary Gilpin received more than a hundred letters of sympathy. They expressed a loss as deeply felt as their indebtedness to her for the selfless care she had given him. H. G. Spicer declared that 'it is to you he has owed the enjoyment in life that has come to him throughout this period during which he has been so crippled.' E. M. Swinburne-Hanham wrote: 'Mr Robinson is the last of my father's friends and I feel a strong link with the past is severed. Dear Gravetye ... so much of Mr Robinson's happiness was due to you.'

Cissy Wallis, the doctor's daughter, addressed her as 'Dearest John Gilpin', which was her nickname in hospital days, in allusion to Cowper's poem. She wrote: 'I can't really believe it is all over because for so many years you and he and Gravetye have stood for that particular kind of charm that cast its spell on us from the time we first came over with Da.' She recalled the thrill of seeing glow-worms on hot summer evenings, and thought she had never met anyone who radiated such perfect calmness as did Mr Robinson. Gravetye, she added, must seem a very empty theatre now that its star was gone, and exclaimed delightedly, 'I can't help thinking how nice he looked the last time I saw him with his little bow tie so jauntily tied!'

From Rhoda Harris came a letter brimming with affection.

Dear, dear Nurse,
How good of you to phone—so many thanks. I longed to ring you up tonight—for *your* sake I don't—but write instead. You will know—& feel—our love & prayers round you—'As the day began to dawn on the first day of the week'—as with my beloved Mother ... it is the hour of the nearest moment to the Greater Life, isn't it?—& the right time for freedom to come. So dear Nurse ... I feel we can share with you very closely—& we do.

She signed it 'From us old 5'.

Another came from 'Sudds' who was Miss Suddaby, so often at Gravetye as an extra nurse. She also had been with William Robinson when he died and stayed on for another few days. 'It was wretched leaving all the beauty of Gravetye last Friday & there was so much to say that my heart was too full to say anything, & passing all the familiar spots through the woods brought many sad thoughts, that I cannot begin to think what it will mean to you as the days go by. I do sincerely hope things will go well with you.'

E. Agnes Druce of Rustington looked forward to what Mary Gilpin's future might be. 'Shall you be living in the dear little house Mr Robinson planned for you some years ago?'

This was Holms Cottage (meaning hollies) which Robinson had commissioned Mervyn Macartney to design. He had Mary Gilpin well in mind when he made his will. He left her life tenancy of Holms Cottage free of rates, taxes and insurance, with underwood for her fires and, whether in his service or not, £1,000 with an annuity of £350, and shares in the London Cremation Co. Ltd. to the value of £100.

To Ernest Markham he left £1,000 and the life tenancy of the Moat, for himself and his widow; to Annie Williams £370, to Mrs Theobald an annuity of £26, to Connie Williams £70, to Mary Clarke £40, with 25 guineas to each of his other indoor and outdoor servants.

A bequest of £100 went to the local cottage hospital, a continuing supply of underwood to the Sackville College almshouses, and £250 in trust to provide the children's annual party at Gravetye.

The Haslett children benefitted handsomely, and he did not forget his Belfast namesake or his god-daughter Rosemary Spalding. To Iris Poynter he left fifty guineas. There were bequests of pictures to various of his friends.

Gravetye Manor itself, its gardens and its woodlands, he left to the nation, to be held and utilized for the purpose of State forestry. There were strict conditions: the house, gardens, orchards and other grounds round about were not to be used for the purpose of lectures, research or technical instruction, 'but the trees, woods and landscapes shall be the only teachers'. The house was to be let and the proceeds go to aid State forestry.

The woodlands were to preserved for the growth of timber, and evergreen forest trees, and as a sanctuary for birds and foxes, badgers and other indigenous animals and birds.

The house and grounds were to be free to the public at least one day a week, the woods on Thursday as before.

He left the residue of his property equally between The Gardeners' Royal Benevolent Institute and the Shipwrecked Fishermen and Mariners' Royal Benevolent Society. The latter may seem a strange bequest, for neither Gravetye nor William Robinson had any connection with the sea or sea-going folk. It happened because he heard a broadcast appeal on the Society's behalf and was deeply touched by it.

36 William Robinson in 1922 at the age of eighty-four

Epilogue

The amount he left was £95,954 gross estate, net £72,783.

The contents of Gravetye were auctioned, the more valuable books, pictures and furniture in London, the remainder at Gravetye itself. Half of West Hoathly village came, some setting foot in the house for the first time and looking curiously at everything there was to be seen, till so recently belonging to the old man who had been their benefactor in so many ways. Local friends came, dealers from near and far. The auctioneer was Jack Mitchell of Turner, Rudge and Turner, East Grinstead, his rostrum a chair on top of a table, a rug round his knees because the house was so cold, although it was July. The wood fires no longer burned in the grates.

The sale lasted for two days. The prices realized pleased the auctioneer. 'Better than they did in London,' was his comment.

Mourning for him passed into thankfulness that William Robinson had ensured Gravetye's safe keeping and that its gardens would still be there 'for the delight of his fellow countrymen', as 'G.M.W., Horsham' phrased it in a newspaper paragraph. But before it was known how the terms of his will would be administered by the Ministry of Agriculture, or even if—because of the cost of maintenance—the gift would be accepted, a clamour broke out in such headlines as GRAVETYE: *What is its Future?*

Frederick Hanbury, whose rock garden at nearby Brockhurst was world famous, wrote to *The Times* appealing for the gardens and house to be handed over to the National Trust. The cost of maintenance could be avoided, he suggested, by letting to a responsible garden lover on suitable terms including a small rental. The land that Mr Robinson thought should go with the house covered about fifty acres, but this included the beautiful Alpine Meadow and the lake, which needed very little attention.

'The preservation of the life's work of this great gardener,' he wrote, 'would form a lasting memorial that we know would be in accordance with his wishes.' He had just visited the garden afresh and was amazed at the great improvements and additions to the plants that had been made up to the end.

His letter was written in June 1935, a month after Robinson's death. The picture was different in 1938, the gardens overgrown and neglected. 'To such a lover of flowers as William Robinson it would have been a grievous disappointment to know that his work would be wasted within three years of his death,' wrote a sorrowful correspondent. He complained that the garden staff was small and inadequate.

What had happened?

[234]

37 Aerial views of the Gravetye Estate showing the manor house and above left the great circular fruit garden. The surrounding woodlands were of Robinson's planting and his rich bequest to the nation

Epilogue

The Forestry Commission had appointed a committee, of which Will Ingwersen was a valuable member, but Percy Picton, Harry Pattenden, Bob Snashfold and, above all, Ernest Markham, were no longer there, to name only four of the faithful team that had kept Gravetye's garden in such perfection. Percy Picton had left in 1932, Harry Pattenden early in 1935, his brother Jim the following year, Bob Snashfold in 1937; and in December of that year Ernest Markham had died at the early age of fifty-seven.

The house lay empty for four years. In November 1939 Captain O. C. W. Johnsen took over the lease. He also took over a wilderness of weeds. He was a keen gardener and installed a head gardener and five other men. Gradually the garden was pulled back from disorder—only to suffer the call-up of the gardeners.

The first Canadian soldiers arrived in England in December 1939. Gravetye was soon taken over for billeting officers and all up the drive was an arsenal of small arms and other war equipment. The War Department was now responsible for dealing with the garden. Tom Pattenden was spared the call-up because he was crippled. He was put to digging up the rose garden for growing vegetables.

With the war over, the Forestry Commission got down to the task of making a working calendar for the woodlands, to carry out the terms of William Robinson's will. He was to be respected, for after all he had pioneered the planting of exotic trees. He had said in his will, 'I give the Estate as evidence of the value of the evergreen forest tree . . . my hope is that the plan will be followed as such trees come from North America and other lands—all to be planted in the forest way and not as specimens.'

The Forestry Commission accepted his wishes.

As for the garden, in 1953 the Johnsens, having returned and again got it into order, relinquished the lease, and once more the place lay empty. From 1955 there were three more years of tenancy, but it was not until it was leased to a local company in 1958 that the future of Gravetye Manor and its garden was assured.

Peter Herbert was installed as managing director. He looked round the place in dismay but some curiosity. It had belonged to William Robinson, a notable amateur gardener and writer on gardening. The house was all right, sound and with many interesting features, though some conversion would have to be done. The once-famous gardens? They were in a deplorable state with weeds and the rotting timbers of countless pergolas. But the bones were there. He set about the job of getting it into acceptable condition, indoors and out.

It was a tough assignment even with all the labour and expertise he needed, but gradually it took shape and the job was finished. He moved in furniture carefully selected to accord with the lovely panelling, the fireplaces, the feel of country-life perfection.

Yet there was more to Gravetye than that. He had glanced through Robinson's books but now began reading them with a closer eye, exploring house and grounds against the chronology of *Gravetye Manor*. Now he began to understand why William Robinson had done this and that, the continual changes he had made to improve, and what he might be doing were he living today. The book was a perfect guide. From it and from the chapters in *The English Flower Garden* Peter Herbert took his cue. He felt that whatever he did in the future he would be on sure ground. For now he was looking at Gravetye through the eyes of William Robinson.

Bibliography

Allan, Mea *E. A. Bowles & his Garden at Myddelton House 1865–1954*. Faber & Faber, 1973

Bailey, L. H. *The Standard Cyclopedia of Horticulture*. 3 vols. Macmillan, 1935

Bowles, E. A. *My Garden in Summer*. T. C. & E. C. Jack, 1914

Duthie, Ruth 'Some Notes on William Robinson'. *Journal of the Garden History Society*, Vol. II, 3

    Addendum to Betty Massingham's 'William Robinson, a Portrait'. See Vol. VI, 2

Elliott, J. Wilkinson *Adventures of a Horticulturist*. Privately printed at Point Loma, California, 1935

Farrer, Reginald *My Rock Garden*. Arnold, 1927

Fletcher, H. R. *The Story of the Royal Horticultural Society, 1804–1968*. Oxford University Press, 1969

Gaunt, William *The Pre-Raphaelite Tragedy*. Jonathan Cape, 1975

Gray, Asa *Manual of the Botany of the Northern United States*. 1st ed. revised. Ivison & Phinney, 1858

    Gray's Manual of Botany. Largely rewritten, Merritt Lyndon Fernald. 8th ed. D. Van Nostrand, 1970

Guillaumin, André *Les Fleurs de Jardins*. Editions Lechevalier, Tome I, 1929

Hadfield, Miles *Pioneers in Gardening*. Routledge & Kegan Paul, 1955

    A History of British Gardening. Spring Books, 1960

    Ed. *The Gardener's Album*. Hulton Press, 1954

Hedrick, U. P. *A History of Horticulture in America, to 1860*. Oxford University Press, New York, 1950

Hellyer, Arthur *The Shell Guide to Gardens*. Heinemann, 1977

Hole, S. Reynolds *The Six of Spades*. Blackwood, 1872

    Memories. Arnold, 1892

    Our Gardens. Dent, 1899

Hunt, Peter *The Shell Gardens Book*. Phoenix House, 1964

Hussey, Christopher *Life of Sir Edwin Lutyens*. Country Life, 1935

Hyams, Edward *The English Garden*. Thames & Hudson, 1964

Ingwersen, Will *Manual of Alpine Plants*. Ingwersen & Dunnsprint, 1978

Bibliography

Kelway, James *Garden Paeonies*. Eyre & Spottiswood, 1954

Le Lièvre, Audrey *Miss Willmott of Warley: her Life and Gardens*. Faber & Faber, 1980

Loudon, J. C. *An Encyclopaedia of Gardening*. Longman, Hurst, Rees, Orme & Brown, 1822

Massingham, Betty *Miss Jekyll: Portrait of a Great Gardener*. Country Life, 1966

   Turn on the Fountains: the Life of Dean Hole. Gollancz, 1974

   'William Robinson, a Portrait'. *Journal of the Garden History Society*, Vol. VI, 1

Morton, Earl of 'The Tree and Garden Books at Gravetye Manor'. *Journal of the Royal Horticultural Society*, Vol. LXXXII, April 1957

Nelson, Charles and Brady, Aidan Eds. *Irish Gardening and Horticulture*. Royal Horticultural Society of Ireland, 1979

Sutton, S. B. *Charles Sprague Sargent of the Arnold Arboretum*. Harvard University Press, 2nd ed. 1856

Synge, Patrick M. Ed. Royal Horticultural Society *Dictionary of Gardening*. Oxford University Press, 2nd ed. 1956

Taylor, Geoffrey *Some Nineteenth Century Gardeners*. Skeffington, 1951

   The Victorian Flower Garden. Skeffington, 1952

Webster, A. D. *The Regent's Park and Primrose Hill*. Greening, 1911

Wolseley, Viscountess 'Historic Houses of Sussex'. *Sussex County Magazine*, No. 16

THE WRITINGS OF WILLIAM ROBINSON

BOOKS (*In the following, dates prefacing titles denote year of first publication: those after titles the edition or editions consulted by the author*)

1868 **Gleanings from French Gardens:** *comprising an account of such features of French Horticulture as are most worthy of adoption in British Gardens*. Frederick Warne, 2nd ed. 1869

1869 **The Parks, Promenades and Gardens of Paris** *described and considered in relation to the wants of our own cities and of public and private gardens*. John Murray, 2nd ed. 1878

1870 **Alpine Flowers for English Gardens.** John Murray, 1870; 3rd ed. 1903

   Mushroom Culture: *its extension and improvement*. Frederick Warne, 1870. Later in 'Robinson's Country Series'.

   The Wild Garden: *or our groves and shrubberies made beautiful by the naturalisation of hardy exotic plants. With a chapter on the garden of British Wild Flowers*. John Murray, 1870; The Scolar Press, 1977

Bibliography

1871 **A Catalogue of Hardy Perennials.** John Murray, 1871
Hardy Flowers: *Descriptions of upwards of thirteen hundred of the most ornamental species, and directions for their arrangement.* Frederick Warne, 1871
The Subtropical Garden: *or beauty of form in the flower garden.* John Murray, 1871
1880 **God's Acre Beautiful:** *or the Cemeteries of the future.* The Garden Office, 1880; 1883 ed. Scribner & Welford
1881 **Asparagus Culture:** *the Best Methods Employed in England and France.* With James Barnes. George Routledge and Sons, 1881. 'Robinson's Country Series'
1883 **The English Flower Garden:** *Style, position and arrangement; followed by a description, alphabetically arranged, of all the plants best suited for its embellishment; their culture, and positions suited for each.* John Murray, 1883. Subsequent editions with different sub-titles. 1st ed. 1883; 3rd ed. 1893; 10th ed. 1906; 15th ed. 1933
1889 **Cremation and Urn Burial:** *or The Cemeteries of the Future.* A cheaper form of *God's Acre Beautiful* and with additions. Cassell, 1889
1892 **Garden Design and Architects' Gardens.** John Murray, 1892
1907 **The Garden Beautiful**, *Home Woods and Home Landscape.* John Murray, 1907
1911 **Gravetye Manor:** *or, Twenty Years' Work round an old Manor House.* John Murray, 1911
1912 **The Virgin's Bower:** *Clematis, Climbing Kinds and their Culture at Gravetye Manor.* John Murray, 1912
1914 'Civil War and Party Lawyers' (Pamphlet). Farm and Home Office, 1914
Home Landscapes. John Murray, 1914
1917 **My Wood Fires and Their Story**. Country Life, 1917
1924 **Wood Fires for the Country House and Cottage.** Extended form of *My Wood Fires* ... John Murray, 1924

PERIODICALS

The Garden. Founded 25 November 1871. Vacated editorial chair 1899. Sold magazine 1919. Magazine incorporated with *Homes and Gardens* 1927
La Semaine Française. Founded 1878. Ceased publication 1883
Gardening (later *Gardening Illustrated*). Founded 1879. Sold magazine 1919. Magazine incorporated with *The Gardeners' Chronicle* 1956
The Garden Annual, Almanack & Address Book. Founded 1881

Bibliography

Farm and Home. Founded 4 March 1882. Taken over by Benn Bros. 1920
Woods and Forests. Founded 1883. Merged with *The Garden* 1886
Cottage Gardening. Founded 12 October 1892. Ceased publication 1898
Flora and Sylva. Founded 1903. Ceased publication 1905

FOREWORDS

The Amateur Gardener's Calendar, Jane Loudon. Ed. and revised 1869 and
    again 1870, with prefaces
The Horticulturist, J. C. Loudon. 1871
The Vegetable Garden, MM Vilmorin-Andrieux. 1885
Scented Flowers and Fragrant Leaves, Donald Macdonald. 1895
French Market-Gardening, John Weathers. 1909
The Herbaceous Garden, Mrs Alice Martineau. 1913
*A Garden Flora: trees and flowers grown in the garden at Nymans, by L. Messel
    1890–1919*, written by his daughter. 1919
Climbing Plants, William Watson. 1915
Clematis, Ernest Markham. 1935

Index

References to plates are in italics

Index

Index

Index

Index

Index

Water lilies, 167–8
West Garden, 154–8, 179
Wood fires, 174–6
Woodland garden, 188
Woodland rides, 182
Gray, Dr Asa, 100, 103, 105, 107, 116, 123, 129; *13*
  Botany for Young People, 129
Gray, Mrs Asa, 100
Great Dixter, 109, 187
Great Fruit Show, 75
Greece, 117, 170, 173
Groom, James, 135
  Apple, The, 135

Hall, Jane, 172
Hanbury, Frederick J., 234
Handfield, Colonel Charles, 20
Harcourt, Sir William, 130
Hardy Flowers, 108, 111, 127, 137, 179
Harpur family, 224
Harpur-Crewe, the Rev. A., 140
Harrington, Earl of, 47
Harris family, 196
  Audrey, 196
  Cecil G., of Moatlands, 196
  Rhoda, 196, 231
  William, 196
Haslett family, *35a*
  Barbara, 222, 226
  Children, 232
  Mary, 222, 224
  Norah (*née* Macan), 224
  Philip, 224
  Rosemary, 222, 226
  Visits to Gravetye, 222–4
  Dr William, 193, 195, 213, 216, 224
Haussmann, Baron Georges Eugène, 57, 61
Hay, Roy, 121
Henley, May, *see* Snashfold
Hennessy, Jane, 226
Henry, Augustine, 201
Herbert, Peter, 236, 237
Hibberd, James Shirley, 49, 125–7
Hibiscus elatus, 48
Higham Court, 144
Highclere, 138
Hippomane mancinella, 47
Hobday, E., 135
  Fruit Culture for Profit, 135
Hole,

Caroline, 122, 160
S. Reynolds, 49, 50, 79, 99, 114, 122–3, 136, 140, 160, 181, 207
  Help with his garden, 160
  Our Gardens, 95
Holland & Hannen, 178
Holmes, Oliver Wendell, 107, 113, 116
Holms Cottage, 174, 232
Home Landscapes, 200
Homes and Gardens, 124, 215–16
Hooker, Joseph D., 23, 98, 105, 107, 117, 119
Hooper, W. H., 97
Horticultural history, 75
Horticulture, revolution in, 229
Hovey, C. M., of Boston, 207
Hugill, J. H. & Co., 174
Hugo, Konig, 169
Hull, 55
  Botanic Garden, 28, 30, 41, 80
Humphreys, Henry Noel, 123, 180
Hunnewell Arboretum, 105
Hunnewell, H. H., 100, 105
Hunt, Holman, 93
Huxley, T. H., 119
Hyde, H., 137

India, 48
Ingram, William, 160
Ingwersen, Walter E. Th., 214
  Paul, 214
  Will, 214
Inner Circle, 25
Inskip, Mr, barrister, 196
Ipomoea bona-nox, 46
Ireland, 36, 56, 98, 106, 152, 170, 172
  Horticulture in, 20
  National Land League, 145
  Royal Horticultural Society, 20

Jalmain & Durand, 72
Jekyll,
  Agnes, 223, 229
  Gertrude, 114, 135–6, 140, 142, 179, 180, 201
    William Robinson attends funeral, 223
  Sir Herbert, 114, 187
Jenkins, nurseryman, 25
Johnsen, Captain O. C. W., 236
Johnson-Walsh, Rev. Sir Hunt, Bt., 20, 172

Index

Index

Index

Index

The Fantasy and Mystery
Stories of F. Scott Fitzgerald

The Fantasy and Mystery Stories of F. Scott Fitzgerald

Selected and Introduced by
PETER HAINING

ROBERT HALE · LONDON

Selection and Introduction © Peter Haining 1991
First published in Great Britain 1991

ISBN 0 7090 4612 X

Robert Hale Limited
Clerkenwell House
Clerkenwell Green
London EC1R 0HT

Photoset in North Wales by
Derek Doyle & Associates, Mold, Clwyd.
Printed in Great Britain by
St Edmundsbury Press, Bury St Edmunds, Suffolk.
Bound by WBC Bookbinders Ltd, Bridgend, Glamorgan.

For
BILL LOFTS
Friend and Critic

'Draw your chair up close to the edge of the precipice and I'll tell you a story ...'

F. Scott Fitzgerald
Notebook, *c*. 1938

Contents

Introduction

In 1918, not long past his twenty-first birthday, F. Scott Fitzgerald wrote a rather idiosyncratic list of the things he was interested in: 'The influence of night, rather bad women, personality, fanaticism, very good women and the supernatural.' Though, at the time, he still had to get his first novel published – indeed, his initial attempt entitled *The Romantic Egotist* had already been turned down by a New York publisher – in those few words he summarized virtually all the themes which in the years that followed were to make him one of the most famous figures of twentieth-century literature.

But while Fitzgerald's classic novels, such as *This Side of Paradise, The Beautiful and the Damned* and *The Great Gatsby*, all of which typify the 'Jazz Age', are as familiar to modern readers as the basic facts of his legendary life style, his fascination with the supernatural – embodying as it does both fantasy and mystery – may come as something of a surprise. Yet the fact remains that he was a writer who was drawn to the subject in his childhood and never abandoned it during his rumbustious life which alternated from drunken playboy to writer of the highest literary talent.

Probably only one of Fitzgerald's fantasy stories is well-known, the novella 'The Diamond as Big as The Ritz' written in 1922, and subsequently used as the title story of a collection of his more typical stories of the lives and loves of America's gilded young men and women of the twenties. But in actual fact this 'wild sort of extravaganza' as Fitzgerald himself called it, was far from his first venture into the realms of fantasia – and its influence was not to stop there, as Malcolm Cowley declared in an introduction to a 1963 collection containing the story:

Written in the winter of 1921–22, 'The Diamond as Big as The Ritz' states a theme that would often recur in his work. A middle-class boy falls in love with the heiress to a great fortune and she returns his love, but the boy is murdered by her family or destroyed by her wealth. 'The Diamond' can have a happy ending – at least for the lovers – because it is a fantasy; but the fable would reappear in *The Great Gatsby* and there it would be carried to its tragic conclusion. Having fallen in love with the rich Mrs Buchanan, Gatsby would be murdered as efficiently as were the visitors to Braddock Washington's diamond mountain.

9

Paul Rosenfeld in his *Men Seen: Twenty-Four Modern Authors* (1925) has spotted a further significance in the tale that it could well be a satire. 'Mr Braddock Washington,' he wrote, 'the richest and most profoundly unsympathetic man in the world, looks dangerously like a jazz age portrait of the father of the country.'

Because it is so readily accessible, 'The Diamond as Big as The Ritz' is not included in these pages – but the earlier fantasy and mystery tales written during Fitzgerald's formative years as well as those of his maturity and decline most certainly are, both as memorial to the man on the fiftieth anniversary of his death, as well as to ensure him a place among the outstanding writers in this genre of fiction, among whom he has so far signally failed to be placed.

The origins of what Robert Sklar in his study *F. Scott Fitzgerald: The Last Laocoön* (1967) has called the writer's 'feeling for the supernatural' can be traced to his youth, and even before that in the influence of his forebears.

Francis Scott Key Fitzgerald the only son of Edward and Mollie Fitzgerald was born on 24 September 1896 in St Paul, Minnesota. On his mother's side, Scott's grandfather had been an Irish immigrant who, by all accounts, was possessed of that instinctive love of folklore and superstition that is the inheritence of all Gaelic men and women; while on his father's side there was an actual skeleton in the cupboard: an aunt, Mrs Suratt, had apparently been hanged for complicity in the murder of President Lincoln!

Scott's father, Edward Fitzgerald, had been raised on a farm in Maryland and was a quiet, rather diffident man who for a time ran a small furniture business until it failed, and then became a salesman for Proctor and Gamble. Mollie Fitzgerald, however, was quite the opposite: an eccentric lady by nature, outspoken in her views, careless in her appearance, and an omnivorous reader. Friends of Scott Fitzgerald later recalled her as 'a witch-like old lady' who always seemed to be going to or from the local library with an armful of books under her arm. Perhaps not surprisingly, her son's attitude towards her alternated between embarrassment and devotion.

Both parents spoiled their precocious and imaginative son – a situation which may partly be explained by the fact that they had lost two of their older children, both girls. From an early age, too, the couple encouraged in him an interest in reading, though while his father favoured literature, his mother had a taste for what Scott later referred to as 'bad books', meaning the lurid, yellow-back fiction of the time.

Like most children, the first books which were read to him were fairy-tales – and the impression they had on him was to remain vivid throughout his life. Indeed, in one of his notebooks written years later can be found an observation inspired by such tales, as well as the evidence that he had something of a sweet tooth.

'In children's books forests are sometimes made out of all-day suckers,' he wrote, 'boulders out of peppermints and rivers out of gently flowing, rippling molasses taffy. Such books are less fantastic than they sound, for such localities exist, and one day a girl, herself little more than a child, sat dejected in the middle of one. It was all hers, she owned it, she owned Candy Town.'

Fitzgerald soon graduated from nursery tales to the adventure stories of Sir Walter Scott and G.A. Henty, by way of a thrilling series of paperback novels with the collective title, *Raiding With Morgan*, which were supplied by his mother. His father read him the poems of Edgar Allan Poe and Lord Byron's 'Prisoner of Chillon' – and 'their mystery echoed in his soul' according to one of his biographers, Andrew Turnbull, who adds that on a trip to Niagara the boy heard 'enchanting voices in the dusk.'

These ghostly voices were to echo through his work when the urge to become a writer consumed him.

A short while later, Fitzgerald senior introduced his pubescent son to the stories of Sherlock Holmes – and by so doing seemingly gave him the inspiration to write his first story, a tale of mystery, scribbled out in an exercise-book in 1908. Years later in 1934, in a letter to a friend, E.S. Oliver in Baltimore, Fitzgerald confessed:

> The first help I ever had in writing in my life was from my father who read an utterly imitative Sherlock Holmes story of mine and pretended to like it.

Though no trace of this composition has survived, it is significant that Fitzgerald's first literary attempt should have been a story of this kind. The plot, apparently, concerned a necklace that had been hidden in a trap-door under a carpet, and described its recovery by the great sleuth of Baker Street. Imitative though the tale may have been – in its author's judgement – it sparked his desire to be a writer: and within a year another story, also a mystery, became his first published work.

The new story was called 'The Mystery of the Raymond Mortgage' and it was published in the October 1909 issue of his school journal, *The St Paul Academy Magazine*. In introducing the story to its readers, a note about the author declared, 'young Scottie is always bubbling over with suppressed knowledge and has excelled in his English classes'. It *didn't* mention that he devoted himself to this study to the exclusion of many of his other lessons, and that several of the teachers had actually caught him writing stories behind the shield of mathematics and Greek textbooks!

According to Andre Le Vot in his biography *F.Scott Fitzgerald* (1984), the youngster's story for the *Academy* magazine 'reflected his taste for the mystery stories he devoured then.' Curiously, in the otherwise reliable *Encyclopedia of Mystery and Detection* (1976), the authors, Chris

Steinbrunner and Otto Penzler, describe the story as 'flawed in plot' and declare that his contribution to the mystery genre was 'negligible'. Another biographer, Arthur Mizener in *The Far Side of Paradise* (1951) is more accurate – as well as generous – in his assessment of this literary début.

'Having become an expert on the detective story on his own initiative,' says Mizener, 'he wrote "The Mystery of the Raymond Mortgage". It is, for a schoolboy, a skilfully plotted little murder story and, in its sedulous imitation of the style of such works, often unconsciously very funny.'

Though we have no record of how Fitzgerald's contemporaries reacted to his fiction, he was encouraged enough at seeing his work in print to produce three more tales for the magazine: two romantic stories set during the Civil War, 'A Debt of Honour' and 'The Room with the Green Blinds'; plus an all-action tale of schoolboy football, American-style entitled 'Reade, Substitute Right Half'.

It was when Fitzgerald entered Princeton University in September 1913 as a seventeen-year-old that he began to write in earnest. Coincidental with this, he came under the influence of two men who furthered his interest in mystery and the supernatural. The first was Father Sigourney Webster Fay, an Episcopalian who had been converted to Catholicism; and the second, a young Irish author and critic, Shane Leslie, a friend of Father Fay.

Aside from being a priest, Father Fay was a man of erudition and learning, and he was to have a profound effect upon young Scott until his sudden death in a flu epidemic in 1919. Leslie, also a Catholic, was then visiting America, and with Fay introduced the Princeton freshman to the apparently disparate traditions of Catholic intellectualism and ghost-stories. Leslie had himself discovered these traditions while studying at Eton where the Provost was the famed ghost-story writer, M.R. James. At Eton, too, he had come across the supernatural works of Robert Hugh Benson and the imaginative tales of H.G. Wells – both of which he promoted at Princeton in general and to Fitzgerald in particular.

Some years later, in 1935, Shane Leslie published his own *Ghost Book* into which he poured 'the drift and silt of a life-long interest in ghosts.' And in introducing the collection, he insisted that it was possible to believe in both religion and ghosts for, 'it is not impossible or uncomfortable to study psychical research while occupying a static view of revealed Faith', he wrote.

Such a belief intrigued and excited the young Fitzgerald, and when Father Fay described a ghost that he had himself seen, Scott's conviction about the supernatural was shaped for life. With the passing months, Fay and Leslie came to nurse high ambitions for their pupil as they read examples of his work – a fact which Shane Leslie confirmed years later in a letter to the *Times Literary Supplement* of 6 November 1959. He wrote,

Monsignor Fay and perhaps myself induced Fitzgerald to believe he was the future Catholic novelist for the United States, a parallel to Hugh Benson in this country.

The first influence of these two men on Fitzgerald's work is to be seen in a short story that he wrote in 1915 entitled 'The Ordeal'. It is concerned with the temptations faced by a young novice about to take his monastic vows – and, apart from its elements of supernaturalism, which earn it a place in this collection, is also of note because of Fitzgerald's statement at this time that he was 'nearly sure that I will become a priest.'

'The Ordeal' was published in the University journal, the *Nassau Literary Magazine*, in June 1915, and the strange elements which emerge during this account of the clash between spiritual good and earthly evil have been described by Andrew Turnbull as 'powerfully dramatised'. It is perhaps only because the author chose to incorporate part of the story into another tale, 'Benediction' which was published by *Smart Set* in February 1920, that the story is today little known, although it is possible that Fitzgerald may have nursed misgivings about it because, as he said in a later letter to Shane Leslie, 'it has come in for the most terrible lashing from the American Catholic intelligentsia.'

Today's reader must judge for himself.

After Fitzgerald left Princeton, joining the regular army in November 1917, he still kept in touch with his two mentors. He corresponded regularly, enthusiastically reporting on his work in progress – in particular, his first novel which he planned to call *The Romantic Egotist*. In February 1918, for instance, he wrote to Shane Leslie from Fort Leavenworth, Kansas enclosing a section of the manuscript.

' "The Devil" is a chapter you can read without knowing the story', he said. 'What do you think of it?'

Leslie responded enthusiastically about the episode, in which the central character, Amory, has a nightmarish encounter with a mysterious, club-footed figure and is then haunted by footsteps in the street which seem to be *leading* rather than following him. The Irish writer promised to recommend the finished book to his own American publisher, Charles Scribner in New York.

Encouraged by these comments, Scott completed the book and in May 1918 dispatched it to Scribner's. At the same time he dropped a line to Shane Leslie with an appropriate aside, 'Well, may Saint Robert Hugh Benson appear to Scribner in a dream!'

Although there was to be no supernatural intervention on Fitzgerald's behalf, for *The Romantic Egotist* was rejected by Scribner's, it was returned with the suggestion that extensive rewriting might well make it publishable. Scott set about doing this with a will – and in September 1919, *This Side of Paradise*, as the work had now been retitled, was accepted. The young man from Minnesota was about to become a published novelist as well as a short-story writer.

One further curious tale remains to be recorded about this period of Scott Fitzgerald's life, and it concerns the death of Father Fay. For Fitzgerald was convinced he had a premonition of the Monsignor's passing.

By the beginning of 1919 Scott had met and fallen in love with the beautiful Zelda Sayre, and on the night of 10 January, as they sat together on a couch in the Sayres' living-room, 'we were seized by uncontrollable fear,' Zelda confessed later in a letter to H.D. Piper. 'The following day we learned of Father Fay's death ...'

It was probably no surprise to those who knew of Fitzgerald's admiration for the father that he decided to dedicate *This Side of Paradise*, 'To Sigourney Fay'.

There is also another story which Fitzgerald wrote during his time at Princeton for the *Nassau Literary Magazine* which can be categorized as fantasy. It is 'Tarquin of Cheapside', published in the magazine in April 1917, and it has the distinction of being the first of his tales to be reviewed. This fact has come to light from a letter Fitzgerald wrote to Maxwell Perkins, his editor at Scribner's, in August 1922:

'Tarquin of Cheapside' first appeared in the *Nassau Literary Magazine*, and Katherine Fullerton Gerould reviewing the issue for the *Daily Princetonian* gave it high praise, called it 'beautifully written' and tickled me with the first public praise my writing has ever had. When H.L.Mencken reprinted it in the *Smart Set* (in February 1921), it drew letters of praise from George O'Neill, the poet, and Zoe Atkins. Structurally, it is almost perfect and next to 'The Offshore Pirate' I like it better than any story I have ever written.

Maxwell Perkins, however, did not share Fitzgerald's estimation of the tale, and asked him to exclude it from his short story collection, *Tales of the Jazz Age*, when this was to be published in September 1922. Perkins explained to his author, 'The crime is a repugnant one for it involves violence, generally requires unconsciousness, and is associated with negroes.'

But Scott, supported by Zelda, upon whose verdicts concerning his work he placed great store, stood by 'Tarquin of Cheapside', and it duly appeared in the book – where once again it caught the eye of critics and readers alike.

'The Offshore Pirate' to which Fitzgerald compared 'Tarquin of Cheapside' was a story that he had written just prior to his marriage to Zelda in April 1920, and again it is a tale with an interesting background that merits a place in this book.

It was early in 1920 while Scott was correcting the galley proofs for *This Side of Paradise* that he had the idea for 'The Offshore Pirate'. It is a mystery-story of a beautiful and wilful young girl, Ardita Farnam, who is cruising off the Florida coast with her wealthy uncle when their yacht is boarded by a group of criminals who have committed some terrible crime and are making their getaway by sea. These desperadoes are led by the dashing Curtis Carlyle, an ambitious poor boy who has turned to crime in his quest for wealth and the love of upper-class girls.

It was a story that flowed from Scott's pen, and the finished item delighted him. When, later, his early short stories were being assessed by the critics and 'The Diamond as Big as The Ritz' was specifically singled-out, Fitzgerald declared, 'One critic has been pleased to like this extravaganza better than anything I have written. Personally, I prefer "The Offshore Pirate".'

When the story was accepted for publication by the prestigious *Saturday Evening Post* and published on 29 May 1920, the public, too, shared the author's pleasure – as James E. Miller has commented in *F.Scott Fitzgerald: His Art and His Technique* (1965):

> 'The Offshore Pirate' could be used to document the fact that Fitzgerald was investing his characters with a glamour which they did not deserve. But the secret of the popular success of his stories is that they served as escape for all the bored five-and-ten-cent store clerks who dreamed of being glamorous Fitzgerald flappers, lavishly courted by disguised millionaire philosophers.

(The story was also reprinted in England in the fashionable *Sovereign Magazine* of February 1922 – from where it has been extracted for this book – and proved equally popular with readers on this side of the Atlantic.)

There are a number of other interesting points about 'The Offshore Pirate'. Initially, Scott had intended to call the story 'The Proud Piracy' and had planned an ending in which the kidnapping which occurs is revealed to have all taken place in Ardita's dream. Wisely, he resisted the temptation to weaken the story with this device. Fitzgerald also did not initially let on that there was a real-life original of his heroine.

She was a girl from St Paul named Ardita Ford who was clearly delighted when this secret emerged. The revelation was made in 1921, just before the story was brought to the screen as a silent movie by MGM directed by Dallas M. Fitzgerald (no relation) starring Viola Dana and Jack Mulhall. Seizing on this, Ardita arranged for a celebrity theatre party to be held in St Paul after the first night's screening, 'So that everyone can see what I am like in the movies!'

'The Offshore Pirate' was also optioned for a musical comedy, and though never produced on the stage, a number of the tunes and lyrics were actually written in 1930 and when played for Fitzgerald impressed him. Four years later, the Hollywood film maker Carl Laemmle also approached Scott with the idea of a 'talkie' version of the story, but this never materialized.

By the time Scott decided to write another tale of fantasy, he and Zelda had moved to New York and he had completed the first draft on his new novel, *The Beautiful and the Damned*. This change of pace from the demands of the novel was called 'His Russet Witch' and he forwarded the manuscript to his agent, Harold Ober, in October 1920, enthusing in an accompanying letter, 'I think it is the best thing I ever wrote.'

Later, when the euphoria of the moment had died down, Scott took another cooler look at what was undeniably an accomplished short story and revised his judgement.

'It was a natural reaction to revel in a story wherein none of the characters need be taken seriously', he said. 'I'm afraid that I was somewhat carried away by the feeling that there was no ordered scheme to which I must conform.'

'His Russet Witch' has been aptly described by Robert Sklar as 'more surreal than real' in the manner in which it recounts the experiences of a bookstore clerk named Merlin Grainger who for forty years continually encounters a mysterious beauty named Caroline who represents for him 'my romantic yearning for a beautiful and perverse woman'. But, as the reader will discover, Merlin's magical fantasy is to be cruelly crushed in the dramatic finale.

The story was published in one of New York's stylish new monthly periodicals, *The Metropolitan Magazine*, in February 1921. And such was the magazine's enthusiasm for Scott's stories that they signed an immediate contract via Harold Ober for six more. 'His Russet Witch' was also optioned to MGM – as was his next fantasy tale, 'The Curious Case of Benjamin Button' – but sadly neither followed 'The Offshore Pirate' on to the screen.

'The Curious Case of Benjamin Button' appeared in the spring of 1922, after the Fitzgeralds had taken their first trip to Europe, then moved back to St Paul, and celebrated the arrival of their daughter, Scottie. In the publisher's announcement for the short story it was also noted that the author had just released his second novel, *The Beautiful and the Damned*, to widespread critical acclaim.

Paul Rosenfeld is just one of several admirers of 'The Curious Case of Benjamin Button'. With this story, he has written, 'a very genuine gift of fantasy arrives in Fitzgerald's work.' The tale was inspired by its author's admiration for a group of fanciful stories by Mark Twain (another mainstream American literary figure who also wrote supernatural tales) and concerns a man who is born old and grows younger the longer he lives.

In a letter to Ober from his home on Goodrich Avenue in St Paul in December 1921, Scott explained that the idea had occurred to him some while before, but on the spur of the moment he had suddenly decided to take two days off to finish it. The recent arrival of Scottie in October may well have been the catalyst, but the story certainly lives up to Fitzgerald's estimate: 'It is a weird thing and I suppose the *Metropolitan* would be most likely to take it.'

In fact, the story was rejected by the magazine in the new year – an accompanying letter explaining that although six of the *Metropolitan's* editors had liked it, 'our readers, however, would be offended.' *Collier's Magazine*, to whom Ober then submitted it, obviously felt their readers were less susceptible to offence by Fitzgerald's fantasy, and published it in their issue of 27 May 1922.

Scott and Zelda Fitzgerald were by this time acknowledged celebrities in St Paul, and their regular parties, especially those which mirrored Scott's love of the fantastic, were legendary. On Friday 13 January 1922, for example, they organized a 'Bad Luck Ball' at the University Club in a room hung with black crêpe. During the evening, copies of a newspaper written by Scott, *The St Paul Dirge – Mortuary Edition* were distributed to the revellers. One front-page story was headlined '*FRIGHTFUL ORGY AT UNIVERSITY CLUB*', while another report stated, 'Business Better, Says Bootlegger.'

But such extravagances, plus the heavy drinking which both Scott and Zelda were now indulging in, were severely taxing their finances. Both were clearly bored with local life and hankered after New York. In fact, Scott had already begun to borrow money from his agent against future royalties from his books and payments for his short stories. As a writer it could be said that he was now coming into his maturity – but the tell-tale signs of the problems both financial and health-wise which lay ahead were also already becoming evident.

A month after *Collier's* publication of the Benjamin Button story, *Smart Set* magazine prominently featured 'The Diamond as Big as The Ritz', and Fitzgerald's mark on fantasy could be said to be assured. For the next two years, though, he turned his back on the genre, and although he continued to write short stories, he also tried his hand at writing a play, *The Vegetable* (which failed in November 1923) and attempted to write himself out of debt with a string of fashionable if unsatisfying non-fiction articles for magazines such as *Vanity Fair* and *Ladies Home Journal* which bore such self-explanatory titles as 'Imagination and a Few Mothers' and 'The Most Disgraceful Thing I Ever Did'.

It was in the spring of 1924 that the Fitzgeralds' restless spirits drove them to cross the Atlantic and begin a period of wandering about Europe. Two fantasies date from this period, 'Rags Martin-Jones and the Pr–nce of W–les' and 'The Adjuster'. Though both were written speedily to help

Scott cope with his mounting debts, they have special qualities which even their author's anxiety and drinking could not dampen.

'Rags Martin-Jones and the Pr–nce of W–les' features John M. Chestnut, a rich, handsome playboy who controls a mysterious network of power and uses it to fulfil the extravagant wishes of his bored girlfriend. It has been described by John A. Higgins in *F.Scott Fitzgerald: A Study of The Stories* (1971) as 'perhaps an unconscious parody of *The Great Gatsby*' – an interesting observation, indeed, for it was written in 1924 shortly before Scott began to work solely on Gatsby. True or not, the story's mixture of an exotic night club, an elevator boy posing as the Prince of Wales travelling incognito, and John Chestnut's curious murder accusation against himself, keeps the whole plot engrossing to the very end. The story appeared in Britain in *Woman's Pictorial* of 18 October 1924 where Fitzgerald was described as 'one of the foremost and cleverest of modern writers.'

'The Adjuster' is a rather more sinister tale about the machinations of a mysterious psychiatrist named Doctor Moon. Arthur Mizener believes this to be one of Fitzgerald's most successful fantasies – listing it with 'The Diamond as Big as The Ritz' and 'A Short Trip Home' – and makes a special point about the symbolism and allegory of the tale. Robert Sklar believes it to be especially significant, 'because it marks Fitzgerald's first explicit exorcising of his flapper creation, the beautiful, young, wilful girl ... Luella Hemple's selfishness has caused her husband's breakdown and her child's death.' Still other experts have seen in it the signs of the marital troubles that were already besetting the Fitzgeralds themselves.

Scott admitted to his agent that the tale 'may seem too gloomy' to be easily placed, but believed it was 'a peach of a story'. His apprehensions were not entirely misplaced, either, for the tale did not find a publisher until September 1925 when it finally appeared in *Red Book Magazine*.

Two events were to highlight Scott Fitzgerald's three-year sojourn in Europe – in 1925 he wrote *The Great Gatsby*, and not long afterwards he became friendly with another famous expatriate American author, Ernest Hemingway, in Paris. In between the rounds of high living and all-night parties, he also began work on a new novel with murder as its central theme.

Scott's basic plot concerned a young man of evil temperament whose father is serving a long prison sentence for a crime of violence, and is himself driven to commit the same act against his unscrupulous and domineering mother while the pair are on vacation in France. It seems probable that a series of events connected with some of Scott's friends had inspired the proposed book, for in a letter to his publishers in New York while working on the manuscript, Fitzgerald commented:

Contemporaries of mine had begun to disappear into the dark maw of violence. A classmate killed his wife and himself on Long Island, another tumbled 'accidentally' from a skyscraper in Philadelphia, another purposefully from a skyscraper in New York. One was killed in a speak-easy in Chicago; another was beaten to death in a speak-easy in New York and crawled home to the Princeton Club to die; still another had his skull crushed by a maniac's axe in an insane asylum where he was confined.

Despite such 'inspiration', Fitzgerald worked disjointedly on the idea for almost four years, somehow never getting near completion. His problems with the idea were indicated by its changing title from, initially, *The World's Fair*, then to *Our Type* and, lastly, *The Boy Who Killed His Mother*. Whether the distractions of the life style he and Zelda were living, or a simple failure to make the plot work, ultimately caused him to discard what would have been his only mystery novel, we shall now never know.

But all was not quite lost, for Scott managed to pour some of the atmosphere of repressed violence and passion that he had planned for the novel into a short story of crime, 'The Dance', which he wrote in the spring of 1926. Set in a small Southern town and narrated by a young New York girl who is sensitive to the 'secret shapes of things' that exist just below the apparently sedate life of the community, the story has a mounting tension that makes it comparable with the best examples to be found in the detective story genre.

Fitzgerald, though, was sceptical of the merits of 'The Dance', and even after Harold Ober had briskly sold it to *Red Book Magazine* (where it was published in June 1926) and it had provided him with some much needed cash, he still wanted to tinker with it and even asked if the title could be changed to 'In a Little Town'. However, Ellery Queen, the doyen of American crime writers and editor of his own magazine, considered it one of the best short stories Fitzgerald ever wrote, and it is from the pages of his famous *Mystery Magazine* where it was prominently featured in the issue of March 1953 that it has been reprinted for this volume. (In August 1940 the story was also sold for broadcasting on the Philip Morris Radio Show – but Scott was dead before the transmission took place.)

The Fitzgeralds' financial plight was a major factor in bringing them back to America in December 1926, where Scott decided to concentrate his energies on the swift returns to be had from writing short stories as well as accepting the blandishments being made to him to move to Hollywood – as a number of his contemporaries had done – to write film scripts.

Not long after his return to his native land he published the appropriately titled 'A Short Trip Home', which again broke new ground in being his first fully fledged ghost-story. In it he again employs some of the supernatural mood he had used in *This Side of Paradise*, but he is now a much more skilful practitioner at this notoriously difficult kind of story to carry off – a verdict that the *Saturday Evening Post* also reached when accepting the story for its Christmas issue of 17 December 1927.

'Frankly, we did not find it easy to reach our decision with reference to "A Short Trip Home" ', an editor of the magazine wrote. 'Ghosts are rather difficult to handle in the *Post*, but the story is so well done that we have not been able to resist it.'

Malcolm Crowley was among those readers also unable to resist the story, seeing it as being 'curiously Japanese in spirit'. He later wrote, 'There are many Japanese legends of re-embodied spirits who try to seduce the living and carry them off to a shadow world. In this case, however, the ghost has a social meaning. The living-dead man in high button shoes represents the lower order of humanity that offers a mysterious threat to the standards and the daughters of the rich people whose mansions rise above them on the hill.'

In my own opinion, the confrontation of the living and the dead on the railroad train in 'A Short Trip Home' is as chilling an episode as any to be found in the works of such masters of the ghost story as Charles Dickens and M.R. James.

The next story in this book, 'Outside the Cabinet-maker's' was also published at Christmas in 1928 in *The Century* magazine. It, too, harks back to childhood and the tales of fairies and ogres that so delighted Fitzgerald – and which he, in turn, related to his daughter.

Scott thought this little fantasy would be ideal for *Woman's Home Companion*, but though one editor on the magazine reported it to be 'delightful' it was none the less rejected, and it was not until several months later that it was bought by *The Century* for just $150. Though, yet again, it was a story the dispirited author held in low regard, it has since delighted every reader fortunate enough to come across a copy, as it has only been reprinted once.

The final decade of Scott Fitzgerald's life – the thirties – has, of course, been exhaustively documented: his wife Zelda's breakdown; his restless travelling both in America and abroad; the publication of *Tender Is The Night* in 1935; and his unhappy last years in Hollywood where he wrote scripts and worked on his novel, *The Last Tycoon*. Arthur Mizener has made an interesting comment that Fitzgerald was rather like his character Cecilia in that final book who 'accepted Hollywood with the resignation of a ghost assigned to a haunted house.'

Yet, despite all his problems at this time, Fitzgerald also wrote several more excellent short stories, three of which evolved from his fascination with fantasy in different forms, and it is these tales which complete this book.

'One Trip Abroad' is one of the most intriguing 'doppelganger' stories I have ever read – and it is doubly fascinating because the two central characters, an American couple Nelson and Nicole Kelly, who visit Europe to find their vision of the good life and instead fall victim to moral and physical decay, are so clearly modelled on Scott and Zelda. The ending of this tale of supernaturalism in which a flash of lightning strikes and the couple realize just *who* the other mysterious man and woman they have repeatedly encountered during their travels really are, is brilliantly handled.

James Miller has pointed out that the story is a treatment in miniature of the major line of action in *Tender Is The Night*.

' "One Trip Abroad",' he writes, 'presents the Dick Divers under the names of Nicole and Nelson Kelly ... as year succeeds year on their trip and one sordid episode follows on the heels of another, the bloom fades and the atmosphere gradually shifts from the shabbily romantic to the sinister.'

Miller's final sentence about the couple's realization who the other elusive pair are I will not quote so as to avoid spoiling the reader's enjoyment of this story, which was published by the *Saturday Evening Post* on 11 October 1930, and again had to wait until after Fitzgerald's death for its true quality to be appreciated.

'The Fiend', the story of a brutal murderer which was published in *Esquire* magazine in January 1935 is an even more neglected tale. It is another example of Scott's interest in crime, which he had continued to discuss in his non-fiction in essays like 'Echoes of the Jazz Age' (November 1931) and 'My Lost City' (July 1932).

In 'Echoes', for instance, he tells us that at the time of the Leopold-Loeb murder, Zelda was 'arrested on the Queensborough Bridge on suspicion of being the "Bob-haired Bandit" '; while in 'My Lost City' he muses, 'Sometimes I imagine myself reading, with curious interest, a *Daily News* of the issue of 1945: *MAN OF FIFTY RUNS AMUCK IN NEW YORK* – Fitzgerald Feathered Many Love Nests, Cutie Avers – Bumped Off By Outraged Gunman.'

The title of 'The Fiend' is suggestive of horror, and it is interesting to learn that while he was in Hollywood, Fitzgerald enjoyed going to watch some of the series of outstanding horror movies produced by Universal Pictures which began with the 1931 production of *Frankenstein*, starring Boris Karloff. Scott, in fact, mentioned the famous English actor in a letter to his daughter Scottie, which he wrote from Hollywood.

'I'm dashing around to a Boris Karloff movie to cheer up', he tells her. 'It is an inspirational thing called "The Corpse in the Breakfast Food"!'

Neither 'The Fiend', which was reprinted in the *Evening Standard* newspaper in London on 29 March 1935, or the final story, 'Shaggy's Morning', which again first appeared in *Esquire* in May 1935, and then on this side of the Atlantic in the *Daily Express* of 1 July 1935, has been collected in the intervening years. 'Shaggy's Morning' is a fanciful story quite unlike any other in this book, in that it is an animal story told from a dog's viewpoint which somehow burlesques that kind of animal yarn at which Scott's friend, Ernest Hemingway, excelled.

Fitzgerald had a childhood horror of cats, but loved dogs, and earlier in his career had written a ballad entitled, 'Dog, Dog, Dog'. In 'Shaggy's Morning', Scott reveals yet another facet of his diverse literary talent which will undoubtedly prove one more surprise for any reader who heretofore has solely associated his name with the Jazz Age.

Scott Fitzgerald died in Hollywood on 21 December 1940, his life extinguished by excess but his undeniable literary talent enshrined in the small clutch of novels and numerous short stories he had written. His body lay, appropriately, in the 'William Wordsworth Room' of a Los Angeles Chapel before it was transported for burial among his father's family in Rockville, Maryland.

After his death, among his possessions were found several notebooks full of scribbled ideas and the incomplete manuscript of *The Last Tycoon*. In both were further instances of his lifelong interest in the fantastic and the mysterious.

Among the ideas he had put down were several for what would have surely made excellent fantasy stories. On one page, for example, he had written: 'Dr X's story about the Emperor of the World'; on the next, 'The Fairy who Fell for a Wax Dummy'; and further on, 'A criminal confesses his crime methods to a reformer, who uses them that same night.'

In another entry he noted the plot for a story about a girl 'whose ear is so sensitive she can hear radio – Man gets her out of insane asylum to use her.' There is even more detail for another plot he has actually given a title: '*A FUNERAL*' – 'His own ashes kept blowing in his eyes. Everything was over by six and nothing remained but a small man to mark the spot. There were no flowers requested or proferred. The corpse stirred faintly during the evening, but otherwise the scene was one of quietude.'

Perhaps, though, the most poignant of all was the final line he had written on the manuscript of *The Last Tycoon*. It read in his unmistakable hand, 'Don't wake the Tarkington ghosts.'

In the pages which follow it has been my pleasure to rewaken some of Fitzgerald's ghosts and reassemble them here to mark the anniversary of his death. At the same time, may Scott's own ghost rest easy in the knowledge that his fame and reputation are now truly assured.

Peter Haining
December 1990

The Mystery of the Raymond Mortgage

When I first saw John Syrel of the New York *Daily News*, he was standing before an open window of my house gazing out on the city. It was about six o'clock and the lights were just going on. All down Thirty-third Street was a long line of gaily illuminated buildings. He was not a tall man, but thanks to the erectness of his posture and the suppleness of his movement, it would take no athlete to tell that he was of fine build. He was twenty-three years old when I first saw him, and was already a reporter on the *News*. He was not a handsome man; his face was clean-shaven, and his chin showed him to be of strong character. His eyes and hair were brown.

As I entered the room he turned around slowly and addressed me in a slow, drawling tone: 'I think I have the honour of speaking to Mr Egan, Chief of Police.' I assented, and he went on: 'My name is John Syrel and my business, to tell you frankly, is to learn all I can about the case of the Raymond mortgage.'

I started to speak but he silenced me with a wave of his hand. 'Though I belong to the staff of the *Daily News*,' he continued, 'I am not here as an agent of the paper.'

'I am not here,' I interrupted coldly, 'to tell every newspaper reporter or adventurer about private affairs. James, show this man out.'

Syrel turned without a word and I heard his steps echo up the driveway.

However, this was not destined to be the last time I ever saw Syrel, as events will show.

The morning after I first saw John Syrel, I proceeded to the scene of the crime to which he had alluded. On the train I picked up a newspaper and read the following account of the crime and theft:

EXTRA
Great Crime Committed in
Suburbs of City
Mayor Proceeding to Scene
of Crime

On the morning of July 1st a crime and serious theft were committed on the outskirts of the city. Miss Raymond was killed

23

and the body of a servant was found outside of the house. Mr Raymond of Santuka Lake was awakened on Tuesday morning by a scream and two revolver shots which proceeded from his wife's room. He tried to open the door but it would not open. He was almost certain the door was locked from the inside, when suddenly it swung open disclosing a room in frightful disorder. On the centre of the floor was a revolver and on his wife's bed was a bloodstain in the shape of a hand. His wife was missing, but on a closer search he found his daughter under the bed, stone dead. The window was broken in two places. Miss Raymond had a bullet wound on her body and her head was fearfully cut. The body of a servant was found outside with a bullet hole through his head. Mrs Raymond has not been found.

The room was upset. The bureau drawers were out as if the murderer had been looking for something. Chief of Police Egan is on the scene of the crime, etc.

Just then the conductor called out 'Santuka!' The train came to a stop, and getting out of the car I walked up to the house. On the porch I met Gregson, who was supposed to be the ablest detective in the force. He gave me a plan of the house which he said he would like to have me look at before we went in.

'The body of the servant,' he said, 'is that of John Standish. He has been with the family twelve years and was a perfectly honest man. He was only thirty-two years old.'

'The bullet which killed him was not found?' I asked.

'No,' he answered, and then, 'Well, you had better come and see for yourself. By the way, there was a fellow hanging around here who was trying to see the body. When I refused to let him in, he went around to where the servant was shot and I saw him go down on his knees on the grass and begin to search. A few minutes later he stood up and leaned against a tree. Then he came up to the house and asked to see the body again. I said he could if he would go away afterwards. He assented, and when he got inside the room he went down on his knees under the bed and hunted around. Then he went over to the window and examined the broken pane carefully. After that he declared himself satisfied and went down towards the hotel.'

After I had examined the room to my satisfaction, I found that I might as well try to see through a millstone as to try to fathom this mystery. As I finished my investigation I met Gregson in the laboratory.

'I suppose you heard about the mortgage,' said he, as he went downstairs. I answered in the negative, and he told me that a valuable mortgage had disappeared from the room in which Miss Raymond was killed. The night before, Mr Raymond had placed the mortgage in a drawer and it had disappeared.

On my way to town that night I met Syrel again, and he bowed cordially to me. I began to feel ashamed of myself for sending him out of my house. As I went into the car the only vacant seat was next to him. I sat down and apologized for my rudeness of the day before. He took it lightly and, there being nothing to say, we sat in silence. At last I ventured a remark.

'What do you think of the case?'

'I don't think anything of it as yet. I haven't had time yet.'

Nothing daunted, I began again. 'Did you learn anything?'

Syrel dug his hand into his pocket and produced a bullet. I examined it.

'Where did you find it?' I asked.

'In the yard,' he answered briefly.

At this I again relapsed into my seat. When we reached the city, night was coming on. My first day's investigation was not very successful.

My next day's investigation was no more successful than the first. My friend Syrel was not at home. The maid came into Mr Raymond's room while I was there and gave notice that she was going to leave. 'Mr Raymond,' she said, 'there was queer noises outside my window last night. I'd like to stay, sir, but it grates on my nerves.'

Beyond this nothing happened, and I came home worn out.

On the morning of the next day I was awakened by the maid who had a telegram in her hand. I opened it and found it was from Gregson. 'Come at once,' it said, 'startling development.'

I dressed hurriedly and took the first car to Santuka. When I reached the Santuka station, Gregson was waiting for me in a runabout. As soon as I got into the carriage Gregson told me what had happened.

'Someone was in the house last night. You know Mr Raymond asked me to sleep there. Well, last night, about one, I began to be very thirsty. I went into the hall to get a drink from the faucet there, and as I was passing from my room (I sleep in Miss Raymond's room) into the hall I heard somebody in Mrs Raymond's room. Wondering why Mr Raymond was up at that time of night I went into the sitting-room to investigate. I opened the door to Mrs Raymond's room. The body of Miss Raymond was lying on the sofa. A man was kneeling beside it. His face was away from me, but I could tell by his figure that he was not Mr Raymond. As I looked he got up softly and I saw him open a bureau drawer. He took something out and put it into his pocket. As he turned around he saw me, and I saw that he was a young man. With a cry of rage he sprang at me, and having no weapon I retreated. He snatched up a heavy Indian club and swung it over my head. I gave a cry which must have alarmed the house, for I knew nothing more till I saw Mr Raymond bending over me.'

'How did this man look?' I asked. 'Would you know him if you saw him again?'

'I think not,' he answered. 'I only saw his profile.'

'The only explanation I can give is this,' said I. 'The murderer was in Miss Raymond's room and when she came in he overpowered her and inflicted the gash. He then made for Mrs Raymond's room and carried her off after having first shot Miss Raymond, who attempted to rise. Outside the house he met Standish, who attempted to stop him and was shot.'

Gregson smiled. 'That solution is impossible,' he said.

As we reached the house I saw John Syrel, who beckoned me aside. 'If you come with me,' he said, 'you will learn something that may be valuable to you.'

I excused myself to Gregson and followed Syrel. As we reached the walk he began to talk.

'Let us suppose that the murderer or murderess escaped from the house. Where would they go? Naturally they wanted to get away. Where did they go? Now, there are two railroad stations near by, Santuka and Lidgeville. I have ascertained that they did not go by Santuka. So did Gregson. I supposed, therefore, that they went by Lidgeville. Gregson didn't. That's the difference. A straight line between here and Lidgeville. At first there was nothing. About two miles farther on I saw some footprints in a marshy hollow. They consisted of three footprints. I took an impression. Here it is. You see this one is a woman's. I have compared it with one of Mrs Raymond's boots. They are identical. The others are mates. They belong to a man.

'I compared the bullet I found, where Standish was killed, with one of the remaining cartridges in the revolver that was found in Mrs Raymond's room. They were mates. Only one shot had been fired and as I had found one bullet, I concluded that either Mrs or Miss Raymond had fired the shot. I preferred to think Mrs Raymond fired it because she had fled.

'Summing these up and also taking into consideration that Mrs Raymond must have had some cause to try to kill Standish, I concluded that John Standish killed Miss Raymond through the window of her mother's room, Friday night. I also conclude that Mrs Raymond after ascertaining that her daughter was dead, shot Standish through the window and killed him. Horrified at what she had done she hid behind the door when Mr Raymond came in. Then she ran down the back stairs. Going outside she stumbled upon the revolver Standish had used and picking it up took it with her. Somewhere between here and Lidgeville she met the owner of these footprints either by accident or design and walked with him to the station where they took the early train for Chicago. The stationmaster did not see the man. He says that only a woman bought a ticket, so I concluded that the young man didn't go. Now you must tell me what Gregson told you.'

'How did you know all this,' I exclaimed, astonished. And then I told him about the midnight visitor. He did not appear to be much astonished, and he said, 'I guess that the young man is our friend of the footprints.

Now you had better get a brace of revolvers and pack your suitcase if you wish to go with me to find this young man and Mrs Raymond, who I think is with him.'

Greatly surprised at what I had heard, I took the first train back to town. I bought a pair of fine Colt revolvers, a dark lantern, and two changes of clothing. We went over to Lidgeville and found that a young man had left on the six o'clock train for Ithaca.

On reaching Ithaca we found that he had changed trains and was now halfway to Princeton, New Jersey. It was five o'clock but we took a fast train and expected to overtake him halfway between Ithaca and Princeton. What was our chagrin when on reaching the slow train, to find he had gotten off at Indianous and was now probably safe.

Thoroughly disappointed, we took the train for Indianous. The ticket seller said that a young man in a light grey suit had taken a bus to the Raswell Hotel. We found the bus which the stationmaster said he had taken, in the street. We went up to the driver and he admitted that he had started for the Raswell Hotel in his cab.

'But,' said the old fellow, 'when I reached there, the fellow had clean disappeared, an' I never got his fare.'

Syrel groaned; it was plain that we had lost the young man. We took the next train for New York and telegraphed to Mr Raymond that we would be down Monday. Sunday night, however, I was called to the phone and recognized Syrel's voice. He directed me to come at once to 534 Chestnut Street. I met him on the doorstep.

'What have you heard?' I asked.

'I have an agent in Indianous,' he replied, 'in the shape of an Arab boy whom I employ for ten cents a day. I told him to spot the woman and today I got a telegram from him (I left him money to send one) saying to come at once. So come on.'

We took the train for Indianous. 'Smidy,' the young Arab, met us at the station.

'You see, sir, it's dis way. You says, "Spot de guy wid dat hack," and I says I would. Dat night a young dude comes out of de house on Pine Street and gives the cab-man a ten-dollar bill. An' den he went back into the house and a minute after he comes out wid a woman, an' den day went down here a little way an' goes into a house farther down the street.'

We followed Smidy down the street until we arrived at a corner house. The ground floor was occupied by a cigar store, but the second floor was evidently for rent. As we stood there a face appeared at the window and, seeing us, hastily retreated.

Syrel pulled a picture from his pocket. 'It's she,' he exclaimed, and calling us to follow he dashed into a little side door. We heard voices upstairs, a shuffle of feet and a noise as if a door had been shut.

'Up the stairs,' shouted Syrel, and we followed him, taking two steps at a bound. As we reached the top landing we were met by a young man.

'What right have you to enter this house?' he demanded.

'The right of the law,' replied Syrel.

'I didn't do it,' broke out the young man. 'It was this way. Agnes Raymond loved me – she did not love Standish – he shot her; and God did not let her murder go unrevenged. It was well Mrs Raymond killed him, for his blood would have been on my hands. I went back to see Agnes before she was buried. A man came in. I knocked him down. I didn't know until a moment ago that Mrs Raymond had killed him.'

'I forgot Mrs Raymond,' screamed Syrel. 'Where is she?'

'She is out of your power forever,' said the young man.

Syrel brushed past him and, with Smidy and me following, burst open the door of the room at the head of the stairs. We rushed in.

On the floor lay a woman, and as soon as I touched her heart I knew she was beyond the doctor's skill.

'She has taken poison,' I said.

Syrel looked around – the young man had gone. And we stood there aghast in the presence of death.

The Ordeal

The hot four o'clock sun beat down familiarly upon the wide stretch of
Maryland country, burning up the long valleys, powdering the winding
road into fine dust and glaring on the ugly slated roof of the monastery.
Into the gardens it poured hot, dry, lazy, bringing with it, perhaps, some
quiet feeling of content, unromantic and cheerful. The walls, the trees,
the sanded walks, seemed to radiate back into the fair cloudless sky the
sweltering late summer heat and yet they laughed and baked happily. The
hour brought some odd sensation of comfort to the farmer in a nearby
field, drying his brow for a moment by his thirsty horse, and to the
lay-brother opening boxes behind the monastery kitchen.

The man walked up and down on the bank above the creek. He had
been walking for half an hour. The lay-brother looked at him quizzically
as he passed and murmured an invocation. It was always hard, this hour
before taking first vows. Eighteen years before one, the world just behind.
The lay-brother had seen many in this same situation, some white and
nervous, some grim and determined, some despairing. Then, when the
bell tolled five, there were the vows and usually the novice felt better. It
was this hour in the country when the world seemed gloriously apparent
and the monastery vaguely impotent. The lay-brother shook his head in
sympathy and passed on.

The man's eyes were bent upon his prayer-book. He was very young,
twenty at the most, and his dark hair in disorder gave him an even more
boyish expression. A light flush lay on his calm face and his lips moved
incessantly. He was not nervous. It seemed to him as if he had always
known he was to become a priest. Two years before, he had felt the vague
stirring, the transcendent sense of seeing heaven in everything, that
warned him softly, kindly that the spring of his life was coming. He had
given himself every opportunity to resist. He had gone a year to college,
four months abroad, and both experiences only increased within him the
knowledge of his destiny. There was little hesitation. He had at first feared
self-committal with a thousand nameless terrors. He thought he loved the
world. Panicky, he struggled, but surer and surer he felt that the last word

had been said. He had his vocation – and then, because he was no coward, he decided to become a priest.

Through the long month of his probation he alternated between deep, almost delirous, joy and the same vague terror at his own love of life and his realization of all he sacrificed. As a favorite child he had been reared in pride and confidence in his ability, in faith in his destiny. Careers were open to him, pleasure, travel, the law, the diplomatic service. When, three months before, he had walked into the library at home and told his father that he was going to become a Jesuit priest, there was a family scene and letters on all sides from friends and relatives. They told him he was ruining a promising young life because of a sentimental notion of self sacrifice, a boyish dream. For a month he listened to the bitter melodrama of the commonplace, finding his only rest in prayer, knowing his salvation and trusting in it. After all, his worst battle had been with himself. He grieved at his father's disappointment and his mother's tears, but he knew that time would set them right.

And now in half an hour he would take the vows which pledged him forever to a life of service. Eighteen years of study – eighteen years where his every thought, every idea would be dictated to him, where his individuality, his physical ego would be effaced and he would come forth strong and firm to work and work and work. He felt strangely calm, happier in fact than he had been for days and months. Something in the fierce, pulsing heat of the sun likened itself to his own heart, strong in its decision, virile and doing its own share in the work, the greatest work. He was elated that he had been chosen, he from so many unquestionably singled out, unceasingly called for. And he had answered.

The words of the prayers seemed to run like a stream into his thoughts, lifting him up peacefully, serenely; and a smile lingered around his eyes. Everything seemed so easy; surely all life was a prayer. Up and down he walked. Then of a sudden something happened. Afterwards he could never describe it except by saying that some undercurrent had crept into his prayer, something unsought, alien. He read on for a moment and then it seemed to take the form of music. He raised his eyes with a start – far down the dusty road a group of negro hands were walking along singing, and the song was an old song that he knew:

> 'We hope ter meet you in heavan whar we'll
>   Part no mo',
>   Whar we'll part no mo'.
> Gawd a'moughty bless you twel we
>   Me–et again.'

Something flashed into his mind that had not been there before. He felt a sort of resentment toward those who had burst in upon him at this time, not because they were simple and primitive, but because they had vaguely disturbed him. That song was old in his life. His nurse had hummed it through the dreamy days of his childhood. Often in the hot summer afternoons he had played it softly on his banjo. It reminded him of so many things: months at the seashore on the hot beach with the gloomy ocean rolling around him, playing with sand castles with his cousin; summer evenings on the big lawn at home when he chased fireflys and the breeze carried the tune over the night to him from the negro-quarters. Later, with new words, it had served as a serenade – and now – well, he had done with that part of life, and yet he seemed to see a girl with kind eyes, old in a great sorrow, waiting, ever waiting. He seemed to hear voices calling, children's voices. Then around him swirled the city, busy with the hum of men; and there was a family that would never be, beckoning him.

Other music ran now as undercurrent to his thoughts: wild, incoherent, music, illusive and wailing, like the shriek of a hundred violins, yet clear and chord-like. Art, beauty, love and life passed in a panorama before him, exotic with the hot perfumes of world-passion. He saw struggles and wars, banners waving somewhere, voices giving hail to a king – and looking at him through it all were the sweet sad eyes of the girl who was now a woman.

Again the music changed; the air was low and sad. He seemed to front a howling crowd who accused him. The smoke rose again around the body of John Wycliffe, a monk knelt at a prie-dieu and laughed because the poor had not bread, Alexander VI pressed once more the poisoned ring into his brother's hand, and the black robed figures of the inquisition scowled and whispered. Three great men said there was no God, a million voices seemed to cry, 'Why! Why! must we believe?' Then as in a crystal he seemed to hear Huxley, Nietzsche, Zola, Kant cry, 'I will not' – He saw Voltaire and Shaw wild with cold passion. The voices pleaded 'Why?' and the girl's sad eyes gazed at him with infinite longing.

He was in a void above the world – the ensemble, everything called him now. He could not pray. Over and over again he said senselessly, meaninglessly, 'God have mercy, God have mercy.' For a minute, an eternity, he trembled in the void and then – something snapped. They were still there, but the girl's eyes were all wrong, the lines around her mouth were cold and chiselled and her passion seemed dead and earthy.

He prayed, and gradually the cloud grew clearer, the images appeared vague and shadowy. His heart seemed to stop for an instant and then – he was standing by the bank and a bell was tolling five. The reverend superior came down the steps and toward him.

'It is time to go in.' The man turned instantly.

'Yes, Father, I am coming.'

II

The novices filed silently into the chapel and knelt in prayer. The blessed Sacrament in the gleaming monstrance was exposed among the flaming candles at the altar. The air was rich and heavy with incense. The man knelt with the others. A first chord of the magnificat, sung by the concealed choir above, startled him; he looked up. The late afternoon sun shone through the stained glass window of St Francis Xavier on his left and fell in red tracery on the cassock of the man in front of him. Three ordained priests knelt at the altar. Above them a huge candle burned. He watched it abstractedly. To the right of him a novice was telling his beads with trembling fingers. The man looked at him. He was about twenty-six with fair hair and green-grey eyes that darted nervously around the chapel. They caught each other's eye and the elder glanced quickly at the altar candle as if to draw attention to it. The man followed his eye and as he looked he felt his scalp creep and tingle. The same unsummoned instinct filled him that had frightened him half an hour ago on the bank. His breath came quicker. How hot the chapel was. It was too hot; and the candle was wrong – wrong – everything suddenly blurred. The man on his left caught him.

'Hold up,' he whispered, 'they'll postpone you. Are you better? Can you go through with it?'

He nodded vaguely and turned to the candle. Yes, there was no mistake. Something was there, something played in the tiny flame, curled in the minute wreath of smoke. Some evil presence was in the chapel, on the very altar of God. He felt a chill creeping over him, though he knew the room was warm. His soul seemed paralyzed, but he kept his eyes riveted on the candle. He knew that he must watch it. There was no one else to do it. He must not take his eyes from it. The line of novices rose and he mechanically reached his feet.

'*Per omnia saecula, saeculorum.* Amen.'

Then he felt suddenly that something corporeal was missing – his last earthly support. He realized what it was. The man on his left had gone out overwrought and shaken. Then it began. Something before had attacked the roots of his faith; had matched his world-sense against his God-sense, had brought, he had thought, every power to bear against him; but this was different. Nothing was denied, nothing was offered. It could best be described by saying that a great weight seemed to press down upon his innermost soul, a weight that had no essence, mental or physical. A whole spiritual realm evil in its every expression engulfed him. He could not think, he could not pray. As in a dream he heard the voices of the men beside him singing, but they were far away, farther away from him than anything had ever been before. He existed on a plane where there was no prayer, no grace; where he realized only that the forces around him were of hell and where the single candle contained the essence of evil. He felt himself alone pitted against an infinity of temptation. He could bring no parallel to it in his own experience or any other. One fact he knew: one man had succumbed to this weight and he must not – must not. He must look at the candle and look and look until the power that filled it and forced him into this plane died forever for him. It was now or not at all.

He seemed to have no body and even what he had thought was his innermost self was dead. It was something deeper that was he, something that he had never felt before. Then the forces gathered for one final attack. The way that the other novice had taken was open to him. He drew his breath quickly and waited and then the shock came. The eternity and infinity of all good seemed crushed, washed away in an eternity and infinity of evil. He seemed carried helplessly along, tossed this way and that – as in a black limitless ocean where there is no light and the waves grow larger and larger and the sky darker and darker. The waves were dashing him toward a chasm, a maelstrom everlastingly evil, and blindly, unseeingly, desperately he looked at the candle, looked at the flame which seemed like the one black star in the sky of despair. Then suddenly he became aware of a new presence. It seemed to come from the left, seemed consummated and expressed in warm, red tracery somewhere. Then he knew. It was the stained window of St Francis Xavier. He gripped at it spiritually, clung to it and with aching heart called silently for God.

> '*Tantum ergo Sacramentum*
> *Veneremur cernui.*'

The words of the hymn gathered strength like a triumphant paean of glory, the incense filled his brain, his very soul, a gate clanged somewhere and *the candle on the altar went out.*

'*Ego vos absolvo a peccatis tuis in nomine patris, filii, spiritus sancti. Amen.*'

The file of novices started toward the altar. The stained lights from the windows mingled with the candle glow and the eucharist in its golden halo seemed to the man very mystical and sweet. It was very calm. The subdeacon held the book for him. He placed his right hand upon it.

'*In the name of the Father and the Son and of the Holy Ghost –*'

Tarquin of Cheapside

Running footsteps – light, soft-soled shoes made of curious leathery cloth brought from Ceylon setting the pace; thick flowing boots, two pairs, dark blue and gilt, reflecting the moonlight in blunt gleams and splotches, following a stone's throw behind.

Soft Shoes flashes through a patch of moonlight, then darts into a blind labyrinth of alleys and becomes only an intermittent scuffle ahead somewhere in the enfolding darkness. In go Flowing Boots, with short swords lurching and long plumes awry, finding a breath to curse God and the black lanes of London.

Soft Shoes leaps a shadowy gate and crackles through a hedgerow. Flowing Boots leap the gate and crackles through the hedgerow – and there, startlingly, is the watch ahead – two murderous pikemen of ferocious cast of mouth acquired in Holland and the Spanish marches.

But there is no cry for help. The pursued does not fall panting at the feet of the watch, clutching a purse; neither do the pursuers raise a hue and cry. Soft Shoes goes by in a rush of swift air. The watch curse and hesitate, glance after the fugitive, and then spread their pikes firmly across the road and wait for Flowing Boots. Darkness, like a great hand, cuts off the even flow of the moon.

The hand moves off the moon whose pale caress finds again the eaves and lintels, and the watch, wounded and tumbled in the dust. Up the street one of Flowing Boots leaves a black trail of spots until he binds himself, clumsily as he runs, with fine lace caught from his throat.

It was no affair for the watch: Satan was at large tonight and Satan seemed to be he who appeared dimly in front, heel over gate, knee over fence. Moreover, the adversary was obviously travelling near home or at least in that section of London consecrated to his coarser whims, for the street narrowed like a road in a picture and the houses bent over further and further, cooping in natural ambushes suitable for murder and its histrionic sister, sudden death.

Down long and sinuous lanes twisted the hunted and the harriers, always in and out of the moon in a perpetual queen's move over a checker-board of glints and patches. Ahead, the quarry, minus his leather jerkin now and half blinded by drips of sweat, had taken to scanning his ground desperately on both sides. As a result he suddenly slowed short, and retracing his steps a bit scooted up an alley so dark that it seemed that here sun and moon had been in eclipse since the last glacier slipped roaring over the earth. Two hundred yards down he stopped and crammed himself into a niche in the wall where he huddled and panted silently, a grotesque god without bulk or outline in the gloom.

Flowing Boots, two pairs, drew near, came up, went by, halted twenty yards beyond him, and spoke in deep-lunged, scanty whispers:

'I was attune to that scuffle, it stopped.'

'Within twenty paces.'

'He's hid.'

'Stay together now and we'll cut him up.'

The voice faded into a low crunch of a boot, nor did Soft Shoes wait to hear more – he sprang in three leaps across the alley, where he bounded up, flapped for a moment on the top of the wall like a huge bird, and disappeared, gulped down by the hungry night at a mouthful.

II

> He read at wine, he read in bed,
> He read aloud, had he the breath,
> His every thought was with the dead,
> And so he read himself to death.

Any visitor to the old James the First graveyard near Peat's Hill may spell out this bit of doggerel, undoubtedly one of the worst recorded of an Elizabethan, on the tomb of Wessel Caxter.

This death of his, says the antiquary, occurred when he was thirty-seven, but as this story is concerned with the night of a certain chase through darkness, we find him still alive, still reading. His eyes were somewhat dim, his stomach somewhat obvious – he was a misbuilt man and indolent – oh, Heavens! But an era is an era, and in the reign of Elizabeth, by the grace of Luther, Queen of England, no man could help but catch the spirit of enthusiasm. Every loft in Cheapside published its *Magnum Folium* (or magazine) of the new blank verse; the Cheapside Players would produce anything on sight as long as it 'got away from those reactionary miracle plays,' and the English Bible had run through seven 'very large' printings in as many months.

So Wessel Caxter (who in his youth had gone to sea) was now a reader of all on which he could lay hands – he read manuscripts in holy friendship; he dined rotten poets; he loitered about the shops where the *Magna Folia* were printed, and he listened tolerantly while the young playwrights wrangled and bickered among themselves, and behind each other's backs made bitter and malicious charges of plagiarism or anything else they could think of.

To-night he had a book, a piece of work which, though inordinately versed, contained, he thought, some rather excellent political satire. 'The Faerie Queene' by Edmund Spenser lay before him under the tremulous candle-light. He had ploughed through a canto; he was beginning another:

> THE LEGEND OF BRITOMARTIS OR OF CHASTITY
> It falls me here to write of Chastity.
> The fayrest vertue, far above the rest ...

A sudden rush of feet on the stairs, a rusty swing-open of the thin door, and a man thrust himself into the room, a man without a jerkin, panting, sobbing, on the verge of collapse.

'Wessel,' words choked him, 'stick me away somewhere, love of Our Lady!'

Caxter rose, carefully closing his book, and bolted the door in some concern.

'I'm pursued,' cried out Soft Shoes. 'I vow there's two short-witted blades trying to make me into mincemeat and near succeeding. They saw me hop the back wall!'

'It would need,' said Wessel, looking at him curiously, 'several battalions armed with blunderbusses, and two or three Armadas, to keep you reasonably secure from the revenges of the world.'

Soft Shoes smiled with satisfaction. His sobbing gasps were giving way to quick, precise breathing; his hunted air had faded to a faintly perturbed irony.

'I feel little surprise,' continued Wessel.

'They were two such dreary apes.'

'Making a total of three.'

'Only two unless you stick me away. Man, man, come alive; they'll be on the stairs in a spark's age.'

Wessel took a dismantled pike-staff from the corner, and raising it to the high ceiling, dislodged a rough trap-door opening into a garret above.

'There's no ladder.'

He moved a bench under the trap, upon which Soft Shoes mounted, crouched, hesitated, crouched again, and then leaped amazingly upward. He caught at the edge of the aperture and swung back and forth for a moment, shifting his hold; finally doubled up and disappeared into the darkness above. There was a scurry, a migration of rats, as the trap-door was replaced; ... silence.

Wessel returned to his reading-table, opened to the Legend of Britomaris or of Chastity – and waited. Almost a minute later there was a scramble on the stairs and an intolerable hammering at the door. Wessel sighed and, picking up his candle, rose.

'Who's there?'

'Open the door!'

'Who's there?'

An aching blow frightened the frail wood, splintered it around the edge. Wessel opened it a scarce three inches, and held the candle high. His was to play the timorous, the super-respectable citizen, disgracefully disturbed.

'One small hour of the night for rest. Is that too much to ask from every brawler and –'

'Quiet gossip! Have you seen a perspiring fellow?'

The shadows of two gallants fell in immense wavering outlines over the narrow stairs; by the light Wessel scrutinized them closely. Gentlemen, they were, hastily but richly dressed – one of them wounded severely in the hand, both radiating a sort of furious horror. Waving aside Wessel's ready miscomprehension, they pushed by him into the room and with their swords went through the business of poking carefully into all suspected dark spots in the room, further extending their search to Wessel's bedchamber.

'Is he hid here?' demanded the wounded man fiercely.

'Is who here?'

'Any man but you.'

'Only two others that I know of.'

For a second Wessel feared that he had been too damned funny, for the gallants made as though to prick him through.

'I heard a man on the stairs,' he said hastily, 'full five minutes ago, it was. He most certainly failed to come up.'

He went on to explain his absorption in 'The Faerie Queene' but, for the moment at least, his visitors, like the great saints, were anaesthetic to culture.

'What's been done?' inquired Wessel.

'Violence!' said the man with the wounded hand. Wessel noticed that his eyes were quite wild. 'My own sister. Oh, Christ in heaven, give us this man!'

Wessel winced.

'Who is the man?'

'God's word! We know not even that. What's that trap door up there!' he added suddenly.

'It's nailed down. It's not been used for years.' He thought of the pole in the corner and quailed in his belly, but the utter despair of the two men dulled their astuteness.

'It would take a ladder for any one not a tumbler,' said the wounded man listlessly.

His companion broke into hysterical laughter.

'A tumbler. Oh a tumbler. Oh –'

Wessel stared at them in wonder.

'That appeals to my most tragic humour,' cried the man, 'that no one – oh, no one – could get up there but a tumbler.'

The gallant with the wounded hand snapped his good fingers impatiently.

'We must go next door – and then on –'

Helplessly they went as two walking under a dark and storm-swept sky.

Wessel closed and bolted the door and stood a moment by it, frowning in pity.

A low-breathed 'Ha!' made him look up. Soft Shoes had already raised the trap and was looking down into the room. His rather elfish face squeezed into a grimace, half of distaste, half of sardonic amusement.

'They take off their heads with their helmets,' he remarked in a whisper, 'but as for you and me, Wessel, we are two cunning men.'

'Now you be cursed,' cried Wessel vehemently. 'I knew you for a dog, but when I hear even the half of a tale like this, I know you for such a dirty cur that I am minded to club your skull.'

Soft Shoes stared at him, blinking.

'At all events,' he replied finally, 'I find dignity impossible in this position.'

With this he let his body through the trap, hung for an instant, and dropped the seven feet to the floor.

'There was a rat considered my ear with the air of a gourmet,' he continued, dusting his hands on his breeches. 'I told him in the rat's peculiar idiom that I was deadly poison, so he took himself off.'

'Let's hear of this night's lechery!' insisted Wessel angrily.

Soft Shoes touched his thumb to his nose and wiggled the fingers derisively at Wessel.

'Street gamin!' muttered Wessel.

'Have you any paper?' demanded Soft Shoes irrelevantly, and then rudely added, 'or can you write?'

'Why should I give you paper?'

'You wanted to hear of the night's entertainment. So you shall, an you give me pen, ink, a sheaf of paper, and a room to myself.'

Wessel hesitated.

'Get out!' he said finally.

'As you will. Yet you have missed a most intriguing story.'

Wessel wavered – he was soft as taffy, that man – gave in. Soft Shoes went into the adjoining room with the begrudged writing materials and precisely closed the door. Wessel grunted and returned to 'The Faerie Queene'; so silence came once more upon the house.

III

Three o'clock went into four. The room paled, the dark outside was shot through with damp and chill, and Wessel, cupping his brain in his hands, bent low over his table, tracing through the pattern of knights and fairies and the harrowing distresses of many girls. There were dragons chortling along the narrow street outside; when the sleepy armorer's boy began his work at half-past five the heavy clink and chank of plate and linked mail swelled to the echo of a marching cavalcade.

A fog shut down at the first flare of dawn, and the room was grayish yellow at six when Wessel tiptoed to his cupboard bedchamber and pulled open the door. His guest turned on him a face pale as parchment in which two distraught eyes burned like great red letters. He had drawn a chair close to Wessel's *prie-dieu* which he was using as a desk; and on it was an amazing stack of closely written pages. With a long sigh Wessel withdrew and returned to his siren, calling himself fool for not claiming his bed here at dawn.

The clump of boots outside, the croaking of old beldames from attic to attic, the dull murmur of morning, unnerved him, and, dozing, he slumped in his chair, his brain, overladen with sound and color, working intolerably over the imagery that stacked it. In this restless dream of his he was one of a thousand groaning bodies crushed near the sun, a helpless bridge for the strong-eyed Apollo. The dream tore at him, scraped along his mind like a ragged knife. When a hot hand touched his shoulder, he awoke with what was nearly a scream to find the fog thick in the room and his guest, a gray ghost of misty stuff, beside him with a pile of paper in his hand.

'It should be a most intriguing tale, I believe, though it requires some going over. May I ask you to lock it away, and in God's name let me sleep?'

He waited for no answer, but thrust the pile at Wessel, and literally poured himself like stuff from a suddenly inverted bottle upon a couch in the corner; slept, with his breathing regular, but his brow wrinkled in a curious and somewhat uncanny manner.

Wessel yawned sleepily and, glancing at the scrawled, uncertain first page, he began reading aloud very softly:

THE RAPE OF LUCRECE
From the besieged Ardea all in post,
Borne by the trustless wings of false desire,
Lust-breathing Tarquin leaves the Roman host –

The Offshore Pirate

I

This story begins on a sea that was a blue dream, as colourful as blue silk stockings, and beneath a sky as blue as the irises of children's eyes. From the western half of the sky the sun was shying little golden discs at the sea – if you gazed intently enough you could see them skip from wave tip to wave tip until they joined a broad collar of golden coin that was collecting half a mile out and would eventually be a dazzling sunset.

About halfway between the shore and the golden collar a white steam yacht, very young and graceful, was riding at anchor, and under a blue and white awning aft a yellow-haired girl reclined in a wicker settee reading *The Revolt of the Angels* by Anatole France. She was about eighteen, slender and supple, with a spoiled alluring mouth and quick grey eyes full of a radiant curiosity.

Suddenly the drowsy silence which enveloped the yacht was broken by the sound of heavy footsteps, and an elderly man, topped with orderly grey hair and clad in a white flannel suit, appeared at the head of the companionway. There he paused for a moment until his eyes became accustomed to the sun, and then, seeing the girl under the awning, he uttered a long even grunt of disapproval.

If he had intended thereby to obtain a rise of any sort he was doomed to disappointment. The girl calmly turned over two pages, turned back one, then very faintly but quite unmistakably yawned.

'Ardita!' said the grey-haired man sternly.

Ardita uttered a small sound indicating nothing.

'Ardita!' he repeated.

'What?'

'Will you listen to me – or shall I get a servant to hold you while I talk to you?'

'Oh, can't you leave me alone for a second?'

'Ardita, I have just received a telephone message from the shore –'

'Telephone?' She showed for the first time a faint interest.

'Yes. Colonel Moreland has called up again to ask me to be sure to bring you in to dinner. His son Toby has come all this way to meet you and

40

he's invited several other young people. For the last time, will you –'

'No,' said Ardita shortly. 'I won't. I came along on this cruise with the one idea of going to Palm Beach, and you knew it, and I absolutely refuse to meet any old colonel or any young Toby or any old young people or to set foot in any other old town in this country. So you either take me to Palm Beach or else go away.'

'Very well. In your infatuation for this man – a man who is notorious for his excesses, a man your father would not have allowed to so much as mention your name – you have reflected the *demi-monde* rather than the circles in which you have presumably grown up. From now on –'

'I know,' interrupted Ardita ironically, 'from now on you go your way and I go mine. I've heard that story before. You know I'd like nothing better.'

'From now on,' he announced grandiloquently, 'you are no niece of mine. I –'

'O-o-o-oh!' The cry was wrung from Ardita with the agony of a lost soul.

'Will you stop boring me? Will you go 'way? Will you jump overboard and drown? Do you want me to throw this book at you?'

'If you dare do any –'

Smack! The *Revolt of the Angels* sailed through the air, missed its target by the length of a short nose and bumped cheerfully down the companionway.

The grey-haired man made an instinctive step backward and then two cautious steps forward. Ardita jumped to her five feet four and stared at him defiantly, her grey eyes blazing.

'Keep off!'

'How dare you?' he cried.

'Because I please!'

'You've grown unbearable! Your disposition –'

'You've made me like it! No child ever has a bad disposition unless it's her family's fault! Whatever I am, you did it.'

Muttering something under his breath, her uncle turned and, walking forward, called in a loud voice for the launch. Then he returned to the awning, where Ardita had again seated herself and resumed her attention to the *Revolt of the Angels*.

'I am going ashore,' he said slowly. 'I will be out again at nine o'clock tonight. When I return we will start for home, where I shall turn you over to your aunt for the rest of your natural, or rather unnatural, life.'

He paused and looked at her, and then all at once something in the utter childishness of her beauty seemed to puncture his anger like an inflated tyre, and render him helpless, uncertain, utterly fatuous.

'Ardita,' he said not unkindly, 'I'm no fool. I've been about. I know men. And, child, confirmed libertines don't reform until they're tired – and then they're not themselves – they're husks of themselves.' He looked at her as if expecting agreement, but receiving no sight or sound of it, he continued. 'Perhaps the man loves you – that's possible. He's loved many women and he'll love many more. Less than a month ago, one month, Ardita, he was involved in a notorious affair with that red-haired woman, Mimi Merril. Why on earth do you want to marry him?'

'I'm sure I couldn't say,' said Ardita shortly. 'Maybe because he's the only man I know, good or bad, who has an imagination and the courage of his convictions. Maybe it's to get away from the young fools that spend their vacuous hours pursuing me around the country.'

'How about the – red-haired woman?'

'He hasn't seen her for six months,' she said angrily. 'Don't you suppose I have enough pride to see to that?'

Too full of words to speak, Mr Farnam cast one utterly condemning glance at his niece and, turning, went quickly down the ladder.

II

Five o'clock rolled down from the sun and plumped soundlessly into the sea. The golden collar widened into a glittering island; and a faint breeze that had been playing with the edges of the awning became suddenly freighted with song. Ardita lifted her head and listened.

With an exclamation she tossed her book to the deck, where it sprawled at a straddle, and hurried to the rail. Fifty feet away a large rowboat was approaching containing seven men, six of them rowing and one standing up in the stern keeping time to their song with an orchestra leader's baton.

The leader's eyes suddenly rested on Ardita, who was leaning over the rail spellbound with curiosity. He made a quick movement with his baton and the singing instantly ceased.

'*Narcissus* ahoy!' he called politely.

'What's the idea of all the discord?' demanded Ardita cheerfully.

By this time the boat was scraping the side of the yacht and a boatman turned round and grasped the ladder. Thereupon the leader left his position in the stern and before Ardita had realized his intention he ran up the ladder and stood breathless before her on the deck.

'The women and children will be spared!' he said briskly. 'All crying babies will be immediately drowned and all males put in irons!'

Digging her hands excitedly down into the pockets of her dress, Ardita stared at him, speechless with astonishment.

He was a young man with a scornful mouth and the bright blue eyes of a healthy baby set in a dark sensitive face. His hair was pitch black, damp and curly – the hair of a Grecian statue gone brunette. He was trimly built, trimly dressed and graceful as an agile quarterback.

'Well, I never!' she said dazedly.

They eyed each other coolly.

'Do you surrender the ship?'

'Is this an outburst of wit?' demanded Ardita. 'Are you an idiot – or just being initiated to some fraternity?'

'I asked you if you surrendered the ship.'

'You'd better get off this yacht!' said Ardita.

'What?' The young man's voice expressed incredulity.

'Get off the yacht! Do you hear me?'

He looked at her for a moment as if considering what she had said.

'No,' said his scornful mouth slowly; 'no, I won't get off the yacht. You can get off if you wish.'

Going to the rail he gave a curt command and immediately the crew of the rowboat scrambled up the ladder and ranged themselves in line before him. Over the shoulder of each was slung a small, heavy-looking white sack, and under their arms they carried large black cases apparently containing musical instruments.

'Ten-*shun!*' commanded the young man, snapping his own heels together crisply. 'Right *driss*! Front! Come here, Babe!'

The smallest man took a quick step forward and saluted.

'Take command, go down below, catch the crew and tie 'em up – all except the engineer. Bring him up to me. Oh, and pile those bags by the rail there.'

'Yes, sir!'

He saluted again, and wheeling about, motioned for the five others to gather about him. Then after a short whispered consultation they all filed noiselessly down the companion-way.

'Now,' said the young man cheerfully to Ardita, who had witnessed this last scene in withering silence, 'if you will swear on your honour as a flapper – which probably isn't worth much – that you'll keep that spoiled little mouth of yours tight shut for forty-eight hours, you can row yourself ashore in our rowboat.'

'Otherwise what?'

'Otherwise you're going to sea in a ship.'

With a little sigh as for a crisis well passed the young man sank into the settee Ardita had lately vacated, and stretched his arms lazily. The corners of his mouth relaxed appreciatively as he looked round at the rich striped awning, the polished brass and the luxurious fittings of the deck.

'What's your name?' he asked presently.

'Farnam.'

'Farnam what?'

'Ardita Farnam.'

'Well, Ardita, no use standing up there and chewing out the insides of your mouth. You ought to break those nervous habits while you're young. Come over here and sit down.'

Ardita took a carved jade case from her pocket, extracted a cigarette and lit it with a conscious coolness, though she knew her hand was trembling a little; then she crossed over with her supple, swinging walk, and sitting down in the other settee, blew a mouthful of smoke at the awning.

'You can't get me off this yacht,' she said steadily; 'and you haven't got very much sense if you think you'll get far with it. My uncle'll have wirelesses zigzagging all over this ocean by half-past six.'

He laughed scornfully.

'If that's advice, you needn't bother. This is part of a plan arranged before I ever knew this yacht existed. If it hadn't been this one it'd have been the next one we passed anchored along the coast.'

'Who are you?' demanded Ardita suddenly. 'And what are you?'

'You've decided not to go ashore?'

'I never even faintly considered it.'

'We're generally known,' he said, 'all seven of us, as Curtis Carlyle and his Six Sailormen, late of the Winter Garden and the Midnight Frolic.'

'You're singers?'

'We were until today. At present, due to those white bags you see there, we're fugitives from justice.'

'What's in the bags?' asked Ardita curiously.

'Well,' he said, 'for the present we'll call it – mud.'

III

Within ten minutes after Curtis Carlyle's interview with a very frightened engineer the yacht *Narcissus* was under way, steaming south through a balmy tropical twilight.

Having given orders for a meal to be prepared and served on deck at seven-thirty, Carlyle rejoined Ardita, and sinking back into his settee, half closed his eyes and fell into a state of profound abstraction.

Ardita scrutinized him carefully – and classed him immediately as a romantic figure. He gave the effect of towering self-confidence erected on a slight foundation – just under the surface of each of his decisions she discerned a hesitancy that was in decided contrast to the arrogant curl of his lips.

'He's not like me,' she thought. 'There's a difference somewhere.'

Being a supreme egotist, Ardita frequently thought about herself; never having had her egotism disputed, she did it entirely naturally and with no distraction from her unquestioned charm. Though she was nineteen, she gave the effect of a high-spirited precocious child, and in the present glow of her youth and beauty all the men and women she had known were but driftwood on the ripples of her temperament. She had met other egotists – in fact, she found that selfish people bored her rather less than unselfish people – but as yet there had not been one she had not eventually defeated and brought to her feet.

But though she recognized an egotist in the settee next to her, she felt none of that usual shutting of doors in her mind which meant clearing ship for action; on the contrary, her instinct told her that this man was somehow completely pregnable and quite defenceless. When Ardita defied convention – and of late it had been her chief amusement – it was from an intense desire to be herself, and she felt that this man on the contrary was preoccupied with his own defiance.

The night deepened. A pale new moon rose slowly out of the sea, and as the shore faded dimly out and dark clouds were blown like leaves along the far horizon, a great haze of moonshine suddenly bathed the yacht and spread an avenue of glittering mail in her swift path. From time to time there was the bright flare of a match as one of them lighted a cigarette, but except for the low undertone of the throbbing engines and the even wash of the waves about the stern, the yacht was quiet as a dream boat star-bound through the heavens. Round them flowed the smell of the night sea, bringing with it an infinite languor.

Carlyle broke the silence at last.

'Lucky girl,' he sighed, 'I've always wanted to be rich – and buy all this beauty.'

Ardita yawned.

'I'd rather be you,' she said frankly.

'You would – for about a day. But you do seem to possess a lot of nerve for a flapper.'

'I wish you wouldn't call me that.'

'Beg your pardon.'

'As to nerve,' she continued slowly, 'it's my one redeeming feature. I'm not afraid of anything in heaven or earth.'

'H'm, I am.'

'To be afraid,' said Ardita, 'a person has either to be very great and strong – or else a coward. I'm neither.' She paused for a moment, and eagerness crept into her tone. 'But I want to talk about you. What on earth have you done – and how did you do it?'

'Why?' he demanded cynically. 'Going to write a story about me?'

'Go on,' she urged. 'Lie to me by the moonlight. Tell a fabulous story.'

A sailor appeared, switched on a string of small lights under the awning and began setting the wicker table for supper. And while they ate cold sliced chicken, salad, artichokes and strawberry jam from the plentiful larder below, Carlyle began to talk, hesitatingly at first, but eagerly as he saw she was interested. Ardita scarcely touched her food as she watched his dark young face – handsome, ironic, faintly in effectual.

He began life as a poor kid, he said. Before he was thirteen he was picking up a living coaxing ragtime out of a battered violin in little cafés. Eight years later the ragtime craze hit the country and he took six darkies on the Orpheum circuit. They were making money – each contract he signed called for more – but, getting tired of troupe work, he went to managers and told them that he wanted to go on as a regular pianist. They laughed at him and told him he was crazy – it would be an artistic suicide. He used to laugh afterward at the phrase 'artistic suicide.' They all used it.

Then he began speculating wildly, and within three weeks he had lost every farthing he had saved.

Presently, in the recital of his adventures, he put a question to the girl. There was no answer. He looked. She had fallen asleep.

IV

In the dense sun-flooded noon of next day a spot in the sea before them resolved casually into a green-and-grey islet, apparently composed of a great granite cliff at its northern end which slanted south through a mile of vivid coppice and grass to a sandy beach melting lazily into the surf. When Ardita, reading in her favourite seat, came to the last page of *The Revolt of the Angels* and slamming the book shut, looked up and saw it, she gave a little cry of delight and called to Carlyle, who was standing moodily by the rail.

'Is this it? Is this where you're going?'

Carlyle shrugged his shoulders carelessly.

'I don't know.' He raised his voice and called up to the acting skipper. 'Babe, is this your island?'

The mulatto's miniature head appeared from round the corner of the deckhouse.

'Yes, sir! This is it.'

Carlyle joined Ardita.

'Looks sort of sporting, doesn't it?'

'Yes,' she agreed; 'but it doesn't look big enough to be much of a hiding-place.'

'You still putting your faith in those wirelesses your uncle was going to have zigzagging round?'

'No,' said Ardita frankly. 'I'm all for you. I'd really like to see you get away.'

He laughed.

'You're our Lucky Lady. We'll have to keep you with us as a mascot – for the present, anyway.'

'You couldn't very well ask me to swim back,' she said coolly. 'If you do, I'm going to start writing shilling shockers, founded on that history of your life you gave me last night.'

He flushed and stiffened slightly. 'Huh,' he said, 'I suppose every other man you meet tells you he loves you?'

Ardita nodded.

'Why shouldn't he? All life is just a progression toward and then a recession from one phrase – "I love you".'

Carlyle laughed and sat down.

'That's very true. That's – that's not bad. Did you make that up?'

'Yes – or rather I found it out. It doesn't mean anything especially. It's just clever.'

'It's the sort of remark,' he said gravely, 'that's typical of your class.'

'Oh,' she interrupted impatiently, 'don't start that lecture on aristocracy again! I distrust people who can be intense at this hour in the morning. Morning's the time to sleep, swim and be careless.'

Ten minutes later they had swung round in a wide circle as if to approach the island from the north.

'There's a trick somewhere,' commented Ardita thoughtfully. 'He can't mean just to anchor up against this cliff.'

They were heading straight in now toward the solid rock, which must have been well over a hundred feet tall, and not until they were within fifty yards off it did Ardita see their objective. Then she clapped her hands in delight. There was a break in the cliff entirely hidden by a curious overlapping of rocks, and through this break the yacht entered and very slowly traversed a narrow channel of crystal-clear water between high grey walls. Then they were riding at anchor in a miniature world of green and gold, a gilded bay smooth as glass and set round with tiny palms, the whole resembling the mirror lakes and twig trees that children set up in sand piles.

'Not so bad!' cried Carlyle excitedly. 'That little half-breed knows his way round this corner of the planet.'

His exuberance was contagious and Ardita became quite jubilant.

'It's an absolutely topping hiding-place!'

'Lordy, yes! It's the sort of island you read about.'

The rowboat was lowered into the golden lake and they pulled ashore.

'Come on,' said Carlyle, as they landed in the slushy sand, 'we'll go exploring.'

The fringe of palms was in turn ringed in by a round mile of flat sandy country. They followed it south, and brushing through a farther rim of tropical vegetation, came out on a pearl-grey virgin beach where Ardita kicked off her brown golf shoes – she seemed to have permanently abandoned stockings – and went wading. Then they sauntered back to the yacht, where the indefatigable Babe had luncheon ready for them.

'What's its name?' asked Ardita – 'the island, I mean?'

'No name 'tall,' chuckled Babe. 'Reckin she jus' island, 'at's all.'

Ardita thought for a moment.

'I'll name it,' she said. 'It'll be the Isle of Illusion.'

'Or of Disillusion,' murmured Carlyle.

'Disillusion, if more people know about it than Babe seems to think.'

In the late afternoon they sat with their backs against great boulders on the highest part of the cliff, and Carlyle sketched for her his vague plans. He was sure they were hot after him by this time. The total proceeds of the coup he had pulled off, and concerning which he still refused to enlighten her, he estimated as just under a quarter of a million. He counted on lying up here several weeks and then setting off southward. The details of coaling and provisioning he was leaving entirely to Babe, who, it seemed, had sailed these seas in every capacity from cabin-boy aboard a coffee trader to virtual first mate on a Chilian pirate craft, whose skipper had long since been hung.

'If he'd been white he'd have been king of South America long ago,' said Carlyle emphatically. 'When it comes to intelligence he's A number 1 at Lloyds. He's got the guile of every race and nationality whose blood is in his veins, and that's half a dozen or I'm a liar. He worships me because I'm the only man in the world who can play better ragtime than he can.'

'What you going to do when you get south?' she interrupted.

'Take ship for India. I want to be a rajah. I mean it. My idea is to go up into Afghanistan somewhere, buy up a palace and a reputation, and then after about five years appear in England with a foreign accent and a mysterious past. But India first. Do you know, they say that all the gold in the world drifts very gradually back to India? Something fascinating about that to me. And I want leisure to read – an immense amount.'

'How about after that?'

'Then,' he answered defiantly, 'comes aristocracy. Laugh if you want to – but at least you'll have to admit that I know what I want – which I imagine is more than you do.'

'On the contrary.' contradicted Ardita, reaching in her pocket for her cigarette case, 'when I met you I was in the midst of a great uproar of all my friends and relatives because I did know what I wanted.'

'What was it?'

'A man.'

He started.

'You mean you were engaged?'

'After a fashion. If you hadn't come aboard I had every intention of slipping ashore yesterday evening – how long ago it seems – and meeting him.'

'But your family disapproved, eh?'

'What there is of it – only a silly uncle and a sillier aunt.'

'I feel rather jealous,' said Carlyle, frowning – and then he laughed.

A pause ensued, a pause which Carlyle found rather awkward, but which Ardita seemed not to notice at all as she sat contentedly enjoying her cigarette and gazing out at the shining sea. After a minute she crawled out on the rock and lay with her face over the edge, looking down.

'Oh, look!' she cried. 'There's a lot of sort of ledges down there. Wide ones of all different heights.'

He joined her, and together they gazed down the dizzy height.

'We'll go swimming to-night!' she said excitedly. 'By moonlight.'

'Wouldn't you rather go in at the beach on the other end?'

'Not a chance. I like to dive. You can use my uncle's bathing suit, only it'll fit you like a sack, because he's a very fat man. I've got a one-piece affair that's shocked the natives everywhere I've shown it.'

'I suppose you're a shark?'

'Yes, I'm pretty good. And I look nice, too. A sculptor last summer told me my calves were worth one hundred pounds.'

There didn't seem to be any answer to this, so Carlyle was silent, permitting himself only a discreet interior smile.

V

When the night crept down in shadowy blue and silver, they threaded the shimmering channel in the rowboat, and tying it to a jutting rock began climbing the cliff together. The first shelf was ten feet up, wide, and furnishing a natural diving platform. There they sat down in the bright moonlight and watched the faint incessant surge of the waters, almost stilled now as the tide set seaward.

'Are you happy?' he asked suddenly.

She nodded.

'Always happy near the sea. You know,' she went on, 'I've been thinking all day that you and I are somewhat alike. We're both rebels – only for different reasons. Two years ago, when I was just eighteen, and you were –'

'Twenty-five.'

'Well, we were both conventional successes. I was an utterly devastating debutante and you were a prosperous musician. But deep in us both was something that made us require more for happiness. I didn't know what I wanted. I went from man to man, restless, impatient, month by month getting less acquiescent and more dissatisfied. I used to sit sometimes chewing at the insides of my mouth and thinking I was going crazy – I had a frightful sense of transiency. I wanted things now – now – now! Here I was – beautiful – I am, aren't I?'

'Yes,' agreed Carlyle tentatively.

Ardita rose suddenly.

'Wait a second. I want to try this delightful-looking sea.'

She walked to the end of the ledge and shot out over the water, doubling up in mid-air and then straightening out and entering the water straight as a blade in a perfect jack-knife dive.

In a minute her voice floated up to him.

'You see, I used to read all day and most of the night. I began to resent society –'

'Come on up here,' he interrupted. 'What on earth are you doing?'

'Just floating round on my back. I'll be up in a minute. Let me tell you. The only thing I enjoyed was shocking people; wearing something quite impossible and quite charming to fancy-dress parties, going round with the fastest men in Town and getting into some of the most hellish scrapes imaginable.'

The sounds of splashing mingled with her words, and then he heard her hurried breathing as she began climbing up the side to the ledge.

'Go on in!' she called.

Obediently he rose and dived. When he emerged, dripping, and made the climb he found that she was no longer on the ledge, but after a frightened second he heard her light laughter from another shelf ten feet up. There he joined her, and they both sat quietly for a moment, their arms clasped round their knees, panting a little from the climb.

'The family were wild,' she said suddenly. 'They tried to marry me off. And then when I'd begun to feel that after all life was scarcely worth living, I found something' – her eyes went skyward exultantly – 'I found something!'

Carlyle waited and her words came with a rush.

'Courage – just that; courage as a rule of life and something to cling to always. I began to build up this enormous faith in myself. I began to see that in all my idols in the past some manifestation of courage had unconsciously been the thing that attracted me. I began separating courage from the other things of life. All sorts of courage – the beaten, bloody prize-fighter coming up for more – I used to make men take me to prize fights; the *déclassé* woman sailing through a nest of cats and looking at them as if they were mud under her feet; the liking what you like always; the utter disregard for other people's opinions – just to live as I liked always and to die in my own way. Did you bring up the cigarettes?'

He handed one over and held a match for her silently.

'Still,' Ardita continued, 'the men kept gathering – old men and young men, my mental and physical inferiors, most of them, but all intensely desiring to have me – to own this rather magnificent proud tradition I'd built up round me. Do you see?'

'Sort of. You never were beaten and you never apologized.'

'Never!'

She sprang to the edge, poised for a moment like a crucified figure against the sky; then describing a dark parabola, plunked without a splash between two silver ripples twenty feet below.

Her voice floated up to him again.

'And courage to me meant ploughing through that dull grey mist that comes down on life. My courage is faith – faith in the eternal resilience of me – that joy'll come back, and hope and spontaneity. And I feel that till it does I've got to keep my lips shut and my chin high and my eyes wide – not necessarily any silly smiling. Oh, I've been through hell without a whine quite often – and the female hell is deadlier than the male.'

'But supposing,' suggested Carlyle, 'that before joy and hope and all that came back the curtain was drawn on you for good?'

Ardita rose, and going to the wall, climbed with some difficulty to the next ledge, another ten or fifteen feet above.

'Why,' she called back, 'then I'd have won!'

He edged out till he could see her.

'Better not dive from there! You'll break your back,' he said quickly.

She laughed.

'Not I!'

Slowly she spread her arms and stood there swan-like, radiating a pride in the young life within her that lit a warm glow in Carlyle's heart.

'We're going through the black air with our arms wide,' she called, 'and our feet straight out behind like a dolphin's tail, and we're going to think we'll never hit the silver down there, till suddenly it'll be all warm round us and full of little kissing, caressing waves.'

Then she was in the air and Carlyle involuntarily held his breath. He had not realized that the dive was nearly forty feet. It seemed an eternity before he heard the swift compact sound as she reached the sea.

And it was with his glad sigh of relief when her light watery laughter curled up the side of the cliff and into his anxious ears that he knew he loved her.

VI

With the long sunny hours Ardita's idea of the episode as incidental, madcap, a sprig of romance in a desert of reality, gradually left her. She dreaded the time when he would strike off southward.

'Take me with you,' said Ardita late one night as they sat lazily in the grass under the shadowy spreading palms. 'I'd love to reappear in ten years as a fabulously wealthy high-caste Indian lady,' she continued.

Carlyle looked at her quickly.

'You can, you know.'

She laughed.

'Is it a proposal of marriage? Extra! Ardita Farnam becomes pirate's bride. Society girl kidnapped by ragtime bank robber.'

'It wasn't a bank.'

'What was it? Why won't you tell me?'

'I don't want to break down your illusions.'

'My dear man, I have no illusions about you.'

'I mean your illusions about yourself.'

She looked up in surprise.

'About myself! What on earth have I got to do with whatever stray felonies you've committed?'

'That remains to be seen.'

She reached over and patted his hand.

'Dear Mr Curtis Carlyle,' she said softly, 'are you in love with me?'

'As if it mattered.'

'But it does – because I think I'm in love with you.'

He looked at her ironically.

'Thus swelling your January total to half a dozen,' he suggested. 'Suppose I ask you to come to India with me?'

'Shall I?'

He shrugged his shoulders.

'We can get married at the first port.'

'What sort of life can you offer me? I don't mean that unkindly, but seriously; what would become of me if the people who want that four thousand pounds reward ever catch up with you?'

'I thought you weren't afraid.'

'I never am – but I won't throw my life away just to show one man I'm not.'

'I wish you'd been poor. Just a little poor girl dreaming over a fence in a warm cow country.'

'Wouldn't it have been nice?'

'I'd have enjoyed astonishing you – watching your eyes open on things. If you only wanted things! Don't you see?'

'I know – like girls who stare into the windows of jewellery stores.'

'Yes – and want the big oblong watch that's platinum and has diamonds all round the edge. Only you'd decide it was too expensive and choose one of white gold for twenty pounds. Then I'd say, "Expensive? I should say not!" And we'd go into the store and pretty soon the platinum one would be gleaming on your wrist.'

'That sounds so nice and vulgar – and fun, doesn't it?' murmured Ardita.

'Doesn't it? Can't you see us travelling round and spending money right and left and being worshipped by lift boys and waiters? Oh, blessed are the simple rich, for they inherit the earth!'

'I honestly wish we were that way.'

'I love you, Ardita,' he said gently.

Her face lost its childish look for a moment and became oddly grave.

'I love to be with you,' she said 'more than with any man I've ever met. And I like your looks and your dark hair and the way you go over the side of the rail when we come ashore. In fact, Curtis Carlyle, I like all the things you do when you're perfectly natural. I think you've got nerve, and you know how I feel about that. Sometimes when you're round I've been tempted to kiss you suddenly and tell you that you were just an idealistic boy with a lot of caste nonsense in his head. Perhaps if I were just a little bit older and a little more bored I'd go with you. As it is, I think I'll go back and marry – that other man.'

Over across the silver lake the figures of the crew writhed and squirmed in the moonlight, like acrobats who, having been too long inactive, must go through their tricks from sheer surplus energy. In single file they marched, weaving in concentric circles, now with their heads thrown back, now bent over their instruments like piping fauns. And from trombone and saxophone ceaselessly whined a blended melody, sometimes riotous and jubilant, sometimes haunting and plaintive.

'Let's dance!' cried Ardita. 'I can't sit still with that perfect jazz going on.'

Taking her hand, he led her out into a broad stretch of hard sandy soil that the moon flooded with great splendour. They floated out like drifting moths under the rich hazy light, and as the fantastic symphony wept and exulted and wavered and despaired Ardita's last sense of reality dropped away and she abandoned her imagination to the dreamy summer scents of tropical flowers and the infinite starry spaces overhead, feeling that if she opened her eyes it would be to find herself dancing with a ghost in a land created by her own fancy.

'This is what I should call an exclusive private dance,' he whispered.

'I feel quite mad – but delightfully mad!'

'We're enchanted. The shades of unnumbered generations of cannibals are watching us from high up on the side of the cliff there.'

'And I'll bet the cannibal women are saying that we dance too close and that it was immodest of me to come without my nose ring.'

They both laughed softly – and then their laughter died as over across the lake they heard the trombones stop in the middle of a bar and the saxophones give a startled moan and fade out.

'What's the matter?' called Carlyle.

After a moment's silence they made out the dark figure of a man rounding the silver lake at a run. As he came closer they saw it was Babe in a state of unusual excitement. He drew up before them and gasped out his news in a breath.

'Ship stan'in' off 'bout half a mile, sah.'

'A ship – what kind of a ship?' demanded Carlyle anxiously.

Dismay was in his voice, and Ardita's heart gave a sudden wrench as she saw his whole face suddenly droop.

'Don't know, sah.'

'Are they landing a boat?'

'No, sah.'

'We'll go up,' said Carlyle.

They ascended the hill in silence, Ardita's hand still resting in Carlyle's as it had when they finished dancing. She felt it clench nervously from time to time as though he were unaware of the contact, but though he hurt her, she made no attempt to remove it. It seemed an hour's climb before they reached the top and crept cautiously across the silhouetted plateau to the edge of the cliff. And after one short look Carlyle involuntarily gave a little cry. It was a revenue boat with six-inch guns mounted fore and aft.

'They know!' he said, with a short intake of breath. 'They know! They picked up the trail somewhere.'

The hours passed and they lay there side by side, very silently, their chins in their hands like dreaming children.

When the colour faded from the sky and lustreless blue changed to leaden grey a commotion was visible on the ship's deck, and they made out a group of officers clad in white duck, gathered near the rail. They had field-glasses in their hands and were attentively examining the islet.

'It's all up,' said Carlyle grimly.

'Damn!' whispered Ardita. She felt tears gathering in her eyes.

'We'll go back to the yacht,' he said, 'I prefer that to being hunted out up here.'

Leaving the plateau, they descended the hill, and reaching the lake, were rowed out to the yacht. Then, pale and weary, they sank into the settees and waited.

Half an hour later, in the dim grey light, the nose of the revenue boat appeared in the channel and stopped. Two boats were lowered casually over the side, one containing an officer and six bluejackets, and the other four rowers and in the stern two grey-haired men in yachting flannels. Ardita and Carlyle stood up and half unconsciously started toward each other.

Suddenly, against the golden furnace low in the east, their two graceful figures melted into one, and he was kissing her spoiled young mouth.

'It's a sort of glory,' he murmured after a second.

She smiled up at him.

'Happy, are you?'

Her sigh was a benediction – an ecstatic surety that she was youth and beauty now as much as she would ever know. For another instant life was radiant and time a phantom and their strength eternal – then there was a bumping, scraping sound as the rowboat scraped alongside.

Up the ladder scrambled the two grey-haired men, the officer and two of the sailors with their hands on their revolvers. Mr. Farnam folded his arms and stood looking at his niece.

'So,' he said, nodding his head slowly.

With a sigh her arms unwound from Carlyle's neck, and her eyes, transfigured and far away, fell upon the boarding party. Her uncle saw her upper lip slowly swell into that arrogant pout he knew so well.

'So,' he repeated savagely. 'So this is your idea of – of romance. A runaway affair, with a – a high-seas pirate.'

Ardita considered him carelessly.

'What an old fool you are!' she said quietly.

And with that she turned, included the two old men, the officer and the two sailors in a curt glance of contempt, and walked proudly down the companion-way.

But had she waited an instant longer she would have heard a sound from her uncle quite unfamiliar in most of their interviews. Her uncle gave vent to a whole-hearted amused chuckle, in which the second old man joined.

The latter turned briskly to Carlyle, who had been regarding this scene with an air of cryptic amusement.

'Well, Toby,' he said genially, 'you incurable, hare-brained, romantic chaser of rainbows, did you find that she was the person you wanted?'

Carlyle smiled confidently.

'Why – naturally,' he said. 'I've been perfectly sure ever since I first heard tell of her wild career. That's why I had Babe send up the rocket last night.'

'I'm glad you did,' said Colonel Moreland. 'And we hoped we'd find you two in some such compromising position.'

'Your father and I sat up all night hoping for the best – or perhaps it's the worst. Lord knows you're welcome to her, my boy. She's run me crazy.'

'Sh!' said Carlyle. 'She's coming on deck.'

Ardita appeared at the head of the companion-way and gave a quick involuntary glance at Carlyle's wrists. A puzzled look came over her face.

'Ardita,' said Carlyle unsteadily.

She swayed a step toward him.

'Ardita,' he repeated breathlessly, 'I must tell you the – the truth. It was all a plant, Ardita. My name isn't Carlyle. It's Moreland, Toby Moreland. The story was invented, Ardita, invented out of thin air.'

She stared at him, bewildered amazement, disbelief and anger flowing in quick waves across her face. The three men held their breaths. Moreland, senior, took a step toward her; Mr. Farnam's mouth dropped a little open as he waited, panic-stricken, for the expected crash.

But it did not come. Ardita's face became suddenly radiant, and with a little laugh she went swiftly to young Moreland and looked up at him without a trace of wrath in her grey eyes.

'Will you swear,' she said quietly, 'that it was entirely a product of your own brain?'

'I swear,' said young Moreland eagerly.

She drew his head down and kissed him gently.

'What an imagination!' she said softly and almost enviously. 'I want you to lie to me just as sweetly as you know how for the rest of my life.'

The negroes' voices floated drowsily back, mingled in an air that she had heard them sing before:

> 'Time is a thief;
> Gladness and grief
> Cling to the leaf
> As it yellows –'

'What was in the bags?' she asked softly.

'Mud,' he answered. 'That was one of the two true things I told you.'

'Perhaps I can guess the other one,' she said; and reaching up on her tiptoes she kissed him.

His Russet Witch

Merlin Grainger was employed by the Moonlight Quill Bookshop, which you may have visited, just around the corner from the Ritz-Carlton on Forty-seventh Street. The Moonlight Quill is, or rather was, a very romantic little store, considered radical and admitted dark. It was spotted interiorly with red and orange posters of breathless exotic intent, and lit no less by the shiny reflecting bindings of special editions than by the great squat lamp of crimson satin that, lighted through all the day, swung overhead. It was truly a mellow bookshop. The words 'Moonlight Quill' were worked over the door in a sort of serpentine embroidery. The windows seemed always full of something that had passed the literary censors with little to spare; volumes with covers of deep orange which offer their titles on little white paper squares. And over all there was the smell of the musk, which the clever, inscrutable Mr Moonlight Quill ordered to be sprinkled about – the smell half of a curiosity shop in Dickens' London and half of a coffee-house on the warm shores of the Bosphorus.

From nine until five-thirty Merlin Grainger asked bored old ladies in black and young men with dark circles under their eyes if they 'cared for this fellow' or were interested in first editions. Did they buy novels with Arabs on the cover, or books which gave Shakespeare's newest sonnets as dictated psychically to Miss Sutton of South Dakota? he sniffed. As a matter of fact, his own taste ran to these latter, but as an employee at the Moonlight Quill he assumed for the working day the attitude of a disillusioned connoisseur.

After he had crawled over the window display to pull down the front shade at five-thirty every afternoon, and said goodbye to the mysterious Mr Moonlight Quill and the lady clerk, Miss McCracken, and the lady stenographer, Miss Masters, he went home to the girl, Caroline. He did not eat supper with Caroline. It is unbelievable that Caroline would have considered eating off his bureau with the collar buttons dangerously near the cottage cheese, and the ends of Merlin's necktie just missing his glass of milk – he had never asked her to eat with him. He ate alone. He went into Braegdort's delicatessen on Sixth Avenue and bought a box of crackers, a tube of anchovy paste, and some oranges, or else a little jar of sausages and some potato salad and a bottled soft drink, and with these in a brown package he went to his room at Fifty-something West Fifty-eighth Street and ate his supper and saw Caroline.

Caroline was a very young and gay person who lived with some older lady and was possibly nineteen. She was like a ghost in that she never existed until evening. She sprang into life when the lights went on in her apartment at about six, and she disappeared, at the latest, about midnight. Her apartment was a nice one, in a nice building with a white stone front, opposite the south side of Central Park. The back of her apartment faced the single window of the single room occupied by the single Mr Grainger.

He called her Caroline because there was a picture that looked like her on the jacket of a book of that name down at the Moonlight Quill.

Now, Merlin Grainger was a thin young man of twenty-five, with dark hair and no moustache or beard or anything like that, but Caroline was dazzling and light, with a shimmering morass of russet waves to take the place of hair, and the sort of features that remind you of kisses – the sort of features you thought belonged to your first love, but know, when you come across an old picture, didn't. She dressed in pink or blue usually, but of late she had sometimes put on a slender black gown that was evidently her especial pride, for whenever she wore it she would stand regarding a certain place on the wall, which Merlin thought must be a mirror. She sat usually in the profile chair near the window, but sometimes honoured the *chaise-longue* by the lamp, and often she leaned 'way back and smoked a cigarette with posturings of her arms and hands that Merlin considered very graceful.

At another time she had come to the window and stood in it magnificently, and looked out because the moon had lost its way and was dripping the strangest and most transforming brilliance into the areaway between, turning the motif of ash-cans and clothes-lines into a vivid impressionism of silver casks and gigantic gossamer cobwebs. Merlin was sitting in plain sight, eating cottage cheese with sugar and milk on it; and so quickly did he reach out for the window cord that he tipped the cottage cheese into his lap with his free hand – and the milk was cold and the sugar made spots on his trousers, and he was sure that she had seen him after all.

Sometimes there were callers – men in dinner coats, who stood and bowed, hat in hand and coat on arm, as they talked to Caroline; then bowed some more and followed her out of the light, obviously bound for a play or for a dance. Other young men came and sat and smoked cigarettes, and seemed trying to tell Caroline something – she sitting either in the profile chair and watching them with eager intentness or else in the *chaise-longue* by the lamp, looking very lovely and youthfully inscrutable indeed.

Merlin enjoyed these calls. Of some of the men he approved. Others won only his grudging toleration, one or two he loathed – especially the most frequent caller, a man with black hair and a black goatee and a pitch-dark soul, who seemed to Merlin vaguely familiar, but whom he was never quite able to recognize.

Now, Merlin's whole life was not 'bound up with this romance he had constructed'; it was not 'the happiest hour of his day.' He never arrived in time to rescue Caroline from 'clutches'; nor did he even marry her. A much stranger thing happened than any of these, and it is this strange thing that will presently be set down here. It began one October afternoon when she walked briskly into the mellow interior of the Moonlight Quill.

It was a dark afternoon, threatening rain and the end of the world, and done in that particularly gloomy grey in which only New York afternoons indulge. A breeze was crying down the streets, whisking along battered newspapers and pieces of things, and little lights were pricking out all the windows – it was so desolate that one was sorry for the tops of sky-scrapers lost up there in the dark green and grey heaven, and felt that now surely the farce was to close, and presently all the buildings would collapse like card houses, and pile up in a dusty, sardonic heap upon all the millions who presumed to wind in and out of them.

At least these were the sort of musings that lay heavily upon the soul of Merlin Grainger, as he stood by the window putting a dozen books back in a row, after a cyclonic visit by a lady with ermine trimmings. He looked out of the window full at the most distressing thoughts – of the early novels of H.G. Wells, of the book of Genesis, of how Thomas Edison had said that in thirty years there would be no dwelling-houses upon the island, but only a vast and turbulent bazaar; and then he set the last book right side up, turned – and Caroline walked coolly into the shop.

She was dressed in a jaunty but conventional walking costume – he remembered this when he thought about it later. Her skirt was plaid, pleated like a concertina; her jacket was a soft but brisk tan; her shoes and spats were brown and her hat, small and trim, completed her like the top of a very expensive and beautifully filled candy box.

Merlin, breathless and startled, advanced nervously toward her.

'Good-afternoon –' he said, and then stopped – why, he did not know, except that it came to him that something very portentous in his life was about to occur, and that it would need no furbishing but silence, and the proper amount of expectant attention. And in that minute before the thing began to happen he had the sense of a breathless second hanging suspended in time: he saw through the glass partition that bounded off the little office the malevolent conical head of his employer, Mr Moonlight Quill, bent over his correspondence. He saw Miss McCracken and Miss Masters as two patches of hair drooping over piles of paper; he saw the crimson lamp overhead, and noticed with a touch of pleasure how really pleasant and romantic it made the book-store seem.

Then the thing happened, or rather it began to happen. Caroline picked up a volume of poems lying loose upon a pile, fingered it absently with her slender white hand, and suddenly, with an easy gesture, tossed it upward toward the ceiling, where it disappeared in the crimson lamp and lodged there, seen through the illuminated silk as a dark, bulging rectangle. This pleased her – she broke into young, contagious laughter, in which Merlin found himself presently joining.

'It stayed up!' she cried merrily. 'It stayed up, didn't it?' To both of them this seemed the height of brilliant absurdity. Their laughter mingled, filled the bookshop, and Merlin was glad to find that her voice was rich and full of sorcery.

'Try another,' he found himself suggesting – 'try a red one.'

At this her laughter increased, and she had to rest her hands upon the stack to steady herself.

'Try another,' she managed to articulate between spasms of mirth. 'Oh, golly, try another!'

'Try two.'

'Yes, try two. Oh, I'll choke if I don't stop laughing. Here it goes.'

Suiting her action to the word, she picked up a red book and sent it in a gentle hyperbola toward the ceiling, where it sank into the lamp beside the first. It was a few minutes before either of them could do more than rock back and forth in helpless glee; but then by mutual agreement they took up the sport anew, this time in unison. Merlin seized a large, specially bound French classic and whirled it upward. Applauding his own accuracy, he took a best-seller in one hand and a book on barnacles in the other, and waited breathlessly while she made her shot. Then the business waxed fast and furious – sometimes they alternated, and, watching, he found how supple she was in every movement; sometimes one of them made shot after shot, picking up the nearest book, sending it off, merely taking time to follow it with a glance before reaching for another. Within three minutes they had cleared a little place on the table, and the lamp of crimson satin was so bulging with books that it was near breaking.

'Silly game, basket-ball,' she cried scornfully as a book left her hand. 'High-school girls play it in hideous bloomers.'

'Idiotic,' he agreed.

She paused in the act of tossing a book, and replaced it suddenly in its position on the table.

'I think we've got room to sit down now,' she said gravely.

They had; they had cleared an ample space for two. With a faint touch of nervousness Merlin glanced toward Mr Moonlight Quill's glass partition, but the three heads were still bent earnestly over their work, and it was evident that they had not seen what had gone on in the shop. So when Caroline put her hands on the table and hoisted herself up Merlin calmly imitated her, and they sat side by side looking very earnestly at each other.

'I had to see you,' she began, with a rather pathetic expression in her brown eyes.

'I know.'

'It was that last time,' she continued, her voice trembling a little, though she tried to keep it steady. 'I was frightened. I don't like you to eat off the dresser. I'm so afraid you'll – you'll swallow a collar button.'

'I did once – almost,' he confessed reluctantly, 'but it's not so easy, you know. I mean you can swallow the flat part easy enough or else the other part – that is, separately – but for a whole collar button you'd have to have a specially made throat.' He was astonishing himself by the debonair appropriateness of his remarks. Words seemed for the first time in his life to run at him shrieking to be used, gathering themselves into carefully arranged squads and platoons, and being presented to him by punctilious adjutants of paragraphs.

'That's what scared me,' she said. 'I knew you had to have a specially made throat – and I knew, at least I felt sure, that you didn't have one.'

He nodded frankly.

'I haven't. It costs money to have one – more money unfortunately than I possess.'

He felt no shame in saying this – rather a delight in making the admission – he knew that nothing he could say or do would be beyond her comprehension; least of all his poverty, and the practical impossibility of ever extricating himself from it.

Caroline looked down at her wrist watch, and with a little cry slid from the table to her feet.

'It's after five,' she cried. 'I didn't realize. I have to be at the Ritz at five-thirty. Let's hurry and get this done. I've got a bet on it.'

With one accord they set to work. Caroline began the matter by seizing a book on insects and sending it whizzing, and finally crashing through the glass partition that housed Mr. Moonlight Quill. The proprietor glanced up with a wild look, brushed a few pieces of glass from his desk, and went on with his letters. Miss McCracken gave no sign of having heard – only Miss Masters started and gave a little frightened scream before she bent to her task again.

But to Merlin and Caroline it didn't matter. In a perfect orgy of energy they were hurling book after book in all directions, until sometimes three or four were in the air at once, smashing against shelves, cracking the glass of pictures on the walls, falling in bruised and torn heaps upon the floor. It was fortunate that no customers happened to come in, for it is certain they would never have come in again – the noise was too tremendous, a noise of smashing and ripping and tearing, mixed now and then with the tinkling of glass, the quick breathing of the two throwers, and the intermittent outbursts of laughter to which both of them periodically surrendered.

At five-thirty Caroline tossed a last book at the lamp, and so gave the final impetus to the load it carried. The weakened silk tore and dropped its cargo in one vast splattering of white and color to the already littered floor. Then with a sigh of relief she turned to Merlin and held out her hand.

'Goodbye,' she said simply.

'Are you going?' He knew she was. His question was simply a lingering wile to detain her and extract for another moment that dazzling essence of light he drew from her presence, to continue his enormous satisfaction in her features, which were like kisses and, he thought, like the features of a girl he had known back in 1910. For a minute he pressed the softness of her hand – then she smiled and withdrew it and, before he could spring to open the door, she had done it herself and was gone out into the turbid and ominous twilight that brooded narrowly over Forty-seventh Street.

I would like to tell you how Merlin, having seen how beauty regards the wisdom of the years, walked into the little partition of Mr Moonlight Quill and gave up his job then and there; thence issuing out into the street a much finer and nobler and increasingly ironic man. But the truth is much more commonplace. Merlin Grainger stood up and surveyed the wreck of the bookshop, the ruined volumes, the torn silk remnants of the once beautiful crimson lamp, the crystalline sprinkling of broken glass which lay in iridescent dust over the whole interior – and then he went to a corner where a broom was kept and began cleaning up and rearranging and, as far as he was able, restoring the shop to its former condition. He found that, though some few of the books were uninjured, most of them had suffered in varying extents. The backs were off some, the pages were torn from others, still others were just slightly cracked in the front, which, as all careless book returners know, makes a book unsaleable, and therefore second-hand.

Nevertheless by six o'clock he had done much to repair the damage. He had returned the books to their original places, swept the floor, and put new lights in the sockets overhead. The red shade itself was ruined beyond redemption, and Merlin thought in some trepidation that the money to replace it might have to come out of his salary. At six, therefore, having done the best he could, he crawled over the front window display to pull down the blind. As he was treading delicately back, he saw Mr Moonlight Quill rise from his desk, put on his overcoat and hat, and emerge into the shop. He nodded mysteriously at Merlin and went toward the door. With his hand on the knob he paused, turned around, and in a voice curiously compounded of ferocity and uncertainty, he said:

'If that girl comes in here again, you tell her to behave.'

With that he opened the door, drowning Merlin's meek 'Yessir' in its creak, and went out.

Merlin stood there for a moment, deciding wisely not to worry about what was for the present only a possible futurity, and then he went into the back of the shop and invited Miss Masters to have supper with him at Pulpat's French Restaurant, where one could still obtain red wine at dinner, despite the Great Federal Government. Miss Masters accepted.

'Wine makes me feel all tingly,' she said.

Merlin laughed inwardly as he compared her to Caroline, or rather as he didn't compare her. There was no comparison.

II

Mr Moonlight Quill, mysterious, exotic, and oriental in temperament was, nevertheless, a man of decision. And it was with decision that he approached the problem of his wrecked shop. Unless he should make an outlay equal to the original cost of his entire stock – a step which for certain private reasons he did not wish to take – it would be impossible for him to continue in business with the Moonlight Quill as before. There was but one thing to do. He promptly turned his establishment from an up-to-the-minute book-store into a second-hand bookshop. The damaged books were marked down from twenty-five to fifty per cent, the name over the door whose serpentine embroidery had once shone so insolently bright, was allowed to grow dim and take on the indescribably vague color of old paint, and, having a strong penchant for ceremonial, the proprietor even went so far as to buy two skull-caps of shoddy red felt, one for himself and one for his clerk, Merlin Grainger. Moreover, he let his goatee grow until it resembled the tail-feathers of an ancient sparrow and substituted for a once dapper business suit a reverence-inspiring affair of shiny alpaca.

In fact, within a year after Caroline's catastrophic visit to the bookshop the only thing in it that preserved any semblance of being up to date was Miss Masters. Miss McCracken had followed in the footsteps of Mr Moonlight Quill and become an intolerable dowd.

For Merlin too, from a feeling compounded of loyalty and listlessness, had let his exterior take on the semblance of a deserted garden. He accepted the red felt skull-cap as a symbol of his decay. Always a young man known as a 'pusher,' he had been, since the day of his graduation from the manual training department of a New York High School, an inveterate brusher of clothes, hair, teeth, and even eyebrows, and had learned the value of laying all his clean socks toe upon toe and heel upon heel in a certain drawer of his bureau, which would be known as the sock drawer.

These things, he felt, had won him his place in the greatest splendor of the Moonlight Quill. It was due to them that he was not still making 'chests useful for keeping things,' as he was taught with breathless practicality in High School, and selling them to whoever had use of such chests – possibly undertakers. Nevertheless when the progressive

Moonlight Quill became the retrogressive Moonlight Quill he preferred to sink with it, and so took to letting his suits gather undisturbed the wispy burdens of the air and to throwing his socks indiscriminately into the shirt drawer, the underwear drawer, and even into no drawer at all. It was not uncommon in his new carelessness to let many of his clean clothes go directly back to the laundry without having ever been worn, a common eccentricity of impoverished bachelors. And this in the face of his favorite magazines, which at that time were fairly staggering with articles by successful authors against the frightful impudence of the condemned poor, such as the buying of wearable shirts and nice cuts of meat, and the fact that they preferred good investments in personal jewelry to respectable ones in four per cent saving-banks.

It was indeed a strange state of affairs and a sorry one for many worthy and God-fearing men. For the first time in the history of the Republic almost any negro north of Georgia could change a one-dollar bill. But as at that time the cent was rapidly approaching the purchasing power of the Chinese ubu and was only a thing you got back occasionally after paying for a soft drink, and could use merely in getting your correct weight, this was perhaps not so strange a phenomenon as it at first seems. It was too curious a state of things, however, for Merlin Grainger to take the step that he did take – the hazardous, almost involuntary step of proposing to Miss Masters. Stranger still that she accepted him.

It was at Pulpat's on Saturday night and over a $1.75 bottle of water diluted with *vin ordinaire* that the proposal occurred.

'Wine makes me feel all tingly, doesn't it you?' chattered Miss Masters gaily.

'Yes,' answered Merlin absently; and then, after a long and pregnant pause: 'Miss Masters – Olive – I want to say something to you if you'll listen to me.'

The tingliness of Miss Masters (who knew what was coming) increased until it seemed that she would shortly be electrocuted by her own nervous reactions. But her 'Yes, Merlin,' came without a sign or flicker of interior disturbance. Merlin swallowed a stray bit of air that he found in his mouth.

'I have no fortune,' he said with the manner of making an announcement. 'I have no fortune at all.'

Their eyes met, locked, became wistful, and dreamy and beautiful.

'Olive,' he told her, 'I love you.'

'I love you too, Merlin,' she answered simply. 'Shall we have another bottle of wine?'

'Yes,' he cried, his heart beating at a great rate. 'Do you mean –'

'To drink to our engagement,' she interrupted bravely. 'May it be a short one!'

'No!' he almost shouted, bringing his fist fiercely down upon the table. 'May it last forever!'

'What?'

'I mean – oh, I see what you mean. You're right. May it be a short one.' He laughed and added, 'My error.'

After the wine arrived they discussed the matter thoroughly.

'We'll have to take a small apartment at first,' he said, 'and I believe, yes, by golly, I know there's a small one in the house where I live, a big room and a sort of a dressing-room-kitchenette and the use of a bath on the same floor.'

She clapped her hands happily, and he thought how pretty she was really, that is, the upper part of her face – from the bridge of the nose down she was somewhat out of true. She continued enthusiastically:

'And as soon as we can afford it we'll take a real swell apartment, with an elevator and a telephone girl.'

'And after that a place in the country – and a car.'

'I can't imagine nothing more fun. Can you?'

Merlin fell silent a moment. He was thinking that he would have to give up his room, the fourth floor rear. Yet it mattered very little now. During the past year and a half – in fact, from the very date of Caroline's visit to the Moonlight Quill – he had never seen her. For a week after that visit her lights had failed to go on – darkness brooded out into the areaway, seemed to grope blindly in at his expectant, uncurtained window. Then the lights had appeared at last, and instead of Caroline and her callers they showed a stodgy family – a little man with a bristly mustache and a full-bosomed woman who spent her evenings patting her hips and rearranging bric-à-brac. After two days of them Merlin had callously pulled down his shade.

No, Merlin could think of nothing more fun than rising in the world with Olive. There would be a cottage in a suburb, a cottage painted blue, just one class below the sort of cottages that are of white stucco with a green roof. In the grass around the cottage would be rusty trowels and a broken green bench and a baby-carriage with a wicker body that sagged to the left. And around the grass and the baby-carriage and the cottage itself, around his whole world there would be the arms of Olive, a little stouter, the arms of her neo-Olivian period, when, as she walked, her cheeks would tremble up and down ever so slightly from too much face-massaging. He could hear her voice now, two spoons' length away:

'I knew you were going to say this to-night, Merlin. I could see –'

She could see. Ah – suddenly he wondered how much she could see. Could she see that the girl who had come in with a party of three men and sat down at the next table was Caroline? Ah, could she see that? Could she see that the men brought with them liquor far more potent than Pulpat's red ink condensed threefold …?

Merlin stared breathlessly, half-hearing through an auditory ether Olive's low, soft monologue, as like a persistent honey-bee she sucked sweetness from her memorable hour. Merlin was listening to the clinking of ice and the fine laughter of all four at some pleasantry – and that laughter of Caroline's that he knew so well stirred him, lifted him, called his heart imperiously over to her table, whither it obediently went. He could see her quite plainly, and he fancied that in the last year and a half she had changed, if ever so slightly. Was it the light or were her cheeks a little thinner and her eyes less fresh, if more liquid, than of old? Yet the shadows were still purple in her russet hair; her mouth hinted yet of kisses, as did the profile that came sometimes between his eyes and a row of books, when it was twilight in the bookshop where the crimson lamp presided no more.

And she had been drinking. The threefold flush in her cheeks was compounded of youth and wine and fine cosmetic – that he could tell. She was making great amusement for the young man on her left and the portly person on her right, and even for the old fellow opposite her, for the latter from time to time uttered the shocked and mildly reproachful cackles of another generation. Merlin caught the words of a song she was intermittently singing –

> 'Just snap your fingers at care,
> Don't cross the bridge 'til you're there –'

The portly person filled her glass with chill amber. A waiter after several trips about the table, and many helpless glances at Caroline, who was maintaining a cheerful, futile questionnaire as to the succulence of this dish or that, managed to obtain the semblance of an order and hurried away ...

Olive was speaking to Merlin –

'When, then?' she asked, her voice faintly shaded with disappointment. He realized that he had just answered no to some question she had asked him.

'Oh, sometime.'

'Don't you – care?'

A rather pathetic poignancy in her question brought his eyes back to her.

'As soon as possible, dear,' he replied with surprising tenderness. 'In two months – in June.'

'So soon?' Her delightful excitement quite took her breath away.

'Oh, yes, I think we'd better say June. No use waiting.'

Olive began to pretend that two months was really too short a time for her to make preparations. Wasn't he a bad boy! Wasn't he impatient, though! Well, she'd show him he mustn't be too quick with *her*. Indeed he was so sudden she didn't exactly know whether she ought to marry him at all.

'June,' he repeated sternly.

Olive sighed and smiled and drank her coffee, her little finger lifted high above the others in true refined fashion. A stray thought came to Merlin that he would like to buy five rings and throw at it.

'By gosh!' he exclaimed aloud. Soon he *would* be putting rings on one of her fingers.

His eyes swung sharply to the right. The party of four had become so riotous that the head-waiter had approached and spoken to them. Caroline was arguing with this head-waiter in a raised voice, a voice so clear and young that it seemed as though the whole restaurant would listen – the whole restaurant except Olive Masters, self-absorbed in her new secret.

'How do you do?' Caroline was saying. 'Probably the handsomest head-waiter in captivity. Too much noise? Very unfortunate. Something'll have to be done about it. Gerald' – she addressed the man on her right – 'the head-waiter says there's too much noise. Appeals to us to have it stopped. What'll I say?'

'Sh!' remonstrated Gerald, with laughter. 'Sh!' and Merlin heard him add in an undertone: 'All the bourgeoisie will be aroused. This is where the floorwalkers learn French.'

Caroline sat up straight in sudden alertness.

'Where's a floorwalker?' she cried. 'Show me a floorwalker.' This seemed to amuse the party, for they all, including Caroline, burst into renewed laughter. The head-waiter, after a last conscientious but despairing admonition, became Gallic with his shoulders and retired into the background.

Pulpat's, as every one knows, has the unvarying respectability of the table d'hôte. It is not a gay place in the conventional sense. One comes, drinks the red wine, talks perhaps a little more and a little louder than usual under the low, smoky ceilings, and then goes home. It closes up at nine-thirty, tight as a drum; the policeman is paid off and given an extra bottle of wine for the missis, the coat-room girl hands her tips to the collector, and then darkness crushes the little round tables out of sight and life. But excitement was prepared for Pulpat's this evening – excitement of no mean variety. A girl with russet, purple-shadowed hair mounted to her table-top and began to dance thereon.

'*Sacré nom de Dieu!* Come down off there!' cried the head-waiter. 'Stop that music!'

But the musicians were already playing so loud that they could pretend not to hear his order; having once been young, they played louder and gayer than ever, and Caroline danced with grace and vivacity, her pink, filmy dress swirling about her, her agile arms playing in supple, tenuous gestures along the smoky air.

A group of Frenchmen at a table near by broke into cries of applause, in which other parties joined – in a moment the room was full of clapping and shouting; half the diners were on their feet, crowding up, and on the outskirts the hastily summoned proprietor was giving indistinct vocal evidence of his desire to put an end to this thing as quickly as possible.

'... Merlin!' cried Olive, awake, aroused at last; 'she's such a wicked girl! Let's get out – now!'

The fascinated Merlin protested feebly that the check was not paid.

'It's all right. Lay five dollars on the table. I despise that girl. I can't *bear* to look at her.' She was on her feet now, tugging at Merlin's arm.

Helplessly, listlessly, and then with what amounted to downright unwillingness, Merlin rose, followed Olive dumbly as she picked her way through the delirious clamor, now approaching its height and threatening to become a wild and memorable riot. Submissively he took his coat and stumbled up half a dozen steps into the moist April air outside, his ears still ringing with the sound of light feet on the table and of laughter all about and over the little world of the café. In silence they walked along toward Fifth Avenue and a bus.

It was not until next day that she told him about the wedding – how she had moved the date forward: it was much better that they should be married on the first of May.

III

And married they were, in a somewhat stuffy manner, under the chandelier of the flat where Olive lived with her mother. After marriage came elation, and then, gradually, the growth of weariness. Responsibility descended upon Merlin, the responsibility of making his thirty dollars a week and her twenty suffice to keep them respectably fat and to hide with decent garments the evidence that they were.

It was decided after several weeks of disastrous and well-nigh humiliating experiments with restaurants that they would join the great army of the delicatessen-fed, so he took up his old way of life again, in that he stopped every evening at Braegdort's delicatessen and bought potatoes in salad, ham in slices, and sometimes even stuffed tomatoes in bursts of extravagance.

Then he would trudge homeward, enter the dark hallway, and climb three rickety flights of stairs covered by an ancient carpet of long obliterated design. The hall had an ancient smell – of the vegetables of 1880, of the furniture polish in vogue when 'Adam-and-Eve' Bryan ran against William McKinley, of *portières* an ounce heavier with dust, from worn-out shoes and lint from dresses turned long since into patch-work quilts. This smell would pursue him up the stairs, revivified and made poignant at each landing by the aura of contemporary cooking, then, as he began the next flight, diminishing into the odour of the dead routine of dead generations.

Eventually would occur the door of his room, which slipped open with indecent willingness and closed with almost a sniff upon his 'Hello, dear! Got a treat for you to-night.'

Olive, who always rode home on the bus to 'get a morsel of air,' would be making the bed and hanging up things. At this call she would come up to him and give him a quick kiss with wide-open eyes, while he held her upright like a ladder, his hands on her two arms, as though she were a thing without equilibrium, and would, once he relinquished hold, fall stiffly backward to the floor. This is the kiss that comes in with the second year of marriage, succeeding the bridegroom kiss (which is rather stagey at best, say those who know about such things, and apt to be copied from passionate movies).

Then came supper, and after that they went out for a walk, up two blocks and through Central Park, or sometimes to a moving picture, which taught them patiently that they were the sort of people for whom life was ordered, and that something very grand and brave and beautiful would soon happen to them if they were docile and obedient to their rightful superiors and kept away from pleasure.

Such was their day for three years. Then change came into their lives: Olive had a baby, and as a result Merlin had a new influx of material resources. In the third week of Olive's confinement, after an hour of nervous rehearsing, he went into the office of Mr Moonlight Quill and demanded an enormous increase in salary.

'I've been here ten years,' he said; 'since I was nineteen. I've always tried to do my best in the interests of the business.'

Mr Moonlight Quill said that he would think it over. Next morning he announced, to Merlin's great delight, that he was going to put into effect a project long premeditated – he was going to retire from active work in the bookshop, confining himself to periodic visits and leaving Merlin as manager with a salary of fifty dollars a week and a one-tenth interest in the business. When the old man finished, Merlin's cheeks were glowing and his eyes full of tears. He seized his employer's hand and shook it violently, saying over and over again:

'It's very nice of you, sir. It's very white of you. It's very, very nice of you.'

So after ten years of faithful work in the store he had won out at last. Looking back, he saw his own progress toward this hill of elation no longer as a sometimes sordid and always gray decade of worry and failing enthusiasm and failing dreams, years when the moonlight had grown duller in the areaway and the youth had faded out of Olive's face, but as a glorious and triumphant climb over obstacles which he had determinedly surmounted by unconquerable will-power. The optimistic self-delusion that had kept him from misery was seen now in the golden garments of stern resolution. Half a dozen times he had taken steps to leave the Moonlight Quill and soar upward, but through sheer faint-heartedness he had stayed on. Strangely enough he now thought that those were times when he had exerted tremendous persistence and had 'determined' to fight it out where he was.

At any rate, let us not for this moment begrudge Merlin his new and magnificent view of himself. He had arrived. At thirty he had reached a post of importance. He left the shop that evening fairly radiant, invested every penny in his pocket in the most tremendous feast that Braegdort's delicatessen offered, and staggered homeward with the great news and four gigantic paper bags. The fact that Olive was too sick to eat, that he made himself faintly but unmistakably ill by a struggle with four stuffed tomatoes, and that most of the food deteriorated rapidly in an iceless ice-box all next day did not mar the occasion. For the first time since the week of his marriage Merlin Grainger lived under a sky of unclouded tranquillity.

The baby boy was christened Arthur, and life became dignified, significant, and, at length, centered. Merlin and Olive resigned themselves to a somewhat secondary place in their own cosmos; but what they lost in personality they regained in a sort of primordial pride. The country house did not come, but a month in an Asbury Park boarding-house each summer filled the gap; and during Merlin's two weeks' holiday this excursion assumed the air of a really merry jaunt – especially when, with the baby asleep in a wide room opening technically on the sea, Merlin strolled with Olive along the thronged board-walk puffing at his cigar and trying to look like twenty thousand a year.

With some alarm at the slowing up of the days and the accelerating of the years, Merlin became thirty-one, thirty-two – then almost with a rush arrived at that age which, with all its washing and panning, can only muster a bare handful of the precious stuff of youth: he became thirty-five. And one day on Fifth Avenue he saw Caroline.

It was Sunday, a radiant, flowerful Easter morning and the avenue was a pageant of lilies and cutaways and happy April-coloured bonnets. Twelve o'clock: the great churches were letting out their people – St Simon's, St Hilda's, the Church of the Epistles, opened their doors like wide mouths until the people pouring forth surely resembled happy laughter as they met and strolled and chattered, or else waved white bouquets at waiting chauffeurs.

In front of the Church of the Epistles stood its twelve vestrymen, carrying out the time-honored custom of giving away Easter eggs full of face-powder to the church-going débutantes of the year. Around them delightedly danced the two thousand miraculously groomed children of the very rich, correctly cute and curled, shining like sparkling little jewels upon their mothers' fingers. Speaks the sentimentalist for the children of the poor? Ah, but the children of the rich, laundered, sweet-smelling, complexioned of the country, and, above all, with soft, in-door voices.

Little Arthur was five, child of the middle class. Undistinguished, unnoticed, with a nose that forever marred what Grecian yearnings his features might have had, he held tightly to his mother's warm, sticky hand, and, with Merlin on his other side, moved upon the home-coming throng. At Fifty-third Street, where there were two churches, the congestion was at its thickest, its richest. Their progress was of necessity retarded to such an extent that even little Arthur had not the slightest difficulty in keeping up. Then it was that Merlin perceived an open landaulet of deepest crimson, with handsome nickel trimmings, glide slowly up to the curb and come to a stop. In it sat Caroline.

She was dressed in black, a tight-fitting gown trimmed with lavender, flowered at the waist with a corsage of orchids. Merlin started and then gazed at her fearfully. For the first time in the eight years since his marriage he was encountering the girl again. But a girl no longer. Her figure was slim as ever – or perhaps not quite, for a certain boyish swagger, a sort of insolent adolescence, had gone the way of the first blooming of her cheeks. But she was beautiful; dignity was there now, and the charming lines of a fortuitous nine-and-twenty; and she sat in the car with such perfect appropriateness and self-possession that it made him breathless to watch her.

Suddenly she smiled – the smile of old, bright as that very Easter and its flowers, mellower than ever – yet somehow with not quite the radiance and infinite promise of that first smile back there in the bookshop nine years before. It was a steelier smile, disillusioned and sad.

But it was soft enough and smile enough to make a pair of young men in cutaway coats hurry over, to pull their high hats off their wetted, iridescent hair; to bring them, flustered and bowing, to the edge of her landaulet, where her lavender gloves gently touched their gray ones. And these two were presently joined by another, and then two more, until there was a rapidly swelling crowd around the landaulet. Merlin would hear a young man beside him say to his perhaps well-favoured companion:

'If you'll just pardon me a moment, there's some one I *have* to speak to. Walk right ahead. I'll catch up.'

Within three minutes every inch of the landaulet, front, back, and side, was occupied by a man – a man trying to construct a sentence clever enough to find its way to Caroline through the stream of conversation. Luckily for Merlin a portion of little Arthur's clothing had chosen the opportunity to threaten a collapse, and Olive had hurriedly rushed him over against a building for some extemporaneous repair work, so Merlin was able to watch, unhindered, the salon in the street.

The crowd swelled. A row formed in back of the first, two more behind that. In the midst, an orchid rising from a black bouquet, sat Caroline enthroned in her obliterated car, nodding and crying salutations and smiling with such true happiness that, of a sudden, a new relay of gentlemen had left their wives and consorts and were striding toward her.

The crowd, now phalanx deep, began to be augmented by the merely curious; men of all ages who could not possibly have known Caroline jostled over and melted into the circle of ever-increasing diameter, until the lady in lavender was the centre of a vast impromptu auditorium.

All about her were faces – clean-shaven, bewhiskered, old, young, ageless, and now, here and there, a woman. The mass was rapidly spreading to the opposite curb, and, as St Anthony's around the corner let out its box-holders, it overflowed to the sidewalk and crushed up against the iron picket-fence of a millionaire across the street. The motors speeding along the avenue were compelled to stop, and in a jiffy were piled three, five, and six deep at the edge of the crowd; auto-buses, top-heavy turtles of traffic, plunged into the jam, their passengers crowding to the edges of the roofs in wild excitement and peering down into the centre of the mass, which presently could hardly be seen from the mass's edge.

The crush had become terrific. No fashionable audience at a Yale-Princeton football game, no damp mob at a world's series, could be compared with the panoply that talked, stared, laughed, and honked about the lady in black and lavender. It was stupendous; it was terrible. A quarter mile down the block a half-frantic policeman called his precinct; on the same corner a frightened civilian crashed in the glass of a fire-alarm and sent in a wild paean for all the fire-engines of the city; up in an apartment high in one of the tall buildings a hysterical old maid telephoned in turn for the prohibition enforcement agent, the special deputies on Bolshevism, and the maternity ward of Bellevue Hospital.

The noise increased. The first fire-engine arrived, filling the Sunday air with smoke, clanging and crying a brazen, metallic message down the high, resounding walls. In the notion that some terrible calamity had overtaken the city, two excited deacons ordered special services immediately and set tolling the great bells of St Hilda's and St Anthony's, presently joined by the jealous gongs of St Simon's and the Church of the Epistles. Even far off in the Hudson and the East River the sounds of the commotion were heard, and the ferry-boats and tugs and ocean liners set up sirens and whistles that sailed in melancholy cadence, now varied, now reiterated, across the whole diagonal width of the city from Riverside Drive to the grey waterfronts of the lower East Side ...

In the centre of her landaulet sat the lady in black and lavender, chatting pleasantly first with one, then with another of that fortunate few in cutaways who had found their way to speaking distance in the first rush. After a while she glanced around her and beside her with a look of growing annoyance.

She yawned and asked the man nearest her if he couldn't run in somewhere and get her a glass of water. The man apologized in some embarrassment. He could not have moved hand or foot. He could not have scratched his own ear ...

As the first blast of the river sirens keened along the air, Olive fastened the last safety-pin in little Arthur's rompers and looked up. Merlin saw her start, stiffen slowly like hardening stucco, and then give a little gasp of surprise and disapproval.

'That woman,' she cried suddenly. 'Oh!'

She flashed a glance at Merlin that mingled reproach and pain, and without another word gathered up little Arthur with one hand, grasped her husband by the other, and darted amazingly in a winding, bumping canter through the crowd. Somehow people gave way before her; somehow she managed to retain her grasp on her son and husband; somehow she managed to emerge two blocks up, battered and dishevelled, into an open space, and, without slowing up her pace, darted down a side-street. Then at last, when uproar had died away into a dim and distant clamor, did she come to a walk and set little Arthur upon his feet.

'And on Sunday, too! Hasn't she disgraced herself enough?' This was her only comment. She said it to Arthur, as she seemed to address her remarks to Arthur throughout the remainder of the day. For some curious and esoteric reason she had never once looked at her husband during the entire retreat.

IV

The years between thirty-five and sixty-five revolve before the passive mind as one unexplained, confusing merry-go-round. True, they are a merry-go-round of ill-gaited and wind-broken horses, painted first in pastel colors, then in dull greys and browns, but perplexing and intolerably dizzy the thing is, as never were the merry-go-rounds of childhood or adolescence, as never, surely, were the certain-coursed, dynamic roller-coasters of youth. For most men and women these thirty years are taken up with a gradual withdrawal from life, a retreat first from a front with many shelters, those myriad amusements and curiosities of youth, to a line with less, when we peel down our ambitions to one ambition, our recreations to one recreation, our friends to a few to whom we are anaesthetic; ending up at last in a solitary, desolate strong point that is not strong, where the shells now whistle abominably, now are but half-heard as, by turns frightened and tired, we sit waiting for death.

At forty, then, Merlin was no different from himself at thirty-five; a larger paunch, a gray twinkling near his ears, a more certain lack of vivacity in his walk. His forty-five differed from his forty by a like margin, unless one mention a slight deafness in his left ear. But at fifty-five the process had become a chemical change of immense rapidity. Yearly he was more and more an 'old man' to his family – senile almost, so far as his wife was concerned. He was by this time complete owner of the bookshop. The mysterious Mr Moonlight Quill, dead some five years and not survived by his wife, had deeded the whole stock and store to him, and there he still spent his days, conversant now by name with almost all that man has recorded for three thousand years, a human catalogue, an authority upon tooling and binding, upon folios and first editions, an accurate inventory of a thousand authors whom he could never have understood and had certainly never read.

At sixty-five he distinctly doddered. He had assumed the melancholy habits of the aged so often portrayed by the second old man in standard Victorian comedies. He consumed vast warehouses of time searching for mislaid spectacles. He 'nagged' his wife and was nagged in turn. He told the same jokes three or four times a year at the family table, and gave his son weird, impossible directions as to his conduct in life. Mentally and materially he was so entirely different from the Merlin Grainger of twenty-five that it seemed incongruous that he should bear the same name.

He worked still in the bookshop with the assistance of a youth, whom, of course, he considered very idle, indeed, and a new young woman, Miss Gaffney. Miss McCracken, ancient and unvenerable as himself, still kept the accounts. Young Arthur was gone into Wall Street to sell bonds, as all the young men seemed to be doing in that day. This, of course, was as it should be. Let old Merlin get what magic he could from his books – the place of young King Arthur was in the countinghouse.

One afternoon at four when he had slipped noiselessly up to the front of the store on his soft-soled slippers, led by a newly formed habit, of which, to be fair, he was rather ashamed, of spying upon the young man clerk, he looked casually out of the front window, straining his faded eyesight to reach the street. A limousine, large, portentous, impressive, had drawn to the curb, and the chauffeur, after dismounting and holding some sort of conversation with persons in the interior of the car, turned about and advanced in a bewildered fashion toward the entrance of the Moonlight Quill. He opened the door, shuffled in, and, glancing uncertainly at the old man in the skull-cap, addressed him in a thick, murky voice, as though his words came through a fog.

'Do you – do you sell additions?'

Merlin nodded.

'The arithmetic books are in the back of the store.'

The chauffeur took off his cap and scratched a close-cropped, fuzzy head.

'Oh, naw. This I want's a detecatif story.' He jerked a thumb back toward the limousine. 'She seen it in the paper. Firs' addition.'

Merlin's interest quickened. Here was possibly a big sale.

'Oh, editions. Yes. We've advertised some firsts, but – detective stories, I – don't – believe – What was the title?'

'I forget. About a crime.'

'About a crime. I have – well, I have *The Crimes of the Borgias* – full morocco, London 1769, beautifully –'

'Naw,' interrupted the chauffeur, 'this was one fella did this crime. She seen you had it for sale in the paper.' He rejected several possible titles with the air of connoisseur.

'"Silver Bones",' he announced suddenly out of a slight pause.

'What?' demanded Merlin, suspecting that the stiffness of his sinews were being commented on.

'Silver Bones. That was the guy that done the crime.'

'Silver Bones?'

'Silver Bones. Indian, maybe.'

Merlin stroked his grizzly cheeks.

'Gees, Mister,' went on the prospective purchaser, 'if you wanna save me an awful bawlin' out jes' try an' think. The old lady goes wile if everything don't run smooth.'

But Merlin's musings on the subject of Silver Bones were as futile as his obliging search through the shelves, and five minutes later a very dejected charioteer wound his way back to his mistress. Through the glass Merlin could see the visible symbols of a tremendous uproar going on in the interior of the limousine. The chauffeur made wild, appealing gestures of his innocence, evidently to no avail, for when he turned around and climbed back into the driver's seat his expression was not a little dejected.

Then the door of the limousine opened and gave forth a pale and slender young man of about twenty, dressed in the attenuation of fashion and carrying a wisp of a cane. He entered the shop, walked past Merlin, and proceeded to take out a cigarette and light it. Merlin approached him.

'Anything I can do for you, sir?'

'Old boy,' said the youth coolly, 'there are several things. You can first let me smoke my ciggy in here out of sight of that old lady in the limousine, who happens to be my grandmother. Her knowledge as to whether I smoke it or not before my majority happens to be a matter of five thousand dollars to me. The second thing is that you should look up your first edition of the *Crime of Sylvester Bonnard* that you advertised in last Sunday's *Times*. My grandmother there happens to want to take it off your hands.'

Detecatif story! Crime of somebody! Silver Bones! All was explained. With a faint deprecatory chuckle, as if to say that he would have enjoyed this had life put him in the habit of enjoying anything, Merlin doddered away to the back of his shop where his treasures were kept, to get this latest investment which he had picked up rather cheaply at the sale of a big collection.

When he returned with it the young man was drawing on his cigarette and blowing out quantities of smoke with immense satisfaction.

'My God!' he said. 'She keeps me so close to her the entire day running idiotic errands that this happens to be my first puff in six hours. What's the world coming to, I ask you, when a feeble old lady in the milk-toast era can dictate to a man as to his personal vices? I happen to be unwilling to be so dictated to. Let's see the book.'

Merlin passed it to him tenderly and the young man, after opening it with a carelessness that gave a momentary jump to the bookdealer's heart, ran through the pages with his thumb.

'No illustrations, eh?' he commented. 'Well, old boy, what's it worth? Speak up! We're willing to give you a fair price, though why I don't know.'

'One hundred dollars,' said Merlin with a frown.

The young man gave a startled whistle.

'Whew! Come on. You're not dealing with somebody from the cornbelt. I happen to be a city-bred man and my grandmother happens to be a city-bred woman, though I'll admit it'd take a special tax appropriation to keep her in repair. We'll give you twenty-five dollars, and let me tell you that's liberal. We've got books in our attic, up in our attic with my old playthings, that were written before the old boy that wrote this was born.'

Merlin stiffened, expressing a rigid and meticulous horror.

'Did your grandmother give you twenty-five dollars to buy this with?'

'She did not. She gave me fifty, but she expects change. I know that old lady.'

'You tell her,' said Merlin with dignity, 'that she has missed a very great bargain.'

'Give you forty,' urged the young man. 'Come on now – be reasonable and don't try to hold us up –'

Merlin had wheeled around with the precious volume under his arm and was about to return it to its special drawer in his office when there was a sudden interruption. With unheard-of magnificence the front door burst rather than swung open, and admitted into the dark interior a regal apparition in black silk and fur which bore rapidly down upon him. The cigarette leaped from the fingers of the urban young man and he gave breath to an inadvertent 'Damn!' – but it was upon Merlin that the entrance seemed to have the most remarkable and incongruous effect – so strong an effect that the greatest treasure of his shop slipped from his hand and joined the cigarette on the floor. Before him stood Caroline.

She was an old woman, an old woman remarkably preserved, unusually handsome, unusually erect, but still an old woman. Her hair was a soft, beautiful white, elaborately dressed and jewelled; her face, faintly rouged à la grande dame, showed webs of wrinkles at the edges of her eyes and two deeper lines in the form of stanchions connected her nose with the corners of her mouth. Her eyes were dim, ill natured, and querulous.

But it was Caroline without a doubt: Caroline's features though in decay; Caroline's figure, if brittle and stiff in movement; Caroline's manner, unmistakably compounded of a delightful insolence and an enviable self assurance; and, most of all, Caroline's voice, broken and shaky, yet with a ring in it that still could and did make chauffeurs want to drive laundry wagons and cause cigarettes to fall from the fingers of urban grandsons.

She stood and sniffed. Her eyes found the cigarette upon the floor.

'What's that?' she cried. The words were not a question – they were an entire litany of suspicion, accusation, confirmation, and decision. She tarried over them scarcely an instant. 'Stand up!' she said to her grandson, 'stand up and blow that nicotine out of your lungs!'

The young man looked at her in trepidation.

'Blow!' she commanded.

He pursed his lips feebly and blew into the air.

'Blow!' she repeated, more peremptorily than before.

He blew again, helplessly, ridiculously.

'Do you realize,' she went on briskly, 'that you've forfeited five thousand dollars in five minutes?'

Merlin momentarily expected the young man to fall pleading upon his knees, but such is the nobility of human nature that he remained standing – even blew again into the air, partly from nervousness, partly, no doubt, with some vague hope of reingratiating himself.

'You ass!' cried Caroline. 'Once more, just once more and you leave college and go to work.'

This threat had such an overwhelming effect upon the young man that he took on an even paler pallor than was natural to him. But Caroline was not through.

'Do you think I don't know what you and your brothers, yes, and your asinine father too, think of me? Well, I do. You think I'm senile. You think I'm soft. I'm not!' She struck herself with her fist as though to prove that she was a mass of muscle and sinew. 'And I'll have more brains left when you've got me laid out in the drawing-room some sunny day than you and the rest of them were born with.'

'But Grandmother –'

'Be quiet. You, a thin little stick of a boy, who if it weren't for my money might have risen to be a journeyman barber out in the Bronx – Let me see your hands. Ugh! The hands of a barber – *you* presume to be smart with *me*, who once had three counts and a bona-fide duke, not to mention half a dozen papal titles pursue me from the city of Rome to the city of New York.' She paused, took breath. 'Stand up! Blow!'

The young man obediently blew. Simultaneously the door opened and an excited gentleman of middle age who wore a coat and hat trimmed with fur, and seemed, moreover, to be trimmed with the same sort of fur himself on upper lip and chin, rushed into the store and up to Caroline.

'Found you at last,' he cried. 'Been looking for you all over town. Tried your house on the 'phone and your secretary told me he thought you'd gone to a bookshop called the Moonlight –'

Caroline turned to him irritably.

'Do I employ you for your reminiscenses?' she snapped. 'Are you my tutor or my broker?'

'Your broker,' confessed the fur-trimmed man, taken somewhat aback. 'I beg your pardon. I came about that phonograph stock. I can sell for a hundred and five.'

'Then do it.'

'Very well. I thought I'd better –'

'Go sell it. I'm talking to my grandson.'

'Very well. I –'

'Goodbye.'

'Goodbye, Madame.' The fur-trimmed man made a slight bow and hurried in some confusion from the shop.

'As for you,' said Caroline, turning to her grandson, 'you stay just where you are and be quiet.'

She turned to Merlin and included his entire length in a not unfriendly survey. Then she smiled and he found himself smiling too. In an instant they had both broken into a cracked but none the less spontaneous chuckle. She seized his arm and hurried him to the other side of the store. There they stopped, faced each other, and gave vent to another long fit of senile glee.

'It's the only way,' she gasped in a sort of triumphant malignity. 'The only thing that keeps old folks like me happy is the sense that they can make other people step around. To be old and rich and have poor descendants is almost as much fun as to be young and beautiful and have ugly sisters.'

'Oh, yes,' chuckled Merlin. 'I know. I envy you.'

She nodded, blinking.

'The last time I was in here, forty years ago,' she said, 'you were a young man and very anxious to kick up your heels.'

'I was,' he confessed.

'My visit must have meant a good deal to you.'

'You have all along,' he exclaimed. 'I thought – I used to think at first that you were a real person – human, I mean.'

She laughed.

'Many men have thought me inhuman.'

'But now,' continued Merlin excitedly, 'I understand. Understanding is allowed to us old people – after nothing much matters. I see now that on a certain night when you danced upon a table-top you were nothing but my romantic yearning for a beautiful and perverse woman.'

Her old eyes were far away, her voice no more than the echo of a forgotten dream.

'How I danced that night! I remember.'

'You were making an attempt at me. Olive's arms were closing about me and you warned me to be free and keep my measure of youth and irresponsibility. But it seemed like an effect gotten up at the last moment. It came too late.'

'You are very old,' she said inscrutably. 'I did not realize.'

'Also I have not forgotten what you did to me when I was thirty-five. You shook me with that traffic tie-up. It was a magnificent effort. The beauty and power you radiated! You became personified even to my wife, and she feared you. For weeks I wanted to slip out of the house at dark and forget the stuffiness of life with music and cocktails and a girl to make me young. But then – I no longer knew how.'

'And now you are so very old.'

With a sort of awe she moved back and away from him.

'Yes, leave me!' he cried. 'You are old also; the spirit withers with the skin. Have you come here only to tell me something I had best forget: that to be old and poor is perhaps more wretched than to be old and rich; to remind me that *my* son hurls my grey failure in my face?'

'Give me my book,' she commanded harshly. 'Be quick, old man!'

Merlin looked at her once more and then patiently obeyed. He picked up the book and handed it to her, shaking his head when she offered him a bill.

'Why go through the farce of paying me? Once you made me wreck these very premises.'

'I did,' she said in anger, 'and I'm glad. Perhaps there had been enough done to ruin *me*.'

She gave him a glance, half disdain, half ill-concealed uneasiness, and with a brisk word to her urban grandson moved toward the door.

Then she was gone – out of his shop – out of his life. The door clicked. With a sigh he turned and walked brokenly back toward the glass partition that enclosed the yellowed accounts of many years as well as the mellowed, wrinkled Miss McCracken.

Merlin regarded her parched, cobwebbed face with an odd sort of pity. She, at any rate, had had less from life than he. No rebellious, romantic spirit cropping out unbidden had, in its memorable moments, given her life a zest and a glory.

Then Miss McCracken looked up and spoke to him:

'Still a spunky old piece, isn't she?'

Merlin started.

'Who?'

'Old Alicia Dare. Mrs. Thomas Allerdyce she is now, of course; has been these thirty years.'

'What? I don't understand you.' Merlin sat down suddenly in his swivel chair; his eyes were wide.

'Why, surely, Mr Grainger, you can't tell me that you've forgotten her, when for ten years she was the most notorious character in New York. Why, one time when she was the correspondent in the Throckmorton divorce case she attracted so much attention on Fifth Avenue that there was a traffic tie-up. Didn't you read about it in the papers.'

'I never used to read the papers.' His ancient brain was whirring.

'Well, you can't have forgotten the time she came in here and ruined the business. Let me tell you I came near asking Mr Moonlight Quill for my salary, and clearing out.'

'Do you mean that – that you *saw* her?'

'Saw her! How could I help it with the racket that went on. Heaven knows Mr Moonlight Quill didn't like it either, but of course *he* didn't say anything. He was daffy about her and she could twist him around her little finger. The second he opposed one of her whims she'd threaten to tell his wife on him. Served him right. The idea of that man falling for a pretty adventuress! Of course he was never rich enough for *her*, even though the shop paid well in those days.'

'But when I saw her,' stammered Merlin, 'that is, when I *thought* I saw her, she lived with her mother.'

'Mother, trash!' said Miss McCracken indignantly. 'She had a woman there she called "Aunty" who was no more related to her than I am. Oh, she was a bad one – but clever. Right after the Throckmorton divorce case she married Thomas Allerdyce, and made herself secure for life.'

'Who was she?' cried Merlin. 'For God's sake what was she – a witch?'

'Why, she was Alicia Dare, the dancer, of course. In those days you couldn't pick up a paper without finding her picture.'

Merlin sat very quiet, his brain suddenly fatigued and stilled. He was an old man now indeed, so old that it was impossible for him to dream of ever having been young, so old that the glamour was gone out of the world, passing not into the faces of children and into the persistent comforts of warmth and life, but passing out of the range of sight and feeling. He was never to smile again or to sit in a long reverie when spring evenings wafted the cries of children in at his window until gradually they became the friends of his boyhood out there, urging him to come and play before the last dark came down. He was too old now even for memories.

That night he sat at supper with his wife and son, who had used him for their blind purposes. Olive said:

'Don't sit there like a death's-head. Say something.'

'Let him sit quiet,' growled Arthur. 'If you encourage him he'll tell us a story we've heard a hundred times before.'

Merlin went upstairs very quietly at nine o'clock. When he was in his room and had closed the door tight he stood by it for a moment, his thin limbs trembling. He knew now that he had always been a fool.

'O Russet Witch!'

But it was too late. He had angered Providence by resisting too many temptations. There was nothing left but heaven, where he would meet only those who, like him, had wasted earth.

The Curious Case of Benjamin Button

I

As long ago as 1860 it was the proper thing to be born at home. At present, so I am told, the high gods of medicine have decreed that the first cries of the young shall be uttered upon the anesthetic air of a hospital, preferably a fashionable one. So young Mr and Mrs Roger Button were fifty years ahead of style when they decided, one day in the summer of 1860, that their first baby should be born in a hospital. Whether this anachronism had any bearing upon the astonishing history I am about to set down will never be known.

I shall tell you what occurred, and let you judge for yourself.

The Roger Buttons held an enviable position, both social and financial, in ante-bellum Baltimore. They were related to the This Family and the That Family, which, as every Southerner knew, entitled them to membership in that enormous peerage which largely populated the Confederacy. This was their first experience with the charming old custom of having babies – Mr Button was naturally nervous. He hoped it would be a boy so that he could be sent to Yale College in Connecticut, at which institution Mr Button himself had been known for four years by the somewhat obvious nickname of 'Cuff.'

On the September morning consecrated to be the enormous event he arose nervously at six o'clock, dressed himself, adjusted an impeccable stock, and hurried forth through the streets of Baltimore to the hospital, to determine whether the darkness of the night had borne in new life upon its bosom.

When he was approximately a hundred yards from the Maryland Private Hospital for Ladies and Gentlemen he saw Doctor Keene, the family physician, descending the front steps, rubbing his hands together with a washing movement – as all doctors are required to do by the unwritten ethics of their profession.

Mr Roger Button, the president of Roger Button & Co., Wholesale Hardware, began to run toward Doctor Keene with much less dignity than was expected from a Southern gentleman of that picturesque period. 'Doctor Keene!' he called. 'Oh, Doctor Keene!'

The doctor heard him, faced around, and stood waiting, a curious expression settling on his harsh, medicinal face as Mr Button drew near.

'What happened?' demanded Mr Button, as he came up in a gasping rush. 'What was it? How is she? A boy? Who is it? What –'

'Talk sense!' said Doctor Keene sharply. He appeared somewhat irritated.

'Is the child born?' begged Mr Button.

Doctor Keene frowned. 'Why, yes, I suppose so – after a fashion.' Again he threw a curious glance at Mr Button.

'Is my wife all right?'

'Yes.'

'Is it a boy or a girl?'

'Here now!' cried Doctor Keene in a perfect passion of irritation, 'I'll ask you to go and see for yourself. Outrageous!' He snapped the last word out in almost one syllable, then he turned away muttering: 'Do you imagine a case like this will help my professional reputation? One more would ruin me – ruin anybody.'

'What's the matter?' demanded Mr Button, appalled. 'Triplets?'

'No, not triplets!' answered the doctor cuttingly. 'What's more, you can go and see for yourself. And get another doctor. I brought you into the world, young man, and I've been physician to your family for forty years, but I'm through with you! I don't want to see you or any of your relatives ever again! Goodbye!'

Then he turned sharply, and without another word climbed into his phaeton, which was waiting at the curbstone, and drove severely away.

Mr Button stood there upon the sidewalk, stupefied and trembling from head to foot. What horrible mishap had occurred? He had suddenly lost all desire to go into the Maryland Private Hospital for Ladies and Gentlemen – it was with the greatest difficulty that, a moment later, he forced himself to mount the steps and enter the front door.

A nurse was sitting behind a desk in the opaque gloom of the hall. Swallowing his shame, Mr Button approached her.

'Good morning,' she remarked, looking up at him pleasantly.

'Good morning. I – I am Mr Button.'

At this a look of utter terror spread itself over the girl's face. She rose to her feet and seemed about to fly from the hall, restraining herself only with the most apparent difficulty.

'I want to see my child,' said Mr Button.

The nurse gave a little scream. 'Oh – of course!' she cried hysterically. 'Upstairs. Right upstairs. Go – *up!*'

She pointed the direction, and Mr Button, bathed in a cool perspiration, turned falteringly, and began to mount to the second floor. In the upper hall he addressed another nurse who approached him, basin in hand. 'I'm Mr Button,' he managed to articulate. 'I want to see my –'

Clank! The basin clattered to the floor and rolled in the direction of the stairs. Clank! Clank! It began a methodical descent as if sharing in the general terror which this gentleman provoked.

'I want to see my child!' Mr Button almost shrieked. He was on the verge of collapse.

Clank! The basin had reached the first floor. The nurse regained control of herself, and threw Mr Button a look of hearty contempt.

'All *right*, Mr Button,' she agreed in a hushed voice. 'Very *well!* But if you *knew* what state it's put us all in this morning! It's perfectly outrageous! The hospital will never have the ghost of a reputation after –'

'Hurry!' he cried hoarsely. 'I can't stand this!'

'Come this way, then, Mr Button.'

He dragged himself after her. At the end of a long hall they reached a room from which proceeded a variety of howls – indeed, a room which, in later parlance, would have been known as the 'crying-room.' They entered. Ranged around the walls were half a dozen white-enameled rolling cribs, each with a tag tied at the head.

'Well,' gasped Mr Button, 'which is mine?'

'There!' said the nurse.

Mr Button's eyes followed her pointing finger, and this is what he saw. Wrapped in a voluminous white blanket, and partially crammed into one of the cribs, there sat an old man apparently about seventy years of age. His sparse hair was almost white, and from his chin dripped a long smoke-coloured beard, which waved absurdly back and forth, fanned by the breeze coming in at the window. He looked up at Mr Button with dim, faded eyes in which lurked a puzzled question.

'Am I mad?' thundered Mr Button, his terror resolving into rage. 'Is this some ghastly hospital joke?'

'It doesn't seem like a joke to us,' replied the nurse severely. 'And I don't know whether you're mad or not – but that is most certainly your child.'

The cool perspiration redoubled on Mr Button's forehead. He closed his eyes, and then, opening them, looked again. There was no mistake – he was gazing at a man of threescore and ten – a *baby* of threescore and ten, a baby whose feet hung over the sides of the crib in which it was reposing.

The old man looked placidly from one to the other for a moment, and then suddenly spoke in a cracked and ancient voice. 'Are you my father?' he demanded.

Mr Button and the nurse started violently.

'Because if you are,' went on the old man querulously, 'I wish you'd get me out of this place – or, at least, get them to put a comfortable rocker in here.'

'Where in God's name did you come from? Who are you?' burst out Mr Button frantically.

'I can't tell you *exactly* who I am,' replied the querulous whine, 'because

I've only been born a few hours – but my last name is certainly Button.'

'You lie! You're an impostor!'

The old man turned wearily to the nurse. 'Nice way to welcome a new-born child,' he complained in a weak voice. 'Tell him he's wrong, why don't you?'

'You're wrong, Mr Button,' said the nurse severely. 'This is your child, and you'll have to make the best of it. We're going to ask you to take him home with you as soon as possible – some time today.'

'Home?' repeated Mr Button incredulously.

'Yes, we can't have him here. We really can't, you know.'

'I'm right glad of it,' whined the old man. 'This is a fine place to keep a youngster of quiet tastes. With all this yelling and howling, I haven't been able to get a wink of sleep. I asked for something to eat' – here his voice rose to a shrill note of protest – 'and they brought me a bottle of milk!'

Mr Button sank down upon a chair near his son and concealed his face in his hands. 'My heavens!' he murmured, in an ecstasy of horror. 'What will people say? What must I do?'

'You'll have to take him home,' insisted the nurse – 'immediately!'

A grotesque picture formed itself with dreadful clarity before the eyes of the tortured man – a picture of himself walking through the crowded streets of the city with this appalling apparition stalking by his side. 'I can't. I can't,' he moaned.

People would stop to speak to him, and what was he going to say? He would have to introduce this – this septuagenarian: 'This is my son, born early this morning.' And then the old man would gather his blanket around him and they would plod on, past the bustling stores, the slave market – for a dark instant Mr Button wished passionately that his son was black – past the luxurious houses of the residential district, past the home for the aged ...

'Come! Pull yourself together,' commanded the nurse.

'See here,' the old man announced suddenly, 'if you think I'm going to walk home in this blanket, you're entirely mistaken.'

'Babies always have blankets.'

With a malicious crackle the old man held up a small white swaddling garment. 'Look!' he quavered. '*This* is what they had ready for me.'

'Babies always wear those,' said the nurse primly.

'Well,' said the old man, 'this baby's not going to wear anything in about two minutes. This blanket itches. They might at least have given me a sheet.'

'Keep it on! Keep it on!' said Mr Button hurriedly. He turned to the nurse. 'What'll I do?'

'Go down town and buy your son some clothes.'

Mr Button's son's voice followed him down into the hall: 'And a cane, father. I want to have a cane.'

Mr Button banged the outer door savagely ...

II

'Good morning,' Mr Button said, nervously, to the clerk in the Chesapeake Dry Goods Company. 'I want to buy some clothes for my child.'

'How old is your child, sir?'

'About six hours,' answered Mr Button, without due consideration.

'Babies' supply department in the rear.'

'Why, I don't think – I'm not sure that's what I want. It's – he's an unusually large-size child. Exceptionally – ah – large.'

'They have the largest child's sizes.'

'Where is the boys' department?' inquired Mr Button, shifting his ground desperately. He felt that the clerk must surely scent his shameful secret.

'Right here.'

'Well –' He hesitated. The notion of dressing his son in men's clothes was repugnant to him. If, say, he could only find a *very* large boy's suit, he might cut off that long and awful beard, dye the white hair brown, and thus manage to conceal the worst, and to retain something of his own self-respect – not to mention his position in Baltimore society.

But a frantic inspection of the boys' department revealed no suits to fit the new-born Button. He blamed the store, of course – in such cases it is the thing to blame the store.

'How old did you say that boy of yours was?' demanded the clerk curiously.

'He's – sixteen.'

'Oh, I beg your pardon. I thought you said six *hours*. You'll find the youths' department in the next aisle.'

Mr Button turned miserably away. Then he stopped, brightened, and pointed his finger toward a dressed dummy in the window display.

'There!' he exclaimed. 'I'll take that suit, out there on the dummy.'

The clerk stared. 'Why,' he protested, 'that's not a child's suit. At least it *is*, but it's for fancy dress. You could wear it yourself!'

'Wrap it up,' insisted his customer nervously. 'That's what I want.'

The astonished clerk obeyed.

Back at the hospital Mr Button entered the nursery and almost threw the package at his son. 'Here's your clothes,' he snapped out.

The old man untied the package and viewed the contents with a quizzical eye.

'They look sort of funny to me,' he complained. 'I don't want to be made a monkey of –'

'You've made a monkey of me!' retorted Mr Button fiercely. 'Never

you mind how funny you look. Put them on – or I'll – or I'll *spank* you.'
He swallowed uneasily at the penultimate word, feeling nevertheless that
it was the proper thing to say.

'All right, father' – this with a grotesque simulation of filial respect –
'you've lived longer; you know best. Just as you say.'

As before, the sound of the word 'father' caused Mr Button to start
violently.

'And hurry.'

'I'm hurrying, father.'

When his son was dressed Mr Button regarded him with depression.
The costume consisted of dotted socks, pink pants, and a belted blouse
with a wide white collar. Over the latter waved the long whitish beard,
drooping almost to the waist. The effect was not good.

'Wait!'

Mr Button seized a hospital shears and with three quick snaps
amputated a large section of the beard. But even with this improvement
the ensemble fell far short of perfection. The remaining brush of scraggly
hair, the watery eyes, the ancient teeth, seemed oddly out of tone with the
gayety of the costume. Mr Button, however, was obdurate – he held out
his hand. 'Come along!' he said sternly.

His son took the hand trustingly. 'What are you going to call me, dad?'
he quavered as they walked from the nursery – 'just "baby" for a while?
till you think of a better name?'

Mr Button grunted. 'I don't know,' he answered harshly. 'I think we'll
call you Methuselah.'

III

Even after the new addition to the Button family had had his hair cut short
and then dyed to a sparse unnatural black, had had his face shaved so
close that it glistened, and had been attired in small-boy clothes made to
order by a flabbergasted tailor, it was impossible for Mr Button to ignore
the fact that his son was a poor excuse for a first family baby. Despite his
aged stoop, Benjamin Button – for it was by this name they called him
instead of by the appropriate but invidious Methuselah – was five feet
eight inches tall. His clothes did not conceal this, nor did the clipping and
dyeing of his eyebrows disguise the fact that the eyes underneath were
faded and watery and tired. In fact, the baby-nurse who had been engaged
in advance left the house after one look, in a state of considerable
indignation.

But Mr Button persisted in his unwavering purpose. Benjamin was a
baby, and a baby he should remain. At first he declared that if Benjamin
didn't like warm milk he could go without food altogether, but he was
finally prevailed upon to allow his son bread and butter, and even oatmeal

by way of a compromise. One day he brought home a rattle and, giving it to Benjamin, insisted in no uncertain terms that he should 'play with it,' whereupon the old man took it with a weary expression and could be heard jingling it obediently at intervals throughout the day.

There can be no doubt, though, that the rattle bored him, and that he found other and more soothing amusements when he was left alone. For instance, Mr Button discovered one day that during the preceding week he had smoked more cigars than ever before – a phenomenon which was explained a few days later when, entering the nursery unexpectedly, he found the room full of faint blue haze and Benjamin, with a guilty expression on his face, trying to conceal the butt of a dark Havana. This, of course, called for a severe spanking, but Mr Button found that he could not bring himself to administer it. He merely warned his son that he would 'stunt his growth.'

Nevertheless he persisted in his attitude. He brought home lead soldiers, he brought toy trains, he brought large pleasant animals made of cotton, and, to perfect the illusion which he was creating – for himself at least – he passionately demanded of the clerk in the toy-store whether 'the paint would come off the pink duck if the baby put it in his mouth.' But despite all his father's efforts, Benjamin refused to be interested. He would steal down the back stairs and return to the nursery with a volume of the *Encyclopaedia Britannica*, over which he would pore through an afternoon, while his cotton cows and his Noah's ark were left neglected on the floor. Against such a stubbornness Mr Button's efforts were of little avail.

The sensation created in Baltimore was, at first, prodigious. What the mishap would have cost the Buttons and their kinsfolk socially cannot be determined, for the outbreak of the Civil War drew the city's attention to other things. A few people who were unfailingly polite racked their brains for compliments to give to the parents – and finally hit upon the ingenious device of declaring that the baby resembled his grandfather, a fact which, due to the standard state of decay common to all men of seventy, could not be denied. Mr and Mrs Roger Button were not pleased, and Benjamin's grandfather was furiously insulted.

Benjamin, once he left the hospital, took life as he found it. Several small boys were brought to see him, and he spent a stiff-jointed afternoon trying to work up an interest in tops and marbles – he even managed, quite accidentally, to break a kitchen window with a stone from a sling shot, a feat which secretly delighted his father.

Thereafter Benjamin contrived to break something every day, but he did these things only because they were expected of him and because he was by nature obliging.

When his grandfather's initial antagonism wore off, Benjamin and that gentleman took enormous pleasure in one another's company. They would sit for hours, these two so far apart in age and experience, and, like old cronies, discuss with tireless monotony the slow events of the day. Benjamin felt more at ease in his grandfather's presence than in his parents' – they seemed always somewhat in awe of him and, despite the dictatorial authority they exercised over him, frequently addressed him and 'Mr'.

He was as puzzled as any one else at the apparently advanced age of his mind and body at birth. He read up on it in the medical journal, but found that no such case had been previously recorded. At his father's urging he made an honest attempt to play with other boys, and frequently he joined in the milder games – football shook him up too much, and he feared that in case of a fracture his ancient bones would refuse to knit.

When he was five he was sent to kindergarten, where he was initiated into the art of pasting green paper on orange paper, of weaving coloured maps and manufacturing eternal cardboard necklaces. He was inclined to drowse off to sleep in the middle of these tasks, a habit which both irritated and frightened his young teacher. To his relief she complained to his parents, and he was removed from the school. The Roger Buttons told their friends that they felt he was too young.

By the time he was twelve years old his parents had grown used to him. Indeed, so strong is the force of custom that they no longer felt that he was different from any other child – except when some curious anomaly reminded them of the fact. But one day a few weeks after his twelfth birthday, while looking in the mirror, Benjamin made, or thought he made, an astonishing discovery. Did his eyes deceive him, or had his hair turned in the dozen years of his life from white to iron-grey under its concealing dye? Was the network of wrinkles on his face becoming less pronounced? Was his skin healthier and firmer, with even a touch of ruddy winter colour? He could not tell. He knew that he no longer stooped and that his physical condition had improved since the early days of his life.

'Can it be –?' he thought to himself, or, rather, scarcely dared to think.

He went to his father. 'I am grown,' he announced determinedly. 'I want to put on long trousers.'

His father hesitated. 'Well,' he said finally, 'I don't know. Fourteen is the age for putting on long trousers – and you are only twelve.'

'But you'll have to admit,' protested Benjamin, 'that I'm big for my age.'

His father looked at him with illusory speculation. 'Oh, I'm not so sure of that,' he said. 'I was as big as you when I was twelve.'

This was not true – it was all part of Roger Button's silent agreement with himself to believe in his son's normality.

Finally a compromise was reached. Benjamin was to continue to dye his hair. He was to make a better attempt to play with boys of his own age.

He was not to wear his spectacles or carry a cane in the street. In return for these concessions he was allowed his first suit of long trousers ...

IV

Of the life of Benjamin Button between his twelfth and twenty-first year I intend to say little. Suffice to record that they were years of normal ungrowth. When Benjamin was eighteen he was erect as a man of fifty; he had more hair and it was of a dark grey; his step was firm, his voice had lost its cracked quaver and descended to a healthy baritone. So his father sent him up to Connecticut to take examinations for entrance to Yale College. Benjamin passed his examination and became a member of the freshman class.

On the third day following his matriculation he received a notification from Mr Hart, the college registrar, to call at his office and arrange his schedule. Benjamin, glancing in the mirror, decided that his hair needed a new application of its brown dye, but an anxious inspection of his bureau drawer disclosed that the dye bottle was not there. Then he remembered – he had emptied it the day before and thrown it away.

He was in a dilemma. He was due at the registrar's in five minutes. There seemed to be no help for it – he must go as he was. He did.

'Good morning,' said the registrar politely. 'You've come to inquire about your son.'

'Why, as a matter of fact, my name's Button –' began Benjamin, but Mr Hart cut him off.

'I'm very glad to meet you, Mr Button. I'm expecting your son here any minute.'

'That's me!' burst out Benjamin. 'I'm a freshman.'

'What!'

'I'm a freshman.'

'Surely you're joking.'

'Not at all.'

The registrar frowned and glanced at a card before him. 'Why, I have Mr Benjamin Button's age down here as eighteen.'

'That's my age,' asserted Benjamin, flushing slightly.

The registrar eyed him wearily. 'Now surely, Mr Button, you don't expect me to believe that.'

Benjamin smiled wearily. 'I am eighteen,' he repeated.

The registrar pointed sternly to the door. 'Get out,' he said. 'Get out of college and get out of town. You are a dangerous lunatic.'

'I am eighteen.'

Mr Hart opened the door. 'The idea!' he shouted. 'A man of your age trying to enter here as a freshman. Eighteen years old, are you? Well, I'll give you eighteen minutes to get out of town.'

Benjamin Button walked with dignity from the room, and half a dozen undergraduates, who were waiting in the hall, followed him curiously with their eyes. When he had gone a little way he turned around, faced the infuriated registrar, who was still standing in the doorway, and repeated in a firm voice: 'I am eighteen years old.'

To a chorus of titters which went up from the group of undergraduates, Benjamin walked away.

But he was not fated to escape so easily. On his melancholy walk to the railroad station he found that he was being followed by a group, then by a swarm, and finally by a dense mass of undergraduates. The word had gone around that a lunatic had passed the entrance examinations for Yale and attempted to palm himself off as a youth of eighteen. A fever of excitement permeated the college. Men ran hatless out of classes, the football team abandoned its practice and joined the mob, professors' wives with bonnets awry and bustles out of position, ran shouting after the procession, from which proceeded a continual succession of remarks aimed at the tender sensibilities of Benjamin Button.

'He must be the Wandering Jew!'

'He ought to go to prep school at his age!'

'Look at the infant prodigy!'

'He thought this was the old men's home.'

'Go up to Harvard!'

Benjamin increased his gait, and soon he was running. He would show them! He *would* go to Harvard, and then they would regret these ill-considered taunts!

Safely on board the train for Baltimore, he put his head from the window. 'You'll regret this!' he shouted.

'Ha-ha!' the undergraduates laughed. 'Ha-ha-ha!' It was the biggest mistake that Yale College had ever made ...

V

In 1880 Benjamin Button was twenty years old, and he signalized his birthday by going to work for his father in Roger Button & Co., Wholesale Hardware. It was in that same year that he began 'going out socially' – that is, his father insisted on taking him to several fashionable dances. Roger Button was now fifty, and he and his son were more and more companionable – in fact, since Benjamin had ceased to dye his hair (which was still grayish) they appeared about the same age, and could have passed for brothers.

One night in August they got into the phaeton attired in their full-dress suits and drove out to a dance at the Shevlins' country house, situated just outside of Baltimore. It was a gorgeous evening. A full moon drenched the road to the lustreless color of platinum, and late-blooming harvest flowers breathed into the motionless air aromas that were like low, half-heard laughter. The open country, carpeted for rods around with bright wheat, was translucent as in the day. It was almost impossible not to be affected by the sheer beauty of the sky – almost.

'There's a great future in the dry-goods business,' Roger Button was saying. He was not a spiritual man – his esthetic sense was rudimentary.

'Old fellows like me can't learn new tricks,' he observed profoundly. 'It's you youngsters with energy and vitality that have the great future before you.'

Far up the road the lights of the Shevlins' country house drifted into view, and presently there was a sighing sound that crept persistently toward them – it might have been the fine plaint of violins or the rustle of the silver wheat under the moon.

They pulled up behind a handsome brougham whose passengers were disembarking at the door. A lady got out, then an elderly gentleman, then another young lady, beautiful as sin. Benjamin started; an almost chemical change seemed to dissolve and recompose the very elements of his body. A rigor passed over him, blood rose into his cheeks, his forehead, and there was a steady thumping in his ears. It was first love.

The girl was slender and frail, with hair that was ashen under the moon and honey-colored under the sputtering gas-lamps of the porch. Over her shoulders was thrown a Spanish mantilla of softest yellow, butterflied in black; her feet were glittering buttons at the hem of her bustled dress.

Roger Button leaned over to his son. 'That,' he said, 'is young Hildegarde Moncrief, the daughter of General Moncrief.'

Benjamin nodded coldly. 'Pretty little thing,' he said indifferently. But when the negro boy had led the buggy away, he added: 'Dad, you might introduce me to her.'

They approached a group of which Miss Moncrief was the centre. Reared in the old tradition, she courtesied low before Benjamin. Yes he might have a dance. He thanked her and walked away – staggered away.

The interval until the time for his turn should arrive dragged itself out interminably. He stood close to the wall, silent, inscrutable, watching with murderous eyes the young bloods of Baltimore as they eddied around Hildegarde Moncrief, passionate admiration in their faces. How obnoxious they seemed to Benjamin; how intolerably rosy! Their curling brown whiskers aroused in him a feeling equivalent to indigestion.

But when his own time came, and he drifted with her out upon the changing floor to the music of the latest waltz from Paris, his jealousies and anxieties melted from him like a mantle of snow. Blind with enchantment, he felt that life was just beginning.

'You and your brother got here just as we did, didn't you?' asked Hildegarde, looking up at him with eyes that were like bright blue enamel.

Benjamin hesitated. If she took him for his father's brother, would it be best to enlighten her? He remembered his experience at Yale, so he decided against it. It would be rude to contradict a lady; it would be criminal to mar this exquisite occasion with the grotesque story of his origin. Later, perhaps. So he nodded, smiled, listened, was happy.

'I like men of your age,' Hildegarde told him. 'Young boys are so idiotic. They tell me how much champagne they drink at college, and how much money they lose playing cards. Men of your age know how to appreciate women.'

Benjamin felt himself on the verge of a proposal – with an effort he choked back the impulse.

'You're just the romantic age,' she continued – 'fifty. Twenty-five is too worldly-wise; thirty is apt to be pale from overwork; forty is the age of long stories that take a whole cigar to tell; sixty is – oh, sixty is too near seventy; but fifty is the mellow age. I love fifty.'

Fifty seemed to Benjamin a glorious age. He longed passionately to be fifty.

'I've always said,' went on Hildegarde, 'that I'd rather marry a man of fifty and be taken care of than marry a man of thirty and take care of *him*.'

For Benjamin the rest of the evening was bathed in a honey-coloured mist. Hildegarde gave him two more dances, and they discovered that they were marvellously in accord on all the questions of the day. She was to go driving with him on the following Sunday, and then they would discuss all these questions further.

Going home in the phaeton just before the crack of dawn, when the first bees were humming and the fading moon glimmered in the cool dew, Benjamin knew vaguely that his father was discussing wholesale hardware.

'... And what do you think should merit our biggest attention after hammers and nails?' the elder Button was saying.

'Love,' replied Benjamin absent-mindedly.

'Lugs?' exclaimed Roger Button. 'Why, I've just covered the question of lugs.'

Benjamin regarded him with dazed eyes just as the eastern sky was suddenly cracked with light, and an oriole yawned piercingly in the quickening trees ...

VI

When, six months later, the engagement of Miss Hildegarde Moncrief to Mr Benjamin Button was made known (I say 'made known,' for General Moncrief declared he would rather fall upon his sword than announce it), the excitement in Baltimore society reached a feverish pitch. The almost forgotten story of Benjamin's birth was remembered and sent out upon the winds of scandal in picaresque and incredible forms. It was said that

Benjamin was really the father of Roger Button, that he was his brother who had been in prison for forty years, that he was John Wilkes Booth in disguise – and, finally, that he had two small conical horns sprouting from his head.

The Sunday supplements of the New York papers played up the case with fascinating sketches which showed the head of Benjamin Button attached to a fish, to a snake, and, finally, to a body of solid brass. He became known, journalistically, as the Mystery Man of Maryland. But the true story, as is usually the case, had a very small circulation.

However, every one agreed with General Moncrief that it was 'criminal' for a lovely girl who could have married any beau in Baltimore to throw herself into the arms of a man who was assuredly fifty. In vain Mr Roger Button published his son's birth certificate in large type in the Baltimore *Blaze*. No one believed it. You had only to look at Benjamin and see.

On the part of the two people most concerned there was no wavering. So many of the stories about her fiancé were false that Hildegarde refused stubbornly to believe even the true one. In vain General Moncrief pointed out to her the high mortality among men of fifty – or, at least, among men who looked fifty; in vain he told her of the instability of the wholesale hardware business. Hildegarde had chosen to marry for mellowness – and marry she did ...

VII

In one particular, at least, the friends of Hildegarde Moncrief were mistaken. The wholesale hardware business prospered amazingly. In the fifteen years between Benjamin Button's marriage in 1880 and his father's retirement in 1895, the family fortune was doubled – and this was due largely to the younger member of the firm.

Needless to say, Baltimore eventually received the couple to its bosom. Even old General Moncrief became reconciled to his son-in-law when Benjamin gave him the money to bring out his *History of the Civil War* in twenty volumes, which had been refused by nine prominent publishers.

In Benjamin himself fifteen years had wrought many changes. It seemed to him that the blood flowed with new vigor through his veins. It began to be a pleasure to rise in the morning, to walk with an active step along the busy, sunny street, to work untiringly with his shipments of hammers and his cargoes of nails. It was in 1890 that he executed his famous business coup: he brought up the suggestion that *all nails used in nailing up the boxes in which nails are shipped are the property of the shippee*, a proposal which became a statute, was approved by Chief Justice Fossile, and saved Roger Button and Company, Wholesale Hardware, more than *six hundred nails every year*.

In addition, Benjamin discovered that he was becoming more and more attracted by the gay side of life. It was typical of his growing enthusiasm for pleasure that he was the first man in the city of Baltimore to own and run an automobile. Meeting him on the street, his contemporaries would stare enviously at the picture he made of health and vitality.

'He seems to grow younger every year,' they would remark. And if old Roger Button, now sixty-five years old, had failed at first to give a proper welcome to his son he atoned at last by bestowing on him what amounted to adulation.

And here we come to an unpleasant subject which it will be well to pass over as quickly as possible. There was only one thing that worried Benjamin Button: his wife had ceased to attract him.

At that time Hildegarde was a woman of thirty-five, with a son, Roscoe, fourteen years old. In the early days of their marriage Benjamin had worshipped her. But, as the years passed, her honey-colored hair became an unexciting brown, the blue enamel of her eyes assumed the aspect of cheap crockery – moreover, and most of all, she had become too settled in her ways, too placid, too content, too anemic in her excitements, and too sober in her taste. As a bride it had been she who had 'dragged' Benjamin to dances and dinners – now conditions were reversed. She went out socially with him, but without enthusiasm, devoured already by that eternal inertia which comes to live with each of us one day and stays with us to the end.

Benjamin's discontent waxed stronger. At the outbreak of the Spanish-American War in 1898 his home had for him so little charm that he decided to join the army. With his business influence he obtained a commission as captain, and proved so adaptable to the work that he was made a major, and finally a lieutenant-colonel just in time to participate in the celebrated charge up San Juan Hill. He was slightly wounded, and received a medal.

Benjamin had become so attached to the activity and excitement of army life that he regretted to give it up, but his business required attention, so he resigned his commission and came home. He was met at the station by a brass band and escorted to his house.

VIII

Hildegarde, waving a large silk flag, greeted him on the porch, and even as he kissed her he felt with a sinking of the heart that these three years had taken their toll. She was a woman of forty now, with a faint skirmish line of gray hairs in her head. The sight depressed him.

Up in his room he saw his reflection in the familiar mirror – he went closer and examined his own face with anxiety, comparing it after a moment with a photograph of himself in uniform taken just before the war.

'Good Lord!' he said aloud. The process was continuing. There was no doubt of it – he looked now like a man of thirty. Instead of being delighted, he was uneasy – he was growing younger. He had hitherto hoped that once he reached a bodily age equivalent to his age in years, the grotesque phenomenon which had marked his birth would cease to function. He shuddered. His destiny seemed to him awful, incredible.

When he came downstairs Hildegarde was waiting for him. She appeared annoyed, and he wondered if she had at last discovered that there was something amiss. It was with an effort to relieve the tension between them that he broached the matter at dinner in what he considered a delicate way.

'Well,' he remarked lightly, 'everybody says I look younger than ever.'

Hildegarde regarded him with scorn. She sniffed. 'Do you think it's anything to boast about?'

'I'm not boasting,' he asserted uncomfortably.

She sniffed again. 'The idea,' she said, and after a moment: 'I should think you'd have enough pride to stop it.'

'How can I?' he demanded.

'I'm not going to argue with you,' she retorted. 'But there's a right way of doing things and a wrong way. If you've made up your mind to be different from everybody else, I don't suppose I can stop you, but I really don't think it's very considerate.'

'But, Hildegarde, I can't help it.'

'You can too. You're simply stubborn. You think you don't want to be like any one else. You always have been that way, and you always will be. But just think how it would be if every one else looked at things as you do – what would the world be like?'

As this was an inane and unanswerable argument Benjamin made no reply, and from that time on a chasm began to widen between them. He wondered what possible fascination she had ever exercised over him.

To add to the breach, he found, as the new century gathered headway, that his thirst for gaiety grew stronger. Never a party of any kind in the city of Baltimore but he was there, dancing with the prettiest of the young married women, chatting with the most popular of the débutantes, and finding their company charming, while his wife, a dowager of evil omen, sat among the chaperons, now in haughty disapproval, and now following him with solemn, puzzled, and reproachful eyes.

'Look!' people would remark. 'What a pity! A young fellow that age tied to a woman of forty-five. He must be twenty years younger than his wife.' They had forgotten – as people inevitably forget – that back in 1880 their mammas and papas had also remarked about this same ill-matched pair.

Benjamin's growing unhappiness at home was compensated for by his many new interests. He took up golf and made a great success of it. He went in for dancing: in 1906 he was an expert at 'The Boston,' and in 1908 he was considered proficient at the 'Maxixe,' while in 1909 his 'Castle Walk' was the envy of every young man in town.

His social activities, of course, interfered to some extent with his business, but then he had worked hard at wholesale hardware for twenty-five years and felt that he could soon hand it on to his son, Roscoe, who had recently graduated from Harvard.

He and his son were, in fact, often mistaken for each other. This pleased Benjamin – he soon forgot the insidious fear which had come over him on his return from the Spanish-American War, and grew to take a naïve pleasure in his appearance. There was only one fly in the delicious ointment – he hated to appear in public with his wife. Hildegarde was almost fifty, and the sight of her made him feel absurd ...

IX

One September day in 1910 – a few years after Roger Button & Co., Wholesale Hardware, had been handed over to young Roscoe Button – a man, apparently about twenty years old, entered himself as a freshman at Harvard University in Cambridge. He did not make the mistake of announcing that he would never see fifty again nor did he mention the fact that his son had been graduated from the same institution ten years before.

He was admitted, and almost immediately attained a prominent position in the class, partly because he seemed a little older than the other freshmen, whose average age was about eighteen.

But his success was largely due to the fact that in the football game with Yale he played so brilliantly, with so much dash and with such a cold, remorseless anger that he scored seven touchdowns and fourteen field goals for Harvard, and caused one entire eleven of Yale men to be carried singly from the field, unconscious. He was the most celebrated man in college.

Strange to say, in his third or junior year he was scarcely able to 'make' the team. The coaches said that he had lost weight, and it seemed to the more observant among them that he was not quite as tall as before. He made no touchdowns – indeed, he was retained on the team chiefly in hope that his enormous reputation would bring terror and disorganization to the Yale team.

In his senior year he did not make the team at all. He had grown so slight and frail that one day he was taken by some sophomores for a freshman, an incident which humiliated him terribly. He became known as something of a prodigy – a senior who was surely no more than sixteen – and he was often shocked at the worldliness of some of his classmates. His studies seemed harder to him – he felt that they were too advanced.

He had heard his classmates speak of St Midas', the famous preparatory school, at which so many of them had prepared for college, and he determined after his graduation to enter himself at St Midas', where the sheltered life among boys his own size would be more congenial to him.

Upon his graduation in 1914 he went home to Baltimore with his Harvard diploma in his pocket. Hildergarde was now residing in Italy, so Benjamin went to live with his son, Roscoe. But though he was welcomed in a general way, there was obviously no heartiness in Roscoe's feeling toward him – there was even perceptible a tendency on his son's part to think that Benjamin, as he moped about the house in adolescent mooniness, was somewhat in the way. Roscoe was married now and prominent in Baltimore life, and he wanted no scandal to creep out in connection with his family.

Benjamin, no longer *persona grata* with the débutantes and younger college set, found himself left much alone, except for the companionship of three or four fifteen-year-old boys in the neighborhood. His idea of going to St Midas' school recurred to him.

'Say,' he said to Roscoe one day, 'I've told you over and over that I want to go to prep school.'

'Well, go, then,' replied Roscoe shortly. The matter was distasteful to him, and he wished to avoid a discussion.

'I can't go alone,' said Benjamin helplessly. 'You'll have to enter me and take me up there.'

'I haven't got time,' declared Roscoe abruptly. His eyes narrowed and he looked uneasily at his father. 'As a matter of fact,' he added, 'you'd better not go on with this business much longer. You better pull up short. You better – you better' – he paused and his face crimsoned as he sought for words – 'you better turn right around and start back the other way. This has gone too far to be a joke. It isn't funny any longer. You – you behave yourself!'

Benjamin looked at him, on the verge of tears.

'And another thing,' continued Roscoe, 'when visitors are in the house I want you to call me "Uncle" – not "Roscoe," but "Uncle," do you understand? It looks absurd for a boy of fifteen to call me by my first name. Perhaps you'd better call me "Uncle" *all* the time, so you'll get used to it.'

With a harsh look at his father, Roscoe turned away ...

X

At the termination of this interview, Benjamin wandered dismally upstairs and stared at himself in the mirror. He had not shaved for three months, but he could find nothing on his face but a faint white down with which it seemed unnecessary to meddle. When he had first come home from

Harvard, Roscoe had approached him with the proposition that he should wear eye-glasses and imitation whiskers glued to his cheeks, and it had seemed for a moment that the farce of his early years was to be repeated. But whiskers had itched and made him ashamed. He wept and Roscoe had reluctantly relented.

Benjamin opened a book of boys' stories. *The Boy Scouts in Bimini Bay*, and began to read. But he found himself thinking persistently about the war. America had joined the Allied cause during the preceding month, and Benjamin wanted to enlist, but, alas, sixteen was the minimum age, and he did not look that old. His true age, which was fifty-seven, would have disqualified him, anyway.

There was a knock at his door, and the butler appeared with a letter bearing a large official legend in the corner and addressed to Mr Benjamin Button. Benjamin tore it open eagerly, and read the enclosure with delight. It informed him that many reserve officers who had served in the Spanish-American War were being called back into service with a higher rank, and it enclosed his commission as brigadier-general in the United States army with orders to report immediately.

Benjamin jumped to his feet fairly quivering with enthusiasm. This was what he had wanted. He seized his cap and ten minutes later he had entered a large tailoring establishment on Charles Street, and asked in his uncertain treble to be measured for a uniform.

'Want to play soldier, sonny?' demanded a clerk, casually.

Benjamin flushed. 'Say! Never mind what I want!' he retorted angrily. 'My name's Button and I live on Mt Vernon Place, so you know I'm good for it.'

'Well,' admitted the clerk, hesitatingly, 'if you're not, I guess your daddy is, all right.'

Benjamin was measured, and a week later his uniform was completed. He had difficulty in obtaining the proper general's insignia because the dealer kept insisting to Benjamin that a nice YWCA badge would look just as well and be much more fun to play with.

Saying nothing to Roscoe, he left the house one night and proceeded by train to Camp Mosby, in South Carolina, where he was to command an infantry brigade. On a sultry April day he approached the entrance to the camp, paid off the taxicab which had brought him from the station, and turned to the sentry on guard.

'Get some one to handle my luggage!' he said briskly.

The sentry eyed him reproachfully. 'Say,' he remarked, 'where you goin' with the general's duds, sonny?'

Benjamin, veteran of the Spanish-American War, whirled upon him with fire in his eye, but with, alas, a changing treble voice.

'Come to attention!' he tried to thunder; he paused for breath – then suddenly he saw the sentry snap his heels together and bring his rifle to the present. Benjamin concealed a smile of gratification, but when he glanced around his smile faded. It was not he who had inspired obedience, but an imposing artillery colonel who was approaching on horseback.

'Colonel!' called Benjamin shrilly.

The colonel came up, drew rein, and looked coolly down at him with a twinkle in his eyes. 'Whose little boy are you?' he demanded kindly.

'I'll soon darn well show you whose little boy I am!' retorted Benjamin in a ferocious voice. 'Get down of that horse!'

The colonel roared with laughter.

'You want him, eh, general?'

'Here!' cried Benjamin desperately. 'Read this.' And he thrust his commission toward the colonel.

The colonel read it, his eyes popping from their sockets.

'Where'd you get this?' he demanded, slipping the document into his own pocket.

'I got it from the Government, as you'll soon find out!'

'You come along with me,' said the colonel with a peculiar look. 'We'll go up to headquarters and talk this over. Come along.'

The colonel turned and began walking his horse in the direction of headquarters. There was nothing for Benjamin to do but follow with as much dignity as possible – meanwhile promising himself a stern revenge.

But this revenge did not materialize. Two days later, however, his son Roscoe materialized from Baltimore, hot and cross from a hasty trip, and escorted the weeping general, *sans* uniform, back to his home.

XI

In 1920 Roscoe Button's first child was born. During the attendant festivities, however, no one thought it 'the thing' to mention that the little grubby boy, apparently about ten years of age who played around the house with lead soldiers and a miniature circus, was the new baby's own grandfather.

No one disliked the little boy whose fresh, cheerful face was crossed with just a hint of sadness, but to Roscoe Button his presence was a source of torment. In the idiom of his generation Roscoe did not consider the matter 'efficient.' It seemed to him that his father, in refusing to look sixty, had not behaved like a 'red-blooded he-man' – this was Roscoe's favorite expression – but in a curious and perverse manner. Indeed, to think about the matter for as much as a half an hour drove him to the edge of insanity. Roscoe believed that 'live wires' should keep young, but carrying it out on such a scale was – was – was inefficient. And there Roscoe rested.

Five years later Roscoe's little boy had grown old enough to play childish games with little Benjamin under the supervision of the same nurse. Roscoe took them both to kindergarten on the same day and Benjamin found that playing with little strips of colored paper, making mats and chains and curious and beautiful designs, was the most fascinating game in the world. Once he was bad and had to stand in the corner – then he cried – but for the most part there were gay hours in the cheerful room, with the sunlight coming in the windows and Miss Bailey's kind hand resting for a moment now and then in his tousled hair.

Roscoe's son moved up into the first grade after a year, but Benjamin stayed on in the kindergarten. He was very happy. Sometimes when other tots talked about what they would do when they grew up a shadow would cross his little face as if in a dim, childish way he realized that those were things in which he was never to share.

The days flowed on in monotonous content. He went back a third year to the kindergarten, but he was too little now to understand what the bright shining strips of paper were for. He cried because the other boys were bigger than he and he was afraid of them. The teacher talked to him, but though he tried to understand he could not understand at all.

He was taken from the kindergarten. His nurse, Nana, in her starched gingham dress, became the centre of his tiny world. On bright days they walked in the park; Nana would point at a great gray monster and say 'elephant,' and Benjamin would say if after her, and when he was being undressed for bed that night he would say it over and over aloud to her: 'Elyphant, elyphant, elyphant.' Sometimes Nana let him jump on the bed, which was fun, because if you sat down exactly right it would bounce you up on your feet again, and if you said 'Ah' for a long time while you jumped you got a very pleasing broken vocal effect.

He loved to take a big cane from the hatrack and go around hitting chairs and tables with it saying: 'Fight, fight, fight.' When there were people there the old ladies would cluck at him, which interested him, and the young ladies would try to kiss him, which he submitted to with mild boredom. And when the long day was done at five o'clock he would go upstairs with Nana and be fed oatmeal and nice soft mushy foods with a spoon.

There were no troublesome memories in his childish sleep; no token came to him of his brave days at college, of the glittering years when he flustered the hearts of many girls. There were only the white, safe walls of his crib and Nana and a man who came to see him sometimes, and a great big orange ball that Nana pointed at just before his twilight bed hour and called 'sun.' When the sun went his eyes were sleepy – there were no dreams, no dreams to haunt him.

The past – the wild charge at the head of his men up San Juan Hill; the first years of his marriage when he worked late into the summer dusk down in the busy city for young Hildegarde whom he loved; the days before that when he sat smoking far into the night in the gloomy old

Button house on Monroe Street with his grandfather – all these had faded like unsubstantial dreams from his mind as though they had never been.

He did not remember. He did not remember clearly whether the milk was warm or cool at his last feeding or how the days passed – there was only his crib and Nana's familiar presence. And then he remembered nothing. When he was hungry he cried – that was all. Through the noons and nights he breathed and over him there were soft mumblings and murmurings that he scarcely heard, and faintly differentiated smells, and light and darkness.

Then it was all dark, and his white crib and the dim faces that moved above him, and the warm sweet aroma of the milk, faded out altogether from his mind.

Rags Martin-Jones and the
Pr–nce of W–les

The *Majestic* came gliding into New York harbour on an autumn morning. She sniffed at the tug-boats and turtle-gaited ferries, winked at a gaudy young yacht and ordered a cattle-boat out of her way with a snarling whistle of steam. Then she drew up at her private dock with all the fuss of a stout lady sitting down, and announced complacently that she had just come from Cherbourg and Southampton with a cargo of the very best people in the world.

The very best people in the world stood on the deck and waved idiotically to their poor relations who were waiting on the dock for gloves from Paris. Before long a great toboggan had connected the *Majestic* with the North American continent and the ship began to disgorge these very best people in the world – who turned out to be cinema stars, missionaries, retired jewellers, British authors, musical comedy twins, the Duchess Mazzini (*née* Goldberg) and, needless to add, Lord and Lady Thingumbob, of Thingumbob Manor.

The deck gradually emptied, but when the last Poiret Madonna had reached shore the photographers still remained at their posts. And the officer in charge of debarkation still stood at the foot of the gangway, glancing first at his watch and then at the deck as if some important part of the cargo was still on board. At last from the watchers on the pier there arose a long-drawn 'Ah-h-h!' as a final entourage began to stream down from deck B.

First came two French maids, one carrying a pair of minute dogs and the other bearing an enormous green parrot in an enormous red cage. After these marched a squad of porters, blind and invisible under innumerable bunches and bouquets of fresh flowers. Another maid followed, leading a sad-eyed orphan child of a French flavour, and close upon its heels walked the second officer, pulling along three neurasthenic wolfhounds, much to their reluctance and his own.

A pause. Then the captain, Sir Howard Deems Macdougall, appeared at the rail, with something that might have been a pile of gorgeous silver fox fur standing by his side.

Rags Martin-Jones, after two years in the capitals of Europe, was returning to her native land! Rags Martin-Jones was not a dog! She was half a girl and half a flower, and as she shook hands with Captain Sir Howard Deems Macdougall she smiled as if someone had told her the newest, freshest joke in the world. All the people who had not already left the pier felt that smile trembling on the morning air and turned around to see. She came slowly down the gangway. Her hat, an expensive, inscrutable experiment, was crushed under her arm so that her scant, French-bobbed hair tossed and flopped a little in the harbour wind. Her face was like seven o'clock on a summer morning, save where she had slipped a preposterous monocle into an eye of clear, childish blue. At every few steps her long lashes would tilt out the monocle and she would laugh, a bored, happy laugh, and replace the supercilious spectacle in the other eye.

Tap! Her one hundred and five pounds reached the pier, and it seemed to sway, and bend from the shock of her beauty. A few porters fainted. A large, sentimental shark which had followed the ship across made a despairing leap to see her once more, and then dived, broken-hearted, back into the deep sea. Rags Martin-Jones had come home.

There was no member of her family there to meet her, for the simple reason that she was the only member of her family left alive. In 1913 her parents had gone down on the *Titanic* together rather than be separated in this world, and so the Martin-Jones fortune of seventy-five millions had been inherited by a very little girl on her tenth birthday. It was what the pessimists always refer to as a 'shame.' Rags Martin-Jones (everybody had forgotten her real name long ago) was now photographed from all sides. The monocle persistently fell out, and she kept laughing and yawning and replacing it, so no very clear picture of her was taken, except by the motion-picture camera. All the photographs, however, included a flustered, handsome young man, with an almost ferocious love-light burning in his eyes, who had met her on the dock. His name was John Chestnut, he was already talked of as a risen star in the financial world, and he had been hopelessly in love with Rags ever since the time when she, like the tides, had come under the influence of the summer moon.

When Rags became really aware of his presence they were walking down the pier, and she looked at him blankly, as though she had never seen him before in this world.

'Rags!' he began. 'Rags –'

'John Chestnut?' she inquired, inspecting him with interest.

'Of course!' he exclaimed angrily. 'Are you trying to pretend you don't know me? That you didn't write to tell me to meet you here?' She laughed. A chauffeur appeared at her elbow, and she twisted out of her coat, revealing a dress made in great, splashy checks of sea-blue and grey. She shook herself like a wet bird.

'I've got a lot of stuff to declare at the customs,' she remarked absently.

'So have I,' said Chestnut anxiously, 'and the first thing I want to declare is that I've loved you, Rags, every minute since you've been away.' She stopped with a groan.

'Please! There were some young men on the boat. The subject's gotten to be a bore.'

'My Heaven!' cried Chestnut. 'Do you mean to say that you class *my* love with what a lot of insolent kids said to you on a boat!' His voice had risen, and several people in the vicinity turned to hear.

'Sh!' she warned him. 'I'm not giving a circus. If you want me to even see you while I'm here you'll have to be less violent.'

But John Chestnut seemed unable to control his voice.

'Do you mean to say' – it trembled to a carrying pitch – 'that you've forgotten what you said on this very pier just twenty-two months ago last Thursday?' Half the passengers from the ship were now watching the scene on the dock, and another little eddy drifted out of the customs house to see.

'John' – her displeasure was increasing – 'if you raise your voice again I'll arrange it so you'll have plenty of chance to cool off. I'm going to the Ritz. Come and see me there this afternoon.'

'But Rags!' he protested hoarsely. 'Listen to me. Twenty-two months ago –' Then the watchers on the dock were treated to a curious sight. A beautiful lady in a checkered dress of sea-blue and grey took a brisk step forward so that her hands came into contact with the excited young man by her side. The young man, retreating instinctively, reached back with his foot, but finding nothing relapsed gently off the thirty-foot dock and plopped into the Hudson River. A shout of alarm went up and there was a rush to the edge just as his head appeared above water. He was swimming easily and, perceiving this, the young lady who had apparently been the cause of the accident leaned over the pier and made a megaphone of her hands.

'I'll be in at half-past four!' she cried. And with a cheerful wave of her hand, which the engulfed gentleman was unable to return, she adjusted her monocle, threw one haughty glance at the gathered crowd and walked leisurely from the scene.

The five dogs, the three maids, the parrot and the French orphan were installed in the largest suite at the Ritz, and Rags tumbled lazily into a steaming bath, where she dozed for the greater part of an hour. At the end of that time she received business calls from a masseuse, a manicurist, a beauty doctor and finally from a Parisian hairdresser who restored the French bob to its original perfection. When John Chestnut arrived at four he found half a dozen lawyers and bankers, the administrators of the Martin-Jones trust fund, waiting in the hall. They had been there since half-past one, and were now in a state of considerable agitation. After one of the maids had subjected him to a severe scrutiny, possibly to be sure that he was thoroughly dry, John was conducted immediately into the presence of M'selle. M'selle was in her bedroom, reclining on the chaise-longue among two dozen silk pillows that had accompanied her across the water. John came into the room somewhat stiffly and greeted her with a formal bow.

'You look better,' she said, raising herself from her pillows and staring at him appraisingly. 'It gave you a colour.' He thanked her coldly for the compliment.

'You ought to go in every morning.' And then she added irrelevantly, 'I'm going back to Paris tomorrow.' John Chestnut gasped.

'I told you in my letter that I didn't intend to stay more than a week, anyhow,' she added.

'But Rags –'

'Why should I? There isn't an interesting man in New York.'

'But listen, Rags – won't you give me a chance? Won't you stay for, say, ten days and get to know me a little?'

'Know you!' Her tone implied that he was already a far too open box.

'Well, what do you want me to be?' he demanded resentfully. 'A cross between an actor and an amusement park?'

'I want a man who's capable of a gallant gesture.'

'Do you want me to express myself entirely in pantomime?'

Rags uttered a disgusted sigh.

'I mean you haven't any imagination,' she explained patiently. 'No Americans have any imagination. Paris is the only city where a civilized person can exist. Paris is the capital of the world.'

'Don't you care for me at all any more?'

'I wouldn't have crossed the Atlantic to see you if I didn't. But as soon as I looked over the Americans on the boat I knew I couldn't marry you. I'd just hate you, John, and the only fun I'd have out of it would be the fun of breaking your heart.' She began to twist herself down among the cushions until she almost disappeared from view.

'I've lost my monocle,' she exclaimed. After an unsuccessful search in the silken depths she discovered the elusive glass hanging down the back of her neck.

'I'd love to be in love,' she went on, replacing the monocle in her childish eye. 'Last spring in Rome I almost eloped with an Indian Rajah, but I took an intense dislike to one of his other wives.'

'Don't talk that rubbish!' cried John, sinking his face into his hands.

'Well, I didn't marry him,' she protested. 'But in one way he had a lot to offer. He was the third richest subject of the British Empire. That's another thing – are you rich?'

'Not as rich as you.'

'There you are. What have you to offer me?'

'Love.'

'Love!' She disappeared again among the cushions. 'Listen, John. Life to me is a series of glistening bazaars, with a merchant in front of each one, rubbing his hands together and saying, "Patronize this place here. Best Bazaar in the world." So I go with my purse full of beauty and money and youth, all prepared to buy. "What have you got for sale?" I ask him, and he rubs his hands together and says, "Well, mademoiselle, today we have some perfectly be-*oo*-tiful love." Sometimes he hasn't even got that in stock, but he sends out for it when he finds I have so much money to spend. Oh, he always gives that to me before I go, and for nothing. That's the one revenge I have.' John Chestnut rose despairingly to his feet and took a step toward the window.

'Don't throw yourself out,' Rags exclaimed quickly.

'I won't.' He tossed away his cigarette.

'It isn't just you,' she said in a softer voice. 'Dull and uninspired as you are, I care for you more than I can say. But life's so stupid here. Nothing ever happens.'

'Well,' he said doggedly, 'just for a change you're to come out with me tonight.'

'Where to?' demanded Rags with scorn.

'I'll take you to the most amusing place in the city.'

'What'll happen? You've got to tell me what'll happen?'

John Chestnut suddenly drew a long breath and looked cautiously around as if he were afraid of being overheard.

'Well, to tell you the truth,' he said in a low, worried tone, 'if everything was known something pretty awful would be liable to happen to *me*.'

She sat upright, and the pillows tumbled about her like leaves.

'Do you mean to imply that there's anything shady in your life?' she cried, with laughter in her voice. 'Do you expect me to believe that? No, John, you'll have your fun by plugging ahead on the beaten path – just plugging ahead.'

Her mouth, a small, insolent rose, dropped the words on him like thorns. John took his hat and coat from the chair and picked up his cane.

'For the last time, will you come along with me tonight and see what we can see?'

'See what? See whom? Is there anything in this country worth seeing?'

'Well,' he said, in a matter-of-fact tone, 'for one thing you'll see the Prince of Wales.'

'What?' She left the chaise-longue at a bound. 'Is he in New York?'

'He will be tonight. Would you care to see him?'

'Would I? I'd give a year of my life to see him for an hour.' Her voice trembled with excitement.

'He's been in Canada. He's down here in cognito. And I happen to know where he's going to be tonight.'

Rags gave a sharp, ecstatic cry: 'Felice! Louise! Nanine!'

The three maids came running. The room seemed to fill suddenly with vibrations of wild, startled light.

'Felice, the car!' cried Rags. 'Louise, my gold dress and the slippers with the real gold heels! The big pearls too, all the pearls, and the egg diamond and the stockings with the sapphire clocks! Nanine, send for the hairdresser on the run! My bath again, ice cold and half full of almond cream! Felice, Tiffany's like lightning, before they close! Find me a bracelet, a brooch, a pendant, anything, it doesn't matter, with the arms of the House of Windsor!' She was fumbling at the buttons of her dress, and as John turned it was already sliding from her shoulders.

'Orchids, for the love of heaven! Four dozen, so I can choose four.'

And then maids flew here and there about the room like frightened birds.

'Perfume, Louise! Bring out all my perfume and my white sable and my diamond garters and the sweet oil for my hands! Here, take these things! This too and this – ouch! – and this!' With becoming modesty John Chestnut closed the outside door. The six trustees, in various postures of fatigue, of ennui, of resignation, of despair, were still cluttering up the outer hall.

'Gentlemen,' announced John Chestnut, 'I fear that Miss Martin-Jones is much too weary from her trip to talk to you this afternoon.'

'This place, for no particular reason, is called the Hole in the Sky.' Rags looked around her. They were on a roof garden wide open to the night. Overhead the true stars winked cold and the moon was a sliver of ice in the dark west. But where they stood it was as warm as June, and the couples dining or dancing on the central floor were unconcerned with the forbidding sky.

'What makes it so warm?' she whispered as they moved toward a table.

'It's some new trick that keeps the warm air from rising. I don't know the principle of the thing, but I know it's open like this even in the middle of winter. Do you see that man at the corner table? That's the heavyweight champion of the world. He knocked out the challenger at five o'clock this afternoon.'

'Where's the Prince of Wales?' she demanded tensely.

John looked around.

He hasn't arrived yet. He won't be here for about half an hour.'

She sighed profoundly. 'It's the first time I've been excited in four years.' Four years – one less than he had loved her. He wondered if when she was sixteen, a wild, lovely child, sitting up all night in restaurants with officers who were to leave for France next day, losing the glamour of life too soon in the old, sad, poignant days of war, she had ever been so lovely as under these amber lights and this dark sky. From her excited eyes to her tiny slipper heels which were striped with layers of real silver and gold, she was like one of those amazing ships that are carved complete in a bottle. She was finished with that delicacy, with that care – as though the long lifetime of some worker in fragility had been used to make her so. John Chestnut wanted to take her up in his hands, turn her this way and that, examine the tip of a slipper or the tip of an ear or squint closely at the fairy stuff from which her lashes were made.

Rags became suddenly aware of the sound of violins and drums, but the music seemed to come from far away, seemed to float over the crisp night and on to the floor with the added remoteness of a dream.

'The orchestra's on another roof,' exclaimed John. 'It's a new idea. Look, the entertainment's beginning.'

He broke off. Just as the light went down for the number, Rags had given a long sigh and leaned forward tensely in her chair. Her eyes were rigid like the eyes of a pointer dog, and John saw that they were fixed on a party that had come through some side entrance and were arranging themselves around a table in the half darkness. The table was shielded with palms, and Rags at first made out only three dim forms. Then she distinguished a fourth who seemed to be placed well behind the other three, a pale oval of a face topped with a glimmer of dark yellow hair.

'Hallo!' ejaculated John. 'There he is now!'

Her breath seemed to die murmurously in her throat. She was dimly aware that the comedian was now standing in a glow of white light on the dancing-floor, that he had been talking for some moments and that there was a constant ripple of laughter in the air. Her eyes remained motionless, enchanted. She saw one of the party bend and whisper to another, and after the low glitter of a match the bright button of a cigarette-end gleamed in the background. How long it was before she moved she did not know. Then the moment was over. The lights returned, the comedian left the floor, and the far-away music began. John leaned toward her. She started. There were now only two men sitting at the table across the floor.

'He's gone!' she exclaimed in quick distress.

'Don't worry; he'll be back. He's got to be awful careful, you see, so he's probably waiting outside with one of his aides until it gets dark again. He's not supposed to be in New York. He's even in Canada under another name.' The lights dimmed again, and almost immediately a dark-haired man appeared out of the darkness and was standing by their table.

'May I introduce myself?' he said rapidly to John in a supercilious British voice. 'Lord Charles Este, of Baron Marchbanks' party.' He glanced at John closely as if to be sure that he appreciated the significance of the name. John nodded.

'The Baron Marchbanks had the pleasure of meeting Mr Martin-Jones on a previous visit here several years ago, and would be honoured if Miss Martin-Jones would join his party for the next number.'

'Very well,' she said, glancing back again interrogatively at John. Again he nodded. Then she rose and, with her heart beating wildly, threaded the tables, making the half circuit of the room, then melted, a slim figure in shimmering gold, into the table set in half darkness.

The number drew to a close, and John Chestnut sat alone at his table, stirring auxiliary bubbles in his glass of champagne. Just as the lights went on there was a soft rasp of gold cloth, and Rags, flushed and breathing quickly, sank into her chair. Her eyes were shining with tears. John looked at her moodily.

'Well, what did he say?'

'He was very quiet.'

'Didn't he say a word?' Her hand trembled as she took up her glass of champagne.

'He just – looked at me while it was dark. And we said a few things, conventional things. He was like his picture, only he looks very bored and tired.'

'Is he leaving New York tonight?'

'In half an hour. He and his aides have a car outside, and they expect to be over the border before dawn.'

Just as she turned back an utterly strange young man who had been standing for a moment in the main entrance came toward them with an air of hurry. He was a deathly pale person in a dishevelled business suit, and he laid a trembling hand on John Chestnut's shoulder.

'Monte!' exclaimed John, starting up so suddenly that he upset his champagne. 'What is it? What's the matter?'

'They've picked up the trail!' said the young man in a shaken whisper. He looked around. 'I've got to speak to you alone.' John got to his feet, and Rags noticed that his face, too, had become white as the napkin in his hand. He excused himself, and they retreated to an unoccupied table a few feet away. Rags watched them curiously for a moment, then she resumed her scrutiny of the table across the floor. Then John returned to the table, and Rags was startled to find that a tremendous change had come over him. He lurched into his chair like a drunken man.

'John! What's the matter?' Instead of answering he reached for the champagne bottle, but his fingers were trembling.

'Rags,' he said unsteadily, 'I'm done for!'

'What do you mean?'

'I'm all through, I tell you.' He managed a sickly smile. 'There's been a warrant out for me for over an hour.'

'What have you done?' she demanded in a frightened voice. 'What's the warrant for?' The lights went out for the next number, and he collapsed suddenly over the table.

'What is it?' she insisted, with rising apprehension. She leaned forward. His answer was barely audible.

'Murder?' She could feel her body grow cold as ice. He nodded. She took hold of both arms and tried to shake him upright as one shakes a coat into place. His eyes were rolling in his head.

'Is it true? Have they got proof?' Again he nodded drunkenly.

'Then you've got to get out of the country now! Do you hear me, John? You've got to get out *now*, before they come looking for you here!' He loosed a wild glance of terror toward the entrance.

'Oh, Heaven!' cried Rags. 'Why don't you do something?' She looked distractedly around the roof. Her eyes strayed here and there in desperation, became suddenly rigid. She drew in her breath sharply, hesitated, and then whispered fiercely into John's ear.

'If I arrange it, will you go to Canada tonight?'

'How?'

'I'll manage if you'll pull yourself together a little. This is Rags talking to you, don't you understand, John? I want you to sit here and not move until I come back!' A minute later she had crossed the room under cover of the darkness.

'Baron Marchbanks!' she whispered softly, standing just behind his chair. He half rose, motioned her to sit down.

'Have you room in your car for two more passengers tonight?' One of the aides looked around abruptly.

'His Lordship's car is full,' he said shortly.

'It's terribly urgent.' Her voice was trembling.

'Well,' said the Prince hesitatingly, 'I don't know.' Lord Charles Este looked at him and shook his head.

'I don't think it'd do, sir. This is a risky matter anyhow, with contrary orders from home. You know we agreed there'd be no complications.' The Prince frowned.

'This isn't a complication,' he objected. Este turned frankly to Rags.

'Why is it urgent?' Rags hesitated.

'Why –' She flushed suddenly. 'It's a runaway marriage.' The Prince laughed.

'Right-o!' he exclaimed. 'That settles it. Este here is just being official. Bring over the lucky man right away. We're leaving shortly, what?' Este looked at his watch.

'Right now!' Rags rushed away. She wanted to move the whole party from the place while the lights were still down.

'Hurry!' she cried in John's ear. 'We're going over the border with the Prince of Wales. You'll be safe by morning.'

He looked up at her with dazed eyes. She hurriedly paid the account and, seizing his arm, piloted him as inconspicuously as possible to the other table, where she introduced him with a word. The Prince acknowledged his presence by shaking hands, the aides nodded, only faintly concealing their displeasure.

'We'd better start,' said Este, looking impatiently at his watch. They were on their feet when suddenly an exclamation broke out from all of them at once. Two policemen and a red-haired man in plain clothes had come in at the main door.

'Out we go!' breathed Este, impelling the party toward the side entrance. 'There's going to be some kind of riot here.' He gasped. Two more bluecoats barred the exit there. They paused uncertainly. The plain-clothes man was beginning a careful inspection of the people at the table. Este looked sharply at Rags and then at John, who shrank back behind the palms.

'There's going to be trouble,' whispered Rags. 'Can't we get out by this entrance?' The Prince, with rising impatience, sat down again in his chair.

'Let me know when you chaps are ready to go.' He smiled at Rags. 'Now, just suppose we all get into trouble just for that jolly face of yours!' Then suddenly the lights went up. The plain-clothes man whirled around quickly and sprang to the middle of the cabaret floor.

'Nobody try to leave this room!' he shouted. 'Sit down, that party behind the palms! Is John Chestnut in this room?' Rags gave a short, involuntary cry.

'Here!' cried the detective to the policeman behind him. 'Take a look at that bunch over there. Hands up, you men!'

'My God!' whispered Este. 'We've got to get out of here!' He turned to the Prince. 'This won't do, Ted. You can't be seen here. I'll try and stall them off while you get to the car.' He took a step toward the side entrance.

'Hands up, there!' cried the plain-clothes man. 'And when I say hands up I mean it! Which one of you's Chestnut?'

'You're mad!' shouted Este. 'We're British subjects. We're not involved in this affair in any way!' A woman screamed somewhere, and there was a general movement toward the lifts, a movement which stopped short before the muzzles of two automatic pistols. A girl next to Rags collapsed in a dead faint to the floor, and at the same moment the music on the other roof began to play.

'Stop that music!' bellowed the plain-clothes man. 'And get some handcuffs on that whole bunch – quick!' Two policemen advanced toward the party, and simultaneously Este and the other aides drew their revolvers and, shielding the Prince as best they could, began to edge toward the side. A shot rang out and then another, followed by a crash of silver and china as half a dozen diners overturned their tables and dropped quickly behind.

The panic became general. There were three shots in quick succession and then a fusillade. Rags saw Este firing coolly at the eight amber lights which lit the roof, and a thick fume of grey smoke began to fill the air. As a strange undertone to the shouting and screaming came the incessant clamour of the distant jazz band. Then in a moment it was all over. A shrill whistle rang out over the roof, and through the smoke Rags saw John Chestnut advancing toward the plain-clothes man, his hands held out in a gesture of surrender. There was a last nervous cry, a shrill clatter as someone inadvertently stepped into a pile of dishes, and then a heavy silence fell on the roof; even the band seemed to have died away.

'It's all over!' John Chestnut's voice rang out wildly on the night air. 'The party's over. Everybody who wants to can go home!' Still there was silence. Rags knew it was the silence of awe. The strain of guilt had driven John Chestnut insane.

'It was a great performance,' he was shouting. 'I want to thank you one and all. If you can find any tables still standing, champagne will be served as long as you care to stay.' It seemed to Rags that the roof and the high stars suddenly began to swim round and round. She saw John take the detective's hand and shake it heartily, and she watched the detective grin and pocket his gun. The music had recommenced, and the girl who had fainted was suddenly dancing with Lord Charles Este in the corner. John was running here and there patting people on the back, and laughing and shaking hands. Then he was coming toward her, fresh and innocent as a child.

'Wasn't it wonderful?' he cried. Rags felt a faintness stealing over her. She groped backward with her hand toward a chair.

'What was it?' she cried dazedly. 'Am I dreaming?'

'Of course not! You're wide awake. I made it up, Rags, don't you see? I made up the whole thing for you. I had it invented! The only thing real about it was my name!' She collapsed suddenly against his coat, clung to his lapels and would have wilted to the floor if he had not caught her quickly in his arms.

'Some champagne – hurry!' he called, and then he shouted at the Prince, who stood near-by: 'Order my car, quick! Miss Rags Martin-Jones has fainted from excitement.'

Miss Rags Martin-Jones sat waiting – waiting for perhaps the first time in her life.

Mr Chestnut wants to know if you'll come right in to his private office.' It was a respectful voice at her elbow.

Obediently her slim feet moved along the carpet into a long, cool, exquisite room. John Chestnut sat at his desk, waiting, and Rags walked to him and put her arms around his shoulder.

'Are you sure *you're* real?' she asked anxiously. 'Are you absolutely *sure?*'

'You only wrote to me a week before you came?' he protested modestly, 'or I could have arranged a revolution.'

'Was the whole thing just *mine*?' she demanded. 'Was it a perfectly useless, gorgeous thing, just for me?'

'Useless?' He considered. 'Well, it started out to be. At the last minute I invited a big restaurant man to be there, and while you were at the other table I sold him the whole idea of the cabaret.' He looked at his watch.

'I've got one more thing to do, and then we've got just time to be married before lunch.' He picked up his telephone to give some brief swift orders, rang off, turned to the wild-eyed girl with a laugh.

'John,' she asked him intently, 'who was the Prince of Wales?' He waited until they were in an outer room, and then pointed to a young secretary who had come politely to his feet. His face was pale, oval, framed in yellow hair. Rags blushed like fire.

'He's from Wessex,' explained John. 'The resemblance is, to say the least, amazing.'

Rags took the monocle from around her neck and threw the ribbon over his head.

'Thank you,' she said simply, 'for the second greatest thrill of my life.'

Then John Chestnut began rubbing his hands together in a commercial gesture.

'Patronize this place, lady,' he besought her. 'Best bazaar in the city!'

'What have you got for sale?'

'Well, m'selle, today we have some perfectly be-*oo*-tiful love.'

'Wrap it up, Mr Merchant,' cried Rags Martin-Jones. 'It looks like a bargain to me.'

The Adjuster

I

At five o'clock the sombre egg-shaped room at the Ritz ripens to subtle melody – the light *clat-clat* of one lump, two lumps, into the cup, and the *ding* of the shining teapots and cream-pots as they kiss elegantly in transit upon a silver tray. There are those who cherish that amber hour above all other hours, for now the pale, pleasant toil of the lilies who inhabit the Ritz is over – the singing decorative part of the day remains.

Moving your eyes around the slightly raised horseshoe balcony you might, one spring afternoon, have seen young Mrs Alphonse Karr and young Mrs Charles Hemple at a table for two. The one in the dress was Mrs Hemple – when I say 'the dress' I refer to that black immaculate affair with the big buttons and the red ghost of a cape at the shoulders, a gown suggesting with faint and fashionable irreverence the garb of a French cardinal, as it was meant to do when it was invented in the Rue de la Paix. Mrs Karr and Mrs Hemple were twenty-three years old, and their enemies said that they had done very well for themselves. Either might have had her limousine waiting at the hotel door, but both of them much preferred to walk home (up Park Avenue) through the April twilight.

Luella Hemple was tall, with the sort of flaxen hair that English country girls should have, but seldom do. Her skin was radiant, and there was no need of putting anything on it at all, but in deference to an antiquated fashion – this was the year 1920 – she had powdered out its high roses and drawn on it a new mouth and new eyebrows – which were no more successful than such meddling deserves. This, of course, is said from the vantage-point of 1925. In those days the effect she gave was exactly right.

'I've been married three years,' she was saying as she squashed out a cigarette in an exhausted lemon. 'The baby will be two years old tomorrow. I must remember to get –'

She took a gold pencil from her case and wrote 'Candles' and 'Things you pull, with paper caps,' on an ivory date-pad. Then, raising her eyes, she looked at Mrs Karr and hesitated.

'Shall I tell you something outrageous?'

'Try,' said Mrs Karr cheerfully.

115

'Even my baby bores me. That sounds unnatural, Ede, but it's true. He doesn't *begin* to fill my life. I love him with all my heart, but when I have him to take care of for an afternoon, I get so nervous that I want to scream. After two hours I begin praying for the moment the nurse'll walk in the door.'

When she had made this confession, Luella breathed quickly and looked closely at her friend. She didn't really feel unnatural at all. This was the truth. There couldn't be anything vicious in the truth.

'It may be because you don't love Charles,' ventured Mrs Karr, unmoved.

'But I do! I hope I haven't given you that impression with all this talk.' She decided that Ede Karr was stupid. 'It's the very fact that I do love Charles that complicates matters. I cried myself to sleep last night because I know we're drifting slowly but surely toward a divorce. It's the baby that keeps us together.'

Ede Karr, who had been married five years, looked at her critically to see if this was a pose, but Luella's lovely eyes were grave and sad.

'And what is the trouble?' Ede inquired.

'It's plural,' said Luella, frowning. 'First, there's food. I'm a vile housekeeper, and I have no intention of turning into a good one. I hate to order groceries, and I hate to go into the kitchen and poke around to see if the ice-box is clean, and I hate to pretend to the servants that I'm interested in their work, when really I never want to hear about food until it comes on the table. You see, I never learned to cook, and consequently a kitchen is about as interesting to me as a – as a boiler-room. It's simply a machine that I don't understand. It's easy to say, "Go to cooking school," the way people do in books – but, Ede, in real life does anybody ever change into a model *Hausfrau* – unless they have to?'

'Go on,' said Ede non-committally. 'Tell me more.'

'Well, as a result, the house is always in a riot. The servants leave every week. If they're young and incompetent, I can't train them, so we have to let them go. If they're experienced, they hate a house where a woman doesn't take an intense interest in the price of asparagus. So they leave – and half the time we eat at restaurants and hotels.'

'I don't suppose Charles likes that.'

'Hates it. In fact, he hates about everything that I like. He's lukewarm about the theatre, hates the opera, hates dancing, hates cocktail parties – sometimes I think he hates everything pleasant in the world. I sat home for a year or so. While Chuck was on the way, and while I was nursing him, I didn't mind. But this year I told Charles frankly that I was still young enough to want some fun. And since then we've been going out whether he wants to or not.' She paused, brooding. 'I'm so sorry for him I don't know what to do, Ede – but if we sat home, I'd just be sorry for myself. And to tell you another true thing, I'd rather that he'd be unhappy than me.'

Luella was not so much stating a case as thinking aloud. She considered that she was being very fair. Before her marriage men had always told her that she was 'a good sport,' and she had tried to carry this fairness into her married life. So she always saw Charley's point of view as clearly as she saw her own.

If she had been a pioneer wife, she would probably have fought the fight side by side with her husband. But here in New York there wasn't any fight. They weren't struggling together to obtain a far-off peace and leisure – she'd had more of either than she could use. Luella, like several thousand other young wives in New York, honestly wanted something to do. If she had had a little more money and a little less love, she could have gone in for horses or for vagarious amour. Or if they had had a little less money, her surplus energy would have been absorbed by hope and even by effort. But the Charles Hemples were in between. They were of that enormous American class who wander over Europe every summer, sneering rather pathetically and wistfully at the customs and traditions and pastimes of other countries, because they have no customs or tradition or pastimes of their own. It is a class sprung yesterday from fathers and mothers who might just as well have lived two hundred years ago.

The tea-hour had turned abruptly into the before-dinner hour. Most of the tables had emptied until the room was dotted rather than crowded with shrill isolated voices and remote, surprising laughter – in one corner the waiters were already covering the tables with white for dinner.

'Charles and I are on each other's nerves.' In the new silence Luella's voice rang out with startling clearness, and she lowered it precipitately. 'Little things. He keeps rubbing his face with his hand – all the time, at table, at the theatre – even when he's in bed. It drives me wild, and when things like that begin to irritate you, it's nearly over.' She broke off and, reaching backward, drew up a light fur around her neck. 'I hope I haven't bored you, Ede. It's on my mind, because tonight tells the story. I made an engagement for tonight – an interesting engagement, a supper after the theatre to meet some Russians, singers or dancers or something, and Charles says he won't go. If he doesn't – then I'm going alone. And that's the end.'

She put her elbows on the table suddenly and, bending her eyes down into her smooth gloves, began to cry, stubbornly and quietly. There was no one near to see, but Ede Karr wished that she had taken her gloves off. She would have reached out consolingly and touched her bare hand. But the gloves were a symbol of the difficulty of sympathizing with a woman to whom life had given so much. Ede wanted to say that it would 'come out all right,' that it wasn't 'so bad as it seemed,' but she said nothing. Her only reaction was impatience and distaste.

A waiter stepped near and laid a folded paper on the table, and Mrs Karr reached for it.

'No, you mustn't,' murmured Luella brokenly. 'No, I invited *you*! I've got the money right here.'

II

The Hemples' apartment – they owned it – was in one of those impersonal white palaces that are known by number instead of names. They had furnished it on their honeymoon, gone to England for the big pieces, to Florence for the bric-à-brac, and to Venice for the lace and sheer linen of the curtains and for the glass of many colours which littered the table when they entertained. Luella enjoyed choosing things on her honeymoon. It gave a purposeful air to the trip, and saved it from ever turning into the rather dismal wandering among big hotels and desolate ruins which European honeymoons are apt to be.

They returned, and life began. On the grand scale. Luella found herself a lady of substance. It amazed her sometimes that the specially created apartment and the specially created limousine were hers, just as indisputably as the mortgaged suburban bungalow out of the *Ladies' Home Journal* and the last year's car that fate might have given her instead. She was even more amazed when it all began to bore her. But it did ...

The evening was at seven when she turned out of the April dusk, let herself into the hall, and saw her husband waiting in the living-room before an open fire. She came in without a sound, closed the door noiselessly behind her, and stood watching him for a moment through the pleasant effective vista of the small *salon* which intervened. Charles Hemple was in the middle thirties, with a young serious face and distinguished iron-grey hair which would be white in ten years more. That and his deep-set, dark-grey eyes were his most noticeable features – women always thought his hair was romantic; most of the time Luella thought so too.

At this moment she found herself hating him a little, for she saw that he had raised his hand to his face and was rubbing it nervously over his chin and mouth. It gave him an air of unflattering abstraction, and sometimes even obscured his words, so that she was continually saying 'What?' She had spoken about it several times, and he had apologized in a surprised way. But obviously he didn't realize how noticeable and how irritating it was, for he continued to do it. Things had now reached such a precarious state that Luella dreaded speaking of such matters any more – a certain sort of word might precipitate the imminent scene.

Luella tossed her gloves and purse abruptly on the table. Hearing the faint sound, her husband looked out toward the hall.

'Is that you, dear?'

'Yes, dear.'

She went into the living-room, and walked into his arms and kissed him tensely. Charles Hemple responded with unusual formality, and then turned her slowly around so that she faced across the room.

'I've brought some one home to dinner.'

She saw then that they were not alone, and her first feeling was of strong relief; the rigid expression on her face softened into a shy, charming smile as she held out her hand.

'This is Doctor Moon – this is my wife.'

A man a little older than her husband, with a round, pale, slightly lined face, came forward to meet her.

'Good evening, Mrs Hemple,' he said. 'I hope I'm not interfering with any arrangements of yours.'

'Oh, no,' Luella cried quickly. 'I'm delighted that you're coming to dinner. We're quite alone.'

Simultaneously she thought of her engagement that night, and wondered if this could be a clumsy trap of Charles' to keep her at home. If it were, he had chosen his bait badly. This man – a tired placidity radiated from him, from his face, from his heavy, leisurely voice, even from the three-year-old shine of his clothes.

Nevertheless, she excused herself and went into the kitchen to see what was planned for dinner. As usual they were trying a new pair of servants, the luncheon had been ill-cooked and ill-served – she would let them go tomorrow. She hoped Charles would talk to them – she hated to get rid of servants. Sometimes they wept, and sometimes they were insolent, but Charles had a way with him. And they were always afraid of a man.

The cooking on the stove, however, had a soothing savour. Luella gave instructions about 'which china,' and unlocked a bottle of precious chianti from the buffet. Then she went in to kiss young Chuck good night.

'Has he been good?' she demanded as he crawled enthusiastically into her arms.

'Very good,' said the governess. 'We went for a long walk over by Central Park.'

'Well, aren't you a smart boy!' she kissed him ecstatically.

'And he put his foot into the fountain, so we had to come home in a taxi right away and change his little shoe and stocking.'

'That's right. Here, wait a minute, *Chuck!*' Luella unclasped the great yellow beads from around her neck and handed them to him. 'You mustn't break mama's beads.' She turned to the nurse. 'Put them on my dresser, will you after he's asleep?'

She felt a certain compassion for her son as she went away – the small enclosed life he led, that all children led, except in big families. He was a dear little rose, except on the days when she took care of him. His face was the same shape as hers; she was thrilled sometimes, and formed new resolves about life when his heart beat against her own.

In her own pink and lovely bedroom, she confined her attentions to her face, which she washed and restored. Doctor Moon didn't deserve a change of dress, and Luella found herself oddly tired, though she had done very little all day. She returned to the living-room, and they went in to dinner.

'Such a nice house, Mrs Hemple,' said Doctor Moon impersonally; 'and let me congratulate you on your fine little boy.'

'Thanks. Coming from a doctor, that's a nice compliment.' She hesitated. 'Do you specialize in children?'

'I'm not a specialist at all,' he said. 'I'm about the last of my kind – a general practitioner.'

'The last in New York, anyhow,' remarked Charles. He had begun rubbing his face nervously, and Luella fixed her eyes on Doctor Moon so that she wouldn't see. But at Charles' next words she looked back at him sharply.

'In fact,' he said unexpectedly, 'I've invited Doctor Moon here because I wanted you to have a talk with him tonight.'

Luella sat up straight in her chair.

'A talk with *me*?'

'Doctor Moon's an old friend of mine, and I think he can tell you a few things, Luella, that you ought to know.'

'Why –' She tried to laugh, but she was surprised and annoyed. 'I don't see, exactly, what you mean. There's nothing the matter with me. I don't believe I've ever felt better in my life.'

Doctor Moon looked at Charles, asking permission to speak. Charles nodded, and his hand went up automatically to his face.

'Your husband has told me a great deal about your unsatisfactory life together,' said Doctor Moon, still impersonally. 'He wonders if I can be of any help in smoothing things out.'

Luella's face was burning.

'I have no particular faith in psychoanalysis,' she said coldly, 'and I scarcely consider myself a subject for it.'

'Neither have I,' answered Doctor Moon, apparently unconscious of the snub; 'I have no particular faith in anything but myself. I told you I am not a specialist, nor, I may add, a faddist of any sort. I promise nothing.'

For a moment Luella considered leaving the room. But the effrontery of the suggestion aroused her curiosity too.

'I can't imagine what Charles has told you,' she said, controlling herself with difficulty, 'much less why. But I assure you that our affairs are a matter entirely between my husband and me. If you have no objections, Doctor Moon, I'd much prefer to discuss something – less personal.'

Doctor Moon nodded heavily and politely. He made no further attempt to open the subject, and dinner proceeded in what was little more than a defeated silence. Luella determined that, whatever happened, she would adhere to her plans for tonight. An hour ago her independence had demanded it, but now some gesture of defiance had become necessary to her self-respect. She would stay in the living-room for a short moment after dinner; then, when the coffee came, she would excuse herself and dress to go out.

But when they did leave the dining-room, it was Charles who, in a quick, unarguable way, vanished.

'I have a letter to write,' he said; 'I'll be back in a moment.' Before Luella could make a diplomatic objection, he went quickly down the corridor to his room and she heard him shut his door.

Angry and confused, Luella poured the coffee and sank into a corner of the couch, looking intently at the fire.

'Don't be afraid, Mrs Hemple,' said Doctor Moon suddenly. 'This was forced upon me. I do not act as a free agent –'

'I'm not afraid of you,' she interrupted. But she knew that she was lying. She was a little afraid of him, if only for his dull insensitiveness to her distaste.

'Tell me about your trouble,' he said very naturally, as though she were not a free agent either. He wasn't even looking at her, and except that they were alone in the room, he scarcely seemed to be addressing her at all.

The words that were in Luella's mind, her will, on her lips, were: 'I'll do no such thing.' What she actually said amazed her. It came out of her spontaneously, with apparently no co-operation of her own.

'Didn't you see him rubbing his face at dinner?' she said despairingly. 'Are you blind? He's become so irritating to me that I think I'll go mad.'

'I see.' Doctor Moon's round face nodded.

'Don't you see I've had enough of home?' Her breasts seemed to struggle for air under her dress. 'Don't you see how bored I am with keeping house, with the baby – everything seems as if it's going on for ever and ever? I want excitement; and I don't care what form it takes or what I pay for it, so long as it makes my heart beat.'

'I see.'

It infuriated Luella that he claimed to understand. Her feeling of defiance had reached such a pitch that she preferred that no one should understand. She was content to be justified by the impassioned sincerity of her desires.

'I've tried to be good, and I'm not going to try any more. If I'm one of those women who wreck their lives for nothing, then I'll do it now. You can call me selfish, or silly, and be quite right; but in five minutes I'm going out of this house and begin to be alive.'

This time Doctor Moon didn't answer, but he raised his head as if he were listening to something that was taking place a little distance away.

'You're not going out,' he said after a moment; 'I'm quite sure you're not going out.'

Luella laughed.

'I *am* going out.'

He disregarded this.

'You see, Mrs Hemple, your husband isn't well. He's been trying to live your kind of life, and the strain of it has been too much for him. When he rubs his mouth –'

Light steps came down the corridor, and the maid, with a frightened expression on her face, tiptoed into the room.

'Mrs Hemple –'

Startled at the interruption, Luella turned quickly.

'Yes?'

'Can I speak to –?' Her fear broke precipitately through her slight training. 'Mr Hemple, he's sick! He came into the kitchen a while ago and began throwing all the food out of the ice-box, and now he's in his room, crying and singing –'

Suddenly Luella heard his voice.

III

Charles Hemple had had a nervous collapse. There were twenty years of almost uninterrupted toil upon his shoulders, and the recent pressure at home had been too much for him to bear. His attitude toward his wife was the weak point in what had otherwise been a strong-minded and well-organized career – he was aware of her intense selfishness, but it is one of the many flaws in the scheme of human relationships that selfishness in women has an irresistible appeal to many men. Luella's selfishness existed side by side with a childish beauty, and, in consequence, Charles Hemple had begun to take the blame upon himself for situations which she had obviously brought about. It was an unhealthy attitude, and his mind had sickened, at length, with his attempts to put himself in the wrong.

After the first shock and the momentary flush of pity that followed it, Luella looked at the situation with impatience. She was 'a good sport' – she couldn't take advantage of Charles when he was sick. The question of her liberties had to be postponed until he was on his feet. Just when she had determined to be a wife no longer, Luella was compelled to be a nurse as well. She sat beside his bed while he talked about her in his delirium – about the days of their engagement, and how some friend had told him then that he was making a mistake, and about his happiness in the early months of their marriage, and his growing disquiet as the gap appeared. Evidently he had been more aware of it than she had thought – more than he ever said.

'Luella!' he would lurch up in bed. 'Luella! Where *are* you?'

'I'm right here, Charles, beside you.' She tried to make her voice cheerful and warm.

'If you want to go, Luella, you'd better go. I don't seem to be enough for you any more.'

She denied this soothingly.

'I've thought it over, Luella, and I can't ruin my health on account of you –' Then quickly, and passionately: 'Don't go, Luella, for God's sake, don't go away and leave me! Promise me you won't! I'll do anything you say if you won't go.'

His humility annoyed her most; he was a reserved man, and she had never guessed at the extent of his devotion before.

'I'm only going for a minute. It's Doctor Moon, your friend, Charles. He came today to see how you were, don't you remember? And he wants to talk to me before he goes.'

'You'll come back?' he persisted.

'In just a little while. There – lie quiet.'

She raised his head and plumped his pillow into freshness. A new trained nurse would arrive tomorrow.

In the living-room Doctor Moon was waiting – his suit more worn and shabby in the afternoon light. She disliked him inordinately, with an illogical conviction that he was in some way to blame for her misfortune, but he was so deeply interested that she couldn't refuse to see him. She hadn't asked him to consult with the specialists, though – a doctor who was so down at the heel ...

'Mrs Hemple.' He came forward, holding out his hand, and Luella touched it, lightly and uneasily.

'You seem well,' he said.

'I am well, thank you.'

'I congratulate you on the way you've taken hold of things.'

'But I haven't taken hold of things at all,' she said coldly. 'I do what I have to –'

'That's just it.'

Her impatience mounted rapidly.

'I do what I have to, and nothing more,' she continued; 'and with no particular goodwill.'

Suddenly she opened up to him again, as she had the night of the catastrophe – realizing that she was putting herself on a footing of intimacy with him, yet unable to restrain her words.

'The house isn't going,' she broke out bitterly. 'I had to discharge the servants, and now I've got a woman in by the day. And the baby has a cold, and I've found out that his nurse doesn't know her business, and everything's just as messy and terrible as it can be!'

'Would you mind telling me how you found out the nurse didn't know her business?'

'You find out various unpleasant things when you're forced to stay around the house.'

He nodded, his weary face turning here and there about the room.

'I feel somewhat encouraged,' he said slowly. 'As I told you, I promise nothing; I only do the best I can.'

Luella looked up at him, startled.

'What do you mean?' she protested. 'You've done nothing for me – nothing at all!'

'Nothing much – yet,' he said heavily. 'It takes time, Mrs Hemple.'

The words were said in a dry monotone that was somehow without offence, but Luella felt that he had gone too far. She got to her feet.

'I've met your type before,' she said coldly. 'For some reason you seem to think that you have a standing here as "the old friend of the family." But I don't make friends quickly, and I haven't given you the privilege of being so' – she wanted to say 'insolent,' but the word eluded her – 'so personal with me.'

When the front door had closed behind him, Luella went into the kitchen to see if the woman understood about the three different dinners – one for Charles, one for the baby, and one for herself. It was hard to do with only a single servant when things were so complicated. She must try another employment agency – this one had begun to sound bored.

To her surprise, she found the cook with hat and coat on, reading a newspaper at the kitchen table.

'Why' – Luella tried to think of the name – 'why, what's the matter, Mrs –'

'Mrs Danski is my name.'

'What's the matter?'

'I'm afraid I won't be able to accommodate you,' said Mrs Danski. 'You see, I'm only a plain cook, and I'm not used to preparing invalid's food.'

'But I've counted on you.'

'I'm very sorry.' She shook her head stubbornly. 'I've got my own health to think of. I'm sure they didn't tell me what kind of a job it was when I came. And when you asked me to clean out your husband's room, I knew it was way beyond my powers.'

'I won't ask you to clean anything,' said Luella desperately. 'If you'll just stay until tomorrow. I can't possibly get anybody else tonight.'

Mrs Danski smiled politely.

'I got my own children to think of, just like you.'

It was on Luella's tongue to offer her more money, but suddenly her temper gave way.

'I've never heard of anything so selfish in my life!' she broke out. 'To leave me at a time like this! You're an old fool!'

'If you'd pay me for my time, I'd go,' said Mrs Danski calmly.

'I won't pay you a cent unless you'll stay!'

She was immediately sorry she had said this, but she was too proud to withdraw the threat.

'You will so pay me!'

'You go out that door!'

'I'll go when I get my money,' asserted Mrs Danski indignantly. 'I got my children to think of.'

Luella drew in her breath sharply, and took a step forward. Intimidated by her intensity, Mrs Danski turned and flounced, muttering, out of the door.

Luella went to the phone and, calling up the agency, explained that the woman had left.

'Can you send me some one right away? My husband is sick and the baby's sick –'

'I'm sorry, Mrs Hemple; there's no one in the office now. It's after four o'clock.'

Luella argued for a while. Finally she obtained a promise that they would telephone to an emergency woman they knew. That was the best they could do until tomorrow.

She called several other agencies, but the servant industry had apparently ceased to function for the day. After giving Charles his medicine, she tiptoed softly into the nursery.

'How's baby?' she asked abstractedly.

'Ninety-nine one,' whispered the nurse, holding the thermometer to the light. 'I just took it.'

'Is that much?' asked Luella, frowning.

'It's just three-fifths of a degree. That isn't so much for the afternoon. They often run up a little with a cold.'

Luella went over to the cot and laid her hand on her son's flushed cheek, thinking, in the midst of her anxiety, how much he resembled the incredible cherub of the 'Lux' advertisement in the bus.

She turned to the nurse.

'Do you know how to cook?'

'Why – I'm not a good cook.'

'Well, can you do the baby's food tonight? That old fool has left, and I can't get anyone, and I don't know what to do.'

'Oh, yes, I can do the baby's food.'

'That's all right, then. I'll try to fix something for Mr Hemple. Please have your door open so you can hear the bell when the doctor comes. And let me know.'

So many doctors! There had scarcely been an hour all day when there wasn't a doctor in the house. The specialist and their family physician every morning, then the baby doctor – and this afternoon there had been Doctor Moon, placid, persistent, unwelcome, in the parlour. Luella went into the kitchen. She could cook bacon and eggs for herself – she had often done that after the theatre. But the vegetables for Charles were a different matter – they must be left to boil or stew or something, and the stove had so many doors and ovens that she couldn't decide which to use. She chose a blue pan that looked new, sliced carrots into it, and covered them with a little water. As she put it on the stove and tried to remember what to do next, the phone rang. It was the agency.

'Yes, this is Mrs Hemple speaking.'

'Why, the woman we sent to you has returned here with the claim that you refused to pay her for her time.'

'I explained to you that she refused to stay,' said Luella hotly. 'She didn't keep her agreement, and I didn't feel I was under any obligation –'

'We have to see that our people are paid,' the agency informed her; 'otherwise we wouldn't be helping them at all, would we? I'm sorry, Mrs Hemple, but we won't be able to furnish you with any one else until this little matter is arranged.'

'Oh, I'll pay, I'll pay!' she cried.

'Of course we like to keep on good terms with our clients –'

'Yes – yes!'

'So if you'll send her money around tomorrow? It's seventy-five cents an hour.'

'But how about tonight?' she exclaimed. 'I've got to have some one tonight.'

'Why – it's pretty late now. I was just going home myself.'

'But I'm Mrs Charles Hemple! Don't you understand? I'm perfectly good for what I say I'll do. I'm the wife of Charles Hemple, of 14 Broadway –'

Simultaneously she realized that Charles Hemple of 14 Broadway was a helpless invalid – he was neither a reference nor a refuge any more. In despair at the sudden callousness of the world, she hung up the receiver.

After another ten minutes of frantic muddling in the kitchen, she went to the baby's nurse, whom she disliked, and confessed that she was unable to cook her husband's dinner. The nurse announced that she had a splitting headache, and that with a sick child her hands were full already, but she consented, without enthusiasm, to show Luella what to do.

Swallowing her humiliation, Luella obeyed orders while the nurse experimented, grumbling, with the unfamiliar stove. Dinner was started after a fashion. Then it was time for the nurse to bathe Chuck, and Luella sat down alone at the kitchen table, and listened to the bubbling perfume that escaped from the pans.

'And women do this every day,' she thought. 'Thousands of women. Cook and take care of sick people – go out to work too.'

But she didn't think of those women as being like her, except in the superficial aspect of having two feet and two hands. She said it as she might have said 'South Sea Islanders wear nose-rings.' She was merely slumming today in her own home, and she wasn't enjoying it. For her, it was merely a ridiculous exception.

Suddenly she became aware of slow approaching steps in the dining-room and then in the butler's pantry. Half afraid that it was Doctor Moon coming to pay another call, she looked up – and saw the nurse coming through the pantry door. It flashed through Luella's mind that the nurse was going to be sick too. And she was right – the nurse had hardly reached the kitchen door when she lurched and clutched at the handle as a winged bird clings to a branch. Then she receded wordlessly to the floor. Simultaneously the doorbell rang; and Luella, getting to her feet, gasped with relief that the baby doctor had come.

'Fainted, that's all,' he said, taking the girl's head into his lap. The eyes fluttered. 'Yep, she fainted, that's all.'

'Everybody's sick!' cried Luella with a sort of despairing humour. 'Everybody's sick but me, doctor.'

'This one's not sick,' he said after a moment. 'Her heart is normal already. She just fainted.'

When she had helped the doctor raise the quickening body to a chair, Luella hurried into the nursery and bent over the baby's bed. She let down one of the iron sides quietly. The fever seemed to be gone now – the flush had faded away. She bent over to touch the small cheek.

Suddenly, Luella began to scream.

IV

Even after her baby's funeral, Luella still couldn't believe that she had lost him. She came back to the apartment and walked around the nursery in a circle, saying his name. Then frightened by grief, she sat down and stared at his white rocker with the red chicken painted on the side.

'What will become of me now?' she whispered to herself. 'Something awful is going to happen to me when I realize that I'll never see Chuck any more!'

She wasn't sure yet. If she waited here till twilight, the nurse might still bring him in from his walk. She remembered a tragic confusion in the midst of which some one had told her that Chuck was dead, but if that was so, then why was his room waiting, with his small brush and comb still on the bureau, and why was she here at all?

'Mrs Hemple.'

She looked up. The weary, shabby figure of Doctor Moon stood in the door.

'You go away,' Luella said dully.

'Your husband needs you.'

'I don't care.'

Doctor Moon came a little way into the room.

'I don't think you understand, Mrs Hemple. He's been calling for you. You haven't any one now except him.'

'I hate you,' she said suddenly.

'If you like. I promised nothing, you know. I do the best I can. You'll be better when you realize that your baby is gone, that you're not going to see him any more.'

Luella sprang to her feet.

'My baby isn't dead!' she cried. 'You lie! You always lie!' Her flashing eyes looked into his and caught something there, at once brutal and kind, that awed her and made her impotent and acquiescent. She lowered her own eyes in tired despair.

'All right,' she said wearily. 'My baby is gone. What shall I do now?'

'Your husband is much better. All he needs is rest and kindness. But you must go to him and tell him what's happened.'

'I suppose you think you made him better,' said Luella bitterly.

'Perhaps. He's nearly well.'

Nearly well – then the last link that held her to her home was broken. This part of her life was over – she could cut it off here, with its grief and oppression, and be off now, free as the wind.

'I'll go to him in a minute,' Luella said in a faraway voice. 'Please leave me alone.'

Doctor Moon's unwelcome shadow melted into the darkness of the hall.

'I can go away,' Luella whispered to herself. 'Life has given me back freedom, in place of what it took away from me.'

But she mustn't linger even a minute, or Life would bind her again and make her suffer once more. She called the apartment porter and asked that her trunk be brought up from the storeroom. Then she began taking things from the bureau and wardrobe, trying to approximate as nearly as possible the possessions that she had brought to her married life. She even found two old dresses that had formed part of her trousseau – out of style now, and a little tight in the hips – which she threw in with the rest. A new life. Charles was well again; and her baby, whom she had worshipped, and who had bored her a little, was dead.

When she had packed her trunk, she went into the kitchen automatically, to see about the preparations for dinner. She spoke to the cook about the special things for Charles and said that she herself was dining out. The sight of one of the small pans that had been used to cook Chuck's food caught her attention for a moment – but she stared at it unmoved. She looked into the ice-box and saw it was clean and fresh inside. Then she went into Charles' room. He was sitting up in bed, and the nurse was reading to him. His hair was almost white now, silvery white, and underneath it his eyes were huge and dark in his thin young face.

'The baby is sick?' he asked in his own natural voice.

She nodded.

He hesitated, closing his eyes for a moment. Then he asked:

'The baby is dead?'

'Yes.'

For a long time he didn't speak. The nurse came over and put her hand on his forehead. Two large, strange tears welled from his eyes.

'I knew the baby was dead.'

After another long wait, the nurse spoke:

'The doctor said he could be taken out for a drive today while there was still sunshine. He needs a little change.'

'Yes.'

'I thought' – the nurse hesitated – 'I thought perhaps it would do you both good, Mrs Hemple, if you took him instead of me.'

Luella shook her head hastily.

'Oh, no,' she said. 'I don't feel able to, today.'

The nurse looked at her oddly. With a sudden feeling of pity for Charles, Luella bent down gently and kissed his cheek. Then, without a word, she went to her own room, put on her hat and coat, and with her suitcase started for the front door.

Immediately she saw that there was a shadow in the hall. If she could get past the shadow, she was free. If she could go to the right or left of it, or order it out of her way! But, stubbornly, it refused to move, and with a little cry she sank down into a hall chair.

'I thought you'd gone,' she wailed. 'I told you to go away.'

'I'm going soon,' said Doctor Moon, 'but I don't want you to make an old mistake.'

'I'm not making a mistake – I'm leaving my mistakes behind.'

'You're trying to leave yourself behind, but you can't. The more you try to run away from yourself, the more you'll have yourself with you.'

'But I've got to go away,' she insisted wildly. 'Out of this house of death and failure!'

'You haven't failed yet. You've only begun.'

She stood up.

'Let me pass.'

'No.'

Abruptly she gave way, as she always did when he talked to her. She covered her face with her hands and burst into tears.

'Go back into that room and tell the nurse you'll take your husband for a drive,' he suggested.

'I can't.'

'Oh, yes.'

Once more Luella looked at him, and knew that she would obey. With the conviction that her spirit was broken at last, she took up her suitcase and walked back through the hall.

V

The nature of the curious influence that Doctor Moon exerted upon her, Luella could not guess. But as the days passed she found herself doing many things that had been repugnant to her before. She stayed at home with Charles; and when he grew better, she went out with him sometimes to dinner, or the theatre, but only when he expressed a wish. She visited the kitchen every day, and kept an unwilling eye on the house, at first with a horror that it would go wrong again, then from habit. And she felt that it was all somehow mixed up with Doctor Moon – it was something he kept telling her about life, or almost telling her, and yet concealing from her, as though he were afraid to have her know.

With the resumption of their normal life, she found that Charles was less nervous. His habit of rubbing his face had left him, and if the world seemed less gay and happy to her than it had before, she experienced a certain peace, sometimes, that she had never known.

Then, one afternoon, Doctor Moon told her suddenly that he was going away.

'Do you mean for good?' she demanded with a touch of panic.

'For good.'

For a strange moment she wasn't sure whether she was glad or sorry.

'You don't need me any more,' he said quietly. 'You don't realize it, but you've grown up.'

He came over and, sitting on the couch beside her, took her hand.

Luella sat silent and tense – listening.

'We make an agreement with children that they can sit in the audience without helping to make the play,' he said, 'but if they still sit in the audience after they're grown, somebody's got to work double time for them, so that they can enjoy the light and glitter of the world.'

'But I want the light and glitter,' she protested. 'That's all there is in life. There can't be anything wrong in wanting to have things warm.'

'Things will still be warm.'

'How?'

'Things will warm themselves from you.'

Luella looked at him, startled.

'It's your turn to be the centre, to give others what was given to you for so long. You've got to give security to young people and peace to your husband, and a sort of charity to the old. You've got to let the people who work for you depend on you. You've got to cover up a few more troubles than you show, and be a little more patient than the average person, and do a little more instead of a little less than your share. The light and glitter of the world is in your hands.'

He broke off suddenly.

'Get up,' he said, 'and go to that mirror and tell me what you see.'

Obediently, Luella got up and went close to a purchase of her honeymoon, a Venetian pier-glass on the wall.

'I see new lines in my face here,' she said, raising her finger and placing it between her eyes, 'and a few shadows at the sides that might be – that are little wrinkles.'

'Do you care?'

She turned quickly. 'No,' she said.

'Do you realize that Chuck is gone? That you'll never see him any more?'

'Yes.' She passed her hands slowly over her eyes. 'But that all seems so vague and far away.'

'Vague and far away,' he repeated; and then: 'And are you afraid of me now?'

'Not any longer,' she said, and she added frankly, 'now that you're going away.'

He moved toward the door. He seemed particularly weary tonight, as though he could hardly move about at all.

'The household here is in your keeping,' he said in a tired whisper. 'If there is any light and warmth in it, it will be your light and warmth; if it is happy, it will be because you've made it so. Happy things may come to you in life, but you must never go seeking them any more. It is your turn to make the fire.'

'Won't you sit down a moment longer?' Luella ventured.

'There isn't time.' His voice was so low now that she could scarcely hear the words. 'But remember that whatever suffering comes to you, I can always help you – if it is something that can be helped. I promise nothing.'

He opened the door. She must find out now what she most wanted to know, before it was too late.

'What have you done to me?' she cried. 'Why have I no sorrow left for Chuck – for anything at all? Tell me; I almost see, yet I can't see. Before you go – tell me who you are!'

'Who am I? –' His worn suit paused in the doorway. His round, pale face seemed to dissolve into two faces, a dozen faces, a score, each one different yet the same – sad, happy, tragic, indifferent, resigned – until threescore Doctor Moons were ranged like an infinite series of reflections, like months stretching into the vista of the past.

'Who am I?' he repeated; 'I am five years.'

The door closed.

At six o'clock Charles Hemple came home, and as usual Luella met him in the hall. Except that now his hair was dead white, his long illness of two years had left no mark upon him. Luella herself was more noticeably changed – she was a little stouter, and there were those lines around her eyes that had come when Chuck died one evening back in 1921. But she was still lovely, and there was a mature kindness about her face at twenty-eight, as if suffering had touched her only reluctantly and then hurried away.

'Ede and her husband are coming to dinner,' she said. 'I've got theatre tickets, but if you're tired, I don't care whether we go or not.'

'I'd like to go.'

She looked at him.

'You wouldn't.'

'I really would.'

'We'll see how you feel after dinner.'

He put his arm around her waist. Together they walked into the nursery where the two children were waiting up to say goodnight.

The Dance

All my life I have had a rather curious horror of small towns: not suburbs; they are quite a different matter – but the little lost cities of New Hampshire and Georgia and Kansas, and upper New York. I was born in New York City, and even as a little girl I never had any fear of the streets or the strange foreign faces – but on the occasions when I've been in the sort of place I'm referring to, I've been oppressed with the consciousness that there was a whole hidden life, a whole series of secret implications, significances and terrors, just below the surface, of which I knew nothing. In the cities everything good or bad eventually comes out, comes out of people's hearts, I mean. Life moves about, moves on, vanishes. In the small towns – those between 5,000 and 25,000 people – old hatreds, old and unforgotten affairs, ghostly scandals and tragedies, seem unable to die, but live on all tangled up with the ebb and flow of outward life.

Nowhere has this sensation come over me more insistently than in the south. Once out of Atlanta and Birmingham and New Orleans, I often have the feeling that I can no longer communicate with the people around me. The men and the girls speak a language wherein courtesy is combined with violence, fanatic morality with corn-drinking recklessness, in a fashion which I can't understand. In *Huckleberry Finn* Mark Twain described some of those towns perched along the Mississippi River, with their fierce feuds and their equally fierce revivals – and some of them haven't fundamentally changed beneath their new surface of flibbers and radios. They are deeply uncivilized to this day.

I speak of the South because it was in a small southern city of this type that I once saw the surface crack for a minute and something savage, uncanny and frightening rear its head. Then the surface closed again – and when I have gone back there since, I've been surprised to find myself as charmed as ever by the magnolia trees and the singing darkies in the street and the sensuous warm nights. I have been charmed, too, by the bountiful hospitality and the languorous easy-going outdoor life and the almost universal good manners. But all too frequently I am the prey of a vivid nightmare that recalls what I experienced in that town five years ago.

Davis – that is not its real name – has a population of about 20,000 people, one-third of them coloured. It is a cotton-mill town, and the workers of that trade, several thousand and gaunt and ignorant 'poor whites', live together in an ill-reputed section known as 'Cotton Hollow'. The population of Davis has varied in its seventy-five years. Once it was under consideration for the capital of the State, and so the older families and their kin form a little aristocracy, even when individually they have sunk to destitution.

That winter I'd made the usual round in New York until about April, when I decided I never wanted to see another invitation again. I was tired and I wanted to go to Europe for a rest; but the baby panic of 1921 hit father's business, and so it was suggested that I go South and visit Aunt Musidora Hale instead.

Vaguely I imagined that I was going to the country, but on the day I arrived the *Davis Courier* published a hilarious old picture of me on its society page, and I found I was in for another season. On a small scale, of course: there were Saturday-night dances at the little country-club with its nine-hole golf-course, and some informal dinner parties and several attractive and attentive boys. I didn't have a dull time at all, and when after three weeks I wanted to go home, it wasn't because I was bored. On the contrary I wanted to go home because I'd allowed myself to get rather interested in a young man named Charley Kincaid, without realizing that he was engaged to another girl.

We'd been drawn together from the first because he was almost the only boy in town who'd gone North to college, and I was still young enough to think that America revolved around Harvard and Princeton and Yale. He liked me too – I could see that; but when I heard that his engagement to a girl named Marie Bannerman had been announced six months before, there was nothing for me except to go away. The town was too small to avoid people, and though so far there hadn't been any talk, I was sure that – well, that if we kept meeting, the emotion we were beginning to feel would somehow get into words. I'm not mean enough to take a man away from another girl.

Marie Bannerman was almost a beauty. Perhaps she would have been a beauty if she'd had any clothes, and if she hadn't used bright pink rouge in two high spots on her cheeks and powdered her nose and chin to a funereal white. Her hair was shining black; her features were lovely; and an affection of one eye kept it always half-closed and gave an air of humourous mischief to her face.

I was leaving on a Monday, and on Saturday night a crowd of us dined at the country-club as usual before the dance. There was Joe Cable, the son of a former governor, a handsome dissipated and yet somehow charming young man; Catherine Jones, a pretty, sharp-eyed girl with an exquisite figure, who under her rouge might have been any age from eighteen to twenty-five; Marie Bannerman; Charley Kincaid; myself and two or three others.

I loved to listen to the genial flow of bizarre neighbourhood anecdote at this kind of party. For instance, one of the girls, together with her entire family, had that afternoon been evicted from her house for non-payment of rent. She told the story wholly without self-consciousness, merely as something troublesome but amusing. And I loved the banter which presumed every girl to be infinitely beautiful and attractive, and every man to have been secretly and hopelessly in love with every girl present from their respective cradles.

'We liked to die laughin'' ... '– said he was fixin' to shoot him without he stayed away.' The girls 'clared to heaven'; the men 'took oath' on inconsequential statements. 'How come you nearly about forgot to come by for me –' and the incessant Honey, Honey, Honey, Honey, until the word seemed to roll like a genial liquid from heart to heart.

Outside, the May night was hot, a still night, velvet, soft-pawed, splattered thick with stars. It drifted heavy and sweet into the large room where we sat and where we would later dance, with no sound in it except the occasional long crunch of an arriving car on the drive. Just at that moment I hated to leave Davis as I never had hated to leave a town before – I felt that I wanted to spend my life in this town, drifting and dancing forever through these long, hot, romantic nights.

Yet horror was already hanging over that little party, was waiting tensely among us, an uninvited guest, and telling off the hours until it could show its pale and blinding face. Beneath the chatter and laughter something was going on, something secret and obscure that I didn't know.

Presently the coloured orchestra arrived, followed by the first trickle of the dance crowd. An enormous red-faced man in muddy knee boots and with a revolver strapped around his waist, clumped in and paused for a moment at our table before going upstairs to the locker-room. It was Bill Abercrombie, the sheriff, the son of Congressman Abercrombie. Some of the boys asked him half-whispered questions, and he replied in an attempt at an undertone.

'Yes ... He's in the swamp all right; farmer saw him near the crossroads store ... Like to have a shot at him myself.'

I asked the boy next to me what was the matter.

'Nigger case,' he said, 'over in Kisco, about two miles from here. He's hiding in the swamp, and they're going in after him tomorrow.'

'What'll they do to him?'

'Hang him, I guess.'

The notion of the forlorn darky crouching dismally in a desolate bog waiting for dawn and death depressed me for a moment. Then the feeling passed and was forgotten.

After dinner Charley Kincaid and I walked out on the veranda – he had just heard that I was going away. I kept as close to the others as I could, answering his words but not his eyes – something inside me was protesting against leaving him on such a casual note. The temptation was strong to let something flicker up between us here at the end. I wanted him to kiss me – my heart promised that if he kissed me, just once, it would accept with equanimity the idea of never seeing him any more; but my mind knew it wasn't so.

The other girls began to drift inside and upstairs to the dressing-room to improve their complexions, and with Charley still beside me, I followed. Just at that moment I wanted to cry – perhaps my eyes were already blurred, or perhaps it was my haste lest they should be, but I opened the door of a small card-room by mistake and with my error the tragic machinery of the night began to function. In the card-room, not five feet from us, stood Marie Bannerman, Charley's fiancée, and Joe Cable. They were in each other's arms, absorbed in a passionate and oblivious kiss.

I closed the door quickly and without glancing at Charley opened the right door and ran upstairs.

A few minutes later Marie Bannerman entered the crowded dressing-room. She saw me and came over, smiling in a sort of mock despair, but she breathed quickly, and the smile trembled a little on her mouth.

'You won't say a word, honey, will you?' she whispered.

'Of course not.' I wondered how that could matter, now that Charley Kincaid knew.

'Who else was it that saw us?'

'Only Charley Kincaid and I.'

'Oh!' She looked a little puzzled; then she added: 'He didn't wait to say anything, honey. When we came out he was just going out the door. I thought he was going to wait and romp all over Joe.'

'How about his romping all over you?' I couldn't help asking.

'Oh, he'll do that.' She laughed wryly. 'But, honey, I know how to handle him. It's just when he's first mad that I'm scared of him – he's got an awful temper.' She whistled reminiscently. 'I know, because this happened once before.'

I wanted to slap her. Turning my back, I walked away on the pretext of borrowing a pin from Katie, the Negro maid. Catherine Jones was claiming the latter's attention with a short gingham garment which needed repair.

'What's that?' I asked.

'Dancing-dress,' she answered shortly, her mouth full of pins. When she took them out, she added: 'It's all come to pieces – I've used it so much.'

'Are you going to dance here tonight?'

'Going to try.'

Somebody had told me that she wanted to be a dancer – that she had taken lessons in New York.

'Can I help you fix anything?'

'No, thanks – unless – can you sew? Katie gets so excited Saturday night that she's no good for anything except fetching pins. I'd be everlasting grateful to you, honey.'

I had reasons for not wanting to go downstairs just yet, and so I sat down and worked on her dress for half an hour. I wondered if Charley had gone home, if I would ever see him again – I scarcely dared to wonder if what he had seen would set him free, ethically. When I went down finally he was not in sight.

The room was now crowded; the tables had been removed and dancing was general. At that time, just after the war, all Southern boys had a way of agitating their heels from side to side, pivoting on the ball of the foot as they danced, and to acquiring this accomplishment I had devoted many hours. There were plenty of stags, almost all of them cheerful with corn-liquor; I refused on an average at least two drinks a dance. Even when it is mixed with a soft drink, as is the custom, rather than gulped from the neck of a warm bottle, it is a formidable proposition. Only a few girls like Catherine Jones took an occasional sip from some boy's flask down at the dark end of the veranda.

I liked Catherine Jones – she seemed to have more energy than these other girls, though Aunt Musidora sniffed rather contemptuously whenever Catherine stopped for me in her car to go to the movies, remarking that she guessed 'the bottom rail had gotten to be the top rail now'. Her family were 'new and common', but it seemed to be that perhaps her very commonness was an asset. Almost every girl in Davis confided in me at one time or another that her ambition was to 'get away to New York', but only Catherine Jones had actually taken the step of studying stage dancing with that end in view.

She was often asked to dance at these Saturday night affairs, something 'classic' or perhaps an acrobatic clog – on one memorable occasion she had annoyed the governing board by a 'shimee' (then the scapegrace of jazz), and the novel and somewhat startling excuse made for her was that she was 'so tight she didn't know what she was doing, anyhow'. She impressed me as a curious girl, and I was eager to see what she would produce tonight.

At twelve o'clock the music always ceased, as dancing was forbidden on

Sunday morning. So at 11.30 a vast fanfaronade of drum and cornet beckoned the dancers and the couples on the verandas, and the ones in the cars outside, and the stragglers from the bar, into the ballroom. Chairs were brought in and galloped up *en masse* and with a great racket to the slightly raised platform. The orchestra had evacuated this and taken a place beside. Then, as the rearward lights were lowered, they began to play a tune accompanied by a curious drumbeat that I had never heard before, and simultaneously Catherine Jones appeared upon the platform. She wore the short, country girl's dress upon which I had lately laboured, and a wide sun bonnet under which her face, stained yellow with powder, looked out at us with rolling eyes and a vacant negroid leer. She began to dance.

I had never seen anything like it before, and until five years later, I wasn't to see it again. It was the Charleston – it must have been the Charleston. I remember the double drum-beat like a shouted 'Hey! Hey!' and the swing of the arms and the odd knock-kneed effect. She had picked it up, heaven knows where.

Her audience, familiar with Negro rhythms, leaned forward eagerly – even to them it was something new, but it is stamped on my mind as clearly and indelibly as though I had seen it yesterday. The figure on the platform swinging and stamping, the excited orchestra, the waiters grinning in the doorway of the bar, and all around, through many windows, the soft languorous Southern night seeping in from swamp and cottonfield and lush foliage and brown, warm streams. At what point a feeling of tense uneasiness began to steal over me I don't know. The dance could scarcely have taken ten minutes; perhaps the first beats of the barbaric music disquieted me – long before it was over, I was sitting rigid in my seat, and my eyes were wandering here and there around the hall, passing along the rows of shadowy faces as if seeking some security that was no longer there.

I'm not a nervous type; nor am I given to panic; but for a moment I was afraid that if the music and the dance didn't stop, I'd be hysterical. Something was happening all about me. I knew it as well as if I could see into these unknown souls. Things were happening, but one thing especially was leaning over so close that it almost touched us, that it did touch us ... I almost screamed as a hand brushed accidentally against my back.

The music stopped. There was applause and protracted cries of encore, but Catherine Jones shook her head definitely at the orchestra leader and made as though to leave the platform. The appeals for more continued – again she shook her head, and it seemed to me that her expression was rather angry. Then a strange incident occurred. At the protracted pleading of someone in the front row, the coloured orchestra leader began the vamp of the tune, as if to lure Catherine Jones into changing her mind. Instead she turned toward him, snapped out: 'Didn't you hear me say no?' and then, surprisingly, slapped his face. The music stopped, and an amused murmur terminated abruptly as a muffled but clearly audible shot rang out.

Immediately we were on our feet, for the sound indicated that it had been fired within or near the house. One of the chaperons gave a little scream, but when some wag called out: 'Caesar's in that henhouse again', the momentary alarm dissolved into laughter. The club manager, followed by several curious couples, went out to have a look about, but the rest were already moving around the floor to the strains of 'Good Night, Ladies', which traditionally ended the dance.

I was glad it was over. The man with whom I had come went to get his car, and calling a waiter, I sent him for my golf-clubs, which were upstairs. I strolled out on the porch and waited, wondering again if Charley Kincaid had gone home.

Suddenly I was aware, in that curious way in which you become aware of something that has been going on for several minutes, that there was a tumult inside. Women were shrieking; there was a cry of 'Oh, my God!', then the sounds of a stampede on the inside stairs, and footsteps running back and forth across the ballroom. A girl appeared from somewhere and pitched forward in a dead faint – almost immediately another girl did the same, and I heard a frantic male voice shouting into a telephone. Then, hatless and pale, a young man rushed out on the porch, and with hands that were cold as ice, seized my arm.

'What is it?' I cried. 'A fire? What's happened?'

'Marie Bannerman's dead upstairs in the women's dressing-room. Shot through the throat!'

The rest of that night is a series of visions that seem to have no connection with one another, that follow each other with the sharp instantaneous transitions of scenes in the movies. There was a group who stood arguing on the porch, in voices now raised, now hushed, about what should be done and how every waiter in the club, 'even old Moses', ought to be given the third degree tonight. That a 'nigger' had shot and killed Marie Bannerman was the instant and unquestioned assumption – in the first unreasoning instant, anyone who doubted it would have been under suspicion. The guilty one was said to be Katie Golstein, the coloured maid, who had discovered the body and fainted. It was said to be 'that nigger they were looking for at Kisco.' It was any darky at all.

Within half an hour people began to drift out, each with his little contribution of new discoveries. The crime had been committed with Sheriff Abercrombie's gun – he had hung it, belt and all, in full view on the wall before coming down to dance. It was missing – they were hunting for it now. Instantly killed, the doctor said – bullet had been fired from only a few feet away.

Then a few minutes later another young man came out and made the announcement in a loud, grave voice: 'They've arrested Charley Kincaid.'

My head reeled. Upon the group gathered on the veranda fell an awed, stricken silence.

'Arrested Charley Kincaid!'

'Charley Kincaid!'

Why, he was one of the best, one of themselves.

'That's the craziest thing I ever heard of!'

The young man nodded, shocked like the rest, but self-important with his information.

'He wasn't downstairs, when Catherine Jones was dancing – he says he was in the men's locker-room. And Marie Bannerman told a lot of girls that they'd had a row, and she was scared of what he'd do.'

Again an awed silence.

'That's the craziest thing I ever heard!' someone said again.

'Charley Kincaid!'

The narrator waited a moment. Then he added:

'He caught her kissing Joe Cable –'

I couldn't keep silence a minute longer.

'What about it?' I cried out. 'I was with him at the time. He wasn't – he wasn't angry at all.'

They looked at me, their faces startled, confused, unhappy. Suddenly the footsteps of several men sounded loud through the ballroom, and a moment later Charley Kincaid, his face dead white, came out the front door between the Sheriff and another man. Crossing the porch quickly, they descended the steps and disappeared in the darkness. A moment later there was the sound of a starting car.

When an instant later far away down the road I heard the eerie scream of an ambulance, I got up desperately and called to my escort, who formed part of the whispering group.

'I've got to go,' I said. 'I can't stand this. Either take me home or I'll find a place in another car.' Reluctantly he shouldered my clubs – the sight of them made me realize that I now couldn't leave on Monday after all – and followed me down the steps just as the black ambulance curved in at the gate – a ghastly shadow on the bright, starry night.

The situation after the first wild surmises, the first burst of unreasoning loyalty to Charley Kincaid, had died away, was outlined by the *Davis Courier* and by most of the State newspapers in this fashion: Marie

Bannerman died in the women's dressing-room of the Davis Country Club from the effects of a shot fired at close quarters from a revolver just after 11.45 o'clock on Saturday night. Many persons had heard the shot; moreover, it had undoubtedly been fired from the revolver of Sheriff Abercrombie, which had been hanging in full sight on the wall of the next room. Abercrombie himself was in the ballroom when the murder took place, as many witnesses could testify. The revolver was not found.

So far as was known, the only man who had been upstairs at the time the shot was fired was Charley Kincaid. He was engaged to Miss Bannerman, but according to several witnesses they had quarrelled seriously that evening. Miss Bannerman herself had mentioned the quarrel, adding that she was afraid and wanted to keep away from him until he cooled off.

Charles Kincaid asserted that at the time the shot was fired he was in the men's locker-room – where, indeed, he was found, immediately after the discovery of Miss Bannerman's body. He denied having had any words with Miss Bannerman at all. He had heard the shot but if he thought anything of it, he thought that 'someone was potting cats out-doors.'

Why had he chosen to remain in the locker-room during the dance?

No reason at all. He was tired. He was waiting until Miss Bannerman wanted to go home.

The body was discovered by Katie Golstein, the coloured maid, who herself was found in a faint when the crowd of girls surged upstairs for their coats. Returning from the kitchen, where she had been getting a bite to eat, Katie had found Miss Bannerman, her dress wet with blood, already dead on the floor.

Both the police and the newspapers attached importance to the geography of the country-club's second storey. It consisted of a row of three rooms – the women's dressing-room and the men's locker-room at either end, and in the middle a room which was used as a cloak-room and for the storage of golf-clubs. The women's and men's rooms had no outlet except into this chamber, which was connected by one stairs with the ball-room below, and by another with the kitchen. According to the testimony of three Negro cooks and the white caddy-master, no one but Katie Golstein had gone up the kitchen stairs that night.

As I remember it after five years, the foregoing is a pretty accurate summary of the situation when Charley Kincaid was accused of first-degree murder and committed for trial. Other people, chiefly Negroes, were suspected (at the loyal instigation of Charley Kincaid's friends), and several arrests were made, but nothing ever came of them, and upon what grounds they were based I have long forgotten. One group, in spite of the disappearance of the pistol, claimed persistently that it was a suicide and suggested some ingenious reasons to account for the absence of the weapon.

Now when it is known Marie Bannerman happened to die so savagely and so violently, it would be easy for me, of all people, to say that I believed in Charley Kincaid all the time. But I didn't. I thought that he had killed her, and at the same time I knew that I loved him with all my heart. That it was I who first happened upon the evidence which set him free was due not to any faith in his innocence but to a strange vividness with which, in moods of excitement, certain scenes stamp themselves on my memory, so that I can remember every detail and how that detail struck me at the time.

It was one afternoon early in July, when the case against Charley Kincaid seemed to be at its strongest, that the horror of the actual murder slipped away from me for a moment and I began to think about other incidents of that same haunted night. Something Marie Bannerman had said to me in the dressing-room persistently eluded me, bothered me – not because I believed it to be important, but simply because I couldn't remember. It was gone from me, as if it had been a part of the fantastic undercurrent of small-town life which I had felt so strongly that evening, the sense that things were in the air, old secrets, old loves and feuds, and unresolved situations, that I could never fully understand. Just for a minute it seemed to me that Marie Bannerman had pushed aside the curtain; then it had dropped into place again – the house into which I might have looked was dark now forever.

Another incident, perhaps less important, also haunted me. The tragic events of a few minutes after had driven it from everyone's mind, but I had a strong impression that for a brief space of time I wasn't the only one to be surprised. When the audience had demanded an encore from Catherine Jones, her unwillingness to dance again had been so acute that she had been driven to the point of slapping the orchestra leader's face. The discrepancy between his offence and the venom of the rebuff recurred to me again and again. It wasn't natural – or, more important, it hadn't seemed natural. In view of the fact that Catherine Jones had been drinking, it was explicable, but it worried me now as it had worried me then. Rather to lay its ghost than to do any investigating, I pressed an obliging young man into service and called on the leader of the band.

His name was Thomas, a very dark, very simple-hearted virtuoso of the traps, and it took less than ten minutes to find out that Catherine Jones' gesture had surprised him as much as it had me. He had known her a long time, seen her at dances since she was a little girl – why, the very dance she did that night was one she had rehearsed with his orchestra a week before. And a few days later she had come to him and said she was sorry.

'I knew she would,' he concluded. 'She's a right good-hearted girl. My sister Katie was her nurse from when she was born up to the time she went to school.'

'Your sister?'

'Katie. She's the maid out at the country-club. Katie Golstein. You been reading 'bout her in the papers in 'at Charley Kincaid case. She's the maid. Katie Golstein. She's the maid at the country-club what found the body of Miss Bannerman.'

'So Katie was Miss Catherine Jones' nurse?'

'Yes ma'am.'

Going home, stimulated but unsatisfied, I asked my companion a quick question.

'Were Catherine and Marie good friends?'

'Oh, yes,' he answered without hesitation. 'All the girls are good friends here, except when two of them are tryin' to get hold of the same man. Then they warm each other up a little.'

'Why do you suppose Catherine hasn't married? Hasn't she got lots of beaux?'

'Off and on. She only likes people for a day or so at a time. That is – all except Joe Cable.'

Now a scene burst upon me, broke over me like a dissolving wave. And suddenly, my mind shivering from the impact, I remembered what Marie Bannerman had said to me in the dressing-room: 'Who else was it that saw?' She had caught a glimpse of someone else, a figure passing so quickly that she could not identify it, out of the corner of her eye.

And suddenly I seemed to see that figure, as if I too had been vaguely conscious of it at the time, just as one is aware of a familiar gait or outline on the street long before there is any flicker of recognition. On the corner of my own eye was stamped a hurrying figure – that might have been Catherine Jones.

But when the shot was fired, Catherine Jones was in full view of over fifty people. Was it credible that Katie Golstein, a woman of fifty, who as a nurse had been known and trusted by three generations of Davis people, would shoot down a young girl in cold blood at Catherine Jones' command?

'But when the shot was fired, Catherine Jones was in full view of over fifty people.'

That sentence beat in my head all night, taking on fantastic variations, dividing itself into phrases, segments, individual words.

'But when the shot was fired – Catherine Jones was in full view – of over fifty people.'

When the shot was fired! What shot? The shot we heard. When the shot was fired ... When the shot was fired ...

The next morning at nine o'clock, with the pallor of sleeplessness buried under a quantity of paint such as I had never worn before or have since, I walked up a rickety flight of stairs to the Sheriff's office.

Abercrombie, engrossed in his morning's mail, looked up curiously as I came in the door.

'Catherine Jones did it,' I cried, struggling to keep the hysteria out of my voice. 'She killed Marie Bannerman with a shot we didn't hear because the orchestra was playing and everybody was pushing up the chairs. The shot we heard was when Katie fired the pistol out of the window after the music was stopped. To give Catherine an alibi!'

I was right – as everyone now knows, but for a week, until Katie Golstein broke down under a fierce and ruthless inquisition, nobody believed me. Even Charley Kincaid, as he afterward confessed, didn't dare to think it could be true.

What had been the relations between Catherine and Joe Cable no one ever knew, but evidently she had determined that his clandestine affair with Marie Bannerman had gone too far.

Then Marie chanced to come into the women's room while Catherine was dressing for her dance – and there again there is a certain obscurity, for Catherine always claimed that Marie got the revolver, threatened her with it and that in the ensuing struggle the trigger was pulled. In spite of everything, I always rather liked Catherine Jones, but in justice it must be said that only a simple-minded and very exceptional jury would have let her off with five years.

And in just about five years from her commitment my husband and I are going to make a round of the New York musical shows and look hard at all the members of the chorus from the very front row.

After the shooting she must have thought quickly. Katie was told to wait until the music stopped, fire the revolver out of the window and then hide it – Catherine Jones neglected to specify where. Katie, on the verge of collapse, obeyed instructions, but she was never able to specify where she had hid the revolver. And no one ever knew until a year later, when Charley and I were on our honeymoon and Sheriff Abercrombie's ugly weapon dropped out of my golf-bag on to a Hot Springs golf-links. The bag must have been standing just outside the dressing-room door; Katie's trembling hand had dropped the revolver into the first aperture she could see.

We live in New York. Small towns make us both uncomfortable. Every day we read about the crimewaves in the big cities, but at least a wave is something tangible that you can provide against. What I dread above all things is the unknown depths, the incalculable ebb and flow, the secret shapes of things that drift through opaque darkness under the surface of the sea.

A Short Trip Home

I was near her, for I had lingered behind in order to get the short walk with her from the living-room to the front door. That was a lot, for she had flowered suddenly and I, being a man and only a year older, hadn't flowered at all, had scarcely dared to come near her in the week we'd been home. Nor was I going to say anything in that walk of ten feet, or touch her; but I had a vague hope she'd do something, give a gay little performance of some sort, personal only in so far as we were alone together.

She had bewitchment suddenly in the twinkle of short hairs on her neck, in the sure, clear confidence that at about eighteen begins to deepen and sing in attractive American girls. The lamplight shopped in the yellow strands of her hair.

Already she was sliding into another world – the world of Joe Jelke and Jim Cathcart waiting for us now in the car. In another year she would pass beyond me for ever.

As I waited, feeling the others outside in the snowy night, feeling the excitement of Christmas week and the excitement of Ellen here, blooming away, filling the room with 'sex appeal' – a wretched phrase to express a quality that isn't like that at all – a maid came in from the dining-room, spoke to Ellen quietly and handed her a note. Ellen read it and her eyes faded down, as when the current grows weak on rural circuits, and smouldered off into space. Then she gave me an odd look – in which I probably didn't show – and without a word, followed the maid into the dining-room and beyond. I sat turning over the pages of a magazine for a quarter of an hour.

Joe Jelke came in, red-faced from the cold, his white silk muffler gleaming at the neck of his fur coat. He was a senior at New Haven, I was a sophomore. He was prominent, a member of Scroll and Keys, and, in my eyes, very distinguished and handsome.

'Isn't Ellen coming?'

'I don't know,' I answered discreetly. 'She was all ready.'

'Ellen!' he called. 'Ellen!'

He had left the front door open behind him and a great cloud of frosty air rolled in from outside. He went halfway up the stairs – he was a familiar in the house – and called again, till Mrs Baker came to the banister and said that Ellen was below. Then the maid, a little excited, appeared in the dining-room door.

'Mr Jelke,' she called in a low voice.

Joe's face fell as he turned toward her, sensing bad news.

'Miss Ellen says for you to go on to the party. She'll come later.'

'What's the matter?'

'She can't come now. She'll come later.'

He hesitated, confused. It was the last big dance of vacation, and he was mad about Ellen. He had tried to give her a ring for Christmas, and failing that, got her to accept a gold mesh bag that must have cost two hundred dollars. He wasn't the only one – there were three or four in the same wild condition, and all in the ten days she'd been home – but his chance came first, for he was rich and gracious and at that moment the 'desirable' boy of St Paul. To me it seemed impossible that she could prefer another, but the rumour was she'd describe Joe as much too perfect. I suppose he lacked mystery for her, and when a man is up against that with a young girl who isn't thinking of the practical side of marriage yet – well –

'She's in the kitchen,' Joe said angrily.

'No, she's not.' The maid was defiant and a little scared.

'She is.'

'She went out the back way, Mr Jelke.'

'I'm going to see.'

I followed him. The Swedish servants washing dishes looked up sideways at our approach and an interested crashing of pans marked our passage through. The storm door, unbolted, was flapping in the wind and as we walked out into the snowy yard we saw the tail-light of a car turn the corner at the end of the back alley.

'I'm going after her,' Joe said slowly. 'I don't understand this at all.'

I was too awed by the calamity to argue. We hurried to his car and drove in a fruitless, despairing zigzag all over the residence section, peering into every machine on the streets. It was half an hour before the futility of the affair began to dawn upon him – St Paul is a city of almost three hundred thousand people – and Jim Cathcart reminded him that we had another girl to stop for. Like a wounded animal he sank into a melancholy mass of fur in the corner, from which position he jerked upright every few minutes and waved himself backward and forward a little in protest and despair.

Jim's girl was ready and impatient, but after what had happened her impatience didn't seem important. She looked lovely though. That's one thing about Christmas vacation – the excitement of growth and change and adventure in foreign parts transforming the people you've known all your life. Joe Jelke was polite to her in a daze – he indulged in one burst of short, loud, harsh laughter by way of conversation – and we drove to the hotel.

The chauffeur approached it on the wrong side – the side on which the line of cars was not putting forth guests – and because of that we came suddenly upon Ellen Baker just getting out of a small coupé. Even before we came to a stop, Joe Jelke had jumped excitedly from the car.

Ellen turned toward us, a faintly distracted look – perhaps of surprise, but certainly not of alarm – in her face; in fact, she didn't seem very aware of us. Joe approached her with a stern, dignified, injured and, I thought, just exactly correct reproof in his expression. I followed.

Seated in the coupé – he had not dismounted to help Ellen out – was a hard thin-faced man of about thirty-five with an air of being scarred, and a slight sinister smile. His eyes were a sort of taunt to the whole human family – they were the eyes of an animal, sleepy and quiescent in the presence of another species. They were helpless yet brutal, unhopeful yet confident. It was as if they felt themselves powerless to originate activity, but infinitely capable of profiting by a single gesture of weakness in another.

Vaguely I placed him as one of the sort of men whom I had been conscious of from my earliest youth as 'hanging around' – leaning with one elbow on the counters of tobacco stores, watching, through heaven knows what small chink of the mind, the people who hurried in and out. Intimate to garages, where he had vague business conducted in undertones, to barber shops and to the lobbies of theatres – in such places, anyhow, I placed the type, if type it was, that he reminded me of. Sometimes his face bobbed up in one of Tad's more savage cartoons, and I had always from earliest boyhood thrown a nervous glance toward the dim borderland where he stood, and seen him watching me and despising me. Once, in a dream, he had taken a few steps toward me, jerking his head back and muttering: 'Say, kid' in what was intended to be a reassuring voice, and I had broken for the door in terror. This was that sort of man.

Joe and Ellen faced each other silently; she seemed, as I have said, to be in a daze. It was cold, but she didn't notice that her coat had blown open; Joe reached out and pulled it together, and automatically she clutched it with her hand.

Suddenly the man in the coupé, who had been watching them silently, laughed. It was a bare laugh, done with the breath – just a noisy jerk of the head – but it was an insult if I had ever heard one; definite and not to be passed over. I wasn't surprised when Joe, who was quick-tempered, turned to him angrily and said:

'What's your trouble?'

The man waited a moment, his eyes shifting and yet staring, and always seeing. Then he laughed again in the same way. Ellen stirred uneasily.

'Who is this – this –' Joe's voice trembled with annoyance.

'Look out now,' said the man slowly.

Joe turned to me.

'Eddie, take Ellen and Catherine in, will you?' he said quickly ... 'Ellen, go with Eddie.'

'Look out now,' the man repeated.

Ellen made a little sound with her tongue and teeth, but she didn't resist when I took her arm and moved her toward the side door of the hotel. It struck me as odd that she should be so helpless, even to the point of acquiescing by her silence in this imminent trouble.

'Let it go, Joe!' I called back over my shoulder. 'Come inside!'

Ellen, pulling against my arm, hurried us on. As we were caught up into the swinging doors I had the impression that the man was getting out of his coupé.

Ten minutes later, as I waited for the girls outside the women's dressing-room, Joe Jelke and Jim Cathcart stepped out of the elevator. Joe was very white, his eyes were heavy and glazed, there was a trickle of dark blood on his forehead and on his white muffler. Jim had both their hats in his hand.

'He hit Joe with brass knuckles,' Jim said in a low voice. 'Joe was out cold for a minute or so. I wish you'd send a bell boy for some witch-hazel and court-plaster.'

It was late and the hall was deserted; brassy fragments of the dance below reached us as if heavy curtains were being blown aside and dropped back into place. When Ellen came out I took her directly downstairs. We avoided the receiving line and went into a dim room set with scraggly hotel palms where couples sometimes sat out during the dance; there I told her what had happened.

'It was Joe's own fault,' she said, surprisingly. 'I told him not to interfere.'

This wasn't true. She had said nothing, only uttered one curious little click of impatience.

'You ran out the back door and disappeared for almost an hour,' I protested. 'Then you turned up with a hard-looking customer who laughed in Joe's face.'

'A hard-looking customer,' she repeated, as if tasting the sound of the words.

'Well, wasn't he? Where on earth did you get hold of him, Ellen?'

'On the train,' she answered. Immediately she seemed to regret this admission. 'You'd better stay out of things that aren't your business, Eddie. You see what happened to Joe.'

Literally I gasped. To watch her, seated beside me, immaculately glowing, her body giving off wave after wave of freshness and delicacy – and to hear her talk like that.

'But that man's a thug!' I cried. 'No girl could be safe with him. He used brass knuckles on Joe – brass knuckles!'

'Is that pretty bad?'

She asked this as she might have asked such a question a few years ago. She looked at me at last and really wanted an answer; for a moment it was as if she were trying to recapture an attitude that had almost departed; then she hardened again. I say 'hardened,' for I began to notice that when she was concerned with this man her eyelids fell a little, shutting other things – everything else – out of view.

That was a moment I might have said something, I suppose, but in spite of everything, I couldn't light into her. I was too much under the spell of her beauty and its success. I even began to find excuses for her – perhaps that man wasn't what he appeared to be; or perhaps – more romantically – she was involved with him against her will to shield some one else. At this point people began to drift into the room and come up to speak to us. We couldn't talk any more, so we went in and bowed to the chaperones. Then I gave her up to the bright restless sea of the dance, where she moved in an eddy of her own among the pleasant islands of colored favors set out on tables and the south winds from the brasses moaning across the hall. After a while I saw Joe Jelke sitting in a corner with a strip of court-plaster on his forehead watching Ellen as if she herself had struck him down, but I didn't go up to him. I felt queer myself – like I feel when I wake up after sleeping through an afternoon, strange and portentous, as if something had gone on in the interval that changed the values of everything and that I didn't see.

The night slipped on through successive phases of cardboard horns, amateur tableaux and flashlights for the morning papers. Then was the grand march and supper, and about two o'clock some of the committee dressed up as revenue agents pinched the party, and a facetious newspaper wad distributed, burlesquing the events of the evening. And all the time out of the corner of my eye I watched the shining orchid on Ellen's shoulder as it moved like Stuart's plume about the room. I watched it with a definite foreboding until the last sleepy groups had crowded into the elevators, and then, bundled to the eyes in great shapeless fur coats, drifted out into the clear dry Minnesota night.

II

There is a sloping mid-section of our city which lies between the residence quarter on the hill and the business district on the level of the river. It is a vague part of town, broken by its climb into triangles and odd shapes – there are names like Seven Corners – and I don't believe a dozen people could draw an accurate map of it, though every one traversed it by trolley, auto or shoe leather twice a day. And though it was a busy section, it would be hard for me to name the business that comprised its activity. There were always long lines of trolley cars waiting to start somewhere; there was a big movie theatre and many small ones with posters of Hoot Gibson and Wonder Dogs and Wonder Horses outside; there were small stores with 'Old King Brady' and 'The Liberty Boys of '76' in the windows, and marbles, cigarettes and candy inside; and – one definite place at least – a fancy costumer whom we all visited at least once a year. Some time during boyhood I became aware that one side of a certain obscure street there were bawdy houses, and all through the district were pawnshops, cheap jewellers, small athletic clubs and gymnasiums and somewhat too blatantly rundown saloons.

The morning after the Cotillion Club party, I woke up late and lazy, with the happy feeling that for a day or two more there was no chapel, no classes – nothing to do but wait for another party tonight. It was crisp and bright – one of those days when you forget how cold it is until your cheek freezes – and the events of the evening before seemed dim and far away. After luncheon I started downtown on foot through a light, pleasant snow of small flakes that would probably fall all afternoon, and I was about half through that halfway section of town – so far as I know, there's no inclusive name for it – when suddenly whatever idle thought was in my head blew away like a hat and I began thinking hard of Ellen Baker. I began worrying about her as I'd never worried about anything outside myself before. I began to loiter, with an instinct to go up on the hill again and find her and talk to her; then I remembered that she was at a tea, and I went on again, but still thinking of her, and harder than ever. Right then the affair opened up again.

It was snowing, I said, and it was four o'clock on a December afternoon, when there is a promise of darkness in the air and the street lamps are just going on. I passed a combination pool parlor and restaurant, with a stove loaded with hot-dogs in the window, and a few loungers hanging around the door. The lights were on inside – not bright lights but just a few pale yellow high up on the ceiling – and the glow they threw out into the frosty dusk wasn't bright enough to tempt you to stare inside. As I went past, thinking hard of Ellen all this time, I took in the quartet of loafers out of the corner of my eye. I hadn't gone half a dozen steps down the street when one of them called to me, not by name but in a way clearly intended for my ear. I thought it was a tribute to my raccoon coat and paid no attention, but a moment later whoever it was called to me again in a peremptory voice. I was annoyed and turned around. There, standing in the group not ten feet away and looking at me with the half-sneer on his face with which he'd looked at Joe Jelke, was the scarred, thin-faced man of the night before.

He had on a black fancy-cut coat, buttoned up to his neck as if he were cold. His hands were deep in his pockets and he wore a derby and high button shoes. I was startled, and for a moment I hesitated, but I was most of all angry, and knowing that I was quicker with my hands than Joe Jelke, I took a tentative step back toward him. The other men weren't looking at me – I don't think they saw me at all – but I knew that this one recognized me; there was nothing casual about his look, no mistake.

'Here I am. What are you going to do about it?' his eyes seemed to say.

I took another step toward him and he laughed soundlessly, but with active contempt, and drew back into the group. I followed. I was going to speak to him – I wasn't sure what I was going to say – but when I came up he had either changed his mind and backed off, or else he wanted me to follow him inside, for he had slipped off and the three men watched my intent approach without curiosity. They were the same kind – sporty, but, unlike him, smooth rather than truculent; I didn't find any personal malice in their collective glance.

'Did he go inside?' I asked.

They looked at one another in that cagey way; a wink passed between them, and after a perceptible pause, one said:

'Who go inside?'

'I don't know his name.'

There was another wink. Annoyed and determined, I walked past them and into the pool room. There were a few people at a lunch counter along one side and a few more playing billiards, but he was not among them.

Again I hesitated. If his idea was to lead me into any blind part of the establishment – there were some half-open doors farther back – I wanted more support. I went up to the man at the desk.

'What became of the fellow who just walked in here?'

Was he on his guard immediately, or was that my imagination?

'What fellow?'

'Thin face – derby hat.'

'How long ago?'

'Oh – a minute.'

He shook his head again. 'Didn't see him,' he said.

I waited. The three men from outside had come in and were lined up beside me at the counter. I felt that all of them were looking at me in a peculiar way. Feeling helpless and increasingly uneasy, I turned suddenly and went out. A little way down the street I turned again and took a good look at the place, so I'd know it and could find it again. On the next corner I broke impulsively into a run, found a taxicab in front of the hotel and drove back up the hill.

Ellen wasn't home. Mrs Baker came downstairs and talked to me. She seemed entirely cheerful and proud of Ellen's beauty, and ignorant of anything being amiss or of anything unusual having taken place the night before. She was glad that vacation was almost over – it was a strain and

Ellen wasn't very strong. Then she said something that relieved my mind enormously. She was glad that I had come in, for of course Ellen would want to see me, and the time was so short. She was going back at half-past eight tonight.

'Tonight!' I exclaimed. 'I thought it was the day after tomorrow.'

'She's going to visit the Brokaws in Chicago,' Mrs Baker said. 'They want her for some party. We just decided it today. She's leaving with the Ingersoll girls tonight.'

I was so glad I could barely restrain myself from shaking her hand. Ellen was safe. It had been nothing all along but a moment of the most casual adventure. I felt like an idiot, but I realized how much I cared about Ellen and how little I could endure anything terrible happening to her.

'She'll be in soon?'

'Any minute now. She just phoned from the University Club.'

I said I'd be over later – I lived almost next door and I wanted to be alone. Outside I remembered I didn't have a key, so I started up the Bakers' driveway to take the old cut we used in childhood through the intervening yard. It was still snowing, but the flakes were bigger now against the darkness, and trying to locate the buried walk I noticed that the Bakers' back door was ajar.

I scarcely know why I turned and walked into that kitchen. There was a time when I would have known the Bakers' servants by name. That wasn't true now, but they knew me, and I was aware of a sudden suspension as I came in – not only a suspension of talk but of some mood or expectation that had filled them. They began to go to work too quickly; they made unnecessary movements and clamour – those three. The parlour maid looked at me in a frightened way and I suddenly guessed she was waiting to deliver another message. I beckoned her into the pantry.

'I know all about this,' I said. 'It's a very serious business. Shall I go to Mrs Baker now, or will you shut and lock that back door?'

'Don't tell Mrs Baker, Mr Stinson!'

'Then I don't want Miss Ellen disturbed. If she is – and if she is I'll know of it –' I delivered some outrageous threat about going to all the employment agencies and seeing she never got another job in the city. She was thoroughly intimidated when I went out; it wasn't a minute before the back door was locked and bolted behind me.

Simultaneously I heard a big car drive up in front, chains crunching on the soft snow; it was bringing Ellen home, and I went in to say goodbye.

Joe Jelke and two other boys were along, and none of the three could manage to take their eyes off her, even to say hello to me. She had one of those exquisite rose skins frequent in our part of the country, and beautiful until the little veins begin to break at about forty; now, flushed with the cold, it was a riot of lovely delicate pinks like many carnations.

She and Joe had reached some sort of reconciliation, or at least he was too far gone in love to remember last night; but I saw that though she laughed a lot she wasn't really paying any attention to him or any of them. She wanted them to go, so that there'd be a message from the kitchen, but I knew that the message wasn't coming – that she was safe. There was talk of the Pump and Slipper dance at New Haven and of the Princeton Prom, and then, in various moods, we four left and separated quickly outside. I walked home with a certain depression of spirit and lay for an hour in a hot bath thinking that vacation was all over for me now that she was gone; feeling, even more deeply than I had yesterday, that she was out of my life.

And something eluded me, some one more thing to do, something that I had lost amid the events of the afternoon, promising myself to go back and pick it up, only to find that it had escaped me. I associated it vaguely with Mrs Baker, and now I seemed to recall that it had poked up its head somewhere in the stream of conversation with her. In my relief about Ellen I had forgotten to ask her a question regarding something she had said.

The Brokaws – that was it – where Ellen was to visit. I knew Bill Brokaw well; he was in my class at Yale. Then I remembered and sat bolt upright in the tub – the Brokaws weren't in Chicago this Christmas; they were at Palm Beach!

Dripping I sprang out of the tub, threw an insufficient union suit around my shoulders and sprang for the phone in my room. I got the connection quick, but Miss Ellen had already started for the train.

Luckily our car was in, and while I squirmed, still damp, into my clothes, the chauffeur brought it around to the door. The night was cold and dry, and we made good time to the station through the hard, crusty snow. I felt queer and insecure starting out this way, but somehow more confident as the station loomed up bright and new against the dark, cold air. For fifty years my family had owned the land on which it was built and that made my temerity seem all right somehow. There was always a possibility that I was rushing in where angels feared to tread, but that sense of having a solid foothold in the past made me willing to make a fool of myself. This business was all wrong – terribly wrong. Any idea I had entertained that it was harmless dropped away now; between Ellen and some vague overwhelming catastrophe there stood me, or else the police and a scandal. I'm no moralist – there was another element here, dark and frightening, and I didn't want Ellen to go through it alone.

There are three competing trains from St Paul to Chicago that all leave within a few minutes of half-past eight. Hers was the Burlington, and as I ran across the station I saw the grating being pulled over and the light above it go out. I knew, though, that she had a drawing-room with the Ingersoll girls, because her mother had mentioned buying the ticket, so she was, literally speaking, tucked in until tomorrow.

The C., M. & St P. gate was down at the other end and I raced for it and made it. I had forgotten one thing, though, and that was enough to keep me awake and worried half the night. This train got into Chicago ten minutes after the other. Ellen had that much time to disappear into one of the largest cities in the world.

I gave the porter a wire to my family to send from Milwaukee, and at eight o'clock next morning I pushed violently by a whole line of passengers, clamoring over their bags parked in the vestibule, and shot out of the door with a sort of scramble over the porter's back. For a moment the confusion of a great station, the voluminous sounds and echoes and cross-currents of bells and smoke struck me helpless. Then I dashed for the exit and toward the only chance I knew of finding her.

I had guessed right. She was standing at the telegraph counter, sending off heaven knows what black lie to her mother, and her expression when she saw me had a sort of terror mixed up with its surprise. There was cunning in it too. She was thinking quickly – she would have liked to walk away from me as if I weren't there, and go about her own business, but she couldn't. I was too matter-of-fact a thing in her life. So we stood silently watching each other and each thinking hard.

'The Brokaws are in Florida,' I said after a minute.

'It was nice of you to take such a long trip to tell me that.'

'Since you've found it out, don't you think you'd better go on to school?'

'Please let me alone, Eddie,' she said.

'I'll go as far as New York with you. I've decided to go back early myself.'

'You'd better let me alone.' Her lovely eyes narrowed and her face took on a look of dumb-animal-like resistance. She made a visible effort, the cunning flickered back into it, then both were gone, and in their stead was a cheerful reassuring smile that all but convinced me.

'Eddie, you silly child, don't you think I'm old enough to take care of myself?' I didn't answer. 'I'm going to meet a man, you understand. I just want to see him today. I've got my ticket East on the five o'clock train. If you don't believe it, here it is in my bag.'

'I believe you.'

'The man isn't anybody that you know and – frankly, I think you're being awfully fresh and impossible.'

'I know who the man is.'

Again she lost control of her face. That terrible expression came back into it and she spoke with almost a snarl:

'You'd better let me alone.'

I took the blank out of her hand and wrote out an explanatory telegram to her mother. Then I turned to Ellen and said a little roughly:

'We'll take the five o'clock train East together. Meanwhile you're going to spend the day with me.'

The mere sound of my own voice saying this so emphatically encouraged me, and I think it impressed her too; at any rate, she submitted – at least temporarily – and came along without protest while I bought my ticket.

When I start to piece together the fragments of that day a sort of confusion begins, as if my memory didn't want to yield up any of it, or my consciousness let any of it pass through. There was a bright, fierce morning during which we rode about in a taxicab and went to a department store where Ellen said she wanted to buy something and then tried to slip away from me by a back way. I had the feeling, for an hour, that someone was following us along Lake Shore Drive in a taxicab, and I would try to catch them by turning quickly or looking suddenly into the chauffeur's mirror; but I could find no one, and when I turned back I could see that Ellen's face was contorted with mirthless, unnatural laughter.

All morning there was a raw, bleak wind off the lake, but when we went to the Blackstone for lunch a light snow came down past the windows and we talked almost naturally about our friends, and about casual things. Suddenly her tone changed; she grew serious and looked me in the eye, straight and sincere.

'Eddie, you're the oldest friend I have,' she said, 'and you oughtn't to find it too hard to trust me. If I promise you faithfully on my word of honor to catch that five o'clock train, will you let me alone a few hours this afternoon?'

'Why?'

'Well – she hesitated and hung her head a little – 'I guess everybody has a right to say – goodbye.'

'You want to say goodbye to that –'

'Yes, yes,' she said hastily; 'just a few hours, Eddie, and I promise faithfully that I'll be on that train.'

'Well, I suppose no great harm could be done in two hours. If you really want to say goodbye –'

I looked up suddenly, and surprised a look of such tense cunning in her face that I winced before it. Her lip was curled up and her eyes were slits again; there wasn't the faintest touch of fairness and sincerity in her whole face.

We argued. The argument was vague on her part and somewhat hard and reticent on mine. I wasn't going to be cajoled again into any weakness or be infected with any – and there was a contagion of evil in the air. She kept trying to imply, without any convincing evidence to bring forward, that everything was all right. Yet she was too full of the thing itself – whatever it was – to build up a real story, and she wanted to catch at any credulous and acquiescent train of thought that might start in my head, and work that for all it was worth. After every reassuring suggestion she threw out she stared at me eagerly, as if she hoped I'd launch into a comfortable moral lecture with the customary sweet at the end – which in this case would be her liberty. But I was wearing her away a little. Two or three times it needed just a touch of pressure to bring her to the point of tears – which, of course, was what I wanted – but I couldn't seem to manage it. Almost I had her – almost possessed her interior attention – then she would slip away.

I bullied her remorselessly into a taxi about four o'clock and started for the station. The wind was raw again, with a sting of snow in it, and the people in the streets, waiting for buses and street cars too small to take them all in, looked cold and disturbed and unhappy. I tried to think how lucky we were to be comfortably off and taken care of, but all the warm, respectable world I had been part of yesterday had dropped away from me. There was something we carried with us now that was the enemy and the opposite of all that; it was in the cabs beside us, the streets we passed through. With a touch of panic, I wondered if I wasn't slipping almost imperceptibly into Ellen's attitude of mind. The column of passengers waiting to go aboard the train were as remote from me as people from another world, but it was I that was drifting away and leaving them behind.

My lower was in the same car with her compartment. It was an old-fashioned car, its lights somewhat dim, its carpets and upholstery full of the dust of another generation. There were half a dozen other travellers, but they made no special impression on me, except that they shared the unreality that I was beginning to feel everywhere around me. We went into Ellen's compartment, shut the door and sat down.

Suddenly I put my arms around her and drew her over to me, just as tenderly as I knew how – as if she were a little girl – as she was. She resisted a little, but after a moment she submitted and lay tense and rigid in my arms.

'Ellen,' I said helplessly, 'you asked me to trust you. You have much more reason to trust me. Wouldn't it help to get rid of all this, if you told me a little?'

'I can't,' she said, very low – 'I mean, there's nothing to tell.'

'You met this man on the train coming home and you fell in love with him, isn't that true?'

'I don't know.'

'Tell me, Ellen. You fell in love with him?'

'I don't know. Please let me alone.'

'Call it anything you want,' I went on, 'he has some sort of hold over you. He's trying to use you; he's trying to get something from you. He's not in love with you.'

'What does that matter?' she said in a weak voice.

'It does matter. Instead of trying to fight this – this thing – you're trying to fight me. And I love you, Ellen. Do you hear? I'm telling you all of a sudden, but it isn't new with me. I love you.'

She looked at me with a sneer on her gentle face; it was an expression I had seen on men who were tight and didn't want to be taken home. But it was human. I was reaching her, faintly and from far away, but no more than before.

'Ellen, I want you to answer me one question. Is he going to be on this train?'

She hesitated; then, an instant too late, she shook her head.

'Be careful, Ellen. Now I'm going to ask you one thing more, and I wish you'd try very hard to answer. Coming West, when did this man get on the train?'

'I don't know,' she said with an effort.

Just at that moment I became aware, with the unquestionable knowledge reserved for facts, that he was just outside the door. She knew it too; the blood left her face and that expression of low-animal perspicacity came creeping back. I lowered my face into my hands and tried to think.

We must have sat there, with scarcely a word, for well over an hour. I was conscious that the lights of Chicago, then of Englewood and of endless suburbs, were moving by, and then there were no more lights and we were out on the dark flatness of Illinois. The train seemed to draw in upon itself; it took on an air of being alone. The porter knocked at the door and asked if he could make up the berth, but I said no and he went away.

After a while I convinced myself that the struggle inevitably coming wasn't beyond what remained of my sanity, my faith in the essential all-rightness of things and people. That this person's purpose was what we call 'criminal,' I took for granted, but there was no need of ascribing to him an intelligence that belonged to a higher plane of human, or inhuman, endeavour. It was still as a man that I considered him, and tried to get at his essence, his self-interest – what took the place in him of a comprehensible heart – but I suppose I more than half knew what I would find when I opened the door.

When I stood up Ellen didn't seem to see me at all. She was hunched into the corner staring straight ahead with a sort of film over her eyes, as if she were in a state of suspended animation of body and mind. I lifted her and put two pillows under her head and threw my fur coat over her knees. Then I knelt beside her and kissed her two hands, opened the door and went out into the hall.

I closed the door behind me and stood with my back against it for a minute. The car was dark save for the corridor lights at each end. There was no sound except the groaning of the couplers, the even click-a-click of the rails and someone's loud sleeping breath farther down the car. I became aware after a moment that the figure of a man was standing by the water cooler just outside the men's smoking room, his derby hat on his head, his coat collar turned up around his neck as if he were cold, his hands in his coat pockets. When I saw him, he turned and went into the smoking room, and I followed. He was sitting in the far corner of the long leather bench; I took the single armchair beside the door.

As I went in I nodded to him and he acknowledged my presence with one of those terrible soundless laughs of his. But this time it was prolonged, it seemed to go on forever, and mostly to cut it short, I asked: 'Where are you from?' in a voice I tried to make casual.

He stopped laughing and looked at me narrowly, wondering what my game was. When he decided to answer, his voice was muffled as though he were speaking through a silk scarf, and it seemed to come from a long way off.

'I'm from St Paul, Jack.'

'Been making a trip home?'

He nodded. Then he took a long breath and spoke in a hard, menacing voice:

'You better get off at Fort Wayne, Jack.'

He was dead. He was dead as hell – he had been dead all along, but what force had flowed through him, like blood in his veins, out to St Paul and back, and was leaving him now. A new outline – the outline of him dead – was coming through the palpable figure that had knocked down Joe Jelke.

He spoke again, with a sort of jerking effort:

'You get off at Fort Wayne, Jack, or I'm going to wipe you out.' He moved his hand in his coat pocket and showed me the outline of a revolver.

I shook my head. 'You can't touch me,' I answered. 'You see, I know.' His terrible eyes shifted over me quickly, trying to determine whether or not I did know. Then he gave a snarl and made as though he were going to jump to his feet.

'You climb off here or else I'm going to get you, Jack!' he cried hoarsely. The train was slowing up for Fort Wayne and his voice rang loud in the comparative quiet, but he didn't move from the chair – he was too weak, I think – and we sat staring at each other while workmen passed up and down outside the window banging the brakes and wheels, and the engine gave out loud mournful pants up ahead. No one got into our car. After a while the porter closed the vestibule door and passed back along the corridor, and we slid out of the murky yellow station light and into the long darkness.

What I remember next must have extended over a space of five or six hours, though it comes back to me as something without any existence in time – something that might have taken five minutes or a year. There began a slow, calculated assault on me, wordless and terrible. I felt what I can only call a strangeness stealing over me – akin to the strangeness I had felt all afternoon, but deeper and more intensified. It was like nothing so much as the sensation of drifting away, and I gripped the arms of the chair convulsively, as if to hang onto a piece in the living world. Sometimes I felt myself going out with a rush. There would be almost a warm relief about it, a sense of not caring; then, with a violent wrench of the will, I'd pull myself back into the room.

Suddenly I realized that from a while back I had stopped hating him, stopped feeling violently alien to him, and with the realization, I went cold and sweat broke out all over my head. He was getting around my abhorrence, as he had got around Ellen coming West on the train; and it was just that strength he drew from preying on people that had brought him up to the point of concrete violence in St Paul, and that, fading and flickering out, still kept him fighting now.

He must have seen that faltering in my heart, for he spoke at once, in a low, even, almost gentle voice: 'You better go now.'

'Oh, I'm not going,' I forced myself to say.

'Suit yourself, Jack.'

He was my friend, he implied. He knew how it was with me and he wanted to help. He pitied me. I'd better go away before it was too late. The rhythm of his attack was soothing as a song: I'd better go away – *and let him get at Ellen.* With a little cry I sat bolt upright.

'What do you want of this girl?' I said, my voice shaking. 'To make a sort of walking hell of her.'

His glance held a quality of dumb surprise, as if I were punishing an animal for a fault of which he was not conscious. For an instant I faltered; then I went on blindly:

'You've lost her; she's put her trust in me.'

His countenance went suddenly black with evil, and he cried: 'You're a liar!' in a voice that was like cold hands.

'She trusts me,' I said. 'You can't touch her. She's safe!'

He controlled himself. His face grew bland, and I felt that curious weakness and indifference begin again inside me. What was the use of all this? What was the use?

'You haven't got much time left,' I forced myself to say, and then, in a flash of intuition, I jumped at the truth. 'You died, or you were killed, not far from here!' – Then I saw what I had not seen before – that his forehead was drilled with a small round hole like a larger picture nail leaves when it's pulled from a plaster wall. 'And now you're sinking. You've only got a few hours. The trip home is over!'

His face contorted, lost all semblance of humanity, living or dead. Simultaneously the room was full of cold air and with a noise that was something between a paroxysm of coughing and a burst of horrible laughter, he was on his feet, reeking of shame and blasphemy.

'Come and look!' he cried. 'I'll show you –'

He took a step toward me, then another and it was exactly as if a door stood open behind him, a door yawning out to an inconceivable abyss of darkness and corruption. There was a scream of mortal agony, from him or from somewhere behind, and abruptly the strength went out of him in a long husky sigh and he wilted to the floor ...

How long I sat there, dazed with terror and exhaustion, I don't know. The next thing I remember is the sleepy porter shining shoes across the room from me, and outside the window the steel fires of Pittsburgh breaking the flat perspective also – something too faint for a man, too heavy for a shadow of the night. There was something extended on the bench. Even as I perceived it it faded off and away.

Some minutes later I opened the door of Ellen's compartment. She was asleep where I had left her. Her lovely cheeks were white and wan, but she lay naturally – her hands relaxed and her breathing regular and clear. What had possessed her had gone out of her, leaving her exhausted but her own dear self again.

I made her a little more comfortable, tucked a blanket around her, extinguished the light and went out.

III

When I came home for Easter vacation, almost my first act was to go down to the billiard parlor near Seven Corners. The man at the cash register quite naturally didn't remember my hurried visit of three months before.

'I'm trying to locate a certain party who, I think, came here a lot some time ago.'

I described the man rather accurately, and when I had finished, the cashier called to a little jockey-like fellow who was sitting near with an air of having something very important to do that he couldn't quite remember.

'Hey, Shorty, talk to this guy, will you? I think he's looking for Joe Varland.'

The little man gave me a tribal look of suspicion. I went and sat near him.

'Joe Varland's dead, fella,' he said grudgingly. 'He died last winter.'

I described him again – his overcoat, his laugh, the habitual expression of his eyes.

'That's Joe Varland you're looking for all right, but he's dead.'

'I want to find out something about him.'

'What you want to find out?'

'What did he do, for instance?'

'How should I know?'

'Look here! I'm not a policeman. I just want some kind of information about his habits. He's dead now and it can't hurt him. And it won't go beyond me.'

'Well' – he hesitated, looking me over – 'he was a great one for travelling. He got in a row in the station in Pittsburgh and a dick got him.'

I nodded. Broken pieces of the puzzle began to assemble in my head.

'Why was he a lot on trains?'

'How should I know, fella?'

'If you can use ten dollars, I'd like to know anything you may have heard on the subject.'

'Well,' said Shorty reluctantly, 'all I know is they used to say he worked the trains.'

'Worked the trains?'

'He had some racket of his own he'd never loosen up about. He used to work the girls travelling alone on the trains. Nobody ever knew much about it – he was a pretty smooth guy – but sometimes he'd turn up here with a lot of dough and he let 'em know it was the janes he got it off of.'

I thanked him and gave him the ten dollars and went out, very thoughtful, without mentioning that part of Joe Varland had made a last trip home.

Ellen wasn't west for Easter, and even if she had been I wouldn't have gone to her with the information, either – at least I've seen her almost every day this summer and we've managed to talk about everything else. Sometimes, though, she gets silent about nothing and wants to be very close to me, and I know what's in her mind.

Of course she's coming out this fall, and I have two more years at New Haven; still, things don't look so impossible as they did a few months ago. She belongs to me in a way – even if I lose her she belongs to me. Who knows? Anyhow, I'll always be there.

Outside the Cabinet-maker's

The automobile stopped at the corner of Sixteenth and some dingy-looking street. The lady got out. The man and the little girl stayed in the car.

'I'm going to tell him it can't cost more than twenty dollars,' said the lady.

'All right. Have you the plans?'

'Oh, yes – she reached for her bag in the back seat – 'at least I have now.'

'Dites qu'il ne faut pas avoir les forts placards,' said the man. 'Ni le bon bois.'

'All right.'

'I wish you wouldn't talk French,' said the little girl.

'Et il faut avoir un bon "height." L'un des Murphys était comme ça.'

He held his hand five feet from the ground. The lady went through a door lettered 'Cabinet-Maker' and disappeared up a small stairs.

The man and the little girl looked around unexpectantly. The neighbourhood was red brick, vague, quiet. There were a few darkies doing something or other up the street and an occasional automobile went by. It was a fine November day.

'Listen,' said the man to the little girl, 'I love you.'

'I love you too,' said the little girl, smiling politely.

'Listen,' the man continued. 'Do you see that house over the way?'

The little girl looked. It was a flat in back of a shop. Curtains masked most of its interior, but there was a faint stir behind them. On one window a loose shutter banged from back to forth every few minutes. Neither the man nor the little girl had ever seen the place before.

'There's a Fairy Princess behind those curtains,' said the man. 'You can't see her but she's there, kept concealed by an Ogre. Do you know what an Ogre is?'

'Yes.'

'Well, this Princess is very beautiful with long golden hair.'

They both regarded the house. Part of a yellow dress appeared momentarily in the window.

'That's her,' the man said. 'The people who live there are guarding her

162

for the Ogre. He's keeping the King and Queen prisoner ten thousand miles below the earth. She can't get out until the Prince finds the three –' He hesitated.

'And what, Daddy? The three what?'

'The three – Look! There she is again.'

'The three what?'

'The three – the three stones that will release the King and Queen.'

He yawned.

'And what then?'

'Then he can come and tap three times on each window and that will set her free.'

The lady's head emerged from the upper story of the cabinet-maker's.

'He's busy,' she called down. 'Gosh, what a nice day!'

'And what, Daddy?' asked the little girl. 'Why does the Ogre want to keep her there?'

'Because he wasn't invited to the christening. The Prince has already found one stone in President Coolidge's collar-box. He's looking for the second in Iceland. Every time he finds a stone the room where the Princess is kept turns blue. *Gosh!*'

'What, Daddy?'

'Just as you turned away I could see the room turn blue. That means he's found the second stone.'

'Gosh!' said the little girl. 'Look! It turned blue again, that means he's found the third stone.'

Aroused by the competition the man looked around cautiously and his voice grew tense.

'Do you see what I see?' He demanded. 'Coming up the street – there's the Ogre himself, disguised – you know: transformed, like *Mombi* in "The Land of Oz".'

'I know.'

They both watched. The small boy, extraordinarily small and taking very long steps, went to the door of the flat and knocked; no one answered but he didn't seem to expect it or to be greatly disappointed. He took some chalk from his pocket and began drawing pictures under the doorbell.

'He's making magic signs,' whispered the man. 'He wants to be sure that the Princess doesn't get out this door. He must know that the Prince has set the King and Queen free and will be along for her pretty soon.'

The small boy lingered for a moment; then he went to a window and called an unintelligible word. After a while a woman threw the window open and made an answer that the crisp wind blew away.

'She says she's got the Princess locked up,' explained the man.

'Look at the Ogre,' said the little girl. 'He's making magic signs under the window too. And on the sidewalk. Why?'

'He wants to keep her from getting out, of course. That's why he's dancing. That's a charm too – it's a magic dance.'

The Ogre went away, taking very big steps. Two men crossed the street ahead and passed out of sight.

'Who are they, Daddy?'

'They're two of the King's soldiers. I think the army must be gathering over on Market Street to surround the house. Do you know what "surround" means?'

'Yes. Are those men soldiers too?'

'Those too. And I believe that the old one just behind is the King himself. He's keeping bent down low like that so that the Ogre's people won't recognize him.'

'Who is the lady?'

'She's a Witch, a friend of the Ogre's.'

The shutter blew closed with a bang and then slowly opened again.

'That's done by the good and bad fairies,' the man explained. 'They're invisible, but the bad fairies want to close the shutters so nobody can see in and the good ones want to open it.'

'The good fairies are winning now.'

'Yes.' He looked at the little girl. 'You're my good fairy.'

'Yes. Look, Daddy! What is that man?'

'He's in the King's army too.' The clerk of Mr Miller, the jeweller, went by with a somewhat unmartial aspect. 'Hear the whistle? That means they're gathering. And listen – there goes the drum.'

'There's the Queen, Daddy. Look at there. Is that the Queen?'

'No, that's a girl called Miss Television.' He yawned. He began to think of something pleasant that had happened yesterday. He went into a trance. Then he looked at the little girl and saw that she was quite happy. She was six and lovely to look at. He kissed her.

'That man carrying the cake of ice is also one of the King's soldiers,' he said. 'He's going to put the ice on the Ogre's head and freeze his brains so he can't do any more harm.'

Her eyes followed the man down street. Other men passed. A darky in a yellow darky's overcoat drove by with a cart marked The Del Upholstery Co. The shutter banged again and then slowly opened.

'See, Daddy, the good fairies are winning again.'

The man was old enough to know that he would look back to that time – the tranquil street and the pleasant weather and the mystery playing before the child's eyes, mystery which he had created, but whose lustre and texture he could never see or touch any more himself. Again he touched his daughter's cheek instead and in payment fitted another small boy and limping man into the story.

'Oh, I love you,' he said.

'I know, Daddy,' she answered, abstractedly. She was staring at the house. For a moment he closed his eyes and tried to see with her but he couldn't see – those ragged blinds were drawn against him forever. There were only the occasional darkies and the small boys and the weather that reminded him of more glamorous mornings in the past.

The lady came out of the cabinet-maker's shop.

'How did it go?' he asked.

'Good. Il dit qu'il a fait les maisons de poupée pour les Duponts. Il va le faire.'

'Combien?'

'Vingt-cinq. I'm sorry I was so long.'

'Look, Daddy, there go a lot more soldiers!'

They drove off. When they had gone a few miles the man turned around and said, 'We saw the most remarkable thing while you were there.' He summarized the episode. 'It's too bad we couldn't wait and see the rescue.'

'But we did,' the child cried. 'They had the rescue in the next street. And there's the Ogre's body in that yard there. The King and Queen and Prince were killed and now the Princess is queen.'

He had liked his King and Queen and felt that they had been too summarily disposed of.

'You had to have a heroine,' he said rather impatiently.

'She'll marry somebody and make him Prince.'

They rode on abstractedly. The lady thought about the doll's house, for she had been poor and had never had one as a child, the man thought how he had almost a million dollars and the little girl thought about the odd doings on the dingy street that they had left behind.

One Trip Abroad

I

In the afternoon the air became black with locusts, and some of the women shrieked, sinking to the floor of the motorbus and covering their hair with travelling rugs. The locusts were coming north, eating everything in their path, which was not so much in that part of the world; they were flying silently and in straight lines, flakes of black snow. But none struck the windshield or tumbled into the car, and presently humorists began holding out their hands, trying to catch some. After ten minutes the cloud thinned out, passed, and the women emerged from the blankets, dishevelled and feeling silly. And everyone talked together.

Everyone talked; it would have been absurd not to talk after having been through a swarm of locusts on the edge of the Sahara. The Smyrna-American talked to the British widow going down to Biskra to have one last fling with an as-yet-unencountered sheik. The member of the San Francisco Stock Exchange talked shyly to the author. 'Aren't you an author?' he said. The father and daughter from Wilmington talked to the cockney airman who was going to fly to Timbuctoo. Even the French chauffeur turned about and explained in a loud, clear voice: 'Bumble-bees', which sent the trained nurse from New York into shriek after shriek of hysterical laughter.

Amongst the unsubtle rushing together of the travellers there was one interchange more carefully considered. Mr and Mrs Liddell Miles, turning as one person, smiled and spoke to the young American couple in the seat behind:

'Didn't catch any in your hair?'

The young couple smiled back politely.

'No. We survived that plague.'

They were in their twenties, and there was still a pleasant touch of bride and groom upon them. A handsome couple; the man rather intense and sensitive, the girl arrestingly light of hue in eyes and hair, her face without shadows, its living freshness modulated by a lovely confident calm. Mr and Mrs Miles did not fail to notice their air of good breeding, of a specifically 'swell' background, expressed both by their unsophistication and by their ingrained reticence that was not stiffness. If they held aloof, it

was because they were sufficient to each other, while Mr and Mrs Miles'
aloofness toward the other passengers was a conscious mask, a social
attitude, quite as public an affair in its essence as the ubiquitous advances
of the Smyrna-American, who was snubbed by all.

The Mileses had, in fact, decided that the young couple were 'possible'
and, bored with themselves, were frankly approaching them.

'Have you been to Africa before? It's been so utterly fascinating! Are
you going on to Tunis?'

The Mileses, if somewhat worn away inside by fifteen years of a
particular set in Paris, had undeniable style, even charm, and before the
evening arrival at the little oasis town of Bou Saada they had all four
become companionable. They uncovered mutual friends in New York
and, meeting for a cocktail in the bar of the Hotel Transatlantique,
decided to have dinner together.

As the young Kellys came downstairs later, Nicole was conscious of a
certain regret that they had accepted, realizing that now they were
probably committed to seeing a certain amount of their new
acquaintances as far as Constantine, where their routes diverged.

In the eight months of their marriage she had been so very happy that it
seemed like spoiling something. On the Italian liner that had brought
them to Gibraltar they had not joined the groups that leaned desperately
on one another in the bar; instead, they seriously studied French, and
Nelson worked on business contingent on his recent inheritance of half a
million dollars. Also he painted a picture of a smokestack. When one
member of the gay crowd in the bar disappeared permanently into the
Atlantic just this side of the Azores, the young Kellys were almost glad,
for it justified their aloof attitude.

But there was another reason Nicole was sorry they had committed
themselves. She spoke to Nelson about it: 'I passed that couple in the hall
just now.'

'Who – the Mileses?'

'No, that young couple – about our age – the ones that were on the
other motorbus, that we thought looked so nice, in Bir Rabalou after
lunch, in the camel market.'

'They did look nice.'

'Charming,' she said emphatically; 'the girl and man, both. I'm almost
sure I've met the girl somewhere before.'

The couple referred to were sitting across the room at dinner, and
Nicole found her eyes drawn irresistibly toward them. They, too, now had
companions, and again Nicole, who had not talked to a girl of her own age
for two months, felt a faint regret. The Mileses, being formally
sophisticated and frankly snobbish, were a different matter. They had
been to an alarming number of places and seemed to know all the flashing
phantoms of the newspapers.

They dined on the hotel veranda under a sky that was low and full of the presence of a strange and watchful God: around the corners of the hotel the night already stirred with the sounds of which they had so often read but that were even so hysterically unfamiliar – drums from Senegal, a native flute, the selfish, effeminate whine of a camel, the Arabs pattering past in shoes made of old automobile tires, the wail of Magian prayer.

At the desk in the hotel, a fellow passenger was arguing monotonously with the clerk about the rate of exchange, and the inappropriateness added to the detachment which had increased steadily as they went south.

Mrs Miles was the first to break the lingering silence; with a sort of impatience she pulled them with her, in from the night and up to the table.

'We really should have dressed. Dinner's more amusing if people dress, because they feel differently in formal clothes. The English know that.'

'Dress here?' her husband objected. 'I'd feel like that man in the ragged dress suit we passed today, driving the flock of sheep.'

'I always feel like a tourist if I'm not dressed.'

'Well, we are, aren't we?' asked Nelson.

'I don't consider myself a tourist. A tourist is somebody who gets up early and goes to cathedrals and talks about scenery.'

Nicole and Nelson, having seen all the official sights from Fez to Algiers, and taken reels of moving pictures and felt improved, confessed themselves, but decided that their experiences on the trip would not interest Mrs Miles.

'Every place is the same,' Mrs Miles continued. 'The only thing that matters is who's there. New scenery is fine for half an hour, but after that you want your own kind to see. That's why some places have a certain vogue, and then the vogue changes and the people move on somewhere else. The place itself really never matters.'

'But doesn't somebody first decide that the place is nice?' objected Nelson. 'The first ones go there because they like the place.'

'Where were you going this spring?' Mrs Miles asked.

'We thought of San Remo, or maybe Sorrento. We've never been to Europe before.'

'My children, I know both Sorrento and San Remo, and you won't stand either of them for a week. They're full of the most awful English, reading the Daily Mail and waiting for letters and talking about the most incredibly dull things. You might as well go to Brighton or Bournemouth and buy a white poodle and a sunshade and walk on the pier. How long are you staying in Europe?'

'We don't know; perhaps several years.' Nicole hesitated. 'Nelson came into a little money, and we wanted a change. When I was young, my father had asthma and I had to live in the most depressing health resorts with him for years; and Nelson was in the fur business in Alaska and he loathed it; so when we were free we came abroad. Nelson's going to paint and I'm going to study singing.' She looked triumphantly at her husband. 'So far, it's been absolutely gorgeous.'

Mrs Miles decided, from the evidence of the younger woman's clothes, that it was quite a bit of money, and their enthusiasm was infectious.

'You really must go to Biarritz,' she advised them. 'Or else come to Monte Carlo.'

'They tell me there's a great show here,' said Miles, ordering champagne. 'The Ouled Naïls. The concierge says they're some kind of tribe of girls who come down from the mountains and learn to be dancers, and what not, till they've collected enough gold to go back to their mountains and marry. Well, they give a performance tonight.'

Walking over to the Café on the Ouled Naïls afterward, Nicole regretted that she and Nelson were not strolling alone through the ever-lower, ever-softer, ever-brighter night. Nelson had reciprocated the bottle of champagne at dinner, and neither of them was accustomed to so much. As they drew near the sad flute she didn't want to go inside, but rather to climb to the top of a low hill where a white mosque shone clear as a planet through the night. Life was better than any show; closing in toward Nelson, she pressed his hand.

The little cave of a café was filled with the passengers from the two buses. The girls – light-brown, flat-nosed Berbers with fine, deep-shaded eyes – were already doing each one her solo on the platform. They wore cotton dresses, faintly reminiscent of Southern mammies; under these their bodies writhed in a slow nautch, culminating in a stomach dance, with silver belts bobbing wildly and their strings of real gold coins tinkling on their necks and arms. The flute player was also a comedian; he danced, burlesquing the girls. The drummer, swathed in goatskins like a witch doctor, was a true black from the Sudan.

Through the smoke of cigarettes each girl went in turn through the finger movement, like piano playing in the air – outwardly facile, yet after a few moments, so obviously exacting – and then through the very simple languid yet equally precise steps of the feet – these were but preparation to the wild sensuality of the culminated dance.

Afterwards there was a lull. Though the performance seemed not quite over, most of the audience gradually got up to go, but there was a whispering in the air.

'What is it?' Nicole asked her husband.

'Why, I believe – it appears that for a consideration the Ouled Naïls dance in more less – ah – Oriental style – in very little except jewellery.'

'Oh.'

'We're all staying,' Mr Miles assured her jovially. 'After all, we're here to see the real customs and manners of the country; a little prudishness shouldn't stand in our way.'

Most of the men remained, and several of the women. Nicole stood up suddenly.

'I'll wait outside,' she said.

'Why not stay, Nicole? After all, Mrs Miles is staying.'

The flute player was making preliminary flourishes. Upon the raised dais two pale brown children of perhaps fourteen were taking off their cotton dresses. For an instant Nicole hesitated, torn between repulsion and the desire not to appear to be a prig. Then she saw another American woman get up quickly and start for the door. Recognizing the attractive young wife from the other bus, her own decision came quickly and she followed.

Nelson hurried after her. 'I'm going if you go,' he said, but with evident reluctance.

'Please don't bother. I'll wait with the guide outside.'

'Well –' The drum was starting. He compromised: 'I'll only stay a minute. I want to see what it's like.'

Waiting in the fresh night, she found that the incident had hurt her – Nelson's not coming with her at once, giving as an argument the fact that Mrs Miles was staying. From being hurt, she grew angry and made signs to the guide that she wanted to return to the hotel.

Twenty minutes later, Nelson appeared, angry with the anxiety at finding her gone, as well as to hide his guilt at having left her. Incredulous with themselves, they were suddenly in a quarrel.

Much later, when there were no sounds at all in Bou Saada and the nomads in the market place were only motionless bundles rolled up in their burnouses, she was asleep upon his shoulder. Life is progressive, no matter what our intentions, but something was harmed, some precedent of possible non-agreement was set. It was a love match, though, and it could stand a great deal. She and Nelson had passed lonely youths, and now they wanted the taste and smell of the living world; for the present they were finding it in each other.

A month later they were in Sorrento, where Nicole took singing lessons and Nelson tried to paint something new into the Bay of Naples. It was the existence they had planned and often read about. But they found, as so many have found, that the charm of idyllic interludes depends upon one person's 'giving the party' – which is to say, furnishing the background, the experience, the patience, against which the other seems to enjoy again the spells of pastoral tranquillity recollected from childhood. Nicole and Nelson were at once too old and too young, and too American, to fall into immediate soft agreement with a strange land. Their vitality made them restless, for as yet his painting had no direction and her singing no immediate prospect of becoming serious. They said they were not 'getting anywhere' – the evenings were long, so they began to drink a lot of *vin de Capri* at dinner.

The English owned the hotel. They were aged, come South for good weather and tranquillity; Nelson and Nicole resented the mild tenor of their days. Could people be content to talk eternally about the weather, promenade the same walks, face the same variant of macaroni at dinner month after month? They grew bored, and Americans bored are already in sight of excitement. Things came to a head all in one night.

Over a flask of wine at dinner they decided to go to Paris, settle in an apartment and work seriously. Paris promised metropolitan diversion, friends of their own age, a general intensity that Italy lacked. Eager with new hopes, they strolled into the salon after dinner, when, for the tenth time, Nelson noticed an ancient and enormous mechanical piano and was moved to try it.

Across the salon sat the only English people with whom they had had any connection – Gen. Sir Evelyne Fragelle and Lady Fragelle. The connection had been brief and unpleasant – seeing them walking out of the hotel in peignoirs to swim, she had announced, over quite a few yards of floor space, that it was disgusting and shouldn't be allowed.

But that was nothing compared with her response to the first terrific bursts of sound from the electric piano. As the dust of years trembled off the keyboard at the vibration, she shot galvanically forward with the sort of jerk associated with the electric chair. Somewhat stunned himself by the sudden din of Waiting for the Robert E. Lee, Nelson had scarcely sat down when she projected herself across the room, her train quivering behind her, and, without glancing at the Kellys, turned off the instrument.

It was one of those gestures that are either plainly justified, or else outrageous. For a moment Nelson hesitated uncertainly; then, remembering Lady Fragelle's arrogant remark about his bathing suit, he returned to the instrument in her still-billowing wake and turned it on again.

The incident had become international. The eyes of the entire salon fell eagerly upon the protagonists, watching for the next move. Nicole hurried after Nelson, urging him to let the matter pass, but it was too late. From the outraged English table there arose, joint by joint, Gen. Sir Evelyne Fragelle, faced with perhaps his most crucial situation since the relief of Ladysmith.

''T'lee outrageous! – 't'lee outrageous!''

'I beg your pardon,' said Nelson.

'Here for fifteen years!' screamed Sir Evelyne to himself. 'Never heard of anyone doing such a thing before!'

'I gathered that this was put here for the amusement of the guests.'

Scorning to answer, Sir Evelyne knelt, reached for the catch, pushed it the wrong way, whereupon the speed and volume of the instrument tripled until they stood in a wild pandemonium of sound; Sir Evelyne livid with military emotions, Nelson on the point of maniacal laughter.

In a moment the firm hand of the hotel manager settled the matter; the instrument gulped and stopped, trembling a little from its unaccustomed outburst, leaving behind it a great silence in which Sir Evelyne turned to the manager.

'Most outrageous affair ever heard of in my life. My wife turned it off once, and he' – this was his first acknowledgment of Nelson's identity as distinct from the instrument – 'he put it on again!'

'This is a public room in a hotel,' Nelson protested. 'The instrument is apparently here to be used.'

'Don't get in an argument,' Nicole whispered. 'They're old.'

But Nelson said, 'If there's any apology, it's certainly due to me.'

Sir Evelyne's eye was fixed menacingly upon the manager, waiting for him to do his duty. The latter thought of Sir Evelyne's fifteen years of residence, and cringed.

'It is not the habitude to play the instrument in the evening. The clients are each one quiet on his or her table.'

'American cheek!' snapped Sir Evelyne.

'Very well,' Nelson said; 'we'll relieve the hotel of our presence tomorrow.'

As a reaction from this incident, as a sort of protest against Sir Evelyne Fragelle, they went not to Paris but to Monte Carlo after all. They were through with being alone.

II

A little more than two years after the Kellys' first visit to Monte Carlo, Nicole woke up one morning into what, though it bore the same name, had become to her a different place altogether.

In spite of hurried months in Paris or Biarritz, it was now home to them. They had a villa, they had a large acquaintance among the spring and summer crowd – a crowd which, naturally, did not include people on charted trips or the shore parties from Mediterranean cruises; these latter had become for them 'tourists'.

They loved the Riveria in full summer with many friends there and the night open and full of music. Before the maid drew the curtains this morning to shut out the glare, Nicole saw from her window the yacht of T. F. Golding, placid among the swells of the Monacan Bay, as if constantly bound on a romantic voyage not dependent upon actual motion.

The yacht had taken the slow tempo of the coast; it had gone no farther than to Cannes and back all summer, though it might have toured the world. The Kellys were dining on board that night.

Nicole spoke excellent French; she had five new evening dresses and four others that would do; she had her husband; she had two men in love with her, and she felt sad for one of them. She had her pretty face. At

10.30 she was meeting a third man, who was just beginning to be in love with her 'in a harmless way'. At once she was having a dozen charming people to luncheon. All that.

'I'm happy,' she brooded toward the bright blinds. 'I'm young and good-looking, and my name is often in the paper as having been here and there, but really I don't care about shi-shi. I think it's all awfully silly, but if you do want to see people, you might as well see the chic, amusing ones; and if people call you a snob, it's envy, and they know it and everybody knows it.'

She repeated the substance of this to Oscar Dane on the Mont Agel golf course two hours later, and he cursed her quietly.

'Not at all,' he said. 'You're just getting to be an old snob. Do you call that crowd of drunks you run with amusing people? Why, they're not even very swell. They're so hard that they've shifted down through Europe like nails in a sack of wheat, till they stick out of it a little into the Mediterranean Sea.'

Annoyed, Nicole fired a name at him, but he answered: 'Class C. A good solid article for beginners.'

'The Colbys – anyway, her.'

'Third flight.'

'Marquis and Marquise de Kalb.'

'If she didn't happen to take dope and he didn't have other peculiarities.'

'Well, then, where are the amusing people?' she demanded impatiently.

'Off by themselves somewhere. They don't hunt in herds, except occasionally.'

'How about you? You'd snap up an invitation from every person I named. I've heard stories about you wilder than any you can make up. There's not a man that's known you six months that would take your cheque for ten dollars. You're a sponge and a parasite and everything –'

'Shut up for a minute,' he interrupted. 'I don't want to spoil this drive … I just don't like to see you kid yourself,' he continued. 'What passes with you for international society is just about as hard to enter nowadays as the public rooms at the Casino; and if I can make my living by sponging off it, I'm still giving twenty times more than I get. We dead beats are about the only people in it with any stuff, and we stay with it because we have to.'

She laughed, liking him immensely, wondering how angry Nelson would be when he found Oscar had walked off with his nail scissors and his copy of the New York Herald this morning.

'Anyhow,' she thought afterward, as she drove home toward luncheon, 'we're getting out of it all soon, and we'll be serious and have a baby. After this last summer.'

Stopping for a moment at a florist's, she saw a young woman coming out with an armful of flowers. The young woman glanced at her over the heap of colour, and Nicole perceived that she was extremely smart, and then that her face was familiar. It was someone she had known once, but only slightly; the name had escaped her, so she did not nod, and forgot the incident until that afternoon.

They were twelve for luncheon; The Goldings' party from the yacht, Liddell and Cardine Miles, Mr Dane – seven different nationalities she counted; among them an exquisite young Frenchwoman, Madame Delauney, whom Nicole referred to lightly as 'Nelson's girl'. Noel Delauney was perhaps her closest friend; when they made up foursomes for golf or for trips, she paired off with Nelson; but today, as Nicole introduced her to someone as 'Nelson's girl', the bantering phrase filled Nicole with distaste.

She said aloud at luncheon: 'Nelson and I are going to get away from it all.'

Everybody agreed that they, too, were going to get away from it all.

'It's all right for the English,' someone said, 'because they're doing a sort of dance of death – you know, gaiety in the doomed fort, with the Sepoys at the gate. You can see it by their faces when they dance – the intensity. They know it and they want it, and they don't see any future. But you Americans, you're having a rotten time. If you want to wear the green hat or the crushed hat, or whatever it is, you always have to get a little tipsy.'

'We're going to get away from it all,' Nicole said firmly, but something within her argued: 'What a pity – this lovely blue sea, this happy time.' What came afterward? Did one just accept a lessening of tension? It was somehow Nelson's business to answer that. His growing discontent that he wasn't getting anywhere ought to explode into a new life for both of them, or rather a new hope and content with life. That secret should be his masculine contribution.

'Well, children, goodbye.'

'It was a great luncheon.'

'Don't forget about getting away from it all.'

'See you when –'

The guests walked down the path toward their cars. Only Oscar, just faintly flushed on liqueurs, stood with Nicole on the veranda, talking on and on about the girl he had invited up to see his stamp collection. Momentarily tired of people, impatient to be alone, Nicole listened for a moment and then, taking a glass vase of flowers from the luncheon table, went through the French windows into the dark, shadowy villa, his voice following her as he talked on and on out there.

It was when she crossed the first salon, still hearing Oscar's monologue on the veranda, that she began to hear another voice in the next room, cutting sharply across Oscar's voice.

'Ah, but kiss me again,' it said, stopped; Nicole stopped, too, rigid in the silence, now broken only by the voice on the porch.

'Be careful.' Nicole recognized the faint French accent of Noel Delauney.

'I'm tired of being careful. Anyhow, they're on the veranda.'

'No, better the usual place.'

'Darling, sweet darling.'

The voice of Oscar Dane on the veranda grew weary and stopped and, as if thereby released from her paralysis, Nicole took a step – forward or backward, she did not know which. At the sound of her heel on the floor, she heard the two people in the next room breaking swiftly apart.

Then she went in. Nelson was lighting a cigarette; Noel, with her back turned, was apparently hunting for hat or purse on a chair. With blind horror rather than anger, Nicole threw, or rather pushed away from her, the glass vase which she carried. If at anyone, it was at Nelson she threw it, but the force of her feeling had entered the inanimate thing; it flew past him, and Noel Delauney, just turning about, was struck full on the side of her head and face.

'Say, there!' Nelson cried. Noel sank slowly into the chair before which she stood, her hand slowly rising to cover the side of her face. The jar rolled unbroken on the thick carpet, scattering its flowers.

'You look out!' Nelson was at Noel's side, trying to take the hand away to see what had happened.

'*C'est liquide,*' gasped Noel in a whisper. '*Est-ce que c'est le sang?*'

He forced her hand away, and cried breathlessly, 'No, it's just water!' and then, to Oscar, who had appeared in the doorway: 'Get some cognac!' and to Nicole: 'You fool, you must be crazy!'

Nicole, breathing hard, said nothing. When the brandy arrived, there was a continuing silence, like that of people watching an operation, while Nelson poured a glass down Noel's throat. Nicole signalled to Oscar for a drink, and, as if afraid to break the silence without it, they all had a brandy. Then Noel and Nelson spoke at once:

'If you can find my hat –'

'This is the silliest –'

'– I shall go immediately.'

'– thing I ever saw; I –'

They all looked at Nicole, who said: 'Have her car drive right up to the door.' Oscar departed quickly.

'Are you sure you don't want to see a doctor?' asked Nelson anxiously.

'I want to go.'

A minute later, when the car had driven away, Nelson came in and poured himself another glass of brandy. A wave of subsiding tension flowed over him, showing in his face; Nicole saw it, and saw also his gathering will to make the best he could of it.

'I want to know just why you did that,' he demanded. 'No, don't go, Oscar.' He saw the story starting out into the world.

'What possible reason –'

'Oh, shut up!' snapped Nicole.

'If I kissed Noel, there's nothing so terrible about it. It's of absolutely no significance.'

She made a contemptuous sound. 'I heard what you said to her.'

'You're crazy.'

He said it as if she were crazy, and wild rage filled her.

'You liar! All this time pretending to be so square, and so particular what I did, and all the time behind my back you've been playing around with that little –'

She used a serious word, and as if maddened with the sound of it, she sprang toward his chair. In protection against this sudden attack, he flung up his arm quickly, and the knuckles of his open hand struck across the socket of her eye. Covering her face with her hand as Noel had done ten minutes previously, she fell sobbing to the floor.

'Hasn't this gone far enough?' Oscar cried.

'Yes,' admitted Nelson, 'I guess it has.'

'You go on out on the veranda and cool off.'

He got Nicole to a couch and sat beside her, holding her hand.

'Brace up – brace up, baby,' he said, over and over. 'What are you – Jack Dempsey? You can't go around hitting French women; they'll sue you.'

'He told her he loved her,' she gasped hysterically. 'She said she'd meet him at the same place ... Has he gone there now?'

'He's out on the porch, walking up and down, sorry as the devil that he accidentally hit you, and sorry he ever saw Noel Delauney.'

'Oh, yes!'

'You might have heard wrong, and it doesn't prove a thing, anyhow.'

After twenty minutes, Nelson came in suddenly and sank down on his knees by the side of his wife. Mr Oscar Dane, reinforced in his idea that he gave much more than he got, backed discreetly and far from unwillingly to the door.

In another hour, Nelson and Nicole, arm in arm, emerged from their villa and walked slowly down to the Café de Paris. They walked instead of driving, as if trying to return to the simplicity they had once possessed, as if they were trying to unwind something that had become visibly tangled. Nicole accepted his explanations, not because they were credible, but because she wanted passionately to believe them. They were both very quiet and sorry.

The Café de Paris was pleasant at that hour, with sunset drooping through the yellow awnings and the red parasols as through stained glass. Glancing about, Nicole saw the young woman she had encountered that morning. She was with a man now, and Nelson placed them immediately as the young couple they had seen in Algeria, almost three years ago.

'They've changed,' he commented. 'I suppose we have, too, but not so much. They're harder-looking and he looks dissipated. Dissipation always shows in light eyes rather than in dark ones. The girl is *tout ce qu'il y a de chic*, as they say, but there's a hard look in her face too.'

'I like her.'

'Do you want me to go and ask them if they are that same couple?'

'No! That'd be like lonesome tourists do. They have their own friends.'

At that moment people were joining them at their table.

'Nelson, how about tonight?' Nicole asked a little later. 'Do you think we can appear at the Golding's after what's happened?'

'We not only can but we've got to. If the story's around and we're not there, we'll just be handing them a nice juicy subject of conversation ... Hello! What on earth –'

Something strident and violent had happened across the café; a woman screamed and the people at one table were all on their feet, surging back and forth like one person. Then the people at the other tables were standing and crowding forward; for just a moment the Kellys saw the face of the girl they had been watching, pale now, and distorted with anger. Panic-stricken, Nicole plucked at Nelson's sleeve.

'I want to get out, I can't stand any more today. Take me home. Is everybody going crazy?'

On the way home, Nelson glanced at Nicole's face and perceived with a start that they were not going to dinner on the Goldings' yacht after all. Nicole had the beginnings of a well-defined and unmistakable black eye – an eye that by eleven o'clock would be beyond the aid of all the cosmetics in the principality. His heart sank and he decided to say nothing about it until they reached home.

III

There is some wise advice in the catechism about avoiding the occasions of sin, and when the Kellys went up to Paris a month later they made a conscientious list of the places they wouldn't visit any more and the people they didn't want to see again. The places included several famous bars, all the night clubs except one or two that were highly decorous, all the early-morning clubs of every description, and all summer resorts that made whoopee for its own sake – whoopee triumphant and unrestrained – the main attraction of the season.

The people they were through with included three-fourths of those with whom they had passed the last two years. They did this not in snobbishness, but for self-preservation, and not without a certain fear in their hearts that they were cutting themselves off from human contacts forever.

But the world is always curious, and people become valuable merely for their inaccessibility. They found that there were others in Paris who were only interested in those who had separated from the many. The first crowd they had known was largely American, salted with Europeans; the second was largely European, peppered with Americans. This latter crowd was 'society', and here and there it touched the ultimate *milieu*, made up of individuals of high position, of great fortune, very occasionally of genius, and always of power. Without being intimate with the great, they made new friends of a more conservative type. Moreover, Nelson began to paint again; he had a studio, and they visited the studios of Brancusi and Leger and Deschamps. It seemed that they were more part of something than before, and when certain gaudy rendezvous were mentioned, they felt a contempt for their first two years in Europe, speaking of their former acquaintances as 'that crowd' and as 'people who waste your time'.

So, although they kept their rules, they entertained frequently at home and they went out to the houses of others. They were young and handsome and intelligent; they came to know what did go and what did not go, and adapted themselves accordingly. Moreover, they were naturally generous and willing, within the limits of common sense, to pay.

When one went out one generally drank. This meant little to Nicole, who had a horror of losing her *soigné* air, losing a touch of bloom or a ray of admiration, but Nelson, thwarted somewhere, found himself quite as tempted to drink at these small dinners as in the more frankly rowdy world. He was not a drunk, he did nothing conspicuous or sodden, but he was no longer willing to go out socially without the stimulus of liquor. It was with the idea of bringing him to a serious and responsible attitude that Nicole decided after a year in Paris, that the time had come to have a baby.

This was coincidental with their meeting Count Chiki Sarolai. He was an attractive relic of the Austrian court, with no fortune or pretence to any, but with solid social and financial connections in France. His sister was married to the Marquis de la Clos d'Hirondelle, who, in addition to being of the ancient noblesse, was a successful banker in Paris. Count Chiki roved here and there, frankly sponging, rather like Oscar Dane, but in a different sphere.

His penchant was Americans; he hung on their words with a pathetic eagerness, as if they would sooner or later let slip their mysterious formula for making money. After a casual meeting, his interest gravitated to the Kellys. During Nicole's months of waiting he was in the house continually, tirelessly interested in anything that concerned American crime, slang, finance or manners. He came in for a luncheon or dinner when he had no other place to go, and with tacit gratitude he persuaded his sister to call on Nicole, who was immensely flattered.

It was arranged that when Nicole went to the hospital he would stay at the *appartement* and keep Nelson company – an arrangement of which Nicole didn't approve, since they were inclined to drink together. But the day on which it was decided, he arrived with news of one of his brother-in-law's famous canal-boat parties on the Seine, to which the Kellys were to be invited and which, conveniently enough, was to occur three weeks after the arrival of the baby. So, when Nicole moved out to the American Hospital Count Chiki moved in.

The baby was a boy. For a while Nicole forgot all about people and their human status and their value. She even wondered at the fact that she had become such a snob, since everything seemed trivial compared with the new individual that, eight times a day, they carried to her breast.

After two weeks she and the baby went back to the apartment, but Chiki and his valet stayed on. It was understood, with that subtlety the Kellys had only recently begun to appreciate, that he was merely staying until after his brother-in-law's party, but the apartment was crowded and Nicole wished him gone. But her old idea, that if one had to see people they might as well be the best, was carried out in being invited to the de la Clos d'Hirondelles'.

As she lay in her chaise longue the day before the event, Chiki explained the arrangements, in which he had evidently aided.

'Everyone who arrives must drink two cocktails in the American style before they can come aboard – as a ticket of admission.'

'But I thought that very fashionable French – Faubourg St Germain and all that – didn't drink cocktails.'

'Oh, but my family is very modern. We adopt many American customs.'

'Who'll be there?'

'Everyone! Everyone in Paris.'

Great names swam before her eyes. Next day she could not resist dragging the affair into conversation with her doctor. But she was rather offended at the look of astonishment and incredulity that came into his eyes.

'Did I understand you aright?' he demanded. 'Did I understand you to say that you were going to a ball tomorrow?'

'Why, yes,' she faltered. 'Why not?'

'My dear lady, you are not going to stir out of the house for two more weeks; you are not going to dance or do anything strenuous for two more after that.'

'That's ridiculous!' she cried. 'It's been three weeks already! Esther Sherman went to America after –'

'Never mind,' he interrupted. 'Every case is different. There is a complication which makes it positively necessary for you to follow my orders.'

'But the idea is that I'll just go for two hours, because of course I'll have to come home to Sonny –'

'You'll not go for two minutes.'

She knew, from the seriousness of his tone, that he was right, but, perversely, she did not mention the matter to Nelson. She said, instead, that she was tired, that possibly she might not go, and lay awake that night measuring her disappointment against her fear. She woke up for Sonny's first feeding, thinking to herself: 'But if I just take ten steps from a limousine to a chair and just sit half an hour –'

At the last minute the pale green evening dress from Callets, draped across a chair in her bedroom, decided her. She went.

Somewhere, during the shuffle and delay on the gangplank while the guests went aboard and were challenged and drank down their cocktails with attendant gaiety, Nicole realized that she had made a mistake. There was, at any rate, no formal receiving line and, after greeting their hosts, Nelson found her a chair on deck, where presently the faintness disappeared.

Then she was glad she had come. The boat was hung with fragile lanterns, which blended with the pastels of the bridges and the reflected stars in the dark Seine, like a child's dream out of the Arabian Nights. A crowd of hungry-eyed spectators were gathered on the banks. Champagne moved past in platoons like a drill of bottles, while the music, instead of being loud and obtrusive, drifted down from the upper deck like frosting dripping over a cake. She became aware presently that they were not the only Americans there – across the deck were the Liddell Mileses, whom she had not seen for several years.

Other people from that crowd were present, and she felt a faint disappointment. What if this was not the marquis' best party? She remembered her mother's second days at home. She asked Chiki, who was at her side, to point out celebrities, but when she inquired about several people whom she associated with that set, he replied vaguely that they were away, or coming later, or could not be there. It seemed to her that she saw across the room the girl who had made the scene in the Café de Paris at Monte Carlo, but she could not be sure, for with the faint almost imperceptible movement of the boat, she realized that she was growing faint again. She sent for Nelson to take her home.

'You can come right back, of course. You needn't wait for me, because I'm going right to bed.'

He left her in the hands of the nurse, who helped her upstairs and aided her to undress quickly.

'I'm desperately tired,' Nicole said. 'Will you put my pearls away?'

'Where?'

'In the jewel box on the dressing-table.'

'I don't see it,' said the nurse after a minute.

'Then it's in a drawer.'

There was a thorough rummaging of the dressing-table, without result.

'But of course it's there.' Nicole attempted to rise, but fell back, exhausted. 'Look for it, please, again. Everything is in it – all my mother's things and my engagement things.'

'I'm sorry, Mrs Kelly. There's nothing in this room that answers to that description.'

'Wake up the maid.'

The maid knew nothing; then, after a persistent cross-examination, she did know something. Count Sarolai's valet had gone out, carrying his suitcase, half an hour after madame left the house.

Writhing in sharp and sudden pain, with a hastily summoned doctor at her side, it seemed to Nicole hours before Nelson came home. When he arrived, his face was deathly pale and his eyes were wild. He came directly into her room.

'What do you think?' he said savagely. Then he saw the doctor. 'Why, what's the matter?'

'Oh, Nelson, I'm sick as a dog and my jewel box is gone, and Chiki's valet has gone. I've told the police ... Perhaps Chiki would know where the man –'

'Chiki will never come in this house again,' he said slowly. 'Do you know whose party that was? Have you got any idea whose party that was?' He burst into wild laughter. 'It was our party – our party, do you understand? We gave it – we didn't know it, but we did.'

'*Maintenant, monsieur, il ne faut pas exciter madame* – the doctor began.

'I thought it was odd when the marquis went home early, but I didn't suspect till the end. They were just guests – Chiki invited all the people. After it was over, the caterers and musicians began to come up and ask me where to send their bills. And that damn Chiki had the nerve to tell me he thought I knew all the time. He said that all he'd promised was that it would be his brother-in-law's sort of party, and that his sister would be there. He said perhaps I was drunk, or perhaps I didn't understand French – as if we'd ever talked anything but English to him.'

'Don't pay!' she said. 'I wouldn't think of paying.'

'So I said, but they're going to sue – the boat people and the others. They want twelve thousand dollars.'

She relaxed suddenly. 'Oh, go away!' she cried. 'I don't care! I've lost my jewels and I'm sick, sick!'

IV

This is the story of a trip abroad, and the geographical element must not be slighted. Having visited North Africa, Italy, the Riveria, Paris and points in between, it was not surprising that eventually the Kellys should go to Switzerland. Switzerland is a country where very few things begin, but many things end.

Though there was an element of choice in their other ports of call, the Kellys went to Switzerland because they had to. They had been married a little more than four years when they arrived one spring day at the lake that is the centre of Europe – a placid, smiling spot with pastoral hillsides, a backdrop of mountains and waters of postcard blue, waters that are a little sinister beneath the surface with all the misery that had dragged itself here from every corner of Europe. Weariness to recuperate and death to die. There are schools, too, and young people splashing at the sunny plages; there is Bonivard's dungeon and Calvin's city, and the ghosts of Byron and Shelley still sail the dim shores by night; but the Lake Geneva that Nelson and Nicole came to was the dreary one of sanatoriums and rest hotels.

For, as if by some profound sympathy that had continued to exist beneath the unlucky destiny that had pursued their affairs, health had failed them both at the same time; Nicole lay on the balcony of a hotel coming slowly back to life after two successive operations, while Nelson fought for life against jaundice in a hospital two miles away. Even after the reserve force of twenty-nine years had pulled him through, there were months ahead during which he must live quietly. Often they wondered why, of all those who sought pleasure over the face of Europe, this misfortune should have come to them.

'There've been too many people in our lives,' Nelson said. 'We've never been able to resist people. We were so happy the first year when there weren't any people.'

Nicole agreed. 'If we could ever be alone – really alone – we could make up some kind of life for ourselves. We'll try, won't we, Nelson?'

But there were other days when they both wanted company desperately, concealing it from each other. Days when they eyed the obese, the wasted, the crippled and the broken of all nationalities who filled the hotel, seeking for one who might be amusing. It was a new life for them, turning on the daily visits of their two doctors, the arrival of the mail and newspapers from Paris, the little walk into the hillside village or occasionally the descent by funicular to the pale resort on the lake, with its *Kursaal*, its grass beach, its tennis clubs and sight-seeing buses. They read Tauchnitz editions and yellow-jacketed Edgar Wallaces; at a certain hour each day they watched the baby being given its bath; three nights a week there was a tired and patient orchestra in the lounge after dinner, that was all.

And sometimes there was a booming from the vine-covered hills on the other side of the lake, which meant that cannons were shooting at hail-bearing clouds, to save the vineyards from an approaching storm; it came swiftly, first falling from the heavens and then falling again in torrents from the mountains, washing loudly down the roads and stone ditches; it came with a dark, frightening sky and savage filaments of lightning and crashing, world-splitting thunder, while ragged and destroyed clouds fled along before the wind past the hotel. The mountains and the lake disappeared completely; the hotel crouched alone amid tumult and chaos and darkness.

It was during such a storm, when the mere opening of a door admitted a tornado of rain and wind into the hall, that the Kellys for the first time in months saw someone they knew. Sitting downstairs with other victims of frayed nerves, they became aware of two new arrivals – a man and woman whom they recognized as the couple, first seen in Algiers, who had crossed their path several times since. A single unexpressed thought flashed through Nelson and Nicole. It seemed like destiny that at last here in this desolate place they should know them, and watching, they saw other couples eyeing them in the same tentative way. Yet something held the Kellys back. Had they not just been complaining that there were too many people in their lives?

Later, when the storm had dozed off into a quiet rain, Nicole found herself near the girl on the glass veranda. Under cover of reading a book, she inspected the face closely. It was an inquisitive face, she saw at once, possibly calculating; the eyes, intelligent enough, but with no peace in them, swept over people in a single quick glance as though estimating their value. 'Terrible egoist', Nicole thought, with a certain distaste. For the rest, the cheeks were wan, and there were little pouches of ill health under the eyes; these combining with a certain flabbiness of arms and legs to give an impression of unwholesomeness. She was dressed expensively, but with a hint of slovenliness, as if she did not consider the people of the hotel important.

On the whole, Nicole decided she did not like her; she was glad that they had not spoken, but she was rather surprised that she had not noticed these things when the girl crossed her path before.

Telling Nelson her impression at dinner, he agreed with her.

'I ran into the man in the bar, and I noticed we both took nothing but mineral water, so I started to say something. But I got a good look at his face in the mirror and I decided not to. His face is so weak and self-indulgent that it's almost mean – the kind of face that needs half a dozen drinks really to open the eyes and stiffen the mouth up to normal.'

After dinner the rain stopped and the night was fine outside. Eager for the air, the Kellys wandered down into the dark garden; on their way they passed the subjects of their late discussion, who withdrew abruptly down a side path.

'I don't think they want to know us any more than we do them,' Nicole laughed.

They loitered among the wild rose-bushes and the beds of damp-sweet, indistinguishable flowers. Below the hotel, where the terrace fell a thousand feet to the lake, stretched a necklace of lights that was Montreux and Vevey, and then, in a dim pendant, Lausanne; a blurred twinkling across the lake was Evian and France. From somewhere below – probably the *Kursaal* – came the sound of full-bodied dance music – American, they guessed, though now they heard American tunes months late, mere distant echoes of what was happening far away.

Over the Dent du Midi, over a black bank of clouds that was the rearguard of the receding storm, the moon lifted itself and the lake brightened; the music and the far-away lights were like hope, like the enchanted distance from which children see things. In their separate hearts Nelson and Nicole gazed backward to a time when life was all like this. Her arm went through his quietly and drew him close.

'We can have it all again,' she whispered. 'Can't we try, Nelson?'

She paused as two dark forms came into the shadows near-by and stood looking down at the lake below.

Nelson put his arm around Nicole and pulled her closer.

'It's just that we don't understand what's the matter,' she said. 'Why did we lose peace and love and health, one after the other? If we knew, if there was anybody to tell us, I believe we could try. I'd try so hard.'

The last clouds were lifting themselves over the Bernese Alps. Suddenly, with a final intensity, the west flared with pale white lightning. Nelson and Nicole turned, and simultaneously the other couple turned, while for an instant the night was as bright as day. Then darkness and a last low peal of thunder, and from Nicole a sharp, terrified cry. She flung herself against Nelson; even in the darkness she saw that his face was as white and strained as her own.

'Did you see?' she cried in a whisper. 'Did you see them?'

'Yes!'

'They're us! They're us! Don't you see?'

Trembling, they clung together. The clouds merged into the dark mass of mountains; looking around after a moment, Nelson and Nicole saw that they were alone together in the tranquil moonlight.

The Fiend

On June 3, 1895 on a country road near Stillwater, Minnesota, Mrs Crenshaw Engels and her seven-year-old son, Mark, were waylaid and murdered by a fiend, under circumstances so atrocious that, fortunately, it is not necessary to set them down here.

Crenshaw Engels, the husband and father, was a photographer in Stillwater. He was 'a great reader' and considered 'a little unsafe', for he had spoken his mind frankly about the farmer-versus-railroad struggles of the time – but no one denied that he was a devoted family man, and the catastrophe visited upon him hung over the little town for many weeks.

There was a move to lynch the perpetrator of the horror, for Minessota did not permit the capital punishment it deserved, but the instigators were foiled by the big stone penitentiary close at hand.

The cloud hung over Engels' home so that folks went there only in moods of penitence, of fear or guilt, hoping that they would be visited in compensation should their lives ever chance to trek under a black sky. The photography shop suffered also: the routine of being posed, the necessary silences and pauses in the process, permitted the client too much time to regard the prematurely aged face of Crenshaw Engels, and young high school students, married couples, mothers of babies were always glad to escape from the place into the open air.

So Crenshaw's business fell off, and he went through a time of hardship – finally liquidating the lease, the apparatus and the goodwill, and wearing out the money obtained. He sold his house for a little more than its two mortgages, went to board, and took a position clerking in Radamacher's Department Store.

In the sight of his neighbours he had become a man ruined by adversity, a man *manqué*, a man emptied. But in the last opinion they were wrong – he was empty of all save one thing. His memory was long as a Jew's, and though his heart was in the grave he was sane as when his wife and son had started on their last walk that summer morning.

At the first trial he lost control and got at the Fiend, seizing him by the necktie – and had been dragged off with the tie in such a knot that the Fiend was nearly garrotted.

At the second trial he cried aloud once. Afterwards he went to all the members of the State legislature in the county and handed them a bill he had written himself for the introduction of capital punishment – the bill to be retroactive on criminals condemned to life imprisonment. The bill fell through; it was on the day Crenshaw heard this that he got inside the penitentiary by a ruse and was only apprehended in time to be prevented from shooting the Fiend in his cell.

Crenshaw was given a suspended sentence, and for some months it was assumed that the agony was fading gradually from his mind. In fact, when he presented himself to the warden a year after the crime the official was sympathetic to Crenshaw's statement that he had had a change of heart, and felt he could only emerge from the valley of the shadow by forgiveness; that he wanted to help the Fiend, show him the True Path by means of good books and appeals to his buried better nature.

So, after being carefully searched, Crenshaw was permitted to sit for half an hour outside the Fiend's cell.

But had the warden suspected the truth he would not have permitted the visit – for far from forgiving, Crenshaw's plan was to wreak upon the Fiend a mental revenge to replace the physical one of which he was subducted.

When he faced the Fiend in his cell, Crenshaw felt his scalp tingle. From behind the bars a roly-poly man, who somehow made his convict's uniform resemble a business suit, a man with thick brown-rimmed glasses and the trim air of an insurance salesman, looked at him uncertainly. Feeling faint, Crenshaw sat down in the chair that had been brought for him.

'The air round you stinks!' he cried suddenly. 'This whole corridor, this whole prison.'

'I suppose it does,' admitted the Fiend. 'I noticed it too.'

'You'll have time to notice it,' Crenshaw snarled. 'All your life you'll pace up and down stinking in that little cell, with everything getting blacker and blacker. And after that there'll be hell waiting for you. For all eternity you'll be shut in a little space, but in hell it'll be so small that you can't stand up or stretch out.'

'Will it, now?' asked the Fiend, concerned.

'It will!' said Crenshaw. 'You'll be alone with your own vile thoughts in that little space, for ever and ever and ever and ever. You'll itch with corruption, so that you can never sleep, and you'll always be thirsty, with water just out of reach.'

'Will I now?' repeated the Fiend, even more concerned. 'I remember once –'

'All the time you'll be full of horrors,' Crenshaw interrupted. 'You'll be like a person just about to go crazy but can't go crazy. All the time you'll be thinking that it's for ever and ever and ever.'

'That's bad,' said the Fiend shaking his head gloomily. 'That's real bad.'

'Now, listen here to me,' went on Crenshaw. 'I've brought you some books you're going to read. It's arranged that you get no books or papers except what I bring you.'

As a beginning, Crenshaw had brought half a dozen books which his vagarious curiosity had collected over as many years. They comprised a German doctor's thousand case histories of sexual abnormality – cases with no cures, no hopes, no prognoses, cases listed cold; a series of sermons by a New England divine of the Great Revival which pictured the tortures of the damned in hell; a collection of horror stories; and a volume of erotic pieces from each of which the last two pages, containing the consummations, had been torn out; and a volume of detective stories mutilated in the same manner. A tome of the Newgate calendar completed the batch. These Crenshaw handed through the bars – the Fiend took them and put them on his iron cot.

This was the first of Crenshaw's long series of fortnightly visits. Always he brought with him something sombre and menacing to say, something dark and terrible to read – save that once when the Fiend had had nothing to read for a long time he brought him four inspiringly titled books – that proved to have nothing but blank paper inside.

Another time, pretending to concede a point, he promised to bring newspapers – he brought ten copies of the yellowed journal that had reported the crime and the arrest. Sometimes he obtained medical books that showed in colour the red and blue and green ravages of leprosy and skin disease, the mounds of shattered cells, the verminous tissue and brown corrupted blood.

And there was no sewer of the publishing world from which he did not obtain records of all that was gross and vile in man.

Crenshaw could not keep this up indefinitely both because of the expense and because of the exhaustibility of such books.

When five years had passed he leaned towards another form of torture. He built up false hopes in the Fiend with protests of his own change of heart and manoeuvres for a pardon, and then dashed the hopes to pieces.

Or else he pretended to have a pistol with him, or an inflammatory substance that would make the cell a raging inferno and consume the Fiend in two minutes – once he threw a dummy bottle into the cell and listened in delight to the screams as the Fiend ran back and forth waiting for the explosion.

At other times he would pretend grimly that the legislature had passed a new law which provided that the Fiend would be executed in a few hours.

A decade passed. Crenshaw was grey at forty – he was white at fifty, when the alternating routine of his fortnightly visits to the graves of his loved ones and to the penitentiary had become the only part of his life – the long days at Radamacher's were only a weary dream.

Sometimes he went and sat outside the Fiend's cell, with no word said during the half-hour he was allowed to be there. The Fiend too had grown white in twenty years. He was very respectable looking with his horn-rimmed glasses and his white hair. He seemed to have a great respect for Crenshaw, and even when the latter, in a renewal of diminishing vitality, promised him one day that on his very next visit he was going to bring a revolver and end the matter, he nodded gravely as if in agreement, said 'I suppose so; yes, I suppose you're perfectly right,' and did not mention the matter to the guards.

On the occasion of the next visit he was waiting with his hands on the bars of the cell, looking at Crenshaw both hopefully and desperately. At certain tensions and strains death takes on, indeed, the quality of a great adventure, as any soldier can testify.

Years passed. Crenshaw was promoted to floor manager at Radamacher's – there were new generations now that did not know of his tragedy, and regarded him as an austere nonentity. He came into a little legacy, and bought new stones for the graves of his wife and son. He knew he would soon be retired, and while a third decade lapsed through the white winters, the short, sweet, smoky summers, it became more and more plain to him that the time had come to put an end to the Fiend, to avoid any mischance by which the other would survive him.

The moment he fixed upon came at the exact end of thirty years. Crenshaw had long owned the pistol with which it would be accomplished; he had fingered the shells lovingly, and calculated the lodgment of each in the Fiend's body, so that death would be sure, but lingering – he studied the tales of abdominal wounds in the war news, and delighted in the agony that made victims pray to be killed.

After that, what happened to *him* did not matter.

When the day came he had no trouble in smuggling the pistol into the penitentiary. But, to his surprise, he found the Fiend scrunched up upon his cot, instead of waiting for him avidly by the bars.

'I'm sick,' the Fiend said. 'My stomach's been burning me up all morning. They gave me a physic, but now it's worse, and nobody comes.'

Crenshaw fancied momentarily that this was a premonition in the man's bowels of a bullet that would shortly ride ragged through that spot.

'Come up to the bars,' he said, mildly.

'I can't move.'

'Yes, you can.'

'I'm doubled up. All doubled up.'

'Come doubled up, then.'

With an effort the Fiend moved himself, only to fall on his side on the cement floor. He groaned, and then lay quiet for a minute, after which, still bent in two, he began to drag himself a foot at a time toward the bars.

Suddenly Crenshaw set off at a run toward the end of the corridor.

'I want a prison doctor,' he demanded of the guard. 'That man's sick – sick, I tell you.'

'The doctor has –'

'Get him – get him now!'

The guard hesitated, but Crenshaw had become a tolerated, even privileged, person around the prison, and in a moment the guard took down his 'phone and called the infirmary.

All that afternoon Crenshaw waited in the bare area inside the gates, walking up and down with his hands behind his back. From time to time he went to the front entrance and demanded of the guard:

'Any news?'

'Nothing yet. They'll call me when there's anything.'

Late in the afternoon the Warden appeared at the door, looked about, and spotted Crenshaw. The latter, all alert, hastened over.

'He's dead,' the Warden said. 'His appendix burst. They did everything they could.'

'Dead,' Crenshaw repeated.

'I'm sorry to bring you this news. I know how –'

'It's all right,' said Crenshaw, and, licking his lips, 'So he's dead.'

The Warden lit a cigarette.

'While you're here, Mr Engels, I wonder if you can let me have that pass that was issued to you? – I can turn it in to the office. That is – I suppose you won't need it any more.'

Crenshaw took the blue card from his wallet, and handed it over. The Warden shook hands with him.

'One thing more,' Crenshaw demanded as the Warden turned away, 'which is the – the window of the infirmary?'

'It's on the interior court, you can't see it from here.'

'Oh.'

When the Warden had gone Crenshaw still stood there a long time, the tears running out down his face. He could not collect his thoughts, and he began by trying to remember what day it was: Saturday – that was it, the day every other week on which he came to see the Fiend.

He would not see the Fiend two weeks from now.

In a misery of solitude and despair he muttered aloud: 'So he is dead. He has left me.' And then, with a long sigh of mingled grief and fear. 'So now at last I am alone.'

He was still saying that to himself as he passed through the outer gate. He felt the necessity of turning to the guard there and repeating it: 'Now, you see,' he muttered. 'I really am alone.'

His coat caught in the great swing of the outer door, and as the guard opened up to release it he heard a reiteration of the words:

'Now I'm alone – now I'm really alone.'

Shaggy's Morning

I woke up after a lousy dream, and as soon as the old beezer came alive I went around the yard trying to pick up something interesting, but the wind was too strong.

There was an old biscuit in my dish and if there's anything gloomier than one dead biscuit on a windy morning I don't know about it.

The Brain came downstairs early like she usually does ever since she began staying away all day long. I gave her a rush, and I meant it, too. I'm not one of these diggities that think their boss is a god, even if he's an old nigger that smells like everybody that gave him his clothes – but really anybody would have to hand it to the Brain.

Since I grew up and got the idea that they don't go in much for any perfumes except their own, I never had any trouble with her – except the time I brought her that bone in the middle of the night and she hit me in the eye with it.

I was hoping it was about the right day to go out in the country and swim, but nothing doing – she got into her moving room at the usual time and shoved off, and I had to amuse myself. It wasn't the first time I wished I had something regular to do.

My friend across the street was waiting for his chow, which he gets in the morning, so I had a workout with the little squirt next door. He came tearing over, cursing and threatening, because he knew I never hurt him.

'You big, clumsy tub of hair, I could run rings around you, and I'm out to prove it!'

'Yeah?' I said, kind of amused, because he talks as if he meant it, and we went through a routine with a lot of false starts, charges, leg and throat holds, rollaways, and escapes. It was all right, and after, while we were panting plenty, but I don't get much of a workout with him, because he uses up so much time dodging and doing circles. I like a dog to go in and take it. Even a little fellow like him. Once he let a tooth slip and nipped me, and I gave him hell.

'Don't take advantage, or I'll tear your coat off.'

'Aw, don't get sore.'

'Then don't let that tooth slip again.'

While we were resting he said: 'What are you doing this morning?'

'What's on your mind? You won't get me out after some cat again. Some dogs never grow up.'

'It's no cat.'

'Then what is it? Meat – or girls?'

'I'll take you there and you can see for yourself.'

'You're generous all of a sudden. How big's the dog that's there now?'

While we waited for my friend we did some barking – or rather the squirt did most of it. These little tykes can yelp all day without getting hoarse. He made some circles around a bunch of kids heading for school, and I had a laugh when he got a kick in the ribs and gave out a real yelp. I only barked a little in the base to stretch my throat – I'm not one of the kind always shooting off their mouth.

After my friend came out we went with the squirt to see what he'd found. Just like I thought, it was nothing – a garbage can with a lid you could nose off. I got a whiff of some perfume, too, that bucked me up for a minute, but it was yesterday's, so my friend and I roughed up the squirt for wasting our time and went off on our own.

We followed a tall lady for a while – no particular reason except she had a parcel with meat in it – we knew we wouldn't get any, but you never can tell. Sometimes I just feel like shutting my nose and just following somebody pretending they're yours, or that they're taking you somewhere. After a couple of streets I picked up a new perfume.

'There's some romance,' I said.

'Say you got a nose.' He tried for it, but didn't get anything.

'I must be getting old. I can always remember shapes, but I get mixed up on perfume.'

'Shucks, it's just the wind,' I said, to make him feel all right, but he *has* got a weak nose. Now me, I got a fine nose, but I'm weak on shapes. In a minute, though, he got it, and we left the lady and started back down the street at a trot.

Say we must have followed a mile, both of us getting more and more disgusted.

'What's the use?' my friend said. 'Either I'm crazy or we're not following one scent, but about ten.'

'I get about twenty.'

'What say we quit?'

'Well, we're pretty near now.'

We got up on a hill presently and looked down – and, say, I haven't seen so many curs since the dog show.

'Sold,' I says, and we started home.

The Brain wasn't there yet, but the Beard was. He got out that damn pole and tried to kid me again, holding it out and jabbering – a long time ago I figured out that his object is to see if I'm fool enough to jump over it. But I don't bite, just walk round it. Then he tried the trick they all do – held my paws and tried to balance me up on the end of my spine. I never could figure out the point of that one.

He started the music-box, that tune that makes my ear hum and starts me howling – so I lammed it out and down the street. A dog passed me carrying a newspaper looking all pleased with himself – but the one time I tried that racket I forgot what it was I was carrying and started to bury it, and when the Beard saw me. Was he sore!

Pretty soon I saw my friend coming down the street. He was a fine big dog. He stopped and visited for a minute, with a child he knew, and then he saw me, and came running in my direction. What happened next I couldn't see. It was noon, and there were lots of moving rooms at the cross street – the first thing I knew was that one of them had stopped and then another, and that several people had gotten out. I hurried over with some men.

It was my friend, lying on his side and bleeding out of his mouth; his eyes were open, but his breathing was wrong. Everybody was excited, and they pulled him up on the lawn: by and by his little boy and girl ran out of their house and came over and began to cry. I and another dog that knew him well went up to him, and I wanted to lick him, but when I came really close he snarled, 'Scram!' and got half up on his haunches. He thought I was going to eat him just because he was down.

The little boy said, 'Get away, you!' and it made me feel bad because I've never eaten a dog in my life, and would not unless I was very hungry. But of course, I went away so as not to worry him, and waited until they carried him away on a blanket. After that we sniffed at the blood in the street and one dog licked it.

In the front yard I howled. I don't know why – then I went to look for the Brain. When I didn't find her I began to figure that maybe something had happened to her, too, and she wouldn't be back any more. I went up on the porch and waited, but she didn't come, so I scratched on the screen and went in and howled a little at the Beard, who gave me a head scratch.

Presently I went to the door, and there was the Brain, getting out of her moving room – I made a rush for her anyhow, and put my nose in her hand and almost tripped her going upstairs. It was good to know she was home. She gave me dinner – the ground beef again and biscuit and milk and a good bone. I picked out the meat first; then I drank the milk and licked the biscuits, but didn't eat them; then I polished my teeth on the bone and buried it shallow – I must have a hundred bones around here, and I don't know why I save them. I never find them again unless accidentally, but I just can't stand leaving them around.

Afterwards I started to go over and see my friend, but there was nobody around except the little girl sitting in the swing and crying.